MRS. STANTON'S BIBLE

Mrs. Stanton's Bible

KATHI KERN

Cornell University Press

Ithaca and London

First published 2001 by Cornell University Press

Printed in the United States of America

Library of Congress Cataloging-in-Publication Data
Kern, Kathi, 1961–
  Mrs. Stanton's Bible /
Kathi Kern
    p. cm.
  Includes index.
  ISBN 0-8014-3191-3 (cloth : alk. paper)
  1. Stanton, Elizabeth Cady, 1815–1902. 2. Stanton, Elizabeth Cady,
1815–1902 Woman's Bible. 3. Feminists—United States—Biography. 4.
Feminism—Religious aspects—Christianity. 5. Bible—Feminist criticism.
6. Women's rights—United States—History—19th century. 7.
Feminism—United States—History—19th century. I. Title.
  HQ1413.S67 K47 2000
  305.42'092—dc21   00-010756

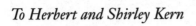

To Herbert and Shirley Kern

Contents

List of Illustrations   viii

Acknowledgments   ix

Introduction   1

1. "The Sunset of Life": Elizabeth Cady Stanton and the
   Polemics of Autobiography   14

2. The "Emasculated Gospel": New Religions, New Bibles,
   and the Battle for Cultural Authority   50

3. Sacred Politics: Religion, Race, and the Transformation
   of the Woman Suffrage Movement in the Gilded Age   92

4. "A Great Feature of the General Uprising": The Revising
   Committee and the *Woman's Bible*   135

5. "The Bigots Promote the Sale": Responses to the *Woman's
   Bible*   172

List of Archival Abbreviations   223

Notes   225

Index   273

Illustrations

Elizabeth Cady Stanton in the 1890s   36

Robert Green Ingersoll   65

The Reverend Thomas DeWitt Talmadge   74

Delegates to the International Council of Women, 1888   105

"American Woman and Her Political Peers" postcard   113

Frances Willard   126

Elizabeth Cady Stanton and Susan B. Anthony   128

Clara Colby   143

Olympia Brown   145

"The Apotheosis of Liberty" cartoon   186

Susan B. Anthony   188

Carrie Chapman Catt   190

Elizabeth Cady Stanton   218

Acknowledgments

Many times in the course of writing this book, I was awed by the generosity of friends and strangers. I am happy at last to thank those who have helped me. One of my oldest debts is to my teachers, particularly Bruce Clayton of Allegheny College, whose model of teaching and scholarship inspired me to study history. At the University of Pennsylvania, I benefited from the insights of Evelyn Brooks-Higginbotham, E. Ann Matter, Bruce Kuklick, Janice Radway, and especially Carroll Smith-Rosenberg. As a student, I thrived (or at least survived) because I was surrounded by a group of contemporaries who taught me much about history, politics, and friendship. I am grateful to Sarah Cornelius, Miriam King, Cindy Himes Gissendanner, Karen Mittelman, Elizabeth Smith, Ellen Somekawa, Karen Erdos, Jackie Pastis, Nancy Berg, and Christine Morrow.

For underwriting the research on this project, I thank the Woodrow Wilson Fellowship Foundation for a National Mellon Fellowship in the Humanities; Research and Graduate Studies at the University of Kentucky; the Kentucky Foundation for Women; the National Endowment for the Humanities; and particularly the editors of the microfilm edition of the Papers of Elizabeth Cady Stanton and Susan B. Anthony: Patricia G. Holland, Ann D. Gordon, Kathleen A. McDonough, and Gail K. Malmgreen. I have benefited, as all scholars of the woman's rights movement have or will, from their careful and prodigious archival work. I am grateful for their patience as I occupied their offices and taxed their brains. Ann Gordon has continued to advise me, and I continue to rely upon her encyclopedic knowledge of Stanton, the woman's rights movement, and the nineteenth century.

My research was also enhanced by the diligence of librarians, archivists, and research assistants. I am particularly indebted to the reference librarians of the University of Kentucky Library who solved mysteries at breakneck speed. I also thank Jeff Flannery at the Library of Congress; Diane Hamer and the staff at the Schlesinger Library, Radcliffe Institute; the librarians at the State Historical Society of Wisconsin; Barbara DeWolf, Clements Library, University of Michigan; Tammy Martin and Roland Baumann, Oberlin College Archives; and the librarians and staff at the Henry E. Huntington Library. For permission to quote from their holdings, I thank the Schlesinger Library, the Huntington Library, and Special Collections and Archives at the University of Kentucky. For their aid in research, I am grateful to James Manasco, Lori Kettering, Julianne Unsel, and especially Amy Gamblin who skillfully found all lost references. In Johnstown, New York, I benefitted from the hospitality and insights of resident historians Noel S. Levee and Lansing Lord, as well as Debbie Callery of the Johnstown Public Library.

Books are worked out in conversation, and I could not have written this one without the friends and colleagues who talked it over with me: Barbara Balliet, Susan Yohn, Claire Potter, Regina Kunzel, and Susan Strasser. Beryl Satter not only shared her research with me; she educated me about New Thought and its importance in the woman's movement. To the scholars in women's history who have supported this project, I offer my heartfelt appreciation: Leila Rupp, Christine Stansell, Nancy Hewitt, Louise Stevenson, Elisabeth Perry, Ann Braude, and Kathy Peiss. For reading and commenting on the manuscript in its various incarnations, I also thank: Karen Tice, Dwight Billings, Ann Gordon, Gail Malmgreen, Rhea Lehman, Susan Worst, Grey Osterud, and an anonymous reader for Cornell University Press. Peter Agree went out of his way to support me and the project. For helping me to navigate the publishing process I am also grateful to Julie Popkin, Roger Haydon, Ange Romeo-Hall, and Kay Scheuer.

I have spent many summers since 1993 working with public school teachers through the auspices of the National Faculty. In particular, the opportunity to work in the Mississippi and Arkansas Delta with groups of black and white teachers has shaped my vision of history. For those rich experiences I thank Dell Upton, Martha Vail, Michael Friedland, Valerie Grim, Jay Tribby, Rob Baird, Karl Raitz, and especially Nan Woodruff, whose model of engaged scholarship and deep appreciation of southern cuisine has forever changed me. Likewise, I am indebted to the fine teachers from Yazoo City, Mississippi, to Juneau, Alaska, who have listened to this work in progress and shared with me their visions of history and love of teaching.

Despite the fact that I contracted food poisoning during my job interview, the University of Kentucky history department has been an ideal place to work. I have been privileged to teach and learn from many fine graduate students including Mary Block, Chad Gregory, Kristen Streater, Melanie Beals Goan, Caroline Light, Julianne Unsel, and Carolyn Dupont. Ed Blum read this work and asked great questions. Kat Williams assisted my research and offered steadfast support. Likewise, I am fortunate to work with historians from whom I have learned much about teaching and writing. I owe a special debt of gratitude to Daniel Blake Smith for his early interest in this project and for modeling excellent work habits. Joanne Pope Melish helped me think about the place of slavery in Stanton's family. I thank George Herring for his wisdom and guidance. Bill Freehling, I thank for his advice, his enthusiasm, and his faith in my work. My colleague in women's history, Patricia Cooper, a careful reader and a gentle editor, helped me to shape this work. Finally, Mark Wahlgren Summers has showered me with generosity in reading, editing, and thinking about this project.

I could not have written this book, or any other, without the love and support of my friends and family. Miriam Davidson shared the evolution of this project over many years and never failed to inquire about the health and well-being of the Woman's Bible "ladies." To my friends, I owe thanks for my continued sanity and for disrupting the isolation that is an inevitable part of writing. I thank Ursula Roma, Karen Jones, Beverly Futrell, Patricia Cooper, Gil Ware, Karen Tice, Dwight Billings, and my tennis partner, Mary Frietag. Joanne Meyerowitz offered encouragement, advice and a good laugh at critical moments. Karla Goldman not only taught me a great deal about nineteenth-century Judaism; she supported me and this project with great enthusiasm. Kate Black shared many a meal with the ghost of Elizabeth Cady Stanton and pronounced her "more interesting than I would have thought." For Kate's wit, keen intelligence, and rich companionship, I am truly grateful. The long-distance phone calls from my brother, Kevin Kern, in which he reported on his discoveries about fatherhood, kept me laughing through the final stages of writing. Since I was a child, my grandfather Kenneth Springer, now aged ninety-five, has shared with me his wealth of stories and ignited my love of history. Finally, my deepest thanks go to my parents, Herbert and Shirley Kern, who inspire me with their zest for life. For their generosity of spirit and their unwavering love, I dedicate this book to them.

K. K.

MRS. STANTON'S BIBLE

Introduction

> This book may be read for generations to come, and your word
> will stand as well as mine, to help or hinder the development of
> a grand womanhood.
>
> ELIZABETH CADY STANTON
> to the *Woman's Bible* Revising Committee, June 15, 1895

For Elizabeth Cady Stanton, the moving force behind the first American woman's rights convention, in Seneca Falls in 1848, and a great crusader in the cause over the half-century that followed, time brought its share of frustrations. Hers was a long life, and yet, by the 1880s, it seemed that the cause of equal rights would not be won before that life closed.[1] It was that frustration with the slow pace of political reform that impelled her to open the war on a different front, one scouted out long since. "It is humiliating," she wrote in 1886, "for a woman of my years to stand up before men twenty years younger, and ask them for the privilege of enjoying my rights as a citizen in a Republic. I feel that I can never do it again. . . . We can make no impression on men who accept the theological view of woman as the author of sin, cursed of God, and all that nonsense. The debris of the centuries must be cleared away before our arguments for equality can have the least significance to any of them."[2] And so she took to the task of clearing away "the debris of the centuries." Partially blind and increasingly physically immobile, Stanton continued to use what powers remained to her: an intellectual engagement and abilities as a writer as strong as ever in her lifetime. "When you are 73 years old, you will appreciate my reluctance to leave your own bed, rocking chair & writing desk," she cautioned a friend. "The word 'go' has lost all charm for me. I think my future work must be done with the pen."[3] True to her word, Stanton made her ninth decade her most prolific, publishing an autobiography, countless magazine articles, and the *Woman's Bible*. The appearance of that last work was one final, great stroke in her battle against inequality. It was also the ruin of her historical reputation.

It was not, strictly speaking, a Bible at all, and Stanton did not wield the pen alone. Convinced that acting alone "would not have the same effect," she drafted a committee of women to embark on a collaborative project.[4] Published in two volumes in 1895 and 1898, the *Woman's Bible* was unlike modern attempts to revise the Bible by modifying the dated patriarchal language. Rather, the *Woman's Bible* reprinted particular biblical passages that pertained to women and, following each, presented interpretive commentaries prepared by Stanton and the members of the revising committee. "The orthodox need not shy in terror at it," a journalist wrote. "It seems that it is merely a commentary upon the Bible."[5]

The book's seemingly straightforward approach, however, did not long conceal its radical critique of American culture. For Stanton, women's liberty depended upon their freedom from social and political constraints in every realm of life: the family, the church, and the state. Nominally a suffragist to the end of her days, she found much else to fight for. Losing her faith in the power of women's vote as a vehicle for social change, she began to see women's lack of political rights as symptomatic of a larger, more disturbing problem: the belief in women's subordination rooted in the Bible and taught by the Christian church and clergy. Throughout the last two decades of her life, Stanton wrote trenchant critiques of the Bible, the clergy, and the organized church.[6]

The *Woman's Bible* represented to her the "crowning achievement" of her life.[7] It was a costly one. Stanton hoped her readers would find within the book's pages a compelling analysis of women's dependence on the church, the clergy, and the Bible. She intended the *Woman's Bible* to be both an instrument and a symbol of women's ultimate emancipation. However, the response it evoked was the opposite. The work confirmed the fears of antisuffragists and alienated many of Stanton's sister suffragists as well. As one critic put it, "it does not seem to signify any thing to her that the so-called 'Bible' is sharply criticized by everybody whose opinion she might be expected to value."[8]

The book stirred a particular sensation among those who never read it. In the wake of a flood of denunciations, Stanton remarked that "the clergy denounced it as the work of Satan, though it really was the work of Ellen Battelle Dietrick, Lillie Devereux Blake, Rev. Phebe A. Hanaford, Clara Bewick Colby, Ursula N. Gestefeld, Louisa Southworth, Frances Ellen Burr, and myself."[9] Groups of church-going women also condemned the *Woman's Bible* and purged it from their local libraries. The response was no more friendly in influential reform circles. The National American Woman Suffrage Association—of which Stanton served as honorary president—censured the *Woman's Bible* at its annual meeting in 1896. The book touched a nerve. For many clergy, it signaled the destruction of biblically based norms of femininity and masculinity. For evangelical women, it posed a threat to the moral authority that their faith in the "real" Bible ensured. And for Stanton's political opponents within the woman's movement, the public controversy that the book provoked threatened the movement's fragile coalitions and popular support.

That evangelical church members and suffragists both rejected this revolutionary reading of the Bible reveals its usefulness to the historian. The *Woman's Bible* deeply undermined the social and religious values of the Gilded Age. Stanton and her colleagues used the project to lay bare the contradictions that riddled Victorian conceptions of the ideal woman, an ideal that depended on the notion of woman's "natural" piety.[10] During the nineteenth century, women rooted their claims to public power in their natural piety and the moral authority it inspired. Under the broad banner of women's moral authority, many women united, identified for the first time as women, and experienced their first potent dose of political agency. Unlike most reformers of the period, who absorbed this rhetoric and frequently subverted it to more radical ends, Stanton by the 1880s had rejected it outright. A platform for women's political liberation could never be built upon the faulty foundation of religious faith because it would not bear weight. The corrosive principle of women's subordination was sealed into every plank: the church, the clergy, and the Bible. But by undermining this cornerstone of Victorian culture, Stanton had gone too far. The *Woman's Bible* was seen as a frontal assault on the moral authority of women, and by extension, the moral integrity of the nation. No wonder so many readers moved to suppress it.

The public controversy Stanton ignited with the *Woman's Bible* had the ironic effect of diminishing her historical stature and nearly erasing this telling moment from the historical record. Despite Stanton's own concerted efforts to document her views on religion and its central place in her evolving cultural critique, those who followed her did their best to ignore her words and, in some cases, to censor them. Take her children, for instance. Watching in disbelief as their mother's historical reputation quickly eroded and then threatened to vanish completely, Stanton's children attempted a heroic intervention. When they reissued her autobiography in 1922, her daughter Harriot Stanton Blatch and her son Theodore Stanton removed a controversial chapter titled "Women and Theology," in which their mother chronicled the project of writing the *Woman's Bible*.[11] Their decision, born of devotion and a desire to restore their mother to the prominence she deserved, would not have surprised Elizabeth Cady Stanton, but it would have exasperated her. She emerged from her children's editing with some of her "heresies" suppressed. In the historical record compiled by the succeeding generation of suffragists, she barely emerged at all. These women were tired of answering for Stanton's controversial religious views and her "so-called Bible." In the words of one of her supporters, the next generation were unable to "kill" Stanton outright, but they managed to get her "comfortably laid on the shelf." Stanton's daughter's assessment was even more bleak. According to Harriot Stanton Blatch, in the wake of the *Woman's Bible*, the younger suffrage leaders proceeded to "bury her alive."[12]

One particularly successful strategy for burying Stanton alive was a discursive one. In the histories of the movement prepared by the next generation of suffragists, Stanton was eclipsed by the familiar shadow of her friend and colleague Susan B. Anthony. In fact, as Stanton scholars and biographers have noted, twentieth-century suffragists consciously sought to canonize Anthony and to position her as the sole leader of the nineteenth-century movement.[13] Stanton, earlier labeled "the mother of the movement" for her pioneering role in the Seneca Falls convention, became an apparent victim of matricide as Anthony bore the name that, in the words of one of the younger suffragists, had "become synonymous with the woman suffrage movement in America."[14] Later suffragists could not entirely erase Stanton from her originating role at Seneca Falls, but they tried. In 1923, as suffragists celebrated the seventy-fifth anniversary of the convention, they planned the event without reference to Stanton. As the culmination of their celebration, the suffragists launched a motorcade that began at Seneca Falls and ended at Anthony's home in Rochester, thus symbolically linking Anthony with the Seneca Falls convention, even though she had not attended it.[15] This later generation of suffragists succeeded in shaping the historical record. For much of the twentieth century, Susan B. Anthony would stand alone—most memorably on an ill-fated coin—as the symbol of women's political progress. Temporarily dislocated in the historical shuffle was one of the most important political partnerships of the nineteenth century, the relationship between Stanton and Anthony.[16] But even more profoundly lost was Elizabeth Cady Stanton's unique voice—the voice of a seasoned veteran, not a youthful pioneer—and the radical critique she put forward in the *Woman's Bible*.

While suffragists attempted to extinguish the legacy of Stanton's Bible, opponents of the woman's movement kept the issue alive. Eighteen years after Stanton's death, the *Woman's Bible* was resuscitated by antisuffragists in a last-minute effort to squelch the ratification of the Nineteenth Amendment, the constitutional amendment that enfranchised American women. After thirty-five states had ratified and the amendment stood before the legislature of Tennessee, the final state required for ratification, antisuffragists papered Nashville with handbills simultaneously resurrecting and crucifying the *Woman's Bible*. One broadside advertised the *Woman's Bible* in large block letters and printed choice quotations from the book. "This is the teaching of National Suffrage Leaders. Are you willing for women who hold these views to become political powers in our country?" it demanded. "Every one who believes that the word of God is divinely inspired, who desires to see his State Constitution not violated, and who believes in the purity of the family and the sanctity of marriage and would keep women out of politics"—was urged to work to defeat the woman suffrage amendment. The *Woman's Bible* proved to be the most devastating weapon in the antisuffrage arsenal.[17]

Abbey Crawford Milton, a suffragist from Tennessee, later recorded some of the fierce political battles in Nashville during that hot summer of 1920. The scene of much violence, the Hermitage Hotel was the headquarters of the antisuffragists where, Milton remembered, among the haze of drunken legislators, a woman's "Bible" was on display. "They called it Mrs. Catt's Bible," Milton remembered. "I don't know what it contained that was so awful, but there were 26 ministers of churches in Nashville . . . who were converted against women suffrage by being shown that book." Concerned, though, like many of the book's critics, she had never read it, Milton and her husband approached Carrie Chapman Catt, the nation's most prominent suffragist and the president of the National American Woman Suffrage Association, and urged her to deny her authorship of this Bible. Catt replied that "she had denied it so much that there wasn't any need." "Yes, there is a need," Milton shot back. "You have got to deny it again."[18]

The ironies of history are rich. Carrie Chapman Catt had been the *Woman's Bible*'s chief political opponent when the first volume was published in 1895. At the national convention the following year, Catt had engineered the National American Woman Suffrage Association's denunciation of Stanton and the *Woman's Bible*. And she had been castigated by the liberal press for her action. There was no love lost between Catt and Stanton. Still, it seems that Stanton, long dead and buried, may have had the last laugh. Stanton had had considerable trouble drafting a quorum of women to serve on her revising committee for the project. She especially wanted the assistance of prominent suffragists and, when few cooperated, she resorted to "borrowing" the names of some and listing them as "members" of her committee.[19] Carrie Chapman Catt, much to her surprise, found her own name listed as a member of the *Woman's Bible* Revising Committee in volume one when it was published in 1895. Appalled, Catt protested and forced Stanton to remove her name from future editions. Twenty-five years later, Catt was dogged by this conflict; the "Antis" had dug up a first edition, advertised it as "Mrs. Catt's Bible," and used it skillfully among the clergy. And, try as she might, Mrs. Catt simply could not "deny it" enough. Supporters of woman suffrage were narrowly victorious in Tennessee; the legislature ratified the Nineteenth Amendment by a single vote.[20] And yet, twenty-five years after it first appeared in print, the *Woman's Bible* still wreaked political havoc among supporters of woman's rights.

Stanton's Bible is no longer credited to Mrs. Catt. Today, thanks to the combined work of scholars, biographers, archivists, local historians, film-makers, family members, and activists, Elizabeth Cady Stanton has emerged from obscurity. But the place of the *Woman's Bible* in her life and work has yet to be fully examined. Perhaps because the range of her thought and activities was so effectively muted in the years following her death, she has been able to resurface in our time as the bearer of multiple historical identities. In search of foremothers, different groups of second-wave feminists rediscovered and reinvented Stanton during the 1970s. Championed by theologians as the "doyenne" of feminist biblical criticism, analyzed by historians for her path-breaking contributions to liberal feminist thought, Stanton emerged from the 1970s as the foremother of two distinct feminist traditions with little to say to each other.[21] Historians minimized her religious views, while religious studies scholars treated her political work as background to her theology.[22]

In its most recent incarnation, Stanton's historical reputation has been complicated by scholarly attention to her less-than-progressive views on race.[23] Saddled with a label she and her contemporaries would not have recognized, her historical legacy is jeopardized by the ever-present question: "was she *really* a racist?" The cloud created by this issue threatens to overshadow other aspects of her work. The historian, like the filmmaker, has the power to shape the roles played by historical actors in the production of our collective memory. Theologian, politician, racist, Stanton emerges from the past a fractured, overworked figure with several roles to juggle. That she can simultaneously star in so many different historical dramas tells us something about the richness of her life. But it tells us even more about ourselves, particularly about the arbitrary divisions scholars erect between academic disciplines that serve to splinter the identities of those we study. What different story might we tell if Stanton's struggles with religion were moved from the margins of her significance and placed at the heart of her political evolution? How might we understand Stanton's feminist theology if it were explored as a response to her contemporary political culture, rather than as a starting point for a modern feminist tradition of biblical exegesis? Rather than refracting Stanton's racial views through the lens of late twentieth-century thinking about race, might we gain a new perspective by tracing their reflection in her beliefs about religion and science? In attempting to answer these questions, I argue in this book that religion—or more precisely, Stanton's quest for religious liberty—provides the connective tissue that binds these partial and seemingly separate identities.

Like its author, the *Woman's Bible* has spawned multiple historical legacies. As its strategic use by antisuffragists in 1920 demonstrated, Stanton's Bible continued to be politically charged well into the twentieth century.

Before the century's end, its symbolic power had been summoned by a new generation of feminists. Several editions were reprinted in the early 1970s and marketed through academic channels and women's bookstores. In 1974, the Seattle-based Coalition Task Force on Women and Religion published its edition of the *Woman's Bible*, a reprint made from two volumes that Jane T. Walker of Tacoma, Washington, had inherited from her suffragist mother. Stanton had inscribed the two volumes to Walker's greataunt, Mary Elizabeth Meech, in 1899, and the women of Walker's family had read the books, transported them across the country, and passed them along to future generations. Having enjoyed reading the *Woman's Bible* herself, Walker wrote to the Coalition Task Force, she was "glad to share it with my sister women."[24]

A collection of essays written by coalition members set off Stanton's original text and provided insight into the political context of this 1974 reprint. No longer freighted with the fears evoked by its original publication, the *Woman's Bible* in the early 1970s had become a symbol of hope for reconciling Christianity and feminism. Believing that "Jesus was truly a feminist" and that "Christianity is an Equal Rights religion," the Coalition Task Force embraced Stanton and her Bible because she championed women's "religious equality." The historic silence imposed on women by the church "proved a disaster," wrote one coalition member. "The first to break that silence in a dramatic fashion was Stanton. This she did for us, it is now our privilege as heirs to follow." When the Coalition Task Force began its project in the early 1970s, the *Woman's Bible* had been out of print for decades. The group's work as Stanton's "heirs" was to make her book widely available at a low cost. "Our hope," wrote another member, was that the reprint of the *Woman's Bible* "will prove an important study document for feminist groups, churches, classes and that it will be used in libraries, school, colleges, etc. [as] a 'spring board' for discussion."[25]

Spreading the news of women's religious equality was one kind of political work the *Woman's Bible* might accomplish in the 1970s. But these feminists saw other important parallels between the nineteenth century and their own. Stanton's Bible detailed "the awful slaughter of women as witches, as wives of drunken husbands, as slaves; today we might add the slaughter of women as victims of poverty, of rape, [and] of backroom abortions." In fact, wrote the project editor, Eleanor D. Bilimoria, the interfaith coalition was reprinting Stanton's Bible "not only for its historic importance but also for its contribution to present day developments." Stanton believed that the church had erected insurmountable obstacles to women's progress. To these feminists of the 1970s, her message had "a strangely familiar ring." "In 1974," Bilimoria wrote, "we find specific religious institutions leading and funding opposition to the passage of the Equal Rights Amendment, to the Constitution, [and] pushing amendments to kill the Supreme Court decision on abortion."[26] Once again, the power of the *Woman's Bible* was harnessed for a vital political mission: to counteract right-wing religious attacks on women's liberation.

The *Woman's Bible* also proved a valuable tool for those feminists laboring in the masculine domains of divinity schools and religious studies programs. Pioneering women scholars who developed the field of feminist biblical hermeneutics gave Stanton's Bible its first academic home. These scholars looked to the *Woman's Bible* as the inaugurating point of a modern feminist tradition, the political act of women interpreting the Bible.[27] In fact, the renowned feminist theologian Elisabeth Schüssler Fiorenza suggested that Stanton's arguments for a feminist interpretation of the Bible were relevant to scholars almost a century later: the Bible was still used to subjugate women; women still believed in their own biblically based subordination; and, finally, reform in the legal system would still be meaningless without simultaneous reform in religion.[28] Stanton had begun a discussion of the Bible as a man-made expression of patriarchal culture; the feminist biblical scholars of the 1980s were her logical successors.

Stanton's radicalism impresssed Fiorenza. Stanton had departed from the vast majority of women interpreters of her day by replacing "the main apologetic argument . . . that the true message of the Bible was obstructed by the translations and interpretations of men." While other suffragists focused on separating the "essence of Chrisitanity" from the "accidents of culture," Stanton offered readers, in Fiorenza's words, "a radical hermeneutical perspective": the Bible is not just interpreted to the benefit of patriarchy, it is itself patriarchal. To Fiorenza, Stanton's bold position was an essential starting point for the recovery of a truly feminist biblical perspective. "A biblical theology that does not seriously confront 'the patriarchal stamp' of the Bible . . ." Fiorenza warned risks "using a feminist perspective to rehabilitate the authority of the Bible, rather than to rehabilitate women's theological heritage."[29]

By the 1990s, however, scholarly attention to Stanton's racism had tempered Fiorenza's earlier unqualified praise for Stanton's radicalism. In *Searching the Scriptures*, a collaborative volume prepared in honor of the *Woman's Bible's* centennial in 1995, Fiorenza cautioned against uncritically celebrating the tradition of the *Woman' Bible*:

> Singling out *The Woman's Bible* as *the* milestone in the history of women's biblical interpretation not only risks overlooking the contributions of women of color to biblical hermeneutics. It also continues a white feminist gender discourse inscribed in *The Woman's Bible* that does not recognize the constitutive kyriarchal *differences* among and within women. In so

doing, it is not only in danger of perpetuating a feminist historical discourse that celebrates the work of those nineteenth-century feminists with "fair skin" and forgets or represses feminist achievements of women from the "Dark Continent" but also in danger of perpetuating the cultural myth of "true womanhood."[30]

In making these claims, Fiorenza attempted to strike a balance between embracing Stanton "as the foremost heroic foremother of women biblical interpreters" and distancing herself from "the essentialist cultural tradition of *The Woman's Bible*."[31] For Fiorenza, Stanton survived history as a "foremost foremother," acknowledged by modern feminist theologians despite her limited vision. However, Fiorenza found it more difficult to reconcile the theological radicalism of the *Woman's Bible* with its "essentialist cultural tradition," which Fiorenza defines as "the Western universalist claims that all women have a special, essential nature in common and that all women are defined in the same way in their otherness to men."[32] Fiorenza notes, "the recognition that Cady Stanton's work was 'racist and classist' cautions white feminists in religion not to adopt the conceptual approach of *The Woman's Bible*."[33] Contemporary feminist interpreters can correct this flaw, Fiorenza argues, by exposing the limits of the categories Stanton and her generation of reformers relied upon, particularly the deceptively exclusive and singular (rather than plural) category of "woman," which worked to mask differences of race, class, ethnicity, and religion.

Fiorenza's criticism of the *Woman's Bible*'s essentialist cultural tradition is a valid one that reflected the concerns of feminist scholarship of the 1990s. Stanton's concept of "woman" cannot be stretched to meet the concerns of present day feminists who strive to be, in Fiorenza's words, "inclusive, ecumenical and multicultural."[34] At the same time, however, this critique—necessary to salvage the *Woman's Bible* as a usable, contemporary feminist symbol—fails to appraise the historical text. The value of the *Woman's Bible* as a historical document rises precisely from the context of its production. The *Woman's Bible* was not, after all, written from a single perspective, with one voice and one goal; rather, the book contains multiple and overlapping dialogues. Members of Stanton's revising committee argued with contemporary patriarchal interpretations of the Bible and with each other from their varied religious, social, and ideological perspectives.

The writers of the original *Woman's Bible* were a diverse and eclectic group who not only represented different political views, but brought vastly different life experiences to their work. Several of the women were quite elderly, as was Stanton, at age eighty when volume one appeared; several of the women were not able-bodied; and several lived in poverty. Although white privilege was a common denominator among the members of the revising committee, it did not translate into a unified vision of the Bible, gender, or the work they undertook. In fact, the collaborators brought very different exegetical practices to their work, differed in their acceptance of non-canonical texts, and, finally, argued for vastly different constructions of gender, particularly evident in their disagreements over the gendered constitution of the soul.[35] Situated within the broader cultural debates of the late nineteenth century, the *Woman's Bible* was certainly elitist, and at times anti-Semitic, but even those narrow interpretations were at odds with other views within the book's covers. While the title the "Woman's Bible" may reflect an "essentialist cultural tradition" that Stanton herself at times embraced, the pages of the *Woman's Bible* should not be reduced to this formulation. Read with an eye to nineteenth-century issues and tensions, the *Woman's Bible* still speaks to the diversity of views, experiences, and privileges among the white women who compiled it.

Ironically, just as Stanton was earning a reputation among one group of contemporary scholars as the foremother of feminist theology, for another group she was emerging as the foremost secularist of the nineteenth-century woman's movement. According to the historian Ellen DuBois, a leading interpreter of the woman's rights movement, the antebellum movement had strong religious roots and expended considerable energy in its early years debating with clergy and determining the meanings of the Bible. Under Stanton and Anthony's leadership, however, the movement's primary strategy, and what distinguished it from other venues of women's activism, was that it "bypassed woman's oppression within the family, or private sphere, and demanded instead her admission to citizenship, and through it admission to the public arena." Relying upon the forces of "secularism, individualism, and an emphasis on the similarities of the sexes," Stanton and Anthony circumvented the dominant paradigm of their age—woman's sphere—by applying to women the "liberal definitions of freedom that had always been intended only for men, principles such as economic independence, natural rights, and personal liberty." For DuBois, the quest for political equality was "at the core of radical feminism" in the nineteenth century because it represented a direct assault on the "male monopoly of the public sphere," an assault that sent "shockwaves" reverberating through the culture.[36]

While DuBois identified religious roots that flowered into a predominantly secular political radicalism, other scholars have emphasized the persistent, invasive, and entangled nature of those religious roots in the antebellum period.[37] In contrast, we know considerably less about the role religious ideas played in the suffrage movement of the late nineteenth century, a period that has been called "the doldrums" of the woman's rights movement.[38] In fact, we have a much richer, more complex picture of the movement immediately before and after "the doldrums." Ellen DuBois has readily admitted, "I had always shied away from this period because I find its politics less personally congenial than the democratic radicalism of the Reconstruction years."[39] The period of the *Woman's Bible* controversy boasted few tangible victories for the cause. As Aileen Kraditor pointed out in 1965, while the suffrage movement in this era became increasingly "expedient" in its call for women's vote, it became increasingly racist and intolerant as well.[40] In the historiographical vacuum created by a desire to pass quickly through "the doldrums" to arrive at, in DuBois's words, "the revival of suffrage militancy" in the early twentieth century, we are left with a partial, less than satisfying understanding of this period.[41] Only by exploring it as a crucial moment of political accommodation can we adequately explain the persistence of a conservative National American Woman Suffrage Association and why militant feminists of the twentieth century chose either to try to radicalize it or to abandon it altogether.

This historical gap in our understanding begs further inquiry. We know comparatively more about the rise of the Woman's Christian Temperance Union and its particular brand of Christian politics, which both joined and threatened to overwhelm the much smaller and increasingly "secular" woman's suffrage movement. But there is much more to the story than this familiar tale. Given the paucity of recent historical work on the suffrage movement in this era, coupled with the comparatively rich documentation of the successes of the WCTU, we are left with a sense that the battles of the late nineteenth century were waged between evangelicals and "secularists."[42] If we examine the thought of the "secularists," however, we will find an impressive array of religious ideas, practices, and allegiances. Furthermore, those who attempted to silence the "secularists" were occasionally evangelicals, but more often were younger women of the movement who were not zealously religious in their orientation. They were politically pragmatic, however, and worked to censor any but the most mainstream, widely held religious ideas from the movement.

In this work I offer a piece that is missing from the larger historiographical puzzle by looking carefully at both religion and secularism, particularly as they affected Stanton's thought and the woman's movement at the end of the nineteenth century. We need to begin by historicizing the terms "secular" and "secularism," whose meanings have shifted over time. To readers today the term "secular" connotes an absence of all things religious. For Stanton and her contemporaries, in contrast, "secularism" took its place among the various new religious alternatives of the day and offered a critique of religion that nevertheless underscored its importance in nineteenth-century society. The *Woman's Bible* and the controversy it generated provide a clear and telling lens on the suffrage movement of "the doldrums." Not only does the Bible controversy situate suffragists in the broader cultural debates of the period; it illuminates the long-forgotten connections between radical politics and religious experimentation in the "secular" wing of the movement. One of the many stories that might be told about the *Woman's Bible* is the systematic marginalization of the movement's most creative thinkers, Stanton as well as the younger women who worked with her on the revising committee. The largely successful effort to purge the movement of its religious and political radicals was one painful example of the taming of American reform that characterized the Gilded Age.

In addition, I hope to explain how it is that Elizabeth Cady Stanton can, for her followers today, occupy two very different and seemingly contradictory subject positions: theologian and secularist. By and large, this calls for a work of restoration: to restore the political context to Stanton's theology and to restore the religious impulse to her secularism. I begin by trying to understand the place of religion in Stanton's evolving analysis of women's oppression, and particularly in the ways she retold her own life story near its end. From the challenges of her childhood to the political disappointments of her later years, her ongoing quest for religious liberty was the frame Stanton placed around her experiences.

This is not to say that Stanton was an atheist. Rather, she took a dim view of the way Christianity inspired fear in children and the way clergy used the Bible to limit the scope of women's activities. Stanton believed in God, but not in one who would arbitrarily limit women to a designated sphere. Where the Bible directly contradicted her on this point, as in the words of Paul, she did not hesitate to suggest a remedy: "The writings of Paul, like our State Constitutions, are susceptible of various interpretations," she wrote in 1855. "But when the human soul is roused with holy indignation against injustice and oppression, it stops not to translate human parchments, but follows out the law of its inner being written by the finger of God in the first hour of its Creation."[43] Stanton understood moral zeal. But like the radical abolitionists whose heightened religious righteousness prohibited them from working within the established churches, she confronted the hypocrisy of "woman's sphere" and its religious underpinnings head-on.

In this campaign, Stanton hoped to decimate the cultural roots of women's inequality. Over the course of fifty-four years of public activism, she continually lamented that woman was "the chief support of the church and clergy; the very powers that make her emancipation impossible."[44] The combined forces of the church and the clergy lacked traditional political power, but they wielded considerable control over woman's psyche by continually reminding her that through Eve, woman "was the author of original sin and the fall of man." Nothing short of a cultural revolution was necessary to correct that perception and, Stanton argued, "It would take forces outside the church to do that."[45]

At age eighty, Stanton might have rested on her laurels as a suffrage "pioneer," doted upon by a younger generation. Instead, she was emboldened by her seniority to serve, as she liked to say, as a "free lance," to needle the suffrage movement for its growing religious conservatism. It was not a role that endeared her either to younger reformers or to the public. Stanton spent these years increasingly isolated, in her words, as "a leader of thought rather than numbers."[46] In the short run, her religious radicalism cost her dearly. In the long run, she never doubted that history would redeem her.

The survival of Stanton's Bible and its impressive ability to resonate with different people in different historical contexts reveal the extent to which, over a century later, we are still hard at work determining the relationship of feminism to Christianity. But this book is not about that. Rather, I am committed to placing the *Woman's Bible* back in the context in which it was written, produced, repudiated, and—at least occasionally—read. Indeed, the importance of the *Woman's Bible* goes well beyond what it symbolizes to readers today. The relationship of this text to its context reveals a vital story about the past. It is a story about Stanton and her Bible; it is a story about the evolution of the movement for woman's rights; it is a story about the spiritual crisis of the turn of the century.

In one way, the controversy generated by the *Woman's Bible* seems oddly out of step with the explosive crises of its era, decades wracked by economic depression, the birth of Jim Crow segregation, and the emergence of an imperialist state.[47] And yet, history continues to teach us that it is in these very moments of political and economic upheaval that we can expect a resurgence of new forms of orthodoxy as well as the scapegoating of those who seem to undermine traditional values. The *Woman's Bible* and the controversy it generated both encapsulated the anxiety of an age and deflected attention from more pressing concerns. In this sense, they can tell us something about the turn of the last century and our time as well.

1

"The Sunset of Life":
Elizabeth Cady Stanton and
the Polemics of Autobiography

> I can truly say . . . that all the cares and anxieties, the trials and disappointments of my whole life, are light, when balanced with my sufferings in childhood and youth from the theological dogmas which I sincerely believed, and the gloom connected with everything associated with the name of religion.
>
> ELIZABETH CADY STANTON,
> *Eighty Years and More* (1898)

By the time Elizabeth Cady Stanton completed her autobiography, she had for all practical purposes retired from public appearances. At the age of eighty-three, she authored her memoir and compiled the second volume of her controversial *Woman's Bible*, bringing the total number of books published since her eightieth birthday to three. Gregarious, funny, and smart, Stanton had devoted decades to political organizing, speaking tours, and polemical writing for the cause of women's emancipation. Now, ensconced in her New York apartment where she hired a "girl" to read to her several hours a day, she was taking a break from all command performances because, as she told her son, "my eyes grow dimmer and legs weaker from month to month."[1] In point of fact, she had not attended a suffrage convention in six years. She was frustrated, and not just by her diminishing strength. Unlike Stanton herself, the woman suffrage movement had grown conservative as it aged, and Stanton felt she could no longer maneuver within its narrow confines. She confided to her former colleague Victoria Woodhull, "I begin to feel discouraged as to the old line of attack. . . . All my fifty years' work seem to have borne little fruit." The trouble, she told Woodhull, was "with women themselves."[2]

A half-century of reform work had taught Stanton a few things about politics, religion, and the relations between the sexes, vital lessons she had en-

14

capsulated for her readers in her books. While she claimed, as a reformer, that her political work had "borne little fruit," she held out hope that as an author, she might yet resolve the trouble "with women themselves." To that end she spent life as an octogenarian "busy writing alternately on this autobiography and 'The Woman's Bible.' "[3] Stanton's memoir and her *Woman's Bible* had a great deal in common. Not only had Stanton written them simultaneously; she offered in them a similar polemic on nineteenth-century religion, politics, and women's condition: "that the religious superstitions of women perpetuate their bondage more than all adverse influences." In the *Woman's Bible*, Stanton located her argument for Christianity's devastating impact on women in the Bible itself, in the misogyny she detected in biblical texts. In her autobiography, she framed the consequences of Christianity in the details of her life story, in the tale of a young woman who rejected the church and Bible as part of her natural progression toward maturity. Stanton had tried and failed to achieve this very progression for the woman's rights movement generally. She now hoped to inspire her readers to take up her cause and demand "justice, liberty and equality in the Church as well as in the State" (*Eighty Years*, 467–468).

Of the two books, her memoir was the more immediately successful vehicle for her views. No doubt, for many readers, Stanton's humor and her storytelling couched the political polemic in more comfortable terms. Like most memoirs, Stanton's autobiography operated on several levels at once. On the most basic, it provided readers with the familiar outlines of her life and political career.[4] Her story began with her birth in 1815 in upstate New York and ended with her eightieth birthday celebration in 1895, a gala event at New York's Metropolitan Opera House, which was attended by thousands of faithful followers. In between those two bookends, Stanton artfully arranged the chapters of her life.

She grew up the daughter of Margaret Livingston Cady, from a prominent New York family, and Daniel Cady, a lawyer, member of Congress, and state supreme court justice in Johnstown, New York. The fourth living child in a line of eleven, only six of whom survived to adulthood, Elizabeth had one brother, Eleazer, who was nine years her senior. His death in 1826 would be the defining moment of her childhood, but her earliest memory was of the birth of her younger sister Catherine in 1820. As her nurse carried her to meet her latest sibling, she heard family friends whisper, "What a pity it is she's a girl." The five-year-old Elizabeth felt compassion for the little newborn, greeted by such remarks, but she "did not understand at that time that girls were considered an inferior order of beings" (4). Her early years of childhood, when she first was exposed to "the humiliation of the distinctions made on the ground of sex," provided rich material for her ensuing career as an activist.

Her life as a young woman was shaped by her dual attraction to the anti-slavery movement and to one of its talented young orators, Henry Brewster Stanton, whom she married over her father's objections in 1840 (71).[5] Pioneers of the "working vacation," Elizabeth and her new husband spent their honeymoon at the World Antislavery Convention in London. This event would take on mythic proportions in her life story and in the history of the woman's rights movement. Citing "Scriptural texts," the British organizers of the convention prohibited women from speaking and literally marginalized them at the meeting by seating them in a balcony. Sequestered with the other women, Stanton made the acquaintance of the legendary Quaker preacher Lucretia Mott, as well as other American antislavery luminaries. "These were the first women I had ever met who believed in the equality of the sexes and who did not believe in the popular orthodox religion," Stanton remembered (83).[6] They made a lasting impact.

When the Stantons returned from Europe they settled initially in Elizabeth's hometown of Johnstown, New York. In Stanton's words, "the puzzling questions of theology and poverty that had occupied so much of my thoughts, now gave place to the practical one, 'what to do with a baby'" (112). In nineteen years of marriage, she bore a total of seven. As Henry developed a career in law, the Stantons moved twice: first to the busy, "enthusiastically literary" city of Boston in 1843, and then in 1847 to the comparatively remote location of Seneca Falls, New York, which Stanton disparaged as "somewhat depressing." After that move, according to the chronology in her memoir, once the "novelty of housekeeping had passed away," Stanton, in conjunction with several of her Quaker neighbors and the visiting Lucretia Mott, issued a call for a woman's rights convention to be held in Seneca Falls on July 19–20, 1848 (145).[7] As they launched their fledgling movement for woman's rights, Stanton repeatedly shocked her more cautious colleagues with her outspoken pronouncements, some religious, some political, but apparently none more revolutionary than her insistence on women's right "to the elective franchise," the vote.

Stanton would not live to see the acquisition of this "sacred" right, but she and her colleagues made headway in other areas. Although she only sporadically attended conventions herself, she applauded the national woman's rights meetings held annually in cities throughout the Northeast over the next decade and claimed them as the logical successors of her Seneca Falls convention. Stanton and her colleagues also pressed for improvements in New York State's Married Woman's Property Act of 1848, a measure that broadened married women's control of their inheritances and real estate, but primarily benefitted white, middle- and upper-class women. Woman's rights activists specifically sought legislation to entitle women to "ownership" of their own wages, a reform which would have advanced the eco-

nomic and legal rights of a broader base of women. However, such legislation was not passed until after the Civil War.[8] The temperance cause, organized to renounce the consumption of alcohol, was also deeply embedded in
the reform consciousness of her generation, and Stanton took on this campaign as well. She was quickly "decapitated" as the head of the Women's
New York State Temperance Society, however, when she declared that a
husband's chronic drunkenness should be a just cause for divorce.[9]

While Stanton seemed destined to work in more progressive venues than
temperance agitation offered her, her temperance work brought her together with Susan B. Anthony. "Mrs. Stanton," as Anthony always called
her, and the unmarried Miss Anthony, "a mother of ideas rather than of
men," forged a political partnership and an intense friendship that endured
the rest of their lives. "Soon fastened, heart to heart," Stanton wrote in her
autobiography, "with hooks of steel in a friendship that years of confidence
and affection have steadily strengthened, we have labored faithfully together" (156, 187). Their labor often began in Stanton's Seneca Falls home,
where they mounted their front line of defense against the "young savages"
(Stanton's sons) who competed for their time and attention (163). Taking
turns on the "domestic watchtowers," Stanton and Anthony wrote "resolutions, protests, appeals, petitions, agricultural reports, and constitutional arguments" and tried, in Stanton's words, "to secure equal rights to all in the
home as well as the nation." Indeed, Stanton credited Anthony with being
her "good angel" who kept her engaged in the work when she might have
slipped into "narrow family selfishness" (164–165). As colleagues with complementary talents, Stanton and Anthony made a formidable duo. In the
1850s and early 1860s they divided their time between antislavery and an array of injustices affecting women in free states, including women's rights to
wages, child custody, divorce reform, and the ballot.

With the onset of the Civil War, however, Stanton and Anthony turned
their attention to organizing exclusively for the war effort and founded the
Women's Loyal National League. Under their leadership, the association
called for the "immediate emancipation and enfranchisement of the Southern slaves, as the most speedy way of ending the War" (236). Setting up
shop at the Cooper Institute in New York City, where the Stantons by then
lived, Stanton and Anthony circulated petitions and raised cash "to secure
the final and complete consecration of America to freedom." Through their
Republican ally, Senator Charles Sumner, they presented hundreds of thousands of signatures to Congress calling for the abolition of slavery in all
parts of the United States (238–239).[10]

In championing the cause of abolition, Stanton and Anthony assumed,
optimistically, that the "final and complete consecration of America to freedom" would include the woman's ballot, a recognition of the loyal women's

efforts during the war. But their hopes were thwarted. "Deceived" by her Republican allies, Stanton wrote bitterly: "the only way they could open the constitutional door just wide enough to let the black man pass in was to introduce the word 'male' into the national Constitution" (238, 255, 242). This constitutional sleight of hand dealt women's cause a fatal blow, Stanton feared. She and Anthony lobbied aggressively to alter the language of the Fourteenth and Fifteenth Amendments, but their efforts failed. With other abolitionists they had formed a new organization, the American Equal Rights Association, which advocated a policy of "universal suffrage." How would they stand now, confronted with the problematic wording of the Fifteenth Amendment? Unwilling to support a constitutional amendment that enfranchised black men and not women, Stanton and Anthony parted company with their long-time allies within the antislavery movement.[11]

At about the same time, Stanton and Anthony had launched a new venture, a controversial newspaper titled the *Revolution*. An expensive proposition, the newspaper was initially financed by their flamboyant (and notorious) new ally George Francis Train, a Democrat who had stumped for their cause in the campaign for woman suffrage in Kansas in 1867. Before long, however, Train had departed for Ireland, where he turned his efforts and resources to another of his pet campaigns, Irish independence. Without Train's backing the *Revolution* was financially strapped and lasted only a few years. Yet Stanton long considered the period in which she edited the paper "one of the happiest of my life, and I may add the most useful" (257). By this time Stanton had moved her household yet again, to the New York suburb of Tenafly, New Jersey, where, despite constant travel, she maintained a residence for nineteen years. In 1869, out of the broken pieces of their failed coalition with abolitionists, Stanton and Anthony assembled a new woman's rights organization, the National Woman Suffrage Association, for which Stanton served as president and Anthony as vice president. A rival organization formed in the following months, led by Stanton and Anthony's former colleagues in the abolition movement Lucy Stone and Henry Blackwell.

Placing the daily operations of their organization in Anthony's hands, Stanton accepted an engagement as a paid lecturer for the New York Lyceum Bureau, an assignment that kept her on the road for eight months a year. For twelve years she traveled the country and delivered a set of popular addresses in which she translated for a wider audience many of the political concerns of the woman's rights movement. Often, in the afternoons, Stanton would hold meetings exclusively for women on one of her favorite topics, "Marriage and Maternity." Equality within marriage was an essential component of women's emancipation, Stanton argued. But to achieve equality in marital relations, women needed to assert their rights to "self-sovereignty" and "voluntary motherhood," terms she used to articulate women's right to refuse sexual intercourse in order to prevent pregnancy (297).[12]

By 1880, Stanton had retired from the Lyceum and taken on, with Anthony and their suffrage colleague Matilda Joslyn Gage, another publishing project, *The History of Woman Suffrage.* The entire massive task would stretch out over ten years. A combination of historical documents and narrative history, the first volume, a modest 871 pages, appeared in May 1881. "I welcomed it," Stanton wrote, "with the same feeling of love and tenderness as I did my firstborn" (329). After devoting two years to gestating volume two, she decided to take a leave of absence from her suffrage work to visit her "other" children in Europe (337). She relished her escape. At age sixty-eight, Stanton would never return to the movement with quite the same commitment or attention to its day-to-day concerns. Rather, she chose to spend her last two decades among family and deeply engaged in her own writing.

Stanton's frustration with organized religion had long smoldered in her, but her time in Europe, and her distance from the American movement, seemingly freed her to fan that flame with abandon. "If we who do see the absurdities of the old superstitions never unveil them to others," she told one of her English colleagues, "how is the world to make any progress in the theologies? I am in the sunset of life, and I feel it to be my special mission to tell people what they are not prepared to hear, instead of echoing worn-out opinions" (372). People were not prepared to hear, for example, Stanton's answer to her own question: "What has Christianity done for Woman?" (357). (Not much, as it turned out.) People would be even less eager to hear about her plans for a collaboratively authored "Woman's Bible." Still Stanton persisted, convinced that eventually her colleagues would "awake to its importance and offer their services" (393). Just as the nation celebrated Stanton's eightieth birthday in 1895, volume one of her *Woman's Bible* appeared, eliciting "a general disapproval by press and pulpit, and even by women themselves." Unflappable, Stanton was not discouraged by the criticism. In the closing pages of her memoir, she wrote of the *Woman's Bible*: "Like other 'mistakes,' this too, in due time will be regarded as 'a step in progress' " (467).

The completion of her memoirs brought Stanton a great deal of satisfaction. In contrast to the virulent attacks on the *Woman's Bible*, the reviews her autobiography received were quite favorable. Thrilled by the attention, Stanton boasted to a friend that the Sunday New York *Sun* "gave me nearly three columns. They all say as the story of a busy life it is very interesting."[13] While the details of a "busy life" may have obscured the book's political slant for some readers, for her part Stanton rarely missed an opportunity to score points with her story. In a typical example, eager both to sell more books and to convert young readers to her views, she urged a friend in Ann Arbor, Michigan, to place her autobiography "in the hands of every girl in the University."[14]

What did Stanton hope those young Michigan students might find in *Eighty Years and More*? Sandwiched amid her biographical details was a rich filling of entertaining anecdotes, advice literature, and political persuasion. With a well-trained ear for comic timing, Stanton regaled readers with hilarious tales often told at her own expense. But her story was more than entertainment, just as it was more than autobiography. It was a portrait of a life whose retelling was strategic and directed. Published in book form just four years before her death in 1902, Stanton's memoirs drew upon a lifetime of memories. When her autobiographical writings first began to appear in print in 1889 as a weekly column in the suffrage paper *Woman's Tribune*, she called them "Reminiscences," a phrase she retained in the subtitle of the book version. Memory was central to her project. But as many of her biographers would attest, Stanton's memory, in certain respects, was not very good.[15] At least, it was not as reliable as her unfailing gift as a storyteller. By its very nature, memory is selective rather than comprehensive; the survival of some memories hinges on the repression of others.[16] To forge a coherent autobiographical narrative from the already selective evidence of memory requires both erasure and invention. Stanton remembered selectively, omitted some events completely, and created a new form for her life story. Often she embellished a memory to make a good story or to anchor an important point of her argument. At other times her memories served a compensatory purpose: she remembered in order to atone for the past.

In the pages of *Eighty Years and More*, Stanton promised readers "the story of my private life" (xxx). But as I explore in what follows, Stanton revealed her private self only partially. Her readers were never far from her thoughts. Stanton envisioned her readers, like the young women she imagined at the University of Michigan, as potential converts to women's emancipation and her book as a polemical means toward their political conversion. Shaped for a public audience and by a political purpose, her memoir was a personal story, but rarely a private one. Furthermore, it was not always accurate history. The historian Nancy Isenberg, for example, has questioned Stanton's account of the origin of the woman's rights movement. Isenberg argues that Stanton's "master narrative," which moves seamlessly from the World Antislavery Convention of 1840 to the Seneca Falls meeting in 1848, has, among other flaws, a "glaring problem of the eight-year gap" in its chronology. Isenberg suggests that this gap might usefully be explained by turning our historical attention to the numerous other reformers and organizations, many of them religious, who were doing woman's rights work in this era. Stanton's narrative is not untrue, according to Isenberg, but it does offer a particularly politicized version of the past that positions Lucretia Mott as the prophetic figure in the woman's rights movement, Elizabeth Cady Stanton as her sole disciple, and Seneca Falls as the putative "beginning" of the movement, a designation that might rightfully belong to the Woman's Rights Convention of Worcester, Massachusetts, held in 1850.[17] Still, Isenberg writes, scholars have "inherited" Stanton's story, overlooked the questions it raises, and elevated the whole package—Stanton, Seneca Falls, the document it produced, "The Declaration of Sentiments," and, particularly, Stanton's controversial call for the right to vote—"into a coherent and complete explanation . . . of the women's rights campaign."[18]

Stanton was, in the words of her children, "a famous storyteller."[19] Indeed, as Isenberg shows with the account of Seneca Falls, Stanton's stories have been so compelling to generations of readers that family members, biographers, historians, and filmmakers alike have delighted in telling and retelling them. In fact, her narrative grasp on the past has been so tight that at times it has been difficult to free the historical record. With the aim of doing so, I have chosen to examine four stories from Stanton's autobiography that illustrate the varied ways in which she remembered and the license with which she cultivated stories from memories. These forays into Stanton's memoir are not intended simply as illustrations of her creative use of memory, however. Rather, her stories, both those she elected to tell and those she omitted, are key to understanding the effort she exerted on her past to make it "bear fruit" in the present as well as her personal and political evolution and the ideological vision that guided her work, particularly the *Woman's Bible*, during her last decades.

If we are to understand Stanton as she understood herself, then her faults as a historian must be weighed against her merits as a storyteller. For Stanton, as for all writers of memoirs, memory fused her past with her present. Her memories were not her past, but rather her effort to make meaning of it. Her friend Susan B. Anthony once said of Stanton, "she can tangle up chronology to beat any other one who puts pen to paper."[20] Nonetheless, as Stanton retold her stories in the twilight of her career, her process of selection, invention, and erasure was neither arbitrary nor accidental, but well grounded in her lucid present. Stanton may have retired from public life, but she had not resigned herself to the status quo. She believed that her stories—shaped by what one reporter called her "immense anecdotal power"—could change the lives of her readers.[21] But though, in one sense, Stanton used the pages of *Eighty Years and More* to tell countless stories about herself, in another sense only a few of the stories really mattered.

Childhood, especially her own, retained a particular fascination for Stanton. When she read that the popular novelist Marietta Holley was planning a book on the "rights of children," she immediately sent the author a copy of her newly minted autobiography. "What I suffered in childhood from fear of parents, teachers, God & the Devil may give you some points," Stanton volunteered.[22] In her memoir, familiar themes from her childhood reappear again and again and help to contextualize the episodes of her adult life. Most of Stanton's beliefs, values, and political commitments, judging from the autobiography, were forged out the raw material of her childhood. Particularly meaningful for understanding the *Woman's Bible* is Stanton's repeated claim that "all the cares and anxieties, the trials and disappointments" of her life paled in comparison to the religious sufferings of her youth (24). But though religion is a commanding theme in the childhood she authors, it is inextricably linked to elements of race, gender, and politics. As Stanton's memoir assigned meaning to the events of her youth, four plots emerge with "immense anecdotal power": "unacceptable ghosts"; the problem of boyhood; the limits of politics; and the suffocation of religion. These repeated plots well served her life story and her political vision.[23]

Unacceptable Ghosts

In writing about the nature of autobiography, the historian Jacquelyn Dowd Hall has emphasized the inevitability of repression as part of the autobiographer's process: "Turning memories into stories—whether humble life stories or pretentious master narratives—is also a potent form of forgetting. For every narrative depends on the suppression and repression of contrary, disruptive memories—other peoples' memories of the same events, as well as the unacceptable ghosts of our own pasts."[24] While Stanton's omissions, her potent form of forgetting, may not reflect a conscious decision on her part, her silences are deafening. In nearly five hundred pages, Stanton left out a great deal. Her memoir contains little mention of her mother, or of the deaths of many of those close to her: a father, a son, a husband.[25] One erasure, however, stands out from all others. During her childhood, Stanton's father, Daniel Cady, owned a slave. In 1820, when Elizabeth Cady was just five years old, the manuscript census listed attorney Daniel Cady as the "head of the family" and enumerated a household that included: one free white male aged 10–15 (Eleazer, b. May 26, 1806); one free white male aged 45 and upwards (Daniel Cady, b. April 29, 1773); four free white females under age 10 (Harriet, b. October 5, 1810; Elizabeth, b. November 12, 1815; Margaret, b. December 9, 1817; Catherine, b. January 7, 1820); one free white female aged 10–15 (Tryphena, b. September 11, 1804); one free white female aged 26–44 (Margaret Livingston Cady, b. February 18, 1785); and, finally, one male slave aged 26–44.[26] In all likelihood, the person recorded in this census category, "Slaves, Males," was the ubiquitous "Peter" from Stanton's memoir, Peter Teabout, the Cady family's beloved "manservant" who cared for Elizabeth and her sisters as young children.[27]

Stanton's family's slaveholding past has not been a focus of historical inquiry. Stanton's erasure of her family's practice of slavery was complete. She rendered it virtually invisible. Like many Northerners, she engaged in a process the historian Joanne Pope Melish has termed "historical amnesia" regarding the history of slavery in that region.[28] According to her own recollection, Stanton first discovered the horrors of slavery at the home of her abolitionist cousin, Gerrit Smith, in Peterboro, New York. Smith's mansion was, Stanton wrote, "one of the stations on the 'underground railroad' for slaves escaping from bondage" (51). Here she first got caught up in the antislavery debates that animated the public in the 1830s. Here too she met various Southerners, such as James G. Birney, who had emancipated their slaves. But most important, in Smith's home Elizabeth Cady witnessed firsthand the cruelties of slavery when she met Harriet, "a beautiful quadroon girl, about eighteen years of age," who had escaped her master and was sequestered there en route to Canada. In Stanton's recollection, cousin Gerrit prompted Harriet to tell his cousins the truth about slavery: " 'I want you to make good abolitionists of them by telling them the history of your life—what you have seen and suffered in slavery.' " Harriet had escaped her master while he was visiting in Syracuse; she would be with them only one night. " 'You may never have another opportunity of seeing a slave girl face to face, so ask her all you care to know of the system of slavery,' " Gerrit urged them. Harriet's testimony was effective. "We all wept together as she talked," Stanton remembered, "and, when Cousin Gerrit returned to summon us away, we needed no further education to make us earnest abolitionists" (62–63). Embodied in Harriet, the "beautiful quadroon girl," slavery emerged in Stanton's account as distant, exotic, and necessarily shrouded in secrecy. Slavery had no relevance to life in upstate New York; indeed, New York was a safe haven for slaves, their route to freedom. Moreover, as Stanton's memoir would have it, this chance meeting with Harriet was Elizabeth Cady's first, and perhaps only, opportunity to witness slavery "face to face."

In point of fact, the state of New York had maintained slavery and vestiges of slavery well into Stanton's youth. In 1799 the legislature had passed a Gradual Manumission Act, mandating that children born to slaves after July 4, 1799, were born technically "free." These children were, however, obligated to be indentured servants until age twenty-five for girls and age twenty-eight for boys. All those slaves born before 1799 (which would have included the slave in residence at the Cady household) were slaves for life. In 1817 the state passed a Final Abolition Act, to take effect in ten years. This law stipulated that as of July 4, 1827, all New York slaves not previously granted freedom by statutory emancipation were to be freed. Even after the enactment of the Final Abolition Act in 1827, however, conditions of servitude persisted, rendering many of New York's slaves, in the words of the historian Shane White, only "somewhat more independent." In 1827, Stanton was just twelve years old, and she was preoccupied by the concerns of a precocious adolescent. Is it possible that, even with a slave living in the Cady household, she might not have known that over 40 percent of the 152 African Americans of her hometown were categorized as human chattel?[29] Or that in 1827, all remaining slaves were to be freed on the Fourth of July, in her words, one of "the great events of the year" (14)? Certainly this seems possible. Even as a fairly young child, however, Elizabeth spent time playing in her father's law office. She was intensely interested in her father's clients and particularly in the inequities of the legal system as they affected women. With Peter, who "was very fond of attending court," she often traversed the town, stopping frequently at the courthouse and the jail where they visited "our friends the prisoners." "All the lawyers knew him," Stanton remembered (14). Peter, it would appear, was very interested in the workings of the law and perhaps for good reason. It therefore seems unlikely that the enactment of such a major state statute as the Final Abolition, which affected the status of her beloved Peter, would have entirely eluded the highly observant Elizabeth Cady.

One possible explanation for the omission of the event from her autobiography is that, even with the passage of the emancipation statute, Peter's role in Elizabeth's life did not change drastically.[30] In Stanton's recollections, Peter was employed in domestic work. "It seems to me now," she wrote "that his chief business was to discover our whereabouts, get us home to dinner, and take us back to school" (14). Although Stanton's memories of Peter mirror a child's perception and certainly should not be construed to reflect the full range of his activities, it seems clear that he was employed as a servant, not as an agricultural worker or as an artisan. His transition to freedom, therefore, might have been limited by his bleak economic prospects.

Emancipation brought at least one significant change to Peter Teabout's life: he became officially recognized as the head of his own household. As such, the outlines of his life and person have been embossed on the historical record. Born in Albany, New York, sometime between 1775 and 1784—in any case, too early to have qualified for freedom under the Gradual Manumission Act of 1799—Teabout spent most of his adult life as a resident of Johnstown. On the county census for 1845, his name appears immediately before that of Daniel Cady, suggesting that the modest home Teabout shared with his wife Mariah was in close quarters to the Cady mansion. Peter owned the land, one sixteenth of an acre, as well as the frame house valued at one hundred dollars. Periodically, Peter and Mariah shared their home with children and young people. (In 1855, for example, a sixteen-year-old African American woman named Elida Yates lived with the Teabouts.) In 1860, at age 85, Teabout reported his occupation as a "day-laborer."

As much information as it provides about Peter Teabout, however, the census also speaks volumes about the status of free people of color in New York during these years. With the minimal mark of a census-takers's pen, for example, we learn the following about the Teabout household: the number of persons over 21 years who cannot read or write (two); and the number of persons entitled to vote (zero). Peter Teabout was, according to Stanton's memoir, fond of attending court. By 1827, he was no longer a slave, but he remained a spectator, observing citizenship from a distance.[31]

Despite her memory to the contrary, Elizabeth Cady as a child had indeed come face to face with slavery.[32] Her autobiography offers some clues as to how she understood Peter to be someone "other" than a slave. He first appears in her memoir as part of a triumvirate of "colored men . . . who acted as menservants in our youth," but he quickly emerges as the central figure in her early childhood.

"Black as coal and six feet in height," Peter must have cut quite a figure as he strode about Johnstown with three small white girls in tow. Indeed, one of the most fascinating differences between Peter and the escaped slave girl from the South, Harriet, is how Stanton remembers their access to the public sphere. When Elizabeth meets Harriet in Peterboro, the slave girl is disguised as a "Quakeress," hidden in Gerrit Smith's home, and then driven off under cover of darkness in a carriage bound for Oswego, where she would be safely ferried across Lake Ontario into Canada (63). Peter, in contrast, was well known about Johnstown where, according to Stanton's memories, there was no public space he did not inhabit: the hotel, the church, the school, the courthouse, the jail, the millpond, and the great open-air celebrations, including the Fourth of July festivities and the Training Day for the County Militia. In fact, in Stanton's memory, Peter negotiated the Cady girls' access to these spaces and, with his well-regarded "diplomacy," rescued them from trouble and "much disagreeable surveillance." Peter had the confidence of the community and the family as well, Stanton remembered: "As we were deemed perfectly safe under his care, no questions were asked when we got to the house, if we had been with him" (14).

In particular, Stanton remembered Peter taking her and her sisters to the Fourth of July celebrations, where "Peter was in his element" (14). These festivals were magnificent community spectacles. In the 1820s, the historian Mary Ryan has demonstrated, the Fourth of July became "the major secular holiday on the urban calendar."[33] In Stanton's memory, the celebrations commenced at midnight on July 3 with great bonfires and the firing of cannons. Daylight "was ushered in with the ringing of bells, tremendous can-nonading, and a continuous popping of fire-crackers and torpedoes." Next came the quintessential American ritual, the Fourth of July parade, in which soldiers and citizens marched through Johnstown performing their inde-pendence. The parade was followed by an oration, and then the Declaration of Independence was read, never solemnly, but with audience participation, as a rousing, raucous condemnation of the British. Finally, the townspeople gathered for a "great dinner given in the open air under the trees in the grounds of the old courthouse." This celebration was loud and often unruly. Every toast that was made to the Republic was punctuated with the boom of a cannon. Public drunkenness was not uncommon. In fact, as a child, Eliza-beth recoiled from this event in sympathy with the family cook, "whose drunken father always cut antics in the streets" (17–19). Unlike Peter, the young Elizabeth Cady was not "in her element" on the Fourth of July and did not care much for these festivities. But, not wanting to be called a "cow-ard," she followed Peter into the fray. The Fourth of July seemed to hold special appeal for Peter; perhaps he enjoyed the conviviality and the social leveling that took place when an otherwise hierarchical society reveled in its mythic democracy and its unified opposition to "the mother country." Maybe too Peter was anticipating his own freedom. The final abolition of slavery in New York State was scheduled for July 4, 1827, "a date widely cel-ebrated by the black population," as the historian Graham Hodges has noted.[34]

Stanton's memoir also recorded another "great event" called "Training Day" when "everybody went to the race course to see the troops and buy what the farmers had brought in their wagons." Prompted by her memories of Peter and his love of public celebrations, Stanton's recollection of "Train-ing Day" may well have fused the General Training Day with one of the nu-merous festivals organized by African Americans in New York at this time. Peter was a native of Albany where these festivals were legendary. In many northern communities, however, General Training Day or Negro Training Day was an important event in which African Americans from the country-side would gather on the edge of town to watch the black militia perform. Although Stanton makes no specific mention of race, clues from her mem-oir suggest that, as a small child in Peter's care, she may have participated in these African American festivals. Gingerbread, for example, was the food most associated with the various African American holidays. Slaves and free people of color would bake round gingerbread cakes and sell them, for a penny apiece, from the backs of wagons. Stanton remembers the commer-cial exchange with farmers at these events as well as "a peculiar kind of gin-gerbread . . . to which we were treated on those occasions, associated in my mind to this day with military reviews and standing armies" (19).[35] Nothing in Stanton's autobiography explicitly labels the festival an African American holiday, but her association of this event with Peter and the "peculiar" gingerbread, as well as its location at the race track on the outskirts of town, resonates with African American culture in upstate New York at the time. In any case, the larger point to be drawn from Stanton's account of Peter and public celebrations is that these memories, refracted through the lens of childhood, no doubt magnified Peter's freedom and his ease of access to the public sphere. Peter was Elizabeth Cady's chaperone, the adult who accompanied her on virtually every foray she records. His presence as a spectator, of course, did not ensure his equal participation in civil society, but that distinction might not have been discernible by a small child. Where she did notice Peter's unequal status, in the church, it made a lasting impression, as we shall see.

In the story Stanton writes, Peter moved easily in the public sphere, but he seemed equally at home in the privacy of the Cady household. Stanton's memoir contains recollections of the marvelous Christmas festivities Peter would plan and execute for the Cady children. With school out of session, they would gather in the cellar kitchen and play blindman's bluff by firelight to the accompaniment of Peter's violin. Christmas Eve would bring the hanging of stockings and much anticipation of presents from St. Nicholas. On Christmas Day, Peter would load the Cady offspring, and neighboring children as well, onto a long red lumber sleigh and take them out into the country where, led by "Peter's fine tenor voice," they would sing carols and wish a Merry Christmas to all the farmers' children. Back from the jaunt, Peter would begin to ready Christmas dinner, "attired in a white apron and turban." His preparations were likewise filled with pomp and ceremony. The three little Cady girls, dressed in red flannel, were mesmerized. Perched on a big ironing table in the kitchen, they watched Peter's every move as he dressed the turkey. Peter's lieutenant, Jacob, peeled vegetables, as Peter delighted them with "marvelous stories" and flapjacks that he deftly flipped in mid-air and skillfully caught with his skillet. Peter knew how to engage children, to sing and play games, even to turn the most mundane of household activities into entertainment. He was, it seems, the perfect parent. In Stanton's words, "his love for us was unbounded and fully returned. He was the only being, visible or invisible, of whom we had no fear." The Cady girls were completely devoted to him, Stanton remembers; "like Mary's lamb, where'er he went we were sure to go" (15–17).

Noticeably absent from these childhood memories of intimate family scenes are Daniel and Margaret Cady. Peter, who offered Elizabeth safe haven and freedom from fear, stands in stark contrast to her cool and distant parents. "Our parents were as kind, indulgent, and considerate as the Puritan ideas of those days permitted, but fear, rather than love, of God and par-

ents alike, predominated," she wrote (4). In many ways it was Peter's maternal attributes to which Stanton was drawn in her youth: his cooking,
singing, dressing up, decorating, storytelling, and game-playing all made an
impression. In fact, it seems that Stanton patterned her own mothering on
the model she learned from Peter. As a mother and a grandmother, she was
a great lover of games and a legendary storyteller (428).[36] She too felt that
there was no place for fear in childrearing. But even as she praised Peter's
maternal qualities, she also lauded his manliness. The image of Peter
dressed up for church was emblazoned on her memory. "Dressed in a new
suit of blue with gilt buttons, he looked like a prince, as, with head erect, he
walked up the aisle, the grandest specimen of manhood in the whole congregation" (17).[37] Peter was her idealized parent, both mother and father.
She appropriated him for her life story as a child does a parent, with little or
no awareness of the parent's existence apart from the child. As a child, Stanton might have never questioned Peter's "status," bond or free, because she
instinctively understood his place in her life as the one person whose love
for her was, paradoxically, "unbounded." When she was an adult, however,
these questions would have been harder to resist.

Despite the fact that Peter Teabout lived in close proximity to the Cady
family until his death in 1862, he vanishes from Stanton's memoir. His dis-
appearance coincides with her brother's death in 1826. Yet, Stanton offers
no explanation for Peter's vanishing from her story any more than she accounted for his presence in her family to begin with. We learn only that Peter is "at rest now with 'Old Uncle Ned in the place where the good niggers
go' " (5).[38] In the story of her childhood, she transfers her affection to Simon Hosack, the minister who lived next door: he follows Peter as her guiding parental figure.

Deliberately or unconsciously, Stanton shielded her readers from the truth
of her family's slaveholding. But in placing Peter in so prominent a position
in her life story, she begged these questions. Stanton's stories of Peter open a
window into the world of her childhood that might otherwise have been
sealed off. She might have omitted Peter entirely. Some of her biographers
have done so; others have argued that her love of Peter was a source of her
later abolitionism.[39] In Stanton's story, however, Peter serves a particular
purpose: to present a telling contrast to her parents. She could not eliminate
Peter from the story and still underscore the more important lesson to be
drawn from her parents' cool reserve: a childhood dominated by fear of God
and parents rendered children emotionally weak, dependent, and vulnerable
to religious superstition. Peter's intervention saved her from that plight, just
as the Reverend Simon Hosack would save her again in the future.

While it may be impossible to determine with certainty the extent of
Stanton's knowledge of her family's slaveholding, this particular issue does

suggest a more general mindset that framed her memoir, her protectiveness of the past.[40] Unlike many of her abolitionist colleagues—Angelina and Sarah Grimké, for example—Stanton did not elect to use her family's slave-holding as a source of authority for her antislavery convictions. Moreover, her complicated relationship with her father may also have silenced her on this topic.

Daniel Cady, grieving the loss of his only male heir, simultaneously encouraged his daughter to be boylike and lamented the fact that she was not, in actuality, a boy. He was impossible to please, but that only made Elizabeth try harder. She consciously styled herself on his model and became an interpreter of the laws. Even in the womb, she contended in her memoir, she had been influenced by her father. Her gestation coincided with his election to Congress, and Stanton speculated that "perhaps the excitement of a political campaign, in which my mother took the deepest interest, may have had an influence on my prenatal life and given me the strong desire that I have always felt to participate in the rights and duties of government" (2).[41] Yet Daniel Cady was mortified by his daughter's public career, and disinherited her for a time. What he had encouraged in her as a child, he could not tolerate in her as an adult woman.

The revelation of Daniel Cady's slaveholding sheds new insight in another area of father-daughter conflict: his strident opposition to Elizabeth's marriage to Henry Brewster Stanton. Henry B. Stanton's abolitionist views were frequently noted as a major reason for Daniel Cady's disapproval, along with Henry's dismal financial prospects, but the fact that Daniel Cady himself had owned property in people offers a new dimension to our understanding of their struggle. What is striking is that she never exposed him; the daughter never "disowned" the father. Even late in her life when Stanton hinted that perhaps their next-door neighbor in Johnstown had held slaves, she refused to shine the same searchlight on her father's past. Despite Daniel Cady's overt disapproval of his daughter, her marriage, her views, and her political work, she cast her lot with his. She was her father's daughter.

Stanton's protectiveness of the past had other ramifications as well. The slave in the household of her childhood was not the only unacceptable ghost of her past. Often Stanton herself, or the painful memory of her own past behavior, emerged as the unacceptable ghost whose existence had to be repressed. This is one way to understand, for example, her terse, abbreviated memories of Reconstruction. As Stanton told the story of her split with abolitionists, black activists, and the Republican Party in 1869, she and Anthony were "betrayed" by the friends of their cause who promoted black male suffrage in the Fifteenth Amendment. In her refusal to support the amendment, Stanton had taken an uncompromising position, evidenced an alarmingly superficial commitment to "universal suffrage," and used virulently

racist rhetoric. Indeed, many reformers believed that it was Stanton and Anthony who were guilty of betrayal, of betraying their own commitment to
African Americans, but this is not what Stanton remembered.

Stanton's suppression of her unacceptable ghosts allows us to see the ways
in which she was able to minimize, if not erase entirely, her own considerable privilege. This was a defining element in her political analysis as she
aged. Her fatal flaw allowed her to overlook race, class, and other inequalities and to maintain that gender, with its religious underpinnings, was the
most critical handicap *all* women faced. By suppressing the enormous privilege that accompanied her status as a member of a slave-owning, aristocratic
family, Stanton could persuasively argue that women's religious liberty was
the crucial "first step" to the equality of the sexes.

"The Problem of Boyhood"

Even in her advanced years, Stanton remained convinced that life's most
painful lessons about the inequality of the sexes were taught in childhood.
Her privileged childhood was not without tragedy. Margaret and Daniel
Cady buried a total of five sons and one daughter between 1810 and 1828.
Only one son, Eleazer, "the pride of my father's heart," survived to adulthood. When Eleazer died at twenty, Daniel Cady sank into a deep and all-
consuming grief.[42] Elizabeth, by then eleven, tried to comfort her father
who could only respond: " 'Oh my daughter I wish you were a boy!' " (21).

From that point on, the adolescent Elizabeth Cady "pondered the problem of boyhood." Although much of her childhood had been spent in boyish
pursuits, "roaming in the forests and sailing on the millpond," she now wondered if being a boy, or "as near like one as possible," required of her less
play and more study (21).[43] Ultimately she opted for a combination of ath-
leticism and academics: "Resolutions never to be forgotten—destined to
mould my character anew."[44] Her brother had graduated from Union College, and she endeavored to follow in his footsteps by being at the head of
her class at the Johnstown Academy. In pursuing boyhood, Elizabeth found
a worthy mentor in her elderly neighbor, the Reverend Simon Hosack. The
Reverend Hosack's greatest asset—in addition to his personal library, which
he would will to Elizabeth—was that he thought girls were smart. In fact, he
assured her, "I would not give you for all the boys in Christendom" (21).

Unbeknownst to Judge Cady, his adolescent daughter spent her mornings
studying Greek with the minister. At twilight she accompanied her father on
his daily pilgrimage to his son's grave. Leaning against a poplar tree, she
looked on unhappily as her father "threw himself on the grave, with out-
stretched arms, as if to embrace his child" (22). As much as this scene pained

her, however, she had confidence in her plan and continued to make "rapid progress" toward boyhood, intellectually and physically. "I surprised even my teacher," she wrote, "who thought me capable of doing anything. I learned to drive, and to leap a fence and ditch on horseback" (22).[45] As she had hoped, her mastery of her horse impressed her father. "I could leap a four-bar fence very easily and that was a great pleasure to my father," she remembered. Daniel Cady further encouraged her boyhood by discouraging her from sewing, the prototypical female activity by which young women were supposed to distinguish themselves. "He never wanted me to sew. If he saw me sewing anything he said 'lay that thing aside and get some strong Irish girl to do it, you go ride.' "[46] Defying the geographical confines of girlhood, Elizabeth took great pleasure in playing outdoors.[47] Boys provided the model for her childhood adventures, in which she "always acted on the assumption that what we had seen done, we could do" (19).

In a rare mishap, Elizabeth captained a company of girls on a sailing expedition that gradually drifted toward danger. Unable to lift the raft's navigation poles, the girls failed to prevent their vessel from heading over a dam. They held on tight and managed not to capsize. Rescued by Peter, none of the girls was injured. But Elizabeth's pride was severely bruised. A boy at school wrote an essay about the young captain's failed adventure, in which he emphasized "the ignorance of the laws of navigation shown by the officers in command." Elizabeth had failed three crucial tests of boyhood—physical prowess, mastery over nature, and independence—and she felt humiliated. "I did not hear the last of that voyage for a long time," Stanton recalled; "I shed tears many times over that performance" (19).[48]

But though Elizabeth may not have won the battle of the millpond, her preparations for boyhood began to pay off in another realm. At the Johnstown Academy she competed in class with boys several years her senior and eventually won second prize in Greek. Sure that this was just the evidence she needed to persuade her father of girls' essential equality with boys, she burst into his office and presented her trophy, a Greek Testament. Seemingly pleased, he bent down, kissed her on the forehead, and sighed, "Ah, you should have been a boy!" Stung by her father's insensitivity, she sought the shoulder of her reverend neighbor. "He chased my bitter tears away, and soothed me with unbounded praises and visions of future success." It was one of many struggles Elizabeth endured in pursuit of her father's elusive praise. She "taxed every power, hoping someday to hear my father say: 'Well, a girl is as good as a boy, after all.' But he never said it" (22–23).

But the Reverend Simon Hosack said it, repeatedly. In fact, we learn very little else about him, except for all the important ways in which he was unlike Elizabeth's father. Hosack appeared in Stanton's memoir as an idealized father figure who recognized his daughter's talents and did not withhold his praise. "All the love that a man would naturally have for his own child," Stanton wrote, "he bestowed upon me."[49] Knowing that his health was declining, Hosack asked Elizabeth if she would like to have his books once he was gone. "Yes," she replied, "but I would rather you stay . . . for what can I do when you are gone?" (22). Seemingly unencumbered by a life of his own, the Reverend could minister to Elizabeth's pressing needs and compensate for her parents' various failings. With impeccable timing, Hosack always appears at the right moment to offer a shoulder, a comforting word, a Greek lesson, and his final gift to her, his books.

Rendered in its simplicity, the story of Stanton's relationship with Hosack is a powerful one. It became more potent over time. As a memoir writer creating a compelling fiction of her childhood, Stanton edited and simplified her relationship with Hosack to magnify its poetic and narrative power. She distilled their friendship to its essential elements. Hosack exists solely to allow her to begin to believe in herself. Does he have a home? He must, he is the neighbor. Does he have a family? She offered no clue. Does he have a church and parishioners, a vocation other than tutoring his young protégé? We only see him tending his garden. In this case, memory did not fail her; Stanton consciously reduced the parameters of Hosack's life in the published version of her autobiography. In earlier accounts, she had offered her readers much greater detail about her neighbor, most of it tainted with the prejudices of childhood and the times. As it turned out, the neighbor minister was not a lone householder, but in fact, "had a little withered wife and no children, a blind sister-in-law and six negroes who ate him out of house and home."[50] Suddenly Simon Hosack is situated in a crowded household of dependent women and former slaves. What might it have meant to Stanton's narrative of childhood liberation that her rescuer was not only a minister but also a slave owner? Ultimately she decided not to complicate the story.

For Stanton, Hosack's household is not as important as his message to her. "This love of his and this respect that he seemed to have for me as a child cultivated in me a good deal of selfrespect," she wrote.[51] It was an elusive virtue, hard to come by. Indeed, the great tragedy of this story is that the young girl who "should have been a boy" had finally found someone who understood her and he was slipping away. Yes, she wanted his books, but she would rather have had his enduring friendship, with all its suppressed complications. Simon Hosack's legacy of books was richly symbolic of what he meant to her: her independence of her father's judgment, her facility for learning, and, most important, her ability, if not to be a boy, then at least to compete successfully against them.

As a child, Elizabeth Cady was so accustomed to ranking and measuring herself against boys that one wonders if she found girls to be worthy adversaries. Her two years at Emma Willard's Female Seminary suggests that she did not. Derailed from her goal of attending the all-male Union College like her brother, Elizabeth "treaded on her pride" and resigned herself to Miss Willard's, where, she recalled, her only hope of intellectual stimulation came in the unlikely form of dancing, music, and French lessons (35).

Stanton was not particularly fair in this assessment of academic life at Willard's school. Considered a progressive institution for its time, the seminary offered an academic curriculum comparable to colleges for men. Moreover, school records indicate that Elizabeth Cady studied much more than dancing, music, and French. In addition to those pursuits, her curriculum included algebra, botany, writing, Euclidean geometry, logic, criticism, and drawing. A lifelong advocate of co-education, Stanton disparaged the academics at Miss Willard's when her larger objections appeared to have been the school's single-sex setting.[52]

This was not the destiny that she had imagined for herself. "I wanted to run the races with somebody," she wrote; "I wanted to show some boy that I could do more than he could."[53] Not only would the religious environment at Miss Willard's prove enervating to her; Elizabeth Cady gradually withered in the all-girl environment of "petty jealousies." Largely through her own passivity, she ended up the victim of a plagiarism scandal. So dormant were her competitive impulses in the absence of boys that Miss Cady, "susceptible to flattery," apparently thought nothing of it when a classmate asked her to "trade" essays and then proposed that each submit the other's work as her own. Sluggish in her own defense, Elizabeth looked on, confused by her complicity, as her classmate received credit for her own clever essay. The worst was yet to come, however. The essay Elizabeth had received in the trade was not only dull and unimaginative; it was plagiarized from yet another student. When Elizabeth read it aloud before the school assembly, the crime was discovered. "The personification of guilt," Elizabeth froze in stunned silence, unable to mount a defense. She then flew to her room, "too wretched for tears." There in her misery she found comfort in the arms of her "betrayer" who, like Judas, "kissed me again and again" (37–39).

Appealing to Elizabeth's boyish sense of honor, her classmate declared her "a hero" and "a soldier." "'I was so afraid, when you were pressed with questions, that the whole truth would come out and I [would] be forced to stand in your place,'" her friend confessed with relief. "'I am not so brave as you,'" she gushed. "'I could not endure it. . . . Promise that you will save me from the same experience. You are so good and noble I know you will not betray me'" (38). The days of besting boys at Greek were but a dim memory. Now Elizabeth was in a quandary: the affront to her integrity compelled her to come forward; the call to loyalty required that she remain silent and absorb the shame. Competitive self-assertion had been a key component of the boyhood culture she had tried to enter, but unshakable fidelity was the true hallmark of friendship.[54] Indeed, something in her friend's request for loyalty appealed to an even higher sense of obligation: that the strong should protect the weak. Elizabeth acquiesced. Such acts of self-sacrifice were not without their compensations, she conceded: "In this supreme moment of misery and disgrace, her loving words and warm embrace were like balm to my bruised soul and I readily promised all she asked" (38–39).

In retelling this story years later, Stanton claimed that her young friend had "penetrated the weak point in my character. I loved flattery." In the moral confusion that resulted, "I really thought it praiseworthy to shelter her from what I had suffered" (39). But what part of Elizabeth's developing character had her classmate flattered? It was not simply her gifts as a ghost-writer. Rather, what is striking about this story is the friend's ability to speak to Elizabeth's own muted sense of herself as a boy: a hero, a soldier, a protector of the weak. Courage and stoicism were cherished values among young boys of the nineteenth century, but, according to the historian Anthony Rotundo, there was one ultimate act of loyalty that outweighed all others: taking the punishment for a friend.[55]

Although she never betrayed her betrayer, Elizabeth was called to answer for her actions once the plot had been fully uncovered by her teacher. In disbelief, her teacher quizzed her repeatedly: " 'Why did you not defend yourself on the spot?' " " 'I could not speak, neither did I know what to say,' " was all Elizabeth could manage in response (39). The moral ambiguity of the situation rendered her speechless—certainly, she could not find words to explain her conflicted feelings to an adult teacher—but she acted boldly by keeping her word to her friend. Her only reward lay in their mutual alliance. When her friend's duplicity was discovered and the young woman was forced to "stand up before the whole school and take the burden on her own shoulders that she had so cunningly laid on mine," Elizabeth could no longer protect her. "I readily shed the tears for her I could not summon for myself" (40).

One wonders why Stanton told this story. It is hardly flattering. Nor is it funny. In contrast to much of her memoir, the political lessons of this episode are not even clearly drawn. For her part, Stanton labeled it "my first sad lesson in human duplicity." It was a coming-of-age story, Stanton suggested, that cautioned her not to "accept all things as they seemed on the surface" (40). So, too, we might ask what meanings lie beneath its surface. For one, this story captured the nagging ambivalence that Stanton often felt toward other girls and women. As natural as it seemed to challenge other boys, whether in Greek or in athletics, it felt awkward to her to compete with other young women, who were worthy of her protection or her pity but who were rarely her equals. Stanton claimed that the incident with

"Miss ———" (Stanton continued to protect her friend's anonymity sixty-five years after the initial trauma) "destroyed in a measure my confidence in my companions" (40).

Stanton's confidence in other women would be considerably restored in her admiration of Lucretia Mott; in her grown-up, forty-year partnership with Susan B. Anthony; in her lifelong camaraderie with her cousin Elizabeth Smith Miller, with whom she shared a penchant for religious and political radicalism; and, as she aged, in her intellectually charged, emotionally textured relationship with her youngest daughter, Harriot Stanton Blatch. But at other times Stanton seemed to languish in a world of women and no more so than in the decade of the 1890s when she had become convinced that the problem "was with women themselves."[56] Her frustration was reflected in her memoir. The young Stanton found Miss Willard's establishment "dreary and profitless" (40). In her youth and adulthood, she always seemed more alive when she was engaged intellectually with and against men. If we are to judge by her autobiography, men served as her most important mentors as well as her most worthy adversaries. It was the boys of Johnstown Academy against whom she "measured [her] intellectual powers." The Reverend Simon Hosack became her earliest teacher, her brother, her first rival, and her father her most damaging critic. Even the maternal role, that of the selfless caregiver who carried her about town, took her to church, told her stories, and made her pancakes, was filled by a man, her beloved Peter (5, 14, 16, 17, 19). For a woman who privately delighted in the company of other women, her published memoir is rather densely populated by "the sons of Adam."

Ultimately, in Stanton's struggle with the "problem of boyhood," she confronted one of the most critical cultural issues of her era: "woman's nature," women's similarity to or difference from men, and the larger social and political implications of those claims. Like her ongoing struggle with religion, this issue of "woman's nature" continued to perplex Stanton throughout her life. In her presentation of self, she resolved the problem of boyhood in a particular, if paradoxical, way. She framed her unconventional, strong-willed, analytical, and rational mind in a conventionally womanly body whose full head of voluptuous white curls always drew comment. In the early days of her public career, men, in particular, were curious to see what she looked like—literally, how she embodied her transgressive views. At the height of the tension over the Reconstruction amendment debates, a Major James Haggerty found himself attending an Equal Rights convention "in spite of [his] prejudices." Haggerty interrupted the debates over the virtues of universal suffrage to confess: "It would make you laugh to know what I supposed Mrs. Stanton to be before I first saw her. I pictured to myself a very angular old maid, and thought she must be a very bad looking person;

Elizabeth Cady Stanton in the 1890s. State Historical Society of Wisconsin (X3) 12219

for to associate a good looking woman with a strong-minded woman, was to me ridiculous and I would not do it."[57] Haggerty, apparently unable to help himself, articulated what others may have also felt: the alluring appeal of Stanton's womanliness and his inability to resolve without comment its relation with her conventionally masculine views and temperament.

In her adult presentation of self, Stanton seemingly resolved the issue of her own relationship to masculine and feminine performance;[58] in her thinking, however, she continued to vacillate among what must have seemed like a limited set of options. A product of her time and place, Stanton variously drew on seemingly opposing intellectual arguments about gender. During the Reconstruction debates, for example, she asserted the need to "bury the Negro and the woman in the citizen," thus dissolving the particularities of race and gender in the larger commonality of the enfranchised, autonomous individual. At the same time, she asserted the pressing need for the "feminine element" to purify the masculine world of politics. Later on, in the 1880s and 1890s, as she became more enamored of evolutionary ideas of racial difference and alarmed by the growing numbers of "uneducated" male voters, Stanton tended to emphasize white women's similarities to white men. But neither thread of argument—women's inherent similarity to or difference from men—ever disappeared completely from her views.

The "problem of boyhood" was important to the political work Stanton tried to do in the culture, among girls and boys, among women and men. But in her own life, as she aged, the "self" evolved in a manner apart from these relational dichotomies of male and female. As she told the members of the House Judiciary Committee in 1892, at the tender age of seventy-seven: "There is a solitude which each and every one of us has always carried with him, more inaccessible than the ice-cold mountains, more profound than the midnight sea; the solitude of self, our inner being which we call ourself, no eye nor touch of man or angel has ever pierced."[59] The comfort that she ultimately found in the "solitude of self" was, she realized, elusive for most women, who (more often than men) were bound up in the false superstitions of religious faith.

The Limits of Politics

As early as the 1860s, Stanton began telling a story that would, in the popular accounts of her life, acquire mythic proportions. For this "American Stateswoman," interest in revolutionizing the law began as a child in her father's law office.[60] Many of her father's clients were widowed women whose fortunes suffered from the legal practice of coverture, the retention of "old feudal ideas of women and property." When men died, they typically left the bulk of their estates to eldest sons, who were expected to make a home for their widowed mothers. These women, in Stanton's memory, had been cruelly demoted. Although they may have brought all the property into the family, widows soon became dependents, thrown upon the "bounty of an uncongenial daughter-in-law and a dissipated son" (31).[61]

Deeply moved by the predicament of her father's clients, Elizabeth was mystified by his passivity. "As the practice of the law was my father's busi-

ness, I could not exactly understand why he could not alleviate the sufferings of these women." His law books held the answer. Each time she railed
at the injustice of a woman's case, her father would "take down his books
and show me the inexorable statutes." This ritual apparently provided a
great diversion for the young men studying law in Judge Cady's office. For
entertainment, they would search the tomes and "amuse themselves by
reading to me all the worst laws they could find, over which I would laugh
and cry by turns" (31).

One memorable Christmas, Elizabeth entered her father's office and, in
an apparent lapse in her quest for boyhood, proudly displayed a new coral
necklace and bracelet. Immediately, the aspiring lawyers began to speculate
on the future of the jewelry once Elizabeth married. "'If in due time you
should be my wife,'" said one of the students, "'I could take them and lock
them up.'" In an earlier version, Stanton reported that the young man
threatened "to wear them himself."[62] Growing tired of this game, Elizabeth
retaliated. Sneaking into her father's office, she quietly took a pencil to the
law books and carefully marked the offensive laws; she resolved "to cut
every one of them out of the books." Her plan was foiled. A woman who
stood to benefit from her guerrilla action betrayed her confidence before
Elizabeth could make one incision with her scissors. The fact that she was
turned in by "dear old Flora Campbell," herself a victim of the unjust laws of
coverture Elizabeth had planned to excise, was a bitter irony that would
continue to haunt her. Having been warned of the impending assault upon
his library, Daniel Cady took his daughter aside and, without revealing "that
he had discovered [her] secret," explained to her the process by which "laws
were made, the large number of lawyers and libraries there were all over the
State, and that if his library should burn up it would make no difference in
woman's condition" (32).[63] Then, in a rare moment of support for his iconoclastic daughter, Judge Cady, the father, the keeper of the laws, urged Elizabeth onto her future path: " 'When you are grown up, and able to prepare
a speech . . . you must go down to Albany and talk to the legislators; tell
them all you have seen in this office . . . and, if you can persuade them to
pass new laws, the old ones will be a dead letter.' " Whether Daniel Cady
was earnest or just casting about for a pacifying response to a child's persistent and tiresome questions, his daughter took him at his word. Her life's
work was "foreshadowed," Stanton wrote, "by him who was most opposed
to my public career when, in due time, I entered upon it" (32–33).

Stanton told this story many times, and it bore the weight of multiple interpretations. Most often it simply forecasted her ensuing career. "When I
saw that it was no use to cut them [the laws] out," she wrote, "I gave up that
scheme and then my thoughts turned to the time when I would be big
enough to go down to the Legislature."[64] Unable to solve the problem of

women's legal inequities one way, she would plan another. Stanton's biographers too have routinely seized upon this story and its foreshadowing capacity. The episode is often streamlined, however, to omit the business about protecting her jewelry as a motivating factor.[65] It was, perhaps, unseemly for a great woman's rights advocate to launch her career by trying to protect her childhood jewelry, though Stanton did not seem to think so. In most of the versions she told of this story, she simply joined her dual motivations, explaining: "With this constant bantering from the students *and* the sad complaints of the women, my mind was sorely perplexed" (32).[66] Perhaps, as an eleven-year-old child, she realized most keenly only when her own jewelry was threatened that no woman, however elite, was immune to the discrimination of traditional property laws.

In addition to foreshadowing her public career and assigning its primary motivation, the law books story serves to reveal important facets of Elizabeth's relationship with her father. She once volunteered that this moment, when she saw him unable to save women's property, was the first time she realized the limits of her father's power. "This was a remarkable thing to me," she wrote, "for I supposed my father was all powerful, and that such terrible wrongs as these was his business to right."[67] But the fact that Stanton resurrected the story at the very time when she was attacking another "inexorable" set of books, the Bible, suggests another possible meaning. In this story a young daughter is turned from her path of destruction to a more constructive one by her father's calm intervention. Her life's work was not to be characterized by enraged demolition, tearing down (or out) the institutions of injustice. Rather, she would learn to follow the rules: to prepare speeches, to use her mind and her voice to persuade those with power to create new laws in order to shape a more just society. She might be passionate, but she must also be contained, orderly, obedient to the laws her father represented. Above all, she must be patient.

It was a strategy that served her best in her youth. As she aged, it wore thin. Ever the dutiful daughter seeking her father's acceptance, she had followed his advice but what difference had it made? Over her father's strenuous objections and, then with his reluctant legal advice, Stanton prepared for her "first speech before a legislature." There in her father's office, that all-important testing ground for her girlhood aspirations, she practiced her speech advocating married women's property rights before "an audience of one, and that the one of all others whose approbation I most desired, whose disapproval I most feared"(188). Stanton finally made a memorable speech in Albany.[68] When she prepared her memoir, forty years had passed and she was still making speeches, but she had become reluctant to continue: "Think of eighteen years before Congressional committees; forty years before the Legislatures of New York, and nothing gained!" she lamented.[69]

When she returned to Albany in 1885 for yet another speech, her "reflections were sad and discouraging, as I sat there and listened to the speakers and remembered how long we had made our appeals at that bar, from year to year, in vain" (383). Stanton could readily quantify the magnitude of her efforts and the relative paucity of the results. Her father's counsel, that calm intervention that had spared his library, had ultimately failed her. As she entered her eightieth year, Stanton, in some sense, returned to the guerrilla action of her childhood. Petitioning, organizing, and passing resolutions had done little to alter women's legal and political position. It stood to reason that these same tired strategies would probably also fail to make an impact on the church. It was time, again, to take down the "big books."[70]

The Suffocation of Religion

Despite the fact that her earliest influences, Peter and the Reverend Simon Hosack, were deeply religious, Elizabeth, as a young child, found religion suffocating. It seemed to snuff out everything that was fun and spontaneous. Reportedly she said to her nurse, " 'I was wondering why it was that everything we like to do is a sin, and everything we dislike is commanded by God or someone on earth. I am so tired of that everlasting no! no! no!' " (10).

Religion not only stifled her as an individual; the church also offended her sense of justice. According to Stanton's memories, the churches of Johnstown practiced racially segregated seating in 1820s. Peter, a devout Episcopalian, was one of the few African American members of his church.[71] Stanton remembers entering the church with him the first time and being ushered into a "white man's pew." The church sexton instructed Peter to "leave the Judge's children there." " 'Oh,' he said, 'they will not stay there without me.' " Elizabeth and her sisters "instinctively" followed Peter to "the negro pew." Communion was also segregated, owing to the "prejudice against color." Peter knelt alone at the altar to receive communion. But soon he was joined by his young charges, and he would take them in hand as he walked back down the aisle to the "negro pew" by the door (17, 16). The church impressed Stanton as a bastion of prejudice and conservatism. She positively rejoiced when her old, cold, and inhospitable Presbyterian church was turned into a mitten factory, "where the pleasant hum of machinery and the glad faces of men and women have chased the evil spirits to their hiding places" (26). Clearly, in her estimation, warm mittens were preferable to a cold church. Moreover, the renovation provided Stanton yet another rich metaphor for what she hoped might happen to religion more generally in America: it could be replaced by a faith in technology and science.

Stanton's childhood skepticism was further solidified by her failed conversion to evangelical Christianity. Stanton's teenage years coincided with an intense period of Protestant revivalism in America, commonly known as the Second Great Awakening. From Kentucky to New England, Protestants of all stripes engaged in successive periods of revitalization, beginning as early as 1801 and culminating in the early 1830s. Earning the title "the burned-over district" for its smoldering fires of holiness, upstate New York served as the flash point for the nation's revivals.[72]

As a student at Miss Willard's Female Seminary in Troy, sent against her will to that "intellectual Mecca," Elizabeth Cady found herself vulnerable to the "epidemic" of religious revivals that swept the city, "attacking in its worst form the most susceptible" (35, 41). For six weeks, "owing to my gloomy Calvinistic training . . . and my vivid imagination," she fell under the spell of the Reverend Charles Grandison Finney, the legendary revivalist and, in Stanton's words, the peerless "terrifier of human souls." Finney had set up shop in Troy as a guest revivalist at the Reverend Dr. Beaman's church, where many of Elizabeth's schoolmates attended worship services. Elizabeth found Finney irresistible: "I can see him now, his great eyes rolling around the congregation and his arms flying about in the air like those of a windmill." Finney had persuaded Miss Willard's girls of their imminent damnation and each, in turn, dutifully considered herself "a monster of iniquity" and a "miserable, helpless, forsaken worm of the dust." Desperate and confused, Miss Cady approached Dr. Finney for counsel: "'I cannot understand what I am to do,'" she implored. "'If you should tell me to go to the top of the church steeple and jump off, I would readily do it, if thereby I could save my soul; but I do not know how to go to Jesus.'" "'Repent and Believe,'" the Reverend reassured her; "'that is all you have to do to be happy here and hereafter.'" With that message of hope, Elizabeth and her comrades "imagined ourselves converted." But her peace of mind was not restored. It seemed, she worried, "the more sincerely I believe, the more unhappy I am" (41–42).

Her bewilderment and fear reached a climax during an evening service. Finney, with his eyes and arms in motion, enacted a live performance of the "procession to hell." Sinners were "being swept down the rapids, about to make the awful plunge into the burning depths of liquid fire below." His booming voice echoing through the vaulted arches of the church, Finney became the Devil and his "rejoicing hosts" shouting their demonic greetings to the doomed travelers. Suddenly he paused with a powerful silence and pointed: "'There, do you not see them!'" Terrorized, Elizabeth bolted from her seat and stared in the direction of Finney's procession to hell "while the picture glowed before my eyes." In the months that followed, "visions of the lost haunted my dreams," Stanton wrote. She became ill and returned to her home in Johnstown. But the nightmares continued. Elizabeth would wake her father in the middle of the night and beg him to pray for her, "lest I should be cast into the bottomless pit before morning" (41–43).[73]

Ultimately the young woman's hallucinations were removed by a successful conversion, this one to Rationalism. On a six-week trip to Niagara Falls, Elizabeth was rehabilitated by her father, her sister Tryphena, and her brother-in-law Edward Bayard. All mention of religion was taboo; they stuck to a strict regimen of science, moral philosophy, and fresh air. The antidote worked. "After many months of weary wandering in the intellectual labyrinth of 'The Fall of Man,' 'Original Sin,' 'Total Depravity,' 'God's Wrath,' 'Satan's Triumph,' 'The Crucifixion,' 'The Atonement,' and 'Salvation by Faith,' I found my way out of the darkness into the clear sunlight of Truth." Furthermore, Stanton suggests, she never looked back. "My religious superstition gave place to rational ideas based on scientific facts, and in proportion, as I looked at everything from a new standpoint, I grew more and more happy, day by day" (43–44).

Stanton's memory of the crisis of her failed conversion is a powerful one. It set a tone for the rest of her life. It played a shaping role in her politics. And for the readers of her autobiography in the late nineteenth century, it would have resonated with familiar characters and themes. The trouble is, in some sense, it may not be true. Charles Grandison Finney did, in fact, conduct a massive revival in the city of Troy for several months during the Second Great Awakening, but that revival took place in 1827, not 1831, when Elizabeth Cady first appeared on the rolls at Miss Willard's School.[74] In 1827, Elizabeth was still living with her family in Johnstown, grieving her brother's death. When she arrived at Miss Willard's School in Troy, in January 1831, the city was in the throes of another great revival. But Finney remained in Rochester, ministering to the converts of his most famous revival. By mid-February, the revival in Troy continued unabated, but Finney was too ill to continue preaching anywhere. Twice during Elizabeth's schooling, Finney briefly visited the area. The first time was in July 1831, one month after her conversion to rationalism at Niagara Falls. She may well have met Finney, but she was not under his spell for a six-week revival. So what is going on here? Did Stanton invent a traumatic conversion experience, from which she would triumphantly recover, to justify her harsh condemnation of Christianity?

Several possibilities suggest themselves. Finney's presence in Troy during the several years before Elizabeth's arrival may have generated a rich folklore of conversion stories among Miss Willard's pupils. Perhaps older girls passed these tales of hell and damnation on to younger girls as a form of theological hazing. A decade after her alleged conversion, Stanton wrote a speech she titled "Fear." A child who is victimized by the vivid images of a fear-inducing God figured prominently in it: "The child scarce begins to notice before older ones begin to startle, shock and frighten him, and as soon as the mind opens to thought, nursery rhymes, ghost stories and a gloomy theology of a powerful devil and a great God who loves not wicked children is forced upon the universal mind until the most thoughtful and sensitive come to live in constant dread of some undefined terrors here and . . . of judgment to come hereafter. Everywhere is the child's fears played upon, at home, at school, in the sanctuary."[75] Stanton imagined the generic child in this passage to be much younger than the typical teenage student at Miss Willard's. Yet the culture she critiqued, of older children scaring younger ones with ghost stories and "a gloomy theology of a powerful devil," could easily have described the rituals of initiation at her all-girl boarding school. It is entirely possible that the "thoughtful and sensitive" Miss Cady may have been traumatized simply by hearing the accounts of Finney's colorful "procession to hell" from her senior classmates.

Another possible explanation of Stanton's failed conversion story lies in the location of the revival: in Stanton's memoir, Finney appeared in the pulpit of the "Reverend Dr. Beaman's church." In 1826–1827, Finney had been invited to Troy by Nathaniel Sydney Smith Beman (not Beaman), pastor of the city's First Presbyterian Church. Beman believed in Finney's histrionic revival methods and desperately wanted him to breathe life into the lackluster Presbyterians in Troy.[76] He was not disappointed. According to one of Beman's parishioners, Finney proffered a vision of hell that might well have inspired nightmares among the schoolgirls at Miss Willard's. "Look! Look!" Finney thundered: "See the millions of wretches, biting and gnawing their tongues, as they lift their scalding heads from the burning lake! . . . See! see! how they are tossed, and how they howl. . . . Hear them groan, amidst the fiery billows, as they Lash! and Lash! and Lash! their burning shores."[77] The vivid image of the sinners' scalding heads bobbing up and down in hell's lake of fire seems to resonate with Stanton's early memory of Finney's performance. Perhaps the Reverend Beman kept Finney's message afloat in Troy in the years immediately following the revival. Well known for his own controversial methods, he may himself have been the catalyst for Miss Cady's failed conversion in 1831.[78] In the final analysis, I subscribe to the interpretation of Ann D. Gordon, the coeditor of Stanton's papers. In accounting for the discrepancies between Stanton's memory and verifiable fact, Gordon explains: "What matters ultimately to Stanton is not, apparently, whether she recalls events accurately . . . but whether she conveys to people the complicated tensions . . . that accompanied the advent of women's rights."[79]

The need to convey the "complicated tensions" that surrounded her thwarted conversion to evangelical Christianity may have overridden Stanton's accuracy in retelling this vital episode from her past. Even if the "facts" of the story could be documented, however, the authenticity of any individual's "experience" remains subjective and elusive.[80] Where does this leave us, as the inheritors of her story? It seems probable that Elizabeth Cady was caught up in the throes of conversion while a student at Miss Willard's Female Seminary. Although Charles Grandison Finney did not hold a revival in Troy during her time at the school, his residual presence and potent techniques of fostering a conviction of sin persisted and became part of the story Stanton told about herself. Finney was credited with converting a long line of abolitionists among Stanton's contemporaries. It was, for her readers, a recognizable credential. A failed conversion by Finney would have been a choice credential of a different sort, a badge of honor among agnostics. More likely, Elizabeth Cady's aborted conversion should be attributed to the lesser-known Nathaniel Beman, or even to the proselytizing of an animated classmate. Yet even if the event did not unfold exactly as Stanton remembered it, the story encapsulated a powerful, identity-shaping experience that would continue to define her throughout her life. She had been an evangelical Christian, albeit briefly, a worthy position from which to launch her critique of the church. And Stanton's subsequent successful conversion, her journey "out of the darkness and into the clear sunlight of Truth," marked the most important transition in her life. In actuality, that transition—from believer to heretic—was not particularly linear. Certainly it was not accomplished in a six-week sojourn at Niagara Falls, as Stanton insists in her memoir, nor was it completed in the course of her youth.[81] Rather, her struggle with the place of religion in her own life and thought, as well as its place in the wider culture, was literally life long. Even after she had rejected the Bible as a guide to salvation (or even as good advice literature), Stanton continued to draw upon its metaphors, characters, and insights to make her political arguments. And as we will see, even in her overt repudiation of Christianity, Stanton conserved many of the faith's basic premises, especially the ultimate importance of the individual conscience.

Casting the legendary Charles Grandison Finney in the leading role in her doomed conversion, Stanton may have embellished the past, even as she obscured a significant portion of her own personal and historical experience. In considering Stanton's religious experiences as a young person, one can hardly imagine a starker contrast than the one she draws between Simon Hosack, her neighbor minister, and Charles Grandison Finney, whose conversion techniques allegedly terrified her into abandoning Christianity altogether. Without doubt, Hosack was the pivotal figure in Stanton's youth; that he was a minister seems largely irrelevant. Whereas Finney's proselytizing and the fear it induced indelibly marked him as a representative of "the church," Hosack always stood apart from his vocation and congregation in Stanton's memoir. In fact, he was so uninspiring as a minister that his influence over Elizabeth did not predispose her as a child to valuing the church. Rather the key to understanding Hosack is in his legacy to her: his knowledge of Greek and his books, which included the Greek Testament and several Bible commentaries. Not only was Simon Hosack the catalyst for her quest for boyhood, he willed her the tools that she would return to as an adult to dismantle the church and the Bible, the very obstacles to her full humanity.

Stanton's early reform career strengthened her conviction that Simon Hosack was an exception. She spent most of her adult life warring with clergy. Charles Grandison Finney had terrified and immobilized her as a young woman with his vision of hell. But his protégés were worse. Time and time again Stanton found that ministers were her most vocal opponents, in the antislavery movement as well as in the woman's rights campaign. When on her honeymoon in London she attended the World Antislavery Convention, she fairly bristled at the gendered bigotry of the clergy, English and American, who had refused conference participation to women delegates from the United States. She later pointed out that the Old Testament figures of "Deborah, Huldah, Vashti and Esther might have questioned the propriety of calling it a World's Convention, when only half of humanity was represented there." (80). She also remarked that the antislavery ministers "would have been horrified at the idea of burning the flesh of the distinguished women present with red-hot irons, but the crucifixion of their pride and self-respect, the humiliation of the spirit, seemed to them a trifling matter" (82). Her memoir is littered with such "narrow-minded bigoted" clergy. In the weeks after the World Antislavery Convention, Stanton and her husband Henry traveled in Europe in the company of a British minister, the Reverend John Scoble, with whom she did constant battle over "woman's sphere." Although it is not clear whether Stanton emerged victorious in their debates, she did find "intense satisfaction" in the Reverend's seasickness as they crossed the English Channel (103–104).

By the 1890s, ministers had become for Stanton the key obstacles to woman's progress and the benefactors of her damaged self-respect; in her memoir they are the favorite target for criticism. Rarely does she mention a minister weighing in on the side of justice. One of the few exceptions is Theodore Parker, the Boston Unitarian who inspired a generation of Transcendentalists and whose lectures Stanton had once found so "soul satisfying." But as she remembered Parker from the vantage point of old age, even he no longer seemed to her particularly revolutionary. Hosack and Parker aside, Stanton held the clergy collectively responsible for perpetrating a hoax on women; that is, they taught women that their secondary status in life and politics was divinely ordained. The clergy were at fault, but their use of the Bible as their prime evidence of women's intended subordination was particularly galling to her. In her autobiography, Stanton recalls a lyceum tour that took her to Utah and provided her the opportunity to spend five hours alone with a group of Mormon women. Those women, whom Stanton saw as oppressed by the practice of polygamy, served as a perfect example of the barbaric social practices that might result when people took the Bible literally. "I appreciated as never before," Stanton wrote, "the danger in intermeddling with the religious ideas of any people. Their faith finds abundant authority in the Bible, in the example of God's chosen people" (285).[82] While Christianity had redeeming features in Stanton's estimation (she usually enjoyed the music, for example), its potential danger outweighed its potential good.

Even as she prepared her memoir, comfortably at home in the agnosticism of her later years, Stanton had to concede Christianity's one great contribution: "the right of individual conscience and judgment." This aspect of Christianity continued to harmonize with her views. "The reason it took such a hold in the hearts of the people," Stanton wrote, "was because it taught that the individual was primary; the state, the church, society, the family secondary" (231).[83] But the clergy corrupted this basic principle of Christianity. The clergy used the Bible to teach, not the "great doctrine" of individual rights, but rather the so-called divinely inspired inferiority of one class of individuals, women. It was this corruption that Stanton dedicated her work to exposing, subtly and gradually in the autobiography and explicitly and forcefully in the *Woman's Bible*. "When women understand that government and religions are human inventions; that Bibles, prayerbooks, catechisms and encyclical letters are all emanations from the brain of man, they will no longer be oppressed by the injunctions that came to them with the divine authority of 'Thus Saith the Lord' " (285). Of course, for many of her readers, this was heresy.

Rejecting religion as she did, not quietly, but as the central component of her feminism, contributed to the gender transgression that Stanton had begun in her quest for boyhood. Much was made of women's passionate religiosity in this era, and for Stanton to reject Christianity out of hand was to place herself in a category populated mostly by men.

THE Stanton who emerges from *Eighty Years and More* is a character who, from childhood forward, navigates a series of disruptive plots. Her life stories contradict every essential truth of nineteenth-century womanhood. The sacred relationship of mother and child that dominated the popular advice literature of her time, Elizabeth finds only with Peter, her family's "servant." Instead of embracing "woman's sphere," Elizabeth spends her childhood escaping it and venturing into the unsupervised haunts of boyhood. Miss Willard's Female Seminary, the perfect setting for "the female world of love and ritual," proves to be "dreary and profitless" and beset by "petty jealousies."[84] The obligatory "conversion experience," which fueled the zealous reform activities of many women of Stanton's generation, literally made her sick, corrupted her reason, and degraded her spirit. Indeed, at a time when a woman's piety was considered the choice ingredient of her womanhood, Stanton attempted to expose that virtue as immature and fear-induced. Even her confrontation with the law and politics, once so promising as a field of endeavor, proved frustrating and meaningless. She could cut out all the patriarchal laws from her father's law books and "it would make no difference in woman's condition." Or, as she came to believe later in her political life: even if the Constitution were amended to enable women to vote, it would make no difference because women's political and social inequality was "but an outgrowth of [their] status in the Bible."[85]

These were not the dominant fictions from which most nineteenth-century women drew the plots of their lives.[86] And one wonders how Stanton got away with it. Her humor served as her safety valve, reducing the tension in and around her stories. Stanton was a gender heretic, a religious infidel, a defector from respectable reform circles; at the same time, she was also a spinner of yarns, and a stout, good-looking matron who managed not to take herself too seriously.

Carolyn Heilbrun, a scholar of women's autobiography, has argued that women of the nineteenth century essentially "had no models on which to form their lives, nor could they themselves become mentors since they did not tell the truth about their lives."[87] In this sense, Stanton's narrative is very much in keeping with the traditions of women's autobiography. By repressing the "slavery story" Stanton is able to offer an alternative set of stories more suitable to her political analysis. In the first of these, Peter is the surrogate parent whose unbounded love compensates for the fear-induced, religiously inspired, judgmental parenting of her Puritan mother and father. In another story, the escaped slave girl Harriet provides Stanton her first encounter with slavery. Slavery is connected to her family's story only tangentially, and then on the side of its abolition. Cousin Gerrit is an abolitionist; Stanton becomes one too. In a final story, Elizabeth learns from her experiences with Peter that the church is a bastion of racial prejudice. Harmonizing nicely with Stanton's broader critique of religion, this story roots racial prejudice not in the social practices of her family's participation in slavery, but "out there" in an institution already corrupted in her mind and alien to her experience, the church. (It was not even her Presbyterian church, but the Episcopal church.) Only with the suppression of the unacceptable ghost, the story of Peter's slave status, do these other stories become viable.

In other ways, however, Stanton's memoir was truthful, painfully so, even though her narrative method was somewhat deceptive. Just as her humor deflected criticism away from her heresies, Stanton also tempered her radical views by subverting familiar narrative conventions of her day. Instead of the prototypical woman's memoir, which cloaked childhood in nostalgia and suppressed the writer's anger and frustration at the constraints of girlhood, she wrote explicitly of her failed attempts to assume the various mantles of boyhood. She unveiled the painful truth of what happened to little girls and young women when they tried to enact plots that were never intended for them.

An idyllic childhood was typically followed in women's autobiographies by a conversion experience in which God or Jesus called a woman to her vocation and thereby justified "achievement and accomplishment in no other way excusable for a female self."[88] These tales abounded among Stanton's contemporaries. For example, Frances Willard, the long-time leader of the Woman's Christian Temperance Union, was converted by the Holy Spirit to work for woman suffrage.[89] Stanton retained the narrative convention, the conversion story, but she substituted science and reason for the all-powerful voice of God, Jesus, or the Holy Spirit. Like her more spiritually motivated contemporaries, Stanton took up her calling with a prophetic zeal. She would try to convert and save other women, not with religion, but from it:

> Having conversed with many young women in sanitariums, insane asylums, and in the ordinary walks of life, suffering with religious melancholia; having witnessed the agony of young mothers in childbirth, believing they were cursed of God in their maternity, and with painful memories of my own fears and bewilderment in girlhood, I have endeavored to dissipate these religious superstitions from the minds of women and base their faith on science and reason, where I found for myself at last that peace and comfort I could never find in the Bible and the Church.[90]

A missionary who placed her faith in "science and reason," Stanton reinterpreted her calling late in her life and career. Ultimately, it was not her father's law books that needed to be mutilated; it was the book of the Father, the Bible. The Greek Testament, once a symbolic trophy of boyhood, became both the object of her wrath and her most passionate vocation. It must have been deeply satisfying, as an elderly woman, finally to take the scissors to the pages of the Bible, which is literally what she did in launching the *Woman's Bible* project.[91]

The *Woman's Bible* and *Eighty Years and More* were Stanton's dual legacy, in "the sunset of life," to women of her time and to women of the future. These two works—Stanton called them her "twins"—were deeply implicated in each other. The young girl who should have been a boy from *Eighty*

Years and More threw off the faith of her fathers and went on to publish the *Woman's Bible*, as "a step in progress" toward women's emancipation. The aged veteran of the woman's rights movement, the radical octogenarian who had created a *Woman's Bible*, penned a memoir in which she carefully depicted a girl's childhood of skepticism and revolt. Closing that story with the celebration of her eightieth birthday, the seasoned agitator fused the end of her life story with her ultimate argument: politics was a limited field of endeavor; women's liberty from the church and the Bible was the vital issue of the hour. The repudiation of that view, as she recorded it in the final pages of her memoir, had only given her "confidence in my judgment and patience with the opposition of my coadjutors, with whom on so many points I disagree." The limits of politics were crystal clear to her: "It requires no courage now to demand the right of suffrage. . . . But it still requires courage to question the divine inspiration of the Hebrew Writings as to the position of women" (467–468).

Stanton must have felt quite isolated in the work of her final years. Yet, when she began her critique of religion in earnest in the early 1880s, questioning the divine inspiration of Scripture placed her squarely in the middle of the most heated debate in late nineteenth-century culture.

2

The "Emasculated Gospel": New Religions, New Bibles, and the Battle for Cultural Authority

> In a few centuries the women may claim that you were inspired
> by Mrs. God. Let us hope that they will be right.
>
> ROBERT GREEN INGERSOLL
> to Elizabeth Cady Stanton, October 14, 1898

On May 27, 1882, Elizabeth Cady Stanton "eloped" with her daughter Harriot to the south of France. Stanton had finally divorced herself from the oppressive task she had undertaken with Susan B. Anthony: publishing volume two of the *History of Woman Suffrage*. "My only regret is that we have not more experience in book-making," Stanton wrote. Yet, she seemed to regret much more. The work had been painstaking. She had battled illness, and it seemed as if they might not finish the volume on time. Stanton's daughter Harriot, who had been traveling in Europe, was summoned home to help her mother and Miss Anthony complete the project. With the tedious work of producing a thousand-page documentary history behind them, the trip to France "beyond the reach and sound of my beloved Susan and the woman suffrage movement" must have felt like a well-earned reward.

From June to October, mother and daughter settled in as guests at the Convent de la Sagesse in Toulouse. A few minor culinary quibbles aside—"I bemoan the absence of butter," she admitted—Stanton thrived in her new setting. While Harriot studied mathematics at the University of Toulouse, Stanton read, reflected, wrote, walked, and rested. She made a delightful new friend in Professor Nicholas Joly, a zoologist at the university. From Joly, Stanton borrowed a copy of Voltaire's biblical commentaries and pronounced them "amusing to say the least." But perhaps even more inspiring than Voltaire was the tranquillity and spirit of cooperation that suffused the convent. It was, ironically, the perfect site for her developing critique of the church and the Bible. "What a wonderful organization the Catholic Church is!" Stanton wrote effusively in her diary. "In these convents and sister-hoods, it realizes in a measure the principle of co-operation. My dream of the future is co-operation. But is there any other foundation outside of religion on which it can be based? Can a belief grounded on science, common sense, and love of humanity sway the human soul as fears of the torments of hell and promises of the joys of heaven have done?"[1]

Stanton had not declared it officially, but she was taking the first of many extended leaves from the business of the suffrage organization she and Anthony led. When a signed copy of the association's convention resolutions reached her in France, Stanton noted in her diary, "the sight of all those familiar names signed thereto brought tears to my eyes and almost made me ashamed for having dropped out even for one year from the works of such a noble band."[2] Stanton's "dropping out" during these years was a source of constant consternation to Susan B. Anthony, who fretted before each major convention over whether Stanton would actually be in attendance. The necessity of crossing the Atlantic made her presence all the more uncertain. Anthony would later confide to a younger colleague that this worry was, in fact, not entirely new. "All that she says about dreading the journey has been just as true of her on every occasion for the last forty years, as to-day," Anthony sighed. While Stanton enjoyed going places, she detested the discomforts of travel, and according to Anthony she was chronically deterred by *"the condition of her mind . . .* the inertia she has to overcome at the last moment."[3] As Stanton aged, travel became increasingly burdensome; once she arrived somewhere, she was prepared to stay a spell. Her geographic remoteness during these years shaped her polemical writing on religious issues. By the 1880s, Stanton was penning caustic attacks on the church and Bible from the relative isolation of her home, or from France or England. She enjoyed the controversies she ignited in the American press and in the suffrage association, but she did not always have to face them in person.

Stanton could not have chosen a more opportune time to launch her attack on religion. The 1880s and 1890s were marked by intense religious concern. As the rise of science precipitated a "spiritual crisis," one historian of American religion has suggested, "faith was both growing and declining."[4] This era witnessed a resurgence of traditional Protestantism as well as a proliferation of new forms of religious faith. With the onslaught of troubling heresies from abroad, which ranged from the "Old-World" beliefs brought by successive waves of immigrants to modern European challenges to the Bible, American Protestantism labored mightily to revive itself anew—often with an eye to its own market value. With businesslike efficiency, Protestant denominations grew exponentially during the period 1880–1900. Methodists and Episcopalians doubled their memberships; Southern Baptists did nearly as well.[5] Revivals staged by Dwight L. Moody drew record crowds in New York, Philadelphia, and Boston. With a "back to the Scripture" message, Moody had a golden touch for saving common people. But he was also legendary for employing the techniques of the modern corporation, bureaucratization and advertising, to ensure the competitiveness of God's cause when urban dwellers had so many other ways to spend their time and money.[6] In small-town America, where the Chautauqua and the vacation Bible school loomed large, Christians alternately created and were enticed by an array of faith-oriented cultural outlets that funneled their leisure time into religion.[7] Religious publishing was booming at the end of the nineteenth century. The American Bible Society had virtually reached the status of a modern corporation and built an elaborate overseas office in Constantinople. Serving as the headquarters for the society's missionary work in the Near East, the structure also provided a rich symbol of the success of evangelical Christianity and its imperial impulse to Christianize the world.[8] The growth of new faiths also attests to the era's intensely religious character. The rise of faith healer Mary Baker Eddy and her practice of Christian Science is a case in point. Although Eddy's personal fortunes faltered somewhat in the 1880s, her practice spread and its adherents multiplied. New variations on faith healing, especially the Mind Cure and New Thought, became a national rage.[9] Even the popular agnosticism of these years, the repudiation of religion that Stanton, Robert Ingersoll, and other "infidels" called for, kept religion swirling at the center of cultural currents.

The era's heightened religiosity touched Stanton's life in many ways and shaped her analysis of religion. Her frequent trips abroad during these years gave Stanton some distance from the American scene and exposed her to the intellectual critiques of religion emerging in Europe. Particularly influential in her ongoing religious analysis was the extended time she spent in England with her daughter Harriot, who in 1882 married an Englishman, William Henry Blatch, and settled there. Stanton was often a featured attraction at gatherings of British suffragists, though she was alarmed at the considerably slower pace of the British woman's movement and regarded the hold of organized religion as an obstacle to its success. She frequently lamented the lack of vigorous, spontaneous discussion in the British suffrage meetings and the Christian humility of the women as well: "The English women all speak with their bonnets on which destroys the artistic effect of the person [and] the platform [and] all sense of freedom. I suppose they do this in obedience to Paul's directions that when women appear in public they should have their heads covered."[10]

In London in 1883, Stanton was reunited with her fellow American secularists, the Reverend Moncure D. Conway and his wife, Ellen Davis Conway. On this memorable occasion, Moncure Conway invited Stanton to fill the pulpit of his London church. In her speech, titled "Has the Christian Religion Done Aught for Woman?" Stanton, "showed triumphantly it had not. I felt happy and magnetic, hurling my thunder at our worst enemies." By the "facts of history," Stanton "showed clearly that to no form of religion was woman indebted for one impulse of freedom." Indeed, the opposite was true: "through utter perversion of the religious element in their nature . . . women are made the patient, hopeless slaves they are." When it was over, she eagerly reported to Susan B. Anthony: "I never gave a speech I enjoyed more than the two at Prince's Hall and South Place Chapel. Mrs. Conway was delighted and astonished at the audience." In retrospect, as Stanton noted in her autobiography several years later, this speech loomed as a breakthrough or a turning point. "I had been so long oppressed with the degradation of woman under canon law and church discipline," she wrote, "that I had a sense of relief in pouring out my indignation."[11]

Not surprisingly, British women found Stanton's religious indignation problematic. The British suffragist Priscilla Bright McLaren, who was sympathetic to Stanton's agnostic views, wrote to her in 1883, "we should be running our heads against a wall were we to go in all at once for all the rights you advocate. . . . In a young country, you may go ahead; but here, we must head cautiously, not timidly, but wisely."[12] But Stanton was worried about the place of religion in the politics of her "young country" as well. She was distressed by the growing visibility and political power of evangelical women in the American suffrage movement, particularly the meteoric rise of the Woman's Christian Temperance Union. "Most of the women in our movement to-day," she wrote to a colleague in 1886, "care more about their religion, the salvation of their souls, than they do about enfranchisement. To concentrate their interest [and] enthusiasm on their own emancipation, their faith in the old theological superstitions must be unsettled."[13] A fear that this evangelical enthusiasm was gaining ground in the woman's movement may have led Stanton to accelerate her attack on religion. Although she desperately wanted some distance from the day-to-day work of her movement, she did not care to see it taken over by devout Christians.

Stanton's Faith: The Religion of Humanity

Stanton found like-minded reformers in the English Secularist movement. Through her daughter Harriot's connections to Fabian Socialists, Stanton met the secularist Annie Besant, whose radicalism on a variety of religious and gender issues impressed her.[14] Besant was a welcome contrast to the British Positivists, whom Stanton found "though liberal on religious questions, . . . very narrow as to the sphere of woman."[15] In her own country, it would be Stanton's particular contribution to push male-dominated secularist movements to a more radical stance on gender issues as she simultaneously worked at translating and applying the critiques offered by Positivism and Freethought to woman's condition.[16]

Stanton had long been an American exponent of the French philosopher Auguste Comte's Positivism. As the historian William Leach has pointed out, Stanton was drawn to Positivism in the 1860s and published articles on Comte in the *Revolution*.[17] Even after her initial enthusiasm for Comte had diminished, Positivist adaptations of his theories persisted in her later work, including her exegesis in the *Woman's Bible*. Basing his theories on the "immutable laws" of science, Comte argued that the same immutable laws would, ultimately, be discovered to govern human affairs as well, establishing the "positive science of society." The "Religion of Humanity" emerged from his social theory. According to one of its popularizers, the Religion of Humanity founded by the "Master," Comte, prided itself on being "absolutely demonstrable to human reason." It shared no common course with atheism, however. Rather, Positivism held that, through the scientific discovery of immutable sociological laws, "all men and women, no matter under what divisions they exist, are shown to be integral parts of our great organism, one collective personality, one Supreme Being, HUMANITY. It is this being whom we worship, whom we serve."[18]

As Stanton explained to readers of the *Revolution*, "the beauty of Comte's philosophy to us is, that it is based on immutable laws, governing not only the solar system, the vegetable, mineral and animal world, but the human family, all moving in beautiful harmony together." The problem was that society had not yet progressed to that stage in which "beautiful harmony" was possible. The first step in Comte's three-part theory of social development had been achieved. The "retrograde" theological world order had been abolished by the age of revolutions, which Comte termed the "metaphysical" stage of politics. This second phase was only a transitional period, however, an era of agitation and inquiry that would ultimately bring about Comte's new world order, the third and final stage that he called the "organic state." Comte's theory and its periodization appealed to Stanton and other anticlerical reformers because it emphasized the triumph of science over theology. More important, Stanton absorbed from Comte a social theory that privileged women's unique contribution to the world order. Comte argued that the immutable laws had established the principle of the "feminine element," an essential element of the universe that was suffused with feminine morality. Herein lay Comte's appeal to nineteenth-century feminists: he made woman "primal to the reconstruction of the state, the church, and the home"—or that was how Stanton chose to read him.[19] While Comte lauded the intrinsic morality of the feminine element, he himself envisioned it and the women who embodied it functioning exclusively within the home and family. "The original source of all moral influence will be far more effectual when men have done their duty to women by setting them free from the pressure of material necessity, and when women on their side have renounced both power and wealth."[20]

Stanton always rejected such constraints on women's activity. Nevertheless, she adapted Comte to her own theoretical and religious needs. It is perhaps an indication of how desperate she was for a theorist who explicitly privileged women's role in the world order that she could suspend her usually incisive democratic and feminist critical acumen and work within Comte's system. The founding fathers of the American Republic, after all, had been conspicuously silent on women, a criticism she had made, at least implicitly, by "writing women into" the Declaration of Independence in the modified version of it she presented as the "Declaration of Sentiments" at Seneca Falls. Although Comte conceptualized a place for women in his "Positive Science of Society," it was a role not unlike the one Catharine Beecher proposed for wives and mothers in *Domestic Economy*. That is, women were most powerful when they relied upon their vaunted influence and ruled from the home.

Comte's theory was shockingly conservative in other ways that probably disturbed Stanton as well. In Comte's view, the ultimate goal, the organic state, was being delayed because people failed to realize that the metaphysical stage was simply a "necessary provisional" phase in the process, not the desired end result. Although agitation and revolution had been necessary to break up the "extended infantile" reign of the theological state, this metaphysical stage was not to be confused with the new order. The goal of the metaphysical state was to "aid progress" by overthrowing "the ancient system," not to obstruct progress by creating the "appearance of a new and stable system." People were starting to mistake the tools of revolution for a new form of dogma, Comte lamented. The precise dogmas that Comte wanted society to relinquish in order to move forward—the dogma of "unbounded liberty of conscience," the dogma of "equality," and the dogma of the "sovereignty of the people"—corresponded with Stanton's most cherished and sacred beliefs. "Indispensable and salutary as it has been," Comte explained, this litany of dogmas "can never be an organic principle; and, moreover, it constitutes an obstacle to reorganization, now that its activity is no longer absorbed by the demolition of the old political order." While relinquishing these cherished principles might seem like a serious sacrifice, it would be worth it. After all, Comte argued, "the theological and metaphysical philosophies have failed to secure permanent social welfare." The Positive Philosophy, in contrast, had proven its merit through science; it reorganized the physical world, "which had been till then in the same chaotic state that we now deplore, in regard to social science."[21]

Comte's abstract social theories carried with them specific political implications. After his death in 1857, the Positive Religion continued to thrive under the Priesthood of Humanity, ten disciples appointed by the Master. One of these priests, the Reverend Henry Edger, considered the "St. Paul of positivism in the United States," translated the religious theories of the Positive Religion into the vernacular of nineteenth-century politics. In an interview with the New York *World*, for example, Edger was asked if Positivists would "favor any sudden revolution of the present conditions of society." He responded: "No. We would rather seek to bring about just social, and industrial relations gradually and naturally. We would not, for instance, have favored the sudden abolition of slavery. We would rather have instituted a sense of responsibility among the slave owners which would have caused them to so modify their relations with the negroes as that they could have said to the whole world, 'Come and see how benignant, well-balanced, mutually advantageous, are these relations, and improve them if you can!' "[22]

Stanton did not accept such conservative views; rather, she interpreted Comte in her own way. In reference to Edger's similarly regressive views on woman's rights, Stanton responded: "As we read Auguste Comte, we think his disciples do him as great injustice as the disciples of Jesus have done their master, in the narrow application of the universal principles this great leader of thought gave to mankind."[23] She used Comte to defend her political position during the controversial Reconstruction debates over the Thirteenth, Fourteenth, and Fifteenth Amendments. In a speech to the American Equal Rights Society in 1867, Stanton explained in a basic Comtian framework the need for gender and racial equality: "Though it has never been tried, we know an experiment on the basis of equality would be safe; for the laws in the world of morals are as immutable as in the world of matter."[24] However, when controversies began to erupt among reformers over the relative merits of black male or white woman suffrage, Stanton applied Comte more narrowly, arguing, "with the black man we have no new element in government; but with the education and elevation of woman we have a power that is to galvanize the Saxon race with a higher and nobler life."[25]

Some of Comte's disciples took issue with her. The Reverend Henry Edger was alarmed at Stanton's use of Comte and, more generally, at what he saw as her misplaced agitation for woman's rights.[26] Edger reminded American reformers "that even human affairs are subject to inviolable natural laws" and that some social relations depend upon "fundamental conditions which admit of no change." Alas, it would have been preferable, Edger lamented, if women could have been spared the metaphysical state of revolution. If only "the positive instruction [could] have been organized in time to have permitted the female intellect to have passed directly from the theological state to the positive, we should have been spared that dreary wilderness of confusion and disorder into which we are, in fact, at this moment madly rushing." Hopelessly stalled in the metaphysical stage, women are deluded, Edger argued. "Paper laws and paper constitutions and paper ballots are very pretty metaphysical playthings, but it is not they that really rule us."[27]

Stanton's typically pithy response to Edger indicated both her familiarity with Comte's theories and her willingness to jettison those that did not fit her woman's rights perspective. Stanton began her rebuttal by pointing out that male resistance, the "weeping and wailing and gnashing of teeth at the prospective equality of woman," was completely in harmony with the metaphysical state of agitation, hence women simply accept "all that twaddle" with a "placid smile, knowing that by an immutable law the mother of the race in a true civilization must be as independent and self-governing a power as the man by her side." Edger's "sneering at the ballot," however, was another issue entirely. Ballots and constitutions might be " 'a very pretty metaphysical plaything' to a few positive philosophers," but in a true republic, like America, their value was well known. Stanton pointed out that Edger seemed bent on frightening people away from political participation, calling women who believed in the power of "paper ballots" the "victims of delusion." Stanton was not to be scared off. "I for one," she responded, "have no fears of the 'metaphysical transition' of the cold plunge into this sea of trouble in order to secure political rights." In Stanton's view, the agitation of the metaphysical state was indeed going to bring about the organic state, which would be revealed to be a "true Republic." "We have the right theory of government here," she reasoned with confidence, "that all mankind are equal; not equally wise, strong, or good, but that their rights are equally sacred." And, in Stanton's elaboration of Comte, woman was the missing catalytic element. "If there is sex in soul, as Swedenborg, and Comte, and Holcomb, and Edger, all admit, then disorganization is the law everywhere until the feminine element is fully recognized." If, in fact, humanity was stymied in the metaphysical stage, it was only because of men's failure to realize the essential role played by women in giving birth to the new order. "Man might as well hope to create a being in and of himself," she added, drawing an analogy from the immutable law of human reproduction. Stanton pursued Comte's theory to its logical conclusion: "If woman's influence is so imperative as they all admit, in social and theological reconstruction, why not in governmental reconstruction[?] If the principle of humanity cannot be breathed into creeds except by woman, how can it be breathed into codes without her[?]"[28]

The kingdom on earth, Stanton elaborated on Comte, would be brought about by women: "Behold with the coming of woman into this higher sphere of influence, the dawn of a new day, when politics so called, are to be lifted into the world of morals and religion." Stanton envisioned a millennial Republic redeemed and purified by women whose first duty would be to teach every boy and girl "that to vote is the most sacred act of citizenship."[29] As these passages illustrate, Stanton found within Positivism a powerful language for fusing religion, politics, and woman's rights. The republic she envisioned would be founded on the basis of a God-given equality between women and men. The Bible was a useful tool for Stanton in the 1860s and she wielded it skillfully.

Stumping for woman suffrage in the Kansas campaign of 1867, for example, Stanton developed biblical arguments for woman suffrage that drew upon her new commitment to Positivism. "The floods; the confusion of tongues; the plagues of Egypt; the destruction of Sodom and Gomorrah; the judgments of Babylon, the ruin of Ninevah [*sic*]; the tyranny of the Romans; the downfall of Jerusalem with its holy temple; the captivity and distress of Israel are but so many manifestations of the working of immutable laws," she contended, "so many declarations that man is more precious than his works; that God dwells not amid temples, thrones and altars . . . but in the lovely sanctuary of true souls, with men and women who have justice and mercy and walk humbly before the Lord." The most important of the immutable laws, the one "written on the soul of man," is the "gradual unfolding to man himself of his own divine origin." God created man in his own image, Stanton reminded her audience, "male and female and said let them have dominion over the earth" but she pointed out, "never shall man enter into this inheritance until woman is first made whole." For proof that God had intended women's shared power over the earth, Stanton provided numerous biblical examples of women as "rulers of nations, leaders of armies, as prophets, seers called of God to preach and pray last at the cross and first at the sepulcher, to whom a risen Savior gave his first message, 'Go tell my disciples that I am risen from the dead.'"[30]

These speeches were Stanton's most avowedly Christian pronouncements. They stand in stark contrast to both her earlier position of the 1850s—that the writings of Paul were human parchments in need of revision—and her later anticlerical writings. For a brief period it seemed that Stanton, empowered by her faith in Positivism, could argue with conviction that the Bible guaranteed women's equality. But it did not last. Increasingly, her sense that the church had done everything in its power to subjugate women won out. She retained her commitment to Positivist principles, particularly a divine "feminine element," but she rarely relied on the Bible as the primary source of her evidence.

Stanton's application of Positivism evolved over time. By the 1880s she had launched full force into her critique of Christianity as a corrupt system that exerted itself at women's expense. The simultaneous creation of male and female continued to be her starting point, but her emphasis shifted to the centuries of subterfuge that had masked this essential equality. Why, she asked, if God had created man in his own image, male and female, was the feminine element not recognized as part of the Trinity? The acknowledgment of the "equality of sex in the Godhead," she told the Free Religious Association in 1881, was the "cornerstone of the Religion of Humanity." Claiming that the "relation of sex to the very substance of religion [cannot] be overstated," Stanton called for a recasting of the Trinity. She conceded to God the Father as a legitimate representation of the masculine element. But it seemed obvious to her that the Holy Ghost "as the Comforter" implied "the presence of the feminine element, its love, tenderness and mercy" and should be formally recognized as such. The third part of the Trinity, was also problematic and, in her opinion, "should not have been Christ, but the aggregate of humanity, the whole human race." The Positivists were her model. They called for a "church of humanity," which makes woman, and especially the mother, the central figure, the actual Divinity." The suppression of the female divinity, Stanton argued, was what prevented "the divine order on earth" from emerging. This recognition was "the first step for woman's freedom and for that of humanity, when we shall have outgrown the popular idea of a male God . . . then we might see and worship God *in* humanity."[31]

Stanton's feminist adaptation of the Positivist Religion of Humanity remained a central component of her theology into the 1890s. In the speech she prepared for the World Parliament of Religions in 1893, she again asked the question: "what will the next step be?" Time and again she returned to an idea of a moral revolution. She still called for the recognition of both masculine and feminine divinities, but her revolutionary vision had expanded beyond this earlier position. The Religion of Humanity needed to focus on the inequalities of class: "It is folly to talk of a just government and a pure religion, in a nation where the State and the Church alike sustain an aristocracy of wealth and ease, while those who do the hard work of the world have no share in the blessings and riches, that their continued labors have made possible for others to enjoy." The moral revolution desperately needed to engage the educated and wealthy classes to show them that by "false theories of natural rights they are responsible for the poverty, ignorance, and vice of the masses." Stanton called for the obliteration of "false distinctions in society" and claimed that this radical work "is a more practical religion than that of man to his God." The meaning of the word "religion," Stanton wrote, is "to bind again, to unite those who have been separated, to harmonise those who have been in antagonism."[32] Positivism remained, for Stanton, a complete and compelling faith. It provided the basis of her critique of the church and it also offered her a framework for redemptive, collective action. As she liked to say, at last she had found that peace and comfort she could never find in the Bible and in the church.

Mother God: The Spiritual Power of New Thought

In embracing Comte's Positivism, Stanton had found a fitting intellectual and theological perspective for her own evolving views on religion, gender, and politics. She shared Positivists' vision of a world where "science, common sense, and love of humanity" held sway. But as her heated debate with Henry Edger demonstrated, Positivists did not endorse her vision of women's catalytic role in bringing about the new world order. Stanton's reading of Comte helped her develop a compelling critique, but Positivism offered her little in the way of like-minded colleagues. This was, in fact, a recurring theme in Stanton's life. As in her early quest for "boyhood" and her disappointments in the all-girl environment at Miss Willard's Female Seminary, Stanton was often at odds with those around her. Convivial in her temperament, she struggled during the last decades of her life for a kind of companionship that often proved elusive. On the one hand, many of the thinkers whose views on religion she most admired were men who took only a marginal interest in woman's rights. On the other hand, many of the women who shared her political liberalism were far more religious than she could ever be. Stanton could work in alliance with those more spiritually oriented women—on the *Woman's Bible* revising committee, for example— but ultimately, she felt compelled to distance herself from their religious beliefs. Finally, the religion question became centrally important to Stanton at a time when those closest to her simply did not share her passion. By the 1880s, Stanton had collaborated with Susan B. Anthony on a wide array of issues for over thirty years. Anthony, raised a Quaker, did not want to see the religion question divert energy from her drive for woman suffrage. "The religious part has never been mine, you know," she later wrote to Stanton, "and I won't take it up . . . so go ahead in your own way and let me stick to my own."[33]

It was perhaps this search for soul mates that drew a hesitant Stanton toward the practice of Mind Cure and New Thought in the decade of the 1880s. Several new friendships beckoned her into the circles of these popular "new religions." Within the suffrage movement, two younger colleagues were particularly influential in this regard. The English suffragist and writer Frances Lord first introduced Stanton to Theosophy and, later, Mind Cure.

Clara Colby, a young woman from Nebraska and the long-time editor of the *Woman's Tribune*, provided Stanton with political, intellectual, and personal kinship during these years and, in the process, exposed Stanton to the teachings of New Thought.

In unraveling the entangled worldviews of evangelicals and secularists in the nineteenth century, we have often lost a vital third strand of belief that was immensely popular at the time: the belief in spirit. Loosely tied to the antebellum Spiritualist tradition, this third thread of belief, sometimes called the "harmonial" tradition, attracted people who believed in the transformative power of unseen spirit.[34] These believers were not entirely at odds with more traditional faiths. Mary Baker Eddy, the founder of Christian Science, incorporated Christianity and the Bible into her practice of faith healing.[35] Believers in spirit frequently embraced the Bible, but not its "literal" interpretation. Rather, they viewed the Bible as a sacred, inspired text written in an esoteric code that only the power of spirit could decipher. In her guide to healing, *Science and Health with Key to the Scriptures*, Mary Baker Eddy provided readers with a tool to understanding the Bible's hidden meanings. Eddy found numerous errors in the way the Bible had been translated and interpreted. Read correctly with the aid of her Key, the Book of Genesis could provide a solid foundation for the principles of what Eddy called "divine Science." In her reading of the creation story, for example, God symbolically elaborated the crucial distinction in life: between the "eternal mind," which is divine spirit, and the "mortal mind," which is human, finite, and linked to matter.[36]

As the historian Beryl Satter has shown, Eddy, like the Mind Curists and New Thought practitioners who emerged before and after her, was deeply engaged in a debate over the boundaries between mind and matter. Eddy and her earliest competitor, Walter Felt Evans, were both trained by Phineas B. Quimby, a mesmerist who taught that the belief in illness actually created and promoted disease. Mary Baker Eddy elaborated his theory into both a form of health care and a theology. Eddy maintained that the real universe, created by God or the Eternal Mind, was entirely spiritual and unfailingly good. Evil had no place in God's universe. Therefore, the evil that appeared to exist—including bodily illness—was created and projected by the mortal mind. To treat the ill body, the mortal mind had to be convinced that its own assumptions were misguided and then persuaded of the totality of goodness. Walter Felt Evans, the author of *The Mental Cure*, shared some of these assumptions but differed from Eddy in that he popularized the notion of the "Divine Within." Rather than seeking illumination from an external "Eternal Mind," as one did in Eddy's Christian Science, Evans argued that each individual was gifted with an "inner spark" that could be cultivated into divinity.[37]

Both Eddy and Evans had a profound impact on several generations of faith healers who collectively became known as the New Thought movement. Eddy was legendary for training disciples with whom she later parted company. Such was the case with Emma Curtis Hopkins, a faith healer who left Eddy's fold and built an enormous practice in Chicago in the 1880s. Hopkins taught her hybrid healing—based both on Eddy and Evans—to numerous women in the suffrage movement, including Stanton's young friends Frances Lord and Clara Colby.[38] Stanton lumped all of this faith healing together into the category of "Mind Cure," but in fact, all of Stanton's associates who were involved in the movement had ties to Emma Curtis Hopkins. Hopkins initially called her version of faith healing Christian Science. But in the early 1890s Mary Baker Eddy successfully copyrighted the term "Christian Science," forcing dissident students such as Hopkins to cast about for a new label. A number of different terms emerged—Mind Cure, Divine Science, Universal Truth, Harmony—but eventually these pracitioners began to adopt New Thought as an umbrella term for their movement. As Beryl Satter has pointed out, New Thought was particularly attractive to women. Part of the appeal lay in its implicitly feminist theology. For Emma Curtis Hopkins, the presence of spirit within the Bible suggested the female nature of God. Hopkins taught her students to "know that the Mother God is the Holy Spirit of the Scripture. They discern the signs of the times in the uprising of woman and the spiritual interpretation she is giving to all words and movements. . . . They see that the rejection by woman of this old false belief that evil is a necessity . . . is the second coming of the Christ."[39]

Given Positivism's inherent spirituality—particularly the concept of the feminine "element," whose moral power was essential to its millennial promise—Stanton's Positivist faith might have led her further into the debates about mind, matter, spirit, and the soul that preoccupied practitioners of New Thought. But it did not. Certainly, Frances Lord's and Clara Colby's interest in New Thought brought Stanton abreast of these alternative, mystical traditions. Invariably, however, Stanton's skepticism prevailed. She confessed to her cousin, Elizabeth Smith Miller, "I fear we are not sufficiently developed for any phase of the occult science. I have tried faithfully to be spiritualized, but this too solid flesh is my drawback."[40] Stanton's initial reaction to the Mind Cure had in fact been more annoyance than curiosity. Frances Lord had become enthralled with the Mind Cure and had given up helping Stanton with an early draft of the *Woman's Bible* in 1886; in Stanton's words, "I could get no more work out of her."[41] A few months later, however, Stanton gave in to her curiosity and enrolled with her daughter Harriot in a Mind Cure course in England, claiming, "we are not fanatical on the question but searchers after the truth."[42] Apparently, Stanton found the course less than persuasive; soon she disparaged the practice as both a "fantasy" and an "epidemic."[43] When Miller wanted to send Stanton a Mind Cure patient the following year, Stanton protested, saying that she did "not believe that thought 'Can mend a broken bone or antidote a poison.'" Stanton recommended that Miller should instead give the woman Stanton's love and tell her "to think of pleasant things."[44]

The Child of Unbelief: The American Freethought Movement

The rationalist bent of Freethought proved more comfortable to Stanton's "too solid flesh." Here again, her search for the friendship of like-minded thinkers led her into a movement beyond the circles of woman's rights. Drawn mainly from middle-class intellectuals in the Northeast—radical Unitarians, transcendentalists, scientists, members of the liberal professions, and woman's rights advocates—this loose amalgamation of reformers and political liberals organized the Free Religious Association and the Secular Union.[45] In their periodicals, which included the *Index*, the *Boston Investigator*, the *Open Court*, and *Free Thought Magazine*, three central and overlapping themes emerge that lent this movement coherence. First of all, Freethinkers were intrigued by the emerging intellectual challenges to religious beliefs. At the same time, they actively sought out other explanatory theories that could take the place of religion. And finally, they engaged in a social critique of what they perceived to be the declining morality of Christian societies.[46]

Freethinkers were not of one mind on the question of religion. For some, their mission involved challenging religious dogma by studying religions comparatively. Others, particularly Francis Abbott, the editor of the *Index*, were committed to integrating religion and science. The *Index* ran articles on such topics as "Evolution and Its Relation to Evangelical Religion" in an attempt to spell out the implications of Darwinism for Christianity.[47] Many Freethinkers regarded science and religion as entirely compatible; the science of tomorrow could be expected to explain the "miracles" of today. In the view of others, however, science had completely destroyed Christianity, the Bible, and all other vestiges of religious faith. Freethinkers led by Andrew Dickson White, author of *A History of the Warfare of Science with Theology in Christendom* and president of Cornell University, campaigned against Christianity and the Bible. "How long," asked the famous agnostic lecturer, Robert Green Ingersoll, "O how long will mankind worship a book? How long will they grovel in the dust before the ignorant legends of the barbaric past?"[48]

Stanton found these pronouncements extremely satisfying. She devoured the published work of her fellow agnostics, followed their careers in the press, and struck up a friendly correspondence with leading Freethinkers in America and abroad.[49] She became particularly enamored of Ingersoll, the most notorious of American heretics. An attorney by training, Ingersoll was dubbed "Colonel" in deference to his Civil War service in the eleventh Illinois volunteer cavalry regiment. Active in Republican politics after the war, he became a legendary orator. His ability to ignite a crowd led people to speculate that he could have had a successful career in politics, but for his religious heresy. In his later years, Ingersoll settled in New York City, where he and Stanton occasionally visited, exchanged work, and followed each other's exploits in the press. From New York, Stanton wrote to Harriot of a memorable Ingersoll lecture in New Jersey: "The clergy planned to arrest him; they had detectives and sheriffs ready in the theater. But the judges said that nothing could be done unless he was openly obscene or blasphemous. But he was neither, and he made them all laugh and listen, clergymen as well as policemen."[50]

A developing friendship with another gifted lecturer, Benjamin Franklin Underwood, and his wife, Sara Underwood, also connected Stanton to the journals and organizations of the American Freethought movement. Like Ingersoll, Benjamin Underwood had volunteered in the Union army and spent time as a prisoner of war. After the war, he earned a living as a Freethought lecturer, frequently debating clergy on the issue of evolution. A popularizer of Darwin in America, Benjamin Underwood verged on being a materialist; that is, his guiding philosophical framework insisted that physical matter was the only knowable reality. In what must have made for a dynamic marriage, his wife Sara took a different view, more oriented toward New Thought. Sara Underwood believed in the reality of spirit and published a book on *Automatic or Spirit Writing*, a meditative practice in which the writer's hand was guided by spirit. Despite their differences, however, both Underwoods shared Stanton's anticlerical commitments. Stanton deeply valued this alliance. Her religious iconoclasm rendered her increasingly unpopular in more orthodox circles. When her younger suffrage colleagues hesitated to publish her pieces on religion, she began placing her writings in journals with an audience of fellow Freethinkers who were not offended by her critique of the Bible. As the publishers of Freethought periodicals, first the *Index* and later the *Open Court*, the Underwoods delighted in having a contributor of Stanton's stature, and they offered a camaraderie she could not find with mainstream reformers. "You need never fear that your letters are too long," Stanton wrote to Sara in 1885; "I have no thoroughly liberal correspondents among women—hence I specially prize you."[51] When in the same year the Freethinkers Convention invited Stan-

American agnostic and Freethinker Robert Green Ingersoll was a friend and colleague of Stanton's in the 1890s. Stanton asserted that he had "done more in the
last twenty years to emancipate the human soul from crushing superstitions than
all the other influences put together." State Historical Society of Wisconsin (X3)
18057

ton to address the group, she asked Benjamin for advice. Worried that Freethought and free love were still conjoined in the public mind, as they had been before the Civil War because of various experimental utopian communities, Stanton inquired about the agenda of this particular association. "After accepting I had some misgivings about the people in that discussion," she wrote to Benjamin. "As you know them all would I compromise myself in any way by being on their platform?"[52]

Stanton's initial reluctance to "compromise herself" gave way to thorough-going enthusiasm for the Freethought movement. Within its folds, Stanton found support for her rationalist critique of the Bible. One of the Freethinkers' central missions focused on supplanting religious superstition—especially Christianity—with a belief in rational, scientific thought. Drawing on the theories of John Locke, Freethinkers insisted that anything contrary to reason or experience—especially miracles revealed in the Bible—simply could not be true. Neither the Bible nor the church could be relied on as a foundation for truth. Instead, as Stanton herself argued in the pages of the *Free Religious Index*, human reason, logic, and utilitarian needs provided the seeds of truth.[53]

The Freethought movement appealed to Stanton as a feminist as well as a rationalist. She and other women Freethinkers built on the insights of the Reform Rabbi Felix Adler, who founded the Ethical Culture movement.[54] Adler was appalled by the poverty and social conditions he observed in the slums of New York and questioned the morality of modern industrial society. Was God responsible for such a world? Stanton read Adler and had her own belief in the Religion of Humanity confirmed. She wrote in her diary: "He says so well what I have long thought and believed—that religion is life. How much happier life would be, if we made more of man and this world and thought less of future states of which we know nothing." A few months later Stanton met Adler at the Free Religious Association, where they shared the platform. She liked him immensely, noting in her diary, "his views are always so large and noble."[55] Adler's critique served as a corrective to Stanton's earlier enthusiastic embrace of Comte's Positivism. She would never relinquish Positivism entirely, but she did lose some of her earlier optimism about "immutable laws" and their inherent justice. As she wrote to her son Kit: "How anyone, in view of the protracted sufferings of the race, can invest the laws of the universe with a tender loving fatherly intelligence, watching, guiding and protecting humanity, is to me amazing. I see nothing but immutable, inexorable law, grinding the ignorant to powder."[56]

Through speeches, essays, and letters, Stanton crafted a feminist adaptation of Freethought: the campaign for women's equality had to begin by leveling the cultural influence of orthodox Christianity.[57] On this issue, her long-time suffrage colleague and friend Matilda Joslyn Gage was particularly influential. In 1881, when the "may day" call went out for help in completing volume two of the *History of Woman Suffrage*, Gage answered it. The month she spent with Stanton meant interrupting her work on her own project, *Woman, Church and State*, in which Gage developed an extended historical critique of the church as an institution. From that point on, Stanton began to write on some of Gage's favorite topics, particularly "The Matriarchate," a prehistoric period in which women allegedly ruled. Gage was troubled by the feeling that Stanton was stealing her thunder, but the two suffragists agreed in condemning religious superstition and the church's power to control women throughout the ages.[58] The Bible and its clerical interpreters, they believed, contributed powerfully to the degraded condition of women. The Bible was culpable for its misogynist imagery and doctrine of original sin which "dishonored womanhood."[59] According to many Freethinkers, the clergy compounded the obstacles to women's equality by corrupting the truly liberating aspects of Jesus' teachings.

Once she had unleashed her anticlerical passion in Moncure Conway's London chapel, Stanton frequently and fervently inveighed against the clergy. As she wrote to Benjamin Underwood in 1885, "I have passed from the political to the religious phase of this question, for I now see more clearly than ever, that the arch enemy to women's freedom skulks behind the altar."[60] "No class of men," Stanton wrote in the pages of the *Index*, "have such power to pervert the religious sentiments and oppress mankind with gloomy superstitions through life and an undefined dread of the unknown after death."[61] Empowered by its clergy, the church robbed woman of her autonomy by putting man in place of God and by excluding her from all positions of ecclesiastical influence. As Gage argued in *Woman, Church and State*, the church through the centuries had "anathematized her sex, teaching her to feel shame for the very fact of her being; it had not been content with proclaiming a curse upon her creative attributes, but had thrust the sorrows and expiations of man's 'curse' upon her."[62]

It bears noting that Stanton and Gage were responding to an argument particularly popular among Christians, missionaries, reformers, and advocates of American imperialism. That is: Christianity's elevation of women was perceived as an indication of its cultural superiority and its higher evolutionary status. So-called heathen societies allegedly degraded women and would consequently benefit from exposure to American Christian and democratic influence. "Compare . . . woman's condition in lands where Christianity had made little or no advance," the Reverend Thomas DeWitt Talmadge told his congregation in 1885, "The *Burmese sell their wives* and daughters as so many sheep. . . . What mean those white bundles on the ponds and rivers in China in the morning? Infanticide following infanticide. Female children destroyed simply because they are female. Woman harnessed to a plough as an ox. . . . No refinement. No liberty. No hope for this life. No hope for the life to come. Ringed nose. Cramped foot. Disfigured face. Embruted soul."[63] For Freethinkers like Stanton and Gage, this formulation was suspect; women's degradation, they countered, was a defining element of Christianity. In fact, women's degraded status under Christianity had no more potent symbol than the prostitute. "We may well ask the question," Stanton wrote to Sara Underwood in 1885, "when 20,000 girls between the ages of 12 [and] 16 are sacrificed annually in the city of London, bought [and] sold to physicians, clergymen, members of Parliament, [and] Princes of the royal blood, we may well ask 'has Christianity benefited woman?' "[64]

Stanton's frontal attacks on the Bible and the church published in the eighties and early nineties served as a rehearsal for the *Woman's Bible*. As Stanton saw it, her task was to rescue women from the self-imposed bondage of blind faith, a condition "that is exasperating to those who see [its] demoralizing influence."[65] This she aimed at in her major writings by stressing her own personal growth from the darkness of childhood superstition into the light of science and reason, a narrative strategy quite popular among Freethinkers. In claiming Stanton as an influential convert, Freethinking colleagues seized upon and enlarged episodes of childhood skepticism to mythological proportions. A review of her autobiography by "T.B.W." (Thaddeus B. Wakeman) related the story of her failed conversion under the spellbinding oratory of Charles Grandison Finney: "How much this sincere, trusting and delicate young woman suffered from these terrors made crushingly real to her by a 'divine and infallible authority' she can only intimate rather than describe, but when she did recover from this cruel delusion, it left her an object in life to which she has been true—the duty of shielding others and especially children and young people from this hellish torture."[66]

For Stanton, the task of liberating women from the shackles of a misogynist religion began, as she claimed it had in her own early experiences, with the assertion of the individual conscience. And how better to effect the conversion of women to science and reason than through the individual reader's contact with the Bible "rightly interpreted"?[67]

"Science" and Biblical Criticism

Stanton intended her critique to take its place among other challenges, both academic and popular, that were eroding the Bible's authority in the late nineteenth century. In her diary in London, she recorded the satisfaction of "dipping" into Charles Darwin's *Descent of Man* and Herbert Spencer's *First*

Principles, which collectively "cleared up many of my ideas on theology and left me more than ever reconciled to rest with many debatable ideas relegated to the unknown."[68] As she wrote to her cousin and fellow skeptic, Elizabeth Smith Miller, "Admit Darwin's theory of evolution, and the whole orthodox system topples to the ground; if there was no Fall, there was no need of a Savior, and the atonement, regeneration and salvation have no significance whatever."[69] Did modern science in general, and Darwinism in particular, pose such a fundamental challenge to the Bible and to theology, or did Stanton seize upon scientific authority to abandon ideas she had long doubted?[70]

Like the Bible itself, "science" had multiple and changing meanings in the late nineteenth century. Just at the time that scientists were professionalizing and encoding stricter rules as to what qualified as science, the meanings of "science" in the vernacular multiplied in unprecedented fashion. During the antebellum period, science had the status of a hobby; one rarely encountered a "professional" scientist. When Darwin first published his work in England in 1859, America boasted only four or five scientists who could actually understand it. After the Civil War, science became more prominent in the halls of academe, but even then scientists had little control over the term's multiple uses. On the one hand, for such groups as Christian Scientists, "science" was a term directly linked with spirituality, not in opposition to it. For Freethinkers, on the other hand, science encompassed any knowledge based on sources other than spirituality. Freethinkers generously included any technological advance—from use of anesthetics to improved farm machinery—under the rubric of science. Science, however defined or derived, meant progress, the sacred doctrine of Freethinkers. Many, including Stanton, accepted the authority of science on faith alone. Scientists, for their part, were trying mightily to disconnect the study of science from metaphysical concerns. Scientists did not make an issue of denying the supernatural; rather, they tended to base their disciplinary inquiries on the verifiable, physical world, particularly the observation of nature.[71] These competing definitions made for strange bedfellows. Who would expect to find Charles Hodge, the orthodox Presbyterian theologian from Princeton, in theoretical agreement with Mary Baker Eddy in the belief that "science" should not be limited to the "external world"?

The prevailing view of American intellectual culture in this period has largely ignored debate between evangelicals and infidels over science and the Bible, focusing instead on the sometimes triumphant, sometimes tragic, tale of liberal Protestantism. Sydney Ahlstrom, in his classic history of American religion, called this era the "Golden Age of Liberal Theology" and praised American theologians' intellectual flexibility in the face of so many challenges, from the sensational oratory of Robert Ingersoll to the quieter but no less troubling discoveries of Charles Darwin.[72] More recent historians have rather tarnished the Golden Age, lamenting the lack of intellectual vigor among theologians in the wake of Darwin. In *No Place of Grace*, T. J. Jackson Lears argues that liberal theology was undone by the challenges of secularization and consequently unable to mediate modern anxieties. For Lears, secularization resulted from a collective failure of ministers and secular moralists alike, who relaxed all the tensions and "blunted all the sharp edges in Protestant tradition." Once a source of autonomous moral authority, liberal Protestantism was reduced to a "handmaiden of the Positivist world view."[73] The historian James Turner, too, has claimed that the rise of unbelief was in large part the fault of theologians, not scientists. Turner maintains that theologians' reliance on science to prove God's existence—before there was any perceived conflict between science and religion—planted the seeds of disaster that emerged in full bloom during the late nineteenth century. According to the "argument from design" that dominated antebellum "natural theology," God had designed the universe, and scientists and theologians were working cooperatively to understand and reveal His design. Nature revealed God. The natural world was not a haphazard one, but an intricately detailed master plan. Darwin cast doubt on the design argument, or worse, according to Turner: "Darwin punctured it, and its plausibility fizzed away like air from a leaky balloon."[74] Darwin's theory of natural selection, in which simple organisms evolved to more complex ones through competition and adaptation and the unfit simply did not survive, did not point to a Great Designer, or even a very good one. Theologians were left out on a limb, and had to let go of the claim that science or nature proved the existence of God.

But even as science could no longer be relied upon to prove God's existence, its methods were being harnessed for the study of the Bible. Nowhere was the emergence of modern methodologies more troubling to orthodox Christians than in German higher criticism of the Bible. The application of what at the time constituted a rather narrowly defined scientific method to Bible study had begun in German universities in the early nineteenth century. Sharing the basic assumptions of natural science, German higher criticism emphasized studying the development of the Bible to determine the date, authorship, and integrity of the various texts. The treatment of the Bible as a historical artifact, a product whose elements could be analyzed, dated, and authenticated, posed potential problems for religious orthodoxy. American churchmen reacted explosively to the writings of one higher critic, the Anglican bishop John William Colenso from South Africa. His skeptical treatise, *The Pentateuch and the Book of Joshua Critically Examined*, shed doubt on the commonly held belief that Moses had authored the Pentateuch, the first five books of the Bible.[75] And if the integrity of the various texts could be questioned by scientific method, so too could the specific content of those texts. Particularly devastating was the "German heresy," *Das Leben Jesu*, the *Life of Jesus* by David F. Strauss, a work of 1,400 pages that examined virtually all biblical events in terms of their approximation of contemporary standards of truth.[76] One might wonder how the publication of a single book could produce such shock waves. But Strauss had revealed numerous inaccuracies in the New Testament and verged on questioning the very existence of Christ. The implications of the German scholarship were potentially radical, but in Stanton's mind, higher criticism had a major drawback as a political weapon: it was inaccessible to average readers. As she put it, it was "fortunate for the faith thus assailed that the critical and rhetorical style of the ordinary German professor is too heavy for export or general circulation."[77]

Reluctant Apostles of Modernity: The American Revising Committee and the Revised New Testament

The tensions of this era can best be traced through the acrimonious public debate that surrounded the publication of a revised New Testament in 1881, foreshadowing the public outrage over the *Woman's Bible* in the following decade. Indeed, what Stanton deemed the "failures" of the Revised New Testament prompted her to begin the *Woman's Bible*. But the debate generated by the Revised New Testament also provides a vital intellectual and religious context: it illustrates how the threat of new "scientific" knowledge played out among the religiously orthodox in the Gilded Age. Cumulatively, the affronts from Darwin, German higher criticism, and such popular trends as the Christian Science, Freethought, and New Thought movements created an atmosphere in which evangelical biblical scholars felt compelled to respond according to "safe and conservative principles."[78]

Virtually every historical account of this era has posited conservative Charles Hodge as the lone voice of resistance to Darwin; in fact, evangelical scholars of Hodge's stripe abounded. One significant exercise of their authority may be seen in the formation of the American Revising Committee in 1871 to prepare a revision of the New and Old Testaments. Philip Schaff, originator of the committee, assembled a group of conservative theologians widely known for their defense of traditional Calvinism, including some of the most prestigious Bible scholars in America. In contrast to the liberal clergy's growing acceptance of higher criticism, the American Revising Committee, almost to a man, consistently countered the inroads of new methodologies. James Strong, chair of Exegetical Theology at Drew Seminary, defended the Mosaic authorship of the Pentateuch and the historical accuracy of the Genesis creation account. William Henry Green, chair of the Old Testament revision committee, had published an essay titled "The Pentateuch Vindicated from the Aspersions of Bishop Colenso" and in time earned a reputation as the intellectual leader of the ultraconservative school of biblical criticism in the United States. Green's and Strong's views were shared by most members of the American Revising Committee.

Countering the wholesale attack on the Bible's legitimacy as a historical work, the committee marshaled the best in Greek scholarship to correct errors in translation that marred the King James or Authorized Version. As a translation of the Greek, the King James was woefully lacking. As Philip Schaff later put it, "for more than two hundred and fifty years, the English-speaking world has been drinking the water of life 'from the jaw bone of a royal jackass.' "[79] Yet despite their sense of urgency, the American Revising Committee proceeded cautiously. The New Testament committee was determined to improve upon the King James Bible by providing a "neutral" and more accurate translation drawn from a variety of existing Greek manuscripts. At the same time, however, the revisers were committed to preserving the Authorized Version as much as possible, and a two-thirds majority was required for any change to the biblical text.[80] This painstaking task consumed ten years. The committee was, after all, walking a fine line fending off an attack from higher criticism without losing the support of its evangelical constituents who were essentially underwriting the revision.[81] The changes it proposed to the actual text of the King James Bible centered around consistency and grammar, not grand interpretative strokes. No matter: a new Bible was news indeed.

When the revised New Testament was finally released for sale on May 20, 1881, newspapers reported major traffic tie-ups in and around the New York publishing houses and retail stores.[82] Within hours, booksellers had placed street venders on the corners of Wall Street and Broadway barking, "Bibles only a quarter," "The Revised New Testament for only twenty-five cents."[83] With prices ranging from fifteen cents for a paperback to sixteen dollars for the best cloth-bound edition, sales in the city on that first day were estimated at around 300,000. One firm alone sold 175,000 copies. Hundreds of thousands of people in New York simultaneously poring over the Scriptures were bound to have a supernatural effect, one clergyman claimed.[84] Indeed, ministers predicted that the revised version would touch off a religious revival "such as the age has not seen."[85] In the spirit of modernity, the text was even telegraphed to Chicago and run as a supplement to a daily newspaper.[86] The commercial aspects of this publishing event were not lost upon observers, including one Episcopal clergyman who remarked that "everything connected with its first appearance in America was as well managed . . . as if . . . the most accomplished advertiser had had it in hand."[87]

The clergy's infatuation with the new revision was short-lived, and the crass commercialism of selling God's word was just one of many criticisms attending its release. A number of ministers expressed reservations. Some lauded the scholarship of the new revision but doubted they would introduce it into their own churches. As the sensation that surrounded its release subsided, it became apparent that the text of the new version pleased no one. Not surprisingly, the revision was censured by clergy who had opposed the project from its onset. A Catholic priest, the Reverend Thomas A. Becker, reviewing the work in the pages of *Catholic World*, juxtaposed this hopelessly flawed Bible with the strength of the Catholic Church as the true witness of the Christian faith, wondering aloud if "the tendency of the revision among thinking Protestants will . . . make them forsake a sinking craft, leaky, untrustworthy, and floundering, in order to make a safe harbor."[88] Episcopal priests, who had abstained en masse from the project, greeted the revision ambivalently. On the one hand, the interest it aroused offered "proof, that no blasphemer can ignore, of the hold Scriptures have upon the world," wrote the Reverend W. C. Doane. Yet, on the other hand, by making a large number of "needless changes" to the King James Bible, the revised version delivered "into the hands of unbelievers, a weapon of attack upon revealed truth."[89] The noted New York evangelist Thomas DeWitt Talmadge concurred, blasting the enormous number of changes to the Bible and warning, "Satan takes those statistics and with them overthrows the faith of many."[90] Liberal clergy were no more generous in their assessment. Among Universalists, for example, the revision, while preferable to the flawed King James Version, was still viewed as falling short of what "the actual state of . . . science demanded in a translation." The list of detractors even included a dissenting member of the American Revising Committee, G. Vance Smith, who contended that the final result in some ways justified the "doubts and fears of those against the revision" all along.[91]

Critiques by a wide array of reviewers, however, yielded little in the way of substantive theological concerns.[92] Most reviewers focused on the relationship between the revised text and the King James Bible and shared Doane's view that the number of revisions was excessive.[93] The theological aftershocks of those changes were more difficult to measure. After all, the revision was accused simultaneously of liberalizing tendencies and of overly cautious conservatism.[94] While doctrines were, by and large, left intact, certain popular passages of the New Testament were altered to the universal displeasure of reviewers. Changes made in the Lord's Prayer were particularly objectionable. Virtually all reviewers commented on the removal of the doxology: "for thine is the kingdom, the power, and the glory." Some clergy regretted the change and remarked that the public "will not willingly relinquish" the traditional language.[95] Others were incensed by the implication

Thomas DeWitt Talmadge, the legendary New York City evangelist, bitterly opposed the revision of the New Testament in 1881. He claimed that the great masses of people thought the revision a "desecration, profanation, and religious outrage." State Historical Society of Wisconsin (X3) 49419

that the familiar doxology was not divinely inspired. The *New York Times* quoted the Reverend DeWitt Talmadge: "What the Church wants is not critics, but evangelists—not men to knock the doxology out of the Lord's Prayer, but men to bring all nations to the feet of Christ, proclaiming, 'For Thine is the kingdom, the power, and the glory, Amen.' When I began this service [using the new revised version] I stopped at the doxology, but I will never do so again in public or in private unless in dying my breath should give out, and then I will finish it in heaven."[96] These alterations to familiar and beloved passages convinced many that the Bible had been violated.

The committee chairman, Philip Schaff, had lauded the revision for striking a balance between the "scientific language of scholars" and "the vulgar language of the street."[97] But few reviewers concurred. By November 1881, just six months after the initial fanfare, the *New York Times* reported that no church in the city had adopted the revision for public worship. All would agree the new version was more accurate, "painfully so."[98] Ironically, the revisers had vindicated the King James Bible. Urging parishioners to boycott the revision, Talmadge cautioned, "Hold on to your Bible. The old Bible is good enough for me; it is good enough for you. . . . It will take more than 71 revisers to revise the memory of a whole generation of Bible readers." It seemed he might be right. Appealing to xenophobia, Talmadge even questioned the "foreign influence" in the revision. The German-born Schaff came under attack as a man "born and educated in a foreign land" who lacked "the necessary qualifications" to choose an appropriately American committee.[99]

The response to the New Testament of 1881 provides a rare window on the fervor aroused when evangelicals attempted, however cautiously, to accommodate science. The results were universally disastrous. Many reviewers concurred that the scholars' "advanced scientific knowledge" had proved an "impediment" rather than an aid to their task.[100] Popular ambivalence toward science was tellingly expressed as clergymen invoked the law of "the survival of the fittest" alternately to explain the revision's persistence and to forecast its demise.[101]

Religious leaders, whatever their seeming degree of accommodation to scientific methods, ultimately turned their backs on the fruits of modern scholarship and rallied behind the King James Version. Their reasons for resisting the revision were as numerous as the changes made in the old Bible. One concern stood out: the Word had been altered. For many clergy, a theoretical embrace of science was possible, but a scientifically informed Bible was not. The growing "religion of the heart" had no place for a technically accurate Bible. No matter how legitimate and limited its scholarly claims, the revising committee precipitated a crisis of authority among clergy that was essentially theological in nature. The divine inspiration of the Word was profoundly shaken by the revision. The conservatives who rushed to the defense of the traditional text knew that a central principle of received wisdom had been breached; even the moderates who maintained that the numerous small changes in language were trivial and had no theological import were attempting to return to a stance that had been undermined or at least called into question. As the reception of the new Bible demonstrates, the America of the 1880s was not a society growing more secular, placing its faith in science rather than Scripture. Apparently there was plenty of faith to go around. American Protestants, clergymen and the Bible-reading public alike, could settle in with the contradiction: they could embrace the scientific progress of the century and still not tolerate changing a single word of their Bible.[102]

A minority of readers regarded the revision as too timid in its recasting of ancient texts. Among those who were eager to lay eyes on the new text and then bitterly disappointed by it, was Elizabeth Cady Stanton. Believing that, "whatever the Bible may be made to do in Hebrew or Greek, in plain English it does not exalt and dignify woman," Stanton may have hoped that the revisers would undo the damage inflicted by previous translations.[103] On the eve of publising her own Bible, she summed up her evaluation of the revised version: "There were hopes that in the last revision of the New Testament justice might at last be done woman and her equality with man clearly brought out, but they did nothing, and still kept woman in a position that has taken away from her her self-respect."[104] She went right to the heart of the problem: the Apostle Paul. Citing Paul's injunction, "wives, obey your husbands," Stanton concluded: "No symbols or metaphors can twist honor or dignity out of such sentiments. Here, in plain English, woman's position is degraded as in the Old Testament."[105] To be fair, we must acknowledge that Stanton was judging the work of these men by an agenda she had set for them, rather than the goals they had set for themselves. Concerned about the growing influence of evangelicalism and spurred on by the academic and popular attempts to undermine the Bible, Stanton might not have liked the American Revising Committee's work in any case, gender issues aside. Certainly the revision did not crystallize a new understanding of the Scriptures in her mind; her critique of it differed little from her wholesale attack on Christianity throughout this period. What the revised New Testament did was provide Stanton a unique opportunity to voice her concerns. The new Bible was no better than the old. The Bible continued to be problematic for women, Stanton argued, because of what it said about women and also for what informed readers and commentators could manipulate it to say.

From the middle of the nineteenth century, the peculiar status of the Bible simultaneously challenged by scientific developments and commercialized by the rapid growth of the religious publishing market had stimulated a host of biblical commentaries from both believers and nonbelievers.[106] Containing both Scripture and commentaries, most such works were close to interminable, published in multiple volumes or as one encyclopedic tome. Stanton enjoyed retelling the story of the day she had difficulty stepping down from a carriage, forcing her hosts to fetch a copy of Clarke's

"Commentaries" to help her alight.[107] Most of the commentaries claimed to be authoritative, one advertising itself as the "results of modern Biblical research and scholarship. Enriched with the fruits of learning more various and advanced, and of interpretation more critical and exact" than its competitors.[108]

The sheer number of commentaries available suggests that "critical and exact" interpretations encouraged a multiplicity of competing meanings in the Bible. This possibility underscored a gnawing ambivalence in nineteenth-century Protestantism. "We are Protestants," wrote one clergyman. "We claim that it is the right and duty of every Christian to read and interpret the Bible. Why should we shrink from the logical and necessary consequences of our position?"[109] Perhaps, in the words of a Catholic critic, they did so to prevent every reader finding "*in* the Bible that which he brings *to* the dead letter of Scripture."[110] In everyday practice, many Americans resolved this tension by putting their faith in the power of "the Book" to inspire the reading. As the *Watchman*, an evangelical periodical, counseled: "The reader of the Scriptures may find in them much that is puzzling and obscure, but if the Holy Spirit dwells in his heart he will constantly find that the Author of the Book is the best interpreter of its meaning. Does not this explain how it is that an unlettered Christian sometimes has a deeper insight into God's Word than the accomplished scholar? The Book has been interpreted to him by its Author."[111]

Stanton was skeptical. "As the Bible is placed in the hands of children and uneducated men and women to point them in the way of salvation, the letter should have no doubtful meaning. What should we think of guide posts on our highways, if we need a symbolic interpreter at every point to tell us which way to go?" she argued.[112] Robert Ingersoll was even more insistent: "Can God, then, through the Bible, make the same revelation to two men? He cannot. Why? Because the man who reads is the man who inspires. Inspiration is in the man and not the book."[113] Despite the popular belief that the Bible was divinely inspired, the growing number of biblical commentaries profoundly undermined the idea that its meaning was literally apparent.

For that matter, despite the uproar over grammatical changes to the King James Bible, not all Bibles of the time were alike. For example, the religious press advertised a special New Testament for marketing exclusively to immigrants, featuring dual columns: one with the "regular English," the other with a phonetic version. The "regular English" was not one of the prevalent versions; the language had been "reduced to the comprehension and easy acquirement of our foreign peoples."[114] Like the manufacturers and promoters of Bibles, the compilers of biblical commentaries routinely targeted their audiences—Sunday school teachers, ministers, parents, children, immigrants—and adapted the language to fit the audience.

With the publication of multiple Bibles, competing commentaries, and new forms of analysis, the act of reading the Bible became freighted with self-consciousness. Seizing upon this moment when the weight of science and historical criticism had laid open the Bible to multiple readings, nineteenth-century women reformers exploited it to considerable gain. They both decried the imposition of preordained, patriarchal views onto biblical texts and welcomed the opportunity to offer their own readings. Interpretations of the Bible, as woman's rights advocates frequently noted, were not disinterested. Rather, in the words of the great temperance reformer Frances Willard, biblical interpretation was "one of the most time-serving and man-made of all sciences, and one of the most misleading of all arts."[115]

A "Man-Made Science": Gendered Readings of the Bible

While science and higher criticism emboldened Stanton to prepare her own commentary on biblical texts, her work in the *Woman's Bible* also responded to a more popular interpretive tradition wherein the Bible was regularly cited to define contemporary gender roles—a tradition that seemed to survive the skirmishes with modern science unscathed.[116] Frequently, Stanton identified her target as male clergy who invoked Genesis and the New Testament letters of Paul to assert women's subordinate status. But she also resisted the readings of the evangelical women reformers who grounded woman's rights in the Bible without challenging its misogyny or sacred status.

An "emasculated Christianity," charged the *Religious Outlook*, was the direct result of nothing less than an "emasculated Gospel."[117] According to the historian T. J. Jackson Lears, the crisis of authority that characterized the close of the nineteenth century was created by "the moral impotence and spiritual sterility" of a "flaccid" liberal Protestantism.[118] Lears's use of images of male sexual impotence to describe a failure of cultural authority echoes the language of many evangelicals of the time. The cultural anxieties generated by challenges to Christianity were frequently expressed in gendered terms. Liberal Protestantism may have been rendered impotent in the face of an emasculating higher criticism, but some evangelical Protestants responded with a call for "muscular Christianity."[119]

Evangelical clergy shored up the "emasculated Gospel" with a reinvigorated reading of the writings of the Apostle Paul. Extending his work on the controversial revised New Testament, Philip Schaff led British and American revisers in publishing a mammoth, interdenominational *Popular Commentary on the New Testament*. The *Popular Commentary* further revealed that whatever revisions had been made, they did not include a change in the traditional view of woman's place. In his exegesis on Paul, for example, David

Brown, one of the New Testament revisers, offered the common assertion that those familiar passages silencing women were justified by frequent references to Old Testament law. Bible scholars throughout the nineteenth century maintained that Paul used the phrase "as also saith the law" to refer specifically to Genesis 3:16: "Unto the woman, he said, I will greatly multiply thy sorrow and thy conception; in sorrow thou shalt bring forth children; and thy desire shall be to thy husband, and he shall rule over thee." This passage was the biblical foundation for women's status, Brown explained, "of which idea all subsequent passages of the same import are but repetitions and expansions."[120]

Brown's linking of Pauline doctrine and the creation story followed the dominant mode of exegesis in Christian biblical commentaries: the Old and New Testaments were read in light of each other. While most Protestants preferred the New Testament as the more recent dispensation, scholars readily used Old Testament passages to illuminate New Testament meanings. Indeed, many Bible scholars unquestioningly accepted Paul's assertion that Eve's conduct in Genesis fixed woman's status in the Bible and thereafter.

Typically in evangelical commentaries on the Old and New Testaments, Eve was portrayed as responsible for the fall of humanity. Her unfortunate exchange with the serpent was a critical part of this story, but Eve began her existence with a handicap. She was created from Adam's rib. Taking their cue from the book of Timothy, in which Paul explained that woman's subordination was, in part, a result of her creation after Adam, nineteenth-century clergymen championed the "rib" story. The first chapter of Genesis describing a simultaneous creation of man and woman, a favorite text among women reformers, was virtually ignored. Emerging at the eleventh hour from Adam's rib, Eve was made vulnerable to sin, one clergyman explained logically, by "having been but a short time in the world—her limited experience of the animal tribes, and above all, her being alone, unfortified by the presence and counsels of her husband."[121] Unprotected and naive, Eve was the "weaker vessel" and naturally inferior "in knowledge, strength, and presence of mind." As one commentary summarized the situation, "Eve was brought over by desire; Adam, by the persuasions of his wife"; therefore, the "comparative imbecility" of women demonstrates their "unfitness for giving public instruction."[122] Eve's inferiority was so natural, in fact, that the serpent approached her, rather than Adam, because "there was an animal nature in Eve to which the animal nature in an inferior animal could speak."[123] Clearly, evangelical Protestants' "literal" reading of Genesis drew heavily on gendered assumptions about nature—in this case, a woman's "natural animalism,"—to persuade readers of Eve's inferiority. The biblical text was a guide in this process, but the reading was further inspired by cultural understandings of "nature."

Eve's "natural" inferiority inevitably led to her sinfulness; her sinfulness led to her punishment.[124] Evangelical commentators portrayed Eve as the object of God's wrath. Eve and the generations of women to follow, they reasoned, were punished for her sin in two explicit ways: eternal domination by man and the curse of childbirth. In the first penalty, the commentators found themselves tangled in inconsistency. Eve, a being created "naturally subordinate" from Adam's rib, now was punished—by being made subordinate.[125] Scrambling to explain a penalty that seemed to change nothing, commentators argued, in essence, that sin simply brought woman the mortification of knowing that she was man's subordinate.

Childbirth, the "frequent sickness," was the other aspect of Eve's sentence.[126] Drawing on "abundant evidence in human nature of the close connexion of sin and suffering," one commentator maintained that the Bible explained contemporary women's difficulties with childbirth: "the pain and danger connected with it [childbearing] have been increased by the accumulated wrongdoing of mankind. Among the lower animals the process of birth is much easier."[127] Women who witnessed the ineptitude of some physicians in the rapidly expanding field of gynecology might have offered a different explanation for the increased pain and danger associated with childbirth in the nineteenth century. But here again, cultural assumptions about science and nature gendered the clerics' "literal" reading of the Bible.

Yet, as well as a curse, childbirth was woman's only hope for redemption. As the commentator Thomas Scott explained, beginning with Eve, who "is generally supposed to have been saved 'through child-bearing,' " woman's "sorrow was turned into joy, her curse into a blessing."[128] As the Old Testament had rooted both woman's curse and salvation in the *private* realm of sexuality and childbearing, male commentators had little difficulty perpetuating Paul's dictum silencing women in the *public* realm of the church. For many male commentators, Paul's prohibition on women's public speech was irrefutable. Paul's charge to Corinthian women to "keep silence in the churches" could be interpreted more broadly to censure all women's public speech.[129]

Yet male commentators had to admit that in Chapter 11 of 1 Corinthians, Paul had explicitly instructed women on how to pray and prophesy. How should Bible readers reconcile Paul's instruction there with his ban on women's speech? For male commentators like David Brown, resolving this conflict was easy. Women's spiritual gifts were not at issue, only the public display of those gifts. Brown described the Corinthian women's "unseemly" habit of prophesying like men with their heads uncovered, arguing that "by such public appearances woman was drawn out of her natural sphere." According to Brown's logic, Paul first instructed the women on how public prayer should be conducted, clarifying the gender-specific requirements that women be covered, men uncovered. Then, however, Paul prohibited women from exercising this form of public worship. Brown declared that "the decision here given is so explicit and so preemptory, that the only wonder is how any candid reader should question it."[130] His views were echoed by other ministers. Henry J. Van Dyke argued that Paul's prohibitions were universally valid: "He speaks not of Corinthian women, but of women *as such*. . . . The application cannot possibly be restricted to any church or any period of Christianity, because the reason is rooted in the history of creation and in the divinely appointed relation of the sexes."[131]

Commentators granted few exceptions.[132] Women might be allowed public speech so long as it could not be construed as "teaching." Praying, reciting hymns, and reading devotional literature aloud fell within divine law. In other words, women were permitted to read but not to interpret.[133] A second and more popular exception to Paul's ban on women's speech was to allow women to speak, even to teach, in private.[134] In fact, Paul himself made no explicit exceptions regarding women's private teaching in his letters. Women were told they might *learn* in private; "let them ask their husbands at home," Paul wrote to the Corinthians. But male commentators offered no biblical support for their assumption that women could teach in private. They simply assumed it, to fit the commonplace view that women were the appropriate teachers of children. This exception brought Paul into the nineteenth century, but clergy offered it within a fairly narrow range of women's roles, even by Victorian standards. In fact, many of the ideas and formulations offered under the cover of "modern biblical research and scholarship" were cultural antiques. Some of the very commentaries that were quoted, elaborated upon, and reprinted in the 1880s were the same ones that young Elizabeth Cady had received from her neighbor, the Reverend Simon Hosack. The "true woman" of the nineteenth century was nowhere to be found in these pages. But Eve, her cultural predecessor, was resurrected with a vengeance.

Evangelical commentators took as their task the exegesis of all Scripture. Unlike Stanton and other women reformers, they did not isolate the passages referring to women for special consideration. When they came upon such passages, however, evangelical ministers did not hesitate to offer an interpretation about gender, but they usually began such explication by invoking the authority of the Bible itself.

Yet, sensing the tension between those ancient proscriptions and the realities of nineteenth-century women's lives, male clergy increasingly summoned authorities beyond the limits of the text and translated Old Testament law into the modern-day idiom of natural spheres. In fact, appeals to science and nature frequently graced their pages, not to challenge the Bible, but to reinforce it. As one male biblical commentator remarked, "the natural distinctions God has made, we should observe."[135] Despite the seismic eruptions over changing the words of the New Testament, the "Word" simply could not stand alone. Rather, clergy commandeered all the tools of nineteenth-century social and scientific judgment to shape the way the Bible was interpreted.

Resurrecting Woman's Sphere:
The Bible and Women's Declining Status

Ironically, the Bible's embattled status seemed not to undermine its cultural authority in determining a proper code of conduct for women. Quite the opposite: the stability of the Bible in this period had its foundation in the "natural" ideas about gender it so clearly laid out. A new conservatism was apparent among evangelical clergy's readings of the Bible, in part because, as the historian Gail Bederman has demonstrated, ministers had begun to complain that "the women have had charge of the church work long enough." The numerical predominance of women in Protestant churches, which had been a given in antebellum America, became alarming during the late nineteenth century, and men began in earnest to reassert their control.[136] Methodists provided a telling example in 1883. The Methodist Church censured a lay preacher, Anna Oliver, forcing her to give up charge of the church and congregation she had rescued from financial ruin because, as one writer put it, the orthodoxy of the denomination upheld Paul's dictum, "I suffer not a woman to teach."[137] A black Baptist newspaper similarly angered its women readers in 1894 by presenting a series of biblical arguments "restricting women's church work to singing and praying."[138]

Although never uncontested, the religious and domestic rhetoric of "spheres"—whether "separate spheres," "woman's sphere," or "natural spheres"—intensified during the latter part of the nineteenth century. Without a doubt, expanding interpretations of "spheres" rhetoric during these years allowed women new avenues to power. But the reinvigoration of the rhetoric was also spurred by critics who perceived its usefulness for censuring women's public work. And, as historians have amply documented, arguments for "woman's sphere" were more than just rhetoric. They found expression in a multitude of social relationships, ranging from the organization of work to the practice of politics.

Perhaps the hidden blessing in Eve's curse was that responsibility for the moral regeneration of the family accompanied motherhood.[139] Man's increasing unbelief, spurred on by the marketplace, could be corrected by woman's pious influence. Indeed, as the physician Elizabeth Blackwell put it, "male Christianity is in a state of dissolution; but . . . true Christianity is in process of formation and will appear by the initiative of women."[140] The association of religion with the female sphere gave women a measure of moral authority, even if they were discouraged from voicing it publicly.

Typically, historians have introduced the concepts of this ideology en route to a more interesting tale: how women subverted the rhetoric to radical ends. Preserving Christian values in the home, after all, forced women to counter the influence of a public sphere to which they were denied free access. But God's moral authority knew no bounds. The brilliant career of the temperance advocate Frances Willard is a case in point. Willard began as an evangelist, became active in the temperance cause, and then was converted to woman suffrage—a reform she liked to call "home protection" because the ballot in the hands of women would grant them the all-important power to protect their homes from drunken husbands and domestic violence. By the time Willard died in 1898, she had converted thousands of women to the cause of "home protection." Women reformers throughout the nineteenth century adopted this formula wholesale. Religious and domestic "duties" justified public, political activity. No one seemed to object. Like a virus, rhetorical expressions of "woman's sphere" spread rapidly through the decades of reform infecting the language of abolition, suffrage, temperance, moral reform, and other movements.[141]

The flexibility of the woman's sphere concept was both its greatest asset and its fatal flaw. As more and more women used its rhetoric to expand their areas of influence, they found their work countered and their words turned against them. On the occasion of her eightieth birthday, Elizabeth Cady Stanton offered to settle once and for all the question of woman's sphere, so "we may never hear it mentioned again."[142] But not even Stanton could pull that off.

In noting the proliferation of conservative uses of "woman's sphere" at the end of the century, historians have attempted to pin down a material explanation for the resurgence of this language and set of beliefs.[143] In part, the reinvigoration of domestic ideology at the century's close may reflect a real change in demographic patterns and a perceived crisis in reproduction. The renewed emphasis on motherhood as a spiritual, nurturing, and civic duty coincided with the steady decline of fertility rates among middle-class white women. During the course of the nineteenth century, the average number of children born to a white woman surviving menopause fell by nearly half, from seven to slightly under four.[144] The drop in white women's fertility rates, coupled with the increase in the numbers of "new" immigrants entering the country, touched off a race panic among whites. White, educated, middle- and upper-class women were accused en masse of committing "race suicide," specifically of abandoning their procreative responsibilities in favor of narrow self-development. In response to the proliferation of women's activism during the 1880s and 1890s, these decades witnessed a retrenchment of women's opportunities, which found parallel expression in the religious revival of the old, threadbare concept of "woman's sphere."

The year 1887 may serve as a case in point. That year witnessed an important step forward in women's political participation as municipal suffrage was granted to the women of Kansas. But this local victory paled in comparison to the raft of defeats of state bills for woman suffrage in Maine, Michigan, Nebraska, New Hampshire, New York, and Pennsylvania. In addition, the Supreme Court of Washington Territory declared the territorial woman suffrage act unconstitutional. On the federal level, the passage of the Edmunds-Tucker Act, intended to curb the polygamous practices of the Mormon community in Utah, included a provision that disfranchised Mormon women, who had voted since 1870. And finally, the United States Senate rejected the first-ever federal woman suffrage amendment by a two-thirds majority.[145]

Even the high water mark of women's progress during the period, coeducation, began to recede. By 1879 approximately half of the nation's colleges were co-ed, but women were still not guaranteed admittance to the male curriculum, and programs in domestic science took on a larger institutional presence in these years. Women's entrance into elite institutions was loudly protested by male students and, in many cases, was not permitted until the late twentieth century. To earn a Ph.D., women had to study in Europe. Women gained access to schools of law in the 1890s, but not necessarily admittance to the bar. Even in medicine, where perhaps the most dramatic inroads had been made, institutions began serious retrenchment of the numbers of women students by the turn of the century. Western Reserve University, for example, stopped admitting women to its medical school altogether in 1885.[146] Furthermore, progress in women's education was constantly checked by medical opinions predicting a subsequent loss of reproductive function among educated women.

As conservatives shaped the public discourse on the dangers of an educated womanhood, the discussion of divorce took a similar turn. Pamphlets circulated by the National Divorce Reform League from 1889 to 1909 broke the news that the number of divorces granted in the United States was "considerably in excess of the number reported from all the rest of the Christian world."[147] Changes in divorce laws that rendered divorces increasingly accessible to women who were victims of cruelty had been a hard-won victory for the woman's movement. By 1900, women were the petitioners in two-thirds of all divorces granted. But, beginning in the 1880s, women became the target of antidivorce hysteria. Conservatives blaming the epidemic on women's "selfishness" called for more stringent divorce laws. Freethinkers like Stanton, in turn, abandoned their earlier advocacy of a national divorce law and argued that in the current climate of opinion women would be better protected by the maintenance of liberal statutes on the state level.[148]

Amid this social and political backlash directed at women during the depression-wracked, final two decades of the nineteenth century, the domesticity urged by evangelical clergy may seem merely like a noisy echo. But, as in earlier periods, the clergy's resistance to women's changing roles was framed as nothing less than the will of God. Like those who feared women's increased access to education and divorce, the clergy made efforts to enhance women's piety and correct any evidence of irreligion because of an anxiety that the family, if not the entire civilization, was endangered. The new domesticity sounded a lot like the old. Familiar themes abounded in the 1890s celebrating woman's capacity to serve others: "And if, my sisters," comforted one minister, "your lot is cast in the kitchen, you need not take any soil. There is no menial occupation if you are filled with the Holy Ghost." The Bible was still the only true guide, the pastor exhorted: "God has no use, in spiritual work, for any man or woman that does not believe in the divine origin and divine power of His Holy Scriptures."[149] And the Bible still ensured women's silence in the churches and contentment in the home. In an article curiously titled, "The Ministry of Woman," a pastor counseled: "No true woman will complain that her sphere is narrowed, because she is told to keep silence in the churches. It is wide enough, as daughter, as sister, as wife, as mother, as a witness for her Lord outside the glare of publicity, to satisfy the loftiest ambition; and if it is any self-denial to keep silence when the church is assembled for worship, the thought that she is silent in obedience to His command will bring far greater joy to her heart than the clatter of human applause."[150]

Clearly, the old arguments still carried some weight. But evangelical clergy also introduced new arguments that criticized both women's public work and their manipulation of "woman's sphere" to justify it. Earlier in the century ministers had looked on helplessly while women liberated themselves with rhetoric intended to confine them; by the latter part of the century, the clergy had caught on. A new hostility to women in public life was clearly evident. Women would not purify politics as promised, ministers cautioned, because the women who would defile themselves by voting were as shameless, unregenerate, and mean as most men. Women voting in Colorado in 1895 had not swept in Prohibition as predicted, proving to the clergy that "something more than woman's vote is required to reform and regenerate mankind." Indeed, "the liquor and brothel and gambling and Sabbath-desecration interests will see to it that their kind of women will be at the polls in larger numbers than the women on the side of virtue," ministers gloomily predicted. And finally, the clergy asked, what was the effect on the homes of these vicious and incompetent women taking an active part in partisan politics? It "can be better imagined than described," sighed one minister.[151]

Woman's purifying influence in the world, a mainstay of antebellum popular discourse, had become suspect even to its earlier proponents among the clergy. Blasting women who listened to Freethought sermons, the Reverend Thomas DeWitt Talmadge declared: "If after all that Christ and Christianity have done for a woman, she can go again to hear such assaults, she is an awful creature and you had better not come near such a reeking lepress. She needs to be washed, and for three weeks to be soaked in carbonic acid, and for a whole year fumigated, before she is fit for decent society."[152] It was, after all, not a woman's mind or soul, but her body that required purification from religious infidelity. In the century that celebrated progress, not very much had changed.

An "Iconoclastic Weapon": Fighting Back with the Bible

The status of women had been loudly debated throughout the nineteenth century, but rarely with a shrillness matching the religious debates of the Gilded Age. As women's public roles continued to expand, evangelical Bible commentators responded with an intensification of biblical justifications for limiting women's role to the home. Nowhere was this contest more pronounced than in the public debate on women's status published in the pages of biblical commentaries, newspapers, and magazines.

Men of the cloth, however, were not of one mind on the place of the Bible in nineteenth-century Protestantism, let alone its literal or symbolic meanings. These years, long considered the heyday of liberal Protestantism, witnessed liberals and evangelicals in heated debates, which were mirrored and exaggerated in the woman's movement as well. Liberals took on evangelicals with abandon, and vice versa. One liberal minister, upon reading a conservative's claim that the serpent preyed upon Eve "because of her limited experience of animal tribes," shot back: "If anybody can find any worse mental rubbish than that, even in a female lunatic asylum, I will undertake to parallel it with other passages from this depository of masculine wisdom."[153] But the debates went beyond the level of mutual insult. Liberal Protestants, in an effort to adapt the Bible to the increasingly diverse realities of women's lives, countered evangelicals' "literal" readings with their own "symbolic" ones.

In the creation account, for example, the symbolism of the rib story could easily be inverted. One of the most popular renderings among liberal Protestants was borrowed from—but not credited to—the Talmud. In this interpretation, Eve emerged from Adam's rib, "not out of his head to top him, not out of his feet to be trampled on by him, but out of his side to be equal with him."[154] Eve could be rescued from both her unfortunate creation and her impending curse. Women needed to see childbearing not exclusively as a punishment, but as a "word of comfort." And, despite the fears of "race suicide," a woman need not trouble herself with the actual pains of childbirth, as her salvation had already been symbolically achieved by the "extraordinary event of the birth of our Savior in a miraculous manner."[155]

Liberals' efforts at rethinking Genesis were intended as a frontal attack on Paul's authority. It was Frances Willard's belief that the clergy was becoming increasingly progressive in its reading of Paul, a trend she attempted to demonstrate by publishing unsigned commentaries by ministers in her edited collection *Woman in the Pulpit*. As one Congregationalist argued, a literal reading of Paul would "prove *too much*; and would silence every Sunday-school and even public school teacher." Any effort to apply Paul's New Testament commentary to women of the nineteenth century constituted a "flippant misuse" of the Scripture and undermined Paul's "real" meaning, which was "to silence a particular kind of speech and a particular kind of woman."[156]

Paul's reliance on "the fall" to justify women's timeless subordination amounted to flawed logic, according to many liberal clergy. The "good news" of the New Testament complicated Old Testament gender arrangements. "Paradise in Eden was lost by sin; it is being regained throughout the earth by the coming of Christ," maintained one minister. "There is no doctrine more clearly taught in the Scriptures than that Christ came to restore that which was lost by the fall." Science could add its support to this side of the argument and render the creation of woman consistent with evolution by paying special attention to the order of the creation: "if we find God gradually advancing in his work from the inorganic earth to the mineral kingdom, then to the vegetable kingdom, and last of all making man, the fact that woman is made after man suggests her higher qualities rather than man's superiority. . . . It takes an immense amount of ingenuity to make out women's inferiority from the simple scale of creation presented in God's word."[157]

Although conservative commentators insisted on the universality of Paul's pronouncements, liberals took great pains to distinguish Corinthian women from the virtuous women of the nineteenth century. In the pages of nineteenth-century biblical commentary, Corinthian women were charged with a host of offenses: interrupting other speakers with rude inquiries, expressing "their own opinions under cover of seeking information," faking divine inspiration, living sinfully as "unsanctified Asiatic women," and breeding "uncleanliness, and fornication and lasciviousness."[158] Indeed, Paul may well have been justified in this case, liberals argued. As one minister explained, if Frances Willard had only seen what Paul had in mind when he said: let the women "keep silence," undoubtedly even she "would have given a similar recommendation." Corinth, where women "reveled in the excesses of wealth and luxury; where they abandoned themselves to vice and profligacy," held little relevance for contemporary Christian women. To apply Paul's words to women today and "thus bury their talents by apostolic law, is an insult to them and to Paul, and a sin against God."[159]

And what of Paul's various contradictions? The only biblical evidence summoned against women's public speech came from Paul; yet, liberals argued, Paul had made repeated reference to women's preaching. "As if Paul foresaw that his words on the subjection of woman might be tortured into falsehood," one liberal argued, he offered his call for egalitarianism in Galatians: "There can be neither Jew nor Greek, bond nor free, male nor female."[160] Adopting a perspective that was shared by many women reformers, liberal clergy were committed to interpreting the Bible in a way that demonstrated its flexibility in light of modern issues. Its inspired status need not be sacrificed in the process. The Bible was a storehouse of multiple and at times conflicting truths; readers needed only to take care in deriving its "intended" meaning. If conservatives had misread Genesis and Paul to limit woman's rights, liberals simply needed to counter those misreadings with legitimate ones.

Among women reformers, misreadings of Paul had long been under fire. Christian women reformers were anxious to marry woman's rights with New Testament theology. As the Reverend Anna Howard Shaw, a suffrage and temperance leader, argued, the life and works of Paul were a model of inspiration for all women reformers; she characterized Paul as "one of the world's greatest reformers."[161] An ordained minister in the Methodist Protestant Church, Shaw feared that directly challenging the divine inspiration of the Bible could actually cost women their privileged status as reformers, teachers, and moral guardians. Any attempt to emancipate women would have to build upon that status, not undermine it. Christians in the woman's movement were convinced that it was through women's moral superiority that they would achieve social and political emancipation, a theological position known as "progressive orthodoxy." Religion and the woman question were not just reconcilable, they were interdependent. As one writer expressed it: "First, . . . the teaching of the Bible is good; secondly, . . . the liberty of women is good, and these two goods do not contradict but confirm each other."[162] Julia Ward Howe concurred, and called for woman's hand in the building of a "Christian state." She viewed a contemporary political role for women as a return to what God had intended before the fall: "I see the position of woman as wrong and harmful. Wrong to herself since she is pushed one remove further from the divine than man—she, born of the same humanity and divinity with himself."[163] As the *Woman's Bible* would make clear, women reformers saw the fall as reversible and Eve as redeemable. Many were no doubt influenced by the Christian Scientist

Mary Baker Eddy's recasting of Eve. Eddy lauded Eve for her wisdom in being the first to confess her sin in eating the forbidden fruit, and argued that this act of confession entitled her and all women to future glories, including the right to interpret the Bible. Eddy wrote of Eve: "She has already learned that corporeal sense is the serpent. Hence she is first to abandon the belief in the material origin of man and to discern spiritual creation. . . . This enabled woman to be first to interpret the Scriptures in their true sense, which reveals the spiritual origins of man."[164]

Frances Willard would have agreed in part, but she located the "spiritual origins of man" in the "Mother-hearts" of Christian women. Although she ostensibly rejected arguments about women's "nature," attributing them to "ignorance, prejudice and tyranny," Willard nevertheless contended that women's natural piety qualified them not only to teach children, but also to purvey the gospel: "It is men who have taken the simple, loving, tender Gospel of the New Testament, so suited to be the proclamation of a woman's lips, and translated it in terms of sacerdotalism, dogma, and martyrdom. It is men who have given us the dead letter rather than the living Gospel. The mother-heart of God will never be known to the world until translated into terms of speech by mother-hearted women."[165] Many church-going women agreed. Black Baptist women, for example, denominational leaders and ordinary parishioners alike, seized upon the Bible as an "iconoclastic weapon" that could be directed at "popular misconceptions of woman's place in the church and society." Virginia Broughton, for instance, circumvented Paul's efforts to silence women by arguing that a woman's loyalty to God superseded earthly restrictions. According to the historian Evelyn Brooks Higginbotham, black Baptist women offered progressive readings of the Bible and created a uniquely "gendered and racialized representation of orthodoxy."[166] For many black Baptist women, armed with their iconoclastic readings, the Bible remained the chief source of their inspiration and the highest possible authority.

Increasingly, Christian women used discrepancies and inconsistencies in the Bible not to invalidate it, but to privilege their own interpretations. Black Baptist women argued, for example, that women were much more generously disposed to Jesus in his lifetime than men had been. Not only did women bathe his feet and provide other acts of kindness, but no woman betrayed Jesus. Willard too interpreted controversial biblical passages with the view that "Christ, not Paul is the source of all churchly authority and power." Willard even went so far as to suggest that Paul's encouragement "to keep women down and silent" more closely resembled the voice of the Devil than of the Lord.[167] Moreover, Paul had been left to men to interpret. Men had read Paul inconsistently, especially regarding the literal meanings of certain passages. For example, the famous passage from Timothy read as

silencing women—"let a woman learn in quietness with all subjection"—
Willard noted, was preceded in the text with this prescription: "women
adorn themselves in modest apparel, with shamefastness and sobriety; not
with braided hair, and gold or pearls or costly raiment."[168] Ministers, wrote
Willard, "while laying the most solemn emphasis upon the last part of this
command as an unchangeable rule of faith and practices for womankind in
all ages and in all places, pass over the specific commands relative to braided
hair, gold, pearls, and expensive attire, and have a thousand times preached
to women who were violating every one of them, without uttering the
slightest warning or reproof." For Willard, the Bible had not sacrificed its
sacred status, but some misguided clergy had. The true spirit of the Gospel
was permeating the world; consequently, "The old texts stand there,"
Willard wrote, "just as before, but we interpret them less narrowly." "We
need women commentators," she insisted, "to bring out the women's side of
the book; we need the stereoscopic view of truth in general, which can only
be had when woman's eye and man's together shall discern the perspective
of the Bible's full-orbed revelation."[169]

Women reformers who embraced progressive orthodoxy were not of one
mind on the issue of Paul, but they agreed in substance where they differed
in degree. For Christians in the woman's rights movement, women's elevation would inevitably result from the moral authority the Bible assigned to
woman as the agent of salvation. Their challenges to male authority were
thus guided by their faith in the Bible's essential promise of equality, where
woman was "born of the same humanity and divinity" as man.

Elizabeth Cady Stanton had once found such reasoning compelling. As a
lyceum lecturer in the 1870s, she had told her audiences that when considering the question of equal rights, "We must seek the truth . . . in the general spirit of Christianity rather than in isolated texts of Scripture or the customs of oriental nations."[170] As the cultural debates over women and
religion intensified in the 1880s, however, Stanton began to lose her faith in
the spirit of Christianity. "Generation after generation," she told an audience of English reformers, "the time and patience of our most advanced
thinkers is wasted in combatting . . . the bigotry and prejudice of an old
worn out theology."[171] Now that scientists and biblical critics alike possessed
the analytical tools to reinterpret and revise the Bible, Stanton insisted these
tools be used to expose the Bible's most objectionable feature, its demeaning
message about women. But like it or not, with the clergy and her sister reformers all marshaling the Bible's "truth" as their weapon, Stanton had to
concede the Bible's relevance to contemporary life. This was the terrain
over which battles for cultural authority were being waged; Stanton eagerly
joined in the fray. In jest, she wrote to her Freethinking friend Sara Underwood about an "interview" with Paul in Heaven:

What shall we say to Paul when walking some day arm in arm on the banks of the Jordan we meet him face to face[?] Of course we will show our sense of superiority by speaking to him first in a condescending manner. We will wear no marks, veils, no *bonnets*[,] no emblems of subjugation whatever, we will each have a Greek testimonial in hand, discussing perchance his gross ideas on marriage. . . . Then if he airs any of those narrow theories he promulgated in Joppa, Ephesus and Damascus, we will have a discussion.[172]

Stanton went on to list others who might join the afterlife's battle of the sexes and included on the women's side such Old Testament luminaries as Ruth, Naomi, and the prophet Huldah. Upholding the male point of view and helping Paul to defend himself were Solomon, David, Moses, and Aaron, as well as the notorious Reverend W. W. Patton, a rabid antisuffragist and the most recent casualty of Stanton's anticlerical attacks. Penned in a personal letter to a friend, Stanton's fantasy was intended to amuse. It does suggest, however, that Stanton regarded Paul as a contemporary of sorts, an opponent whose views needed to be refuted just like those of the ministers whom she regularly castigated in the press.

No more compelling question confronted Bible readers than the "literal" truth regarding the social relations of the sexes. Hence, Stanton took on Paul; the clergy took on Eve. And in many ways, these biblical characters functioned as thinly disguised surrogates for their respective opponents. Stanton derided clergy at every opportunity. And clergy hurled their thunder at Stanton, "a pronounced unbeliever," and at other women like her who dared challenge the Bible. They cast her in the role of Eve, while she protested their Pauline position and doctrines.

How were average readers of the Bible to make sense of all these controversies when the "trained" interpreters failed to reach agreement? That, of course, was the point of the ongoing debate and commentary: to determine for others meanings which, left to their own devices, they might reject. In the shadow of Darwin, the church seemed to forget its own complex past in which ancient and medieval Christians could boast a healthy acquaintance with different forms of biblical interpretation—allegorical, typological, moral, mystical, as well as historical-literal.[173] For nineteenth-century believers, the Bible's continued survival was tied to determining and defending its "literal" truth: the immutability of the Word and the gendered world they found within it. And, as Elizabeth Cady Stanton would readily testify, nowhere would the Bible prove to be a more divisive issue than in the ranks of the woman's rights movement.

3

Sacred Politics: Religion, Race, and the Transformation of the Woman Suffrage Movement in the Gilded Age

> I would rather live under a government of man alone with religious liberty than under a mixed government without it.
>
> ELIZABETH CADY STANTON
> to Clara Colby, March 25, 1898

On November 12, 1883, her sixty-eighth birthday, Elizabeth Cady Stanton was set to return from her European sojourn. In the following months she and Susan B. Anthony would once again be knee deep in documents, preparing the third volume of their mammoth *History of Woman Suffrage*. But on that particular day in November, Stanton was not eager to leave. During the eighteen months she had been abroad, she had spent precious time with her children and grandchildren, witnessing the marriage of her daughter Harriot and the birth of a grandchild, Nora. As she said good-bye to Harriot, Stanton wrote, "we stood mute, without a tear, hand in hand, gazing into each other's eyes. My legs trembled so that I could scarcely walk to the carriage. The blessed baby was sleeping, one little arm over her head." As Stanton kissed the newborn good-bye, "she in the dawn and I in the sunset of life, I realized how widely the broad ocean would separate us."[1]

In Europe, Stanton had also launched a new chapter in her political work, her public critique of the church and Bible, an idea that had "long been revolving" in her mind. Although she had nervously anticipated her anticlerical debut, she boldly filled pulpits in England and railed against the injustices of the Christian religion. Her Freethinking friend the Reverend Moncure Conway pronounced her a "born preacher."[2]

On her way to Liverpool, where she would board the *Servia* for the crossing, Stanton met up with Susan B. Anthony, who had joined her for the last few months of her English sabbatical. Friends of woman's suffrage in Liverpool hosted a farewell reception for both of them, and there was talk of holding an international council of women. The voyage across the Atlantic was a particularly trying one. With the ship "rolling beyond all endurance," most of the passengers experienced seasickness. Stanton, proudly, did not. For ten days she and Anthony, stationed in the dining saloon, reviewed "all they had seen and heard" in England. As the *Servia* pushed into New York harbor, Stanton was elated. After England's "leaden sky," the "clear bright heavens" that greeted her arrival were breathtaking. "I was unspeakably happy to set foot on my native shores once more."[3]

Stanton brought home with her an interest in a new alternative to organized religion. In England, she had been especially taken with a young "woman of rare culture and research," Frances Lord, an English writer and reformer. Lord shared Stanton's interest in religion and had introduced her to the study of Theosophy, particularly the teachings of the legendary Madame Blavatsky, the reigning inspiration of the British and American Theosophical movements. Politically committed to exposing what she deemed the hypocrisies of the Christian church, Stanton remained, if not a seeker, intensely interested in religious movements. The Positivism she had embraced in the 1860s had carried her far. But twenty years later, the promised "new time coming" had not arrived, and Stanton had begun to question the inherent goodness of Comte's immutable law when all she witnessed suggested that it was "grinding the ignorant to powder." Theosophy offered a more optimistic view, complementing a universal theory of social progress with the prospect of individual transformation. Madame Blavatsky's principles resonated with some of Stanton's residual Positivist beliefs. Blavatsky posited an alternative to "God the Father" reminiscent of Comte's immutable law: an "Omnipresent, Eternal, Boundless, and Immutable PRINCIPLE." Blavatsky also offered theories about the nature of the universe, which she termed "a boundless plane," and the nature of society, a "fundamental identity of all Souls with the Universal Over-Soul." While part of the Over-Soul, each individual soul was on its own singular pilgrimage of reincarnation, a process Stanton once lauded as potentially offering "justice for all."[4]

When Stanton reached New York, she pursued her interest in Theosophy with great enthusiasm. Visiting her cousin Elizabeth Smith Miller in Geneva, Stanton introduced the Miller household to Blavatsky's teachings. For six weeks they dedicated themselves to in-depth study. A component of Blavatsky's analysis fascinating to them was her appropriation of Hindu and Buddhist religious concepts. Stanton and Miller were determined to learn all they could about Eastern religions. Together they read Blavatsky's *Isis Re-*

vealed, Alfred Percy Sinnett's studies of the "Occult World," and *The Perfect Way* by Anna Kingsford. Casting about for "some pilot to start us on the right course," Stanton and Miller invited a teacher from New York City, Gerald Massey, to come to Geneva to instruct them. But an illness prevented Massey's visit, and Stanton's Theosophical training ground to a halt. At the time, Stanton was disappointed, for, she later wrote, "we were very desirous to get a glimpse into the unknown world, and hold converse with the immortals."[5]

By May 1883, however, all thoughts of the immortals were pushed aside as Miss Anthony arrived with a load of "appalling boxes" to begin the compilation of the third volume of the *History of Woman Suffrage*. Stanton and Anthony set up shop at the Cady home in Johnstown, where they sorted through the dizzying array of documents, including scores of unidentified newspaper clippings, congressional reports, and suffrage proceedings. Manuscript chapters written by suffrage colleagues seemed to Stanton "illegible" and a "sore trial to old eyes." Her children bemoaned this use of their mother's talents, "like putting a race horse at the plow." But Stanton and Anthony persevered on and off over the course of three summers and finally completed volume three in 1886.[6]

Her work compiling the history of their movement had a decided impact on Stanton's thinking, inspiring her to revive an earlier strain of religious radicalism. Many of the arguments she would make at the century's close had been made with even greater fervor in the 1840s and 1850s. In fact, it was this sense of "old history" that contributed to Anthony's general lack of interest in the religious questions Stanton pursued. Anthony maintained that the abolitionists had already challenged the Bible sufficiently and Stanton's insistence on continuing that critique seemed misplaced. To many of the younger suffragists as well, the religious radicalism of the antebellum movement was something less than a "usable past."[7] The younger women most active in the movement in the 1880s had been born in the 1840s and 1850s. The religious thinkers of that earlier era—Lucretia Mott, Ernestine Rose, Paulina Wright Davis—were little more to them than the familiar names of "pioneers." In 1895, for example, Anthony was horrified when Carrie Chapman Catt issued a "suffrage calendar" featuring pictures of her predecessors, because the legendary Lucretia Mott's picture appeared at the bottom of the calendar, to Anthony an inversion of the "natural order." "Mrs. Mott, from every point of view, should have stood at the head, Mrs. Stanton second, Lucy Stone third and Anthony at the bottom," Anthony explained. "It is very queer that the young people can't get it into their heads as regards the proper rank of the old soldiers. . . . It seems to me I have said it over and over to Carrie . . . a hundred times, and yet she puts Mrs. Mott at the very bottom. It makes me shiver when I think of it."[8] "Old soldiers," though honored and celebrated by the younger ranks, were not often valued for their ideas, which were presumably too outmoded to apply to the contemporary suffrage movement. This judgment awaited Stanton as well.

Although Stanton introduced revised versions of older ideas into the religious debates of the 1880s, she could not manage, among her current coworkers, to resurrect the earlier radicalism that had generated those critiques. For Stanton and others who had begun their political careers as abolitionists, the clergy had provided an obvious target for feminist agitation. From the 1830s through the 1880s, biblical texts were frequently invoked either to justify or to deny women's right to a public presence. This debate was not relegated to the pages of biblical commentary; it had real-life dimensions in the efforts of clergymen to silence women reformers. At the woman's rights convention at Seneca Falls, reformers included in their "Declaration of Sentiments" a clause decrying a "perverted application of the Scriptures" that excluded women from the clergy.[9] In many of the state and national woman's rights conventions in the 1850s, reformers charged that tyrannical ministers and a misguided reading of Scripture "have driven woman from the pulpit." "The priesthood from Paul down," claimed Abby Price at the 1852 national convention held in Syracuse, "says gravely, 'It is not permitted for woman to speak in the churches' . . . The church places its hands on woman's lips and says to her, 'you shall not *speak*; you shall not be represented; you are not eligible to office because *you are a woman!*' " Lucretia Mott, who belonged to the Society of Friends, laid the blame not on Christianity itself but its manipulative "priestcraft"; they claim that if a woman enters the pulpit, "she disobeys God. Believe it not, my sisters."[10] Clergy of this stripe were derided as "pin-cushion" ministers because they believed that women's role in the church should be confined to sewing societies, which reformers disparaged as apolitical and socially conservative.

Early religious radicals felt compelled to rectify the abuses perpetrated by a perverted Scripture and a corrupt priestcraft. They sought to reconcile woman's rights with the word of God, emphasizing that Scripture in fact supported women preaching in church. Paulina Wright Davis insisted that Paul actually said "to the whole church, woman included, 'Ye may all prophesy, one by one.' " "The Bible," she declared, "is truly democratic . . . recognizing neither male nor female in Christ Jesus."[11] As the historian Nancy Isenberg has argued, religious dissent was the centerpiece of antebellum feminists' collective thinking about "rights." The creation story in Genesis that proclaimed Eve's emergence from Adam's rib had been used to curtail women's rights and to justify their political exclusion. Women religious radicals had countered this reading with an emphasis on the simultaneous creation of man and woman, a passage tucked away at the beginning of Genesis. This story determined woman's "cosovereignty" in every realm of human life, including the state. But as Isenberg points out, the belief in cosovereignty was not simply the elaboration of individual rights; rather, it was an effort to rethink the social contract. Clerical authority had to be challenged whenever and wherever it corrupted the essential equality guaranteed by the Bible. Unlike Stanton, who in the 1880s would see the state as needing protection from the intrusions of religion, many antebellum reformers saw religion and rights as "inextricably linked."[12] In this sense, a thinker such as the temperance leader Frances Willard, who championed the Bible and its position on women, was much more the inheritor of antebellum religious radicalism than Stanton.

Stanton herself had, over time, departed from this tradition of Christian radicalism. In her search for alternative beliefs, she had sacrificed the very quality that made those antebellum arguments for woman's rights so potent: the firm belief that the Bible and "true" Christianity were the foundation of those rights. Stanton's dream of a Religion of Humanity was continually interrupted by the real-life nightmare of women's religious fidelity to an oppressive system of Christianity. By the early 1880s Stanton saw the church and the Bible uncompromisingly, as looming obstacles to woman's liberty that needed to be leveled. Her occasional call for woman's rights grounded in a "true" interpretation of the Bible rang hollow; Stanton was more interested in saving women from the "perversions" of religion. She had become deeply interested in what would later be understood as the "psychological" or "subjective" roots of women's inequality. In her critique, she granted the church, clergy, and Bible enormous authority to influence an individual woman's sense of herself, her intrinsic worth as well as her place in the world. Stanton was convinced that this teaching—that women were an afterthought in creation and had introduced sin into the world—lowered women's assessment of their individual worth. She hoped to counter it by using the National Woman Suffrage Association (NWSA) as a vehicle for education and agitation.

As Stanton returned to the work of the suffrage movement, she and her Freethinking colleagues kept the critique of religion at the forefront of the suffrage agenda. When some NWSA members attempted to demonstrate that the clergy supported their cause, Stanton resisted, pointing out that they would not be able to locate a single minister who had "dissolved his connection with his sect because of woman's degradation." Arguing along lines that would become even more avowedly racist in the years ahead, she contended: "Surely, the subjugation of one half the race is as momentous a question as the slavery of 4,000,000 Africans; yet how quickly the abolitionists split the churches and declared them the bulwarks of American slavery, and how slow women are to see that their arch enemies are skulking behind the altar."[13]

Throughout the early 1880s, NWSA officers toured the country and in local and state meetings repeatedly raised the "religion question." During Stanton's time in England, and later on when she deemed herself too old to go on speaking tours, a core group of her followers—including Olympia Brown, Clara Colby, Lillie Devereux Blake, and Matilda Joslyn Gage—carried the message. Believing, as Francis E. Abbot had written the national convention in 1877, that "if you cannot educate woman as a whole out of Christianity, you cannot educate them as a whole into the demand for equal rights," NWSA leaders attempted to stamp out religious superstition en route to political equality.[14]

NWSA discussions of the role of the church in subjugating women came to a head in 1878 and again in 1885 and 1886, when Stanton, Gage, and Colby introduced convention resolutions asking members, in effect, to leave the church, withdrawing "personal support" from all individuals or institutions who taught that "woman was an afterthought in creation, her sex a misfortune, marriage a condition of subordination, and maternity a curse."[15] While these resolutions enjoyed at least the tepid support of NWSA members in 1885, they occasioned a retort from a Congregationalist minister in Washington, D.C. In a sermon titled "Women and Skepticism," the Reverend W. W. Patton warned that "the enlargement of woman's sphere tended to immorality; that women are governed by their emotions and are incapable as advisors in the world of action."[16] Patton's sermon caused a considerable uproar in the press and among NWSA members, many of whom made a point of attending the Sunday service. Anthony reportedly chastised the Reverend, "Dr. Patton, your mother, if you ever had one, ought to take you across her knee and give you what you deserve—a good spanking." Stanton was delighted to have instigated such a public debate. Reportedly she congratulated the Reverend, saying, "I have been trying for years to make the women understand that the very worst enemies they have are in the pulpit and you have illustrated the truth of my assertion."[17] Later that Sunday the Reverend Olympia Brown, a suffragist and NWSA member, preached a sermon to counter Patton's. "Freedom for women, we are told, leads to immorality. On the contrary, look around you. What is acknowledged to be the great primary cause of licentiousness, of immorality of the time?" she asked her audience of reformers. It was not women's self-sustaining independence that led to immorality. "The story of the prostitute is, in two-thirds of the cases . . . a story of want, a story of poverty, a story of ignorance, a story of betrayal because of her weakness and her dependence," Brown asserted. The cause of immorality, she argued, is that women "have been kept down, that they have been kept poor, until they become the easy victims of licentious men; and while men hold the power in their hands, and while they hold all the remunerative employments for themselves, while they have charge of the wealth of this nation . . . let no man on this earth charge upon women the immorality of the time." Brown's sermon was a triumph within NWSA, but among evangelical clergy observing the woman suffrage movement, it only added insult to injury. The legendary New York evangelist Thomas DeWitt Talmadge preached a sermon two weeks later in response, condemning the immorality of the suffrage movement. Despite Christianity's elevation of woman, Talmadge asserted, "notwithstanding the fact that the only salvation of woman from degradation and woe is the Christian religion . . . I have read that, notwithstanding all that, there were women present at that wholesale bombardment of Christianity, and that long-protracted insult of Jesus Christ. I make no remark in regard to those persons. I make no remark in regard to them. In the silence of your own soul make your observations. If infidelity triumph and Christianity be overthrown, it means the demoralization of society."[18]

By the 1886 national convention, visible opposition to this type of public assault on the clergy was developing within the NWSA. Some members claimed that attacking Christianity undermined the very foundation of the movement, an argument not unlike the one put forth by the rival American Woman Suffrage Association (AWSA), which Stanton charged with catering to "our worst enemies the priests [and] the church."[19] Several members spoke in favor of redirecting the NWSA's energies to achieving the vote, claiming that it was "enough to undertake to change the National Constitution without undertaking to change the Bible."[20] When Helen Gougar of Indiana complained that the public discussion of the resolutions had "done more to cripple my work and that of our suffragists than anything that has happened in the whole history of the woman suffrage movement," many agreed with her.[21] The debates over the resolutions illuminated a growing resistance to Stanton's religious radicalism among the membership and its leaders as well. It also indicated that, at least on the religion question, the memberships of the rival organizations, the NWSA and the AWSA, were not so far apart. Even Stanton and Anthony's long-term political alliance faltered over this issue, for Anthony's commitment to unifying diverse groups of women around the common goal of suffrage reinforced her native lack of enthusiasm for Stanton's controversial critiques of religion.

A False Start: Beginning the *Woman's Bible*

For Stanton, the resistance of women within her own movement to her campaign for religious liberty only underscored the desperate need for a woman's critique of the church and Bible. In the summer of 1886, at home in Tenafly, with her daughter Harriot visiting from England, Stanton welcomed a visit from Frances Lord. Lord's comic monologues and singing delighted the entire family, but Stanton had more serious pursuits in mind. After a few days, she laid before Frances and Harriot "the subject so near my heart," the "Woman's Bible."[22] The perfect guest, Lord immediately went to work searching through the Bible with a concordance. Much to the surprise of all three, she discovered that only about one-tenth of the Bible made any mention of women at all. For two months that summer the threesome pored over several "cheap" Bibles, cutting out passages, pasting them in a blank book, and writing commentaries below.[23]

It took nine years before Stanton's Bible was completed in published form. But the effort, much of which Stanton carried out almost single-handedly, was clearly an act of passionate conviction. That conviction grew out of her increasing certainty that the Bible and its orthodox interpreters constituted a real and oppressive force in the lives of women. "Canon and civil law; priests and legislators; all political parties and religious denominations" alike, Stanton declared, marshaled biblical precedents to justify women's inferior position in law, politics, and religion.[24] Convinced that the majority of women actually believed that there was "some divine authority for their subjection," she envisioned the *Woman's Bible* as a tool to uproot women's deeply entrenched sense of inferiority.[25]

Stanton had other motives as well. She had grown impatient with traditional avenues for reform. She admitted to Antoinette Brown Blackwell that she was "discouraged & disgruntled, & I feel like making an attack on some new quarter of the enemies [*sic*] domain. Our politicians are calm & complacent under our fire, but the clergy jump round the minute you aim a pop gun at them like parched peas on a hot shovel."[26] In some profound sense, politics and politicians had failed her. Beginning with the disappointments of Reconstruction when suffragists were unable to compel legislators to include woman's suffrage in the new constitutional amendments, Stanton had felt "betrayed," both by politicians and by a political process that fed on women's energies without ever compensating them with full citizenship. While Susan B. Anthony homed in on the political process, continually strategizing to win the vote both nationally and in state-wide campaigns, Stanton drifted elsewhere. She did not drop out of politics entirely—Anthony saw to that—but she began casting about for other venues, audiences, and strategies for achieving women's emancipation. After Reconstruction, politics never again drew her in as deeply. In England in 1883, for example, as the British contemplated extending the vote to widows and spinsters, Stanton cautioned that this narrow political gain would not achieve broad emancipation for women. That married women seemingly accepted the virtual representation of their husbands was "the strongest evidence of their own need of emancipation," she wrote. "Any other course is as illusory as was working for the black man's emancipation and enfranchisement at the close of our Civil War."[27] Stanton now sought a course that would not prove illusory. Her campaign against the church, the clergy, and the Bible, she firmly believed, would provide the catalyst to women's emancipation.

The question was whether Stanton would do this work alone or could still muster support for her project within the woman's movement. In the late summer of 1886, she and Frances Lord advertised the formation of a joint committee of British and American women to undertake the revision of biblical scriptures. Stanton proposed that the committee study the Old and New Testaments in the original languages as well as in modern translations to prepare the commentaries. She envisioned a three-part division of labor: a subcommittee of female Greek and Hebrew scholars to derive a more accurate translation of problematic texts; a subcommittee of researchers responsible for biblical history, criticism, and interpretation; and a large committee of women to comment on the "plain English" versions of the Old and New Testaments. Two or three overseeing editors would tie the commentaries together. Finally, Stanton proposed an advisory committee to whom the final project would be submitted for approval.[28]

Stanton's plan was ambitious, but Frances Lord's call to action bordered on the incendiary. Writing in the pages of the Freethought journal the *Index*, Lord declared that the belief in the "plenary inspiration" of the Bible was crude and could be maintained only by "a mind that has never frankly thought at all." Women needed to be faced with the cumulative absurdities of the Bible and forced to ask and answer the question, "If it is not the Book of God . . . [then] whose book is it?" The revising committee would seek the assistance of any and every "scholar and linguist, every anthropologist and mystic" in preparing the "recondite scholarship, for the benefit of women anxious to face their Bible foe." This work, Lord predicted, would produce "a more startling social upheaval than any other force we could point to in the laboratory of modern reform." Women had endured men's "mosquito-buzzing of lies" about the Bible long enough. It was time to turn the tables.[29]

While Lord solicited committee members who could liberate their sisters from "Bible bondage," Stanton took a more moderate approach. She sought women who were "liberal minded" but who also could explicate the orthodox interpretation of any given text and expose its frailties. Differences of opinion among the collaborators would actually enhance the book, Stanton explained to a prospective reviser, by encouraging readers to think for themselves and "to respect the right of individual opinion."[30]

Stanton had great hopes for such a committee, but her colleagues failed her. She wrote countless letters to leading women reformers first inviting them, and later begging them, to join. She even sought the help of former political rivals, hoping to entice prominent, socially conservative reformers to the project. They declined in droves. Prior commitments eliminated a few. Julia Ward Howe and the Reverend Antoinette Brown Blackwell, whose participation would have enhanced the respectability of Stanton's project, claimed to be too busy to take part, Howe with "numerous and heavy" unspecified tasks and Blackwell with a subject "a thousand fold more important than yours," the search for scientific grounds of immortality. The fact that Blackwell, who had studied theology at Oberlin College and had published extensive biblical exegeses in the 1840s and 1850s, was not interested in Stanton's project was revealing. It demonstrated that those "pioneers" who were still alive in 1886 had moved beyond this question. Blackwell had been one of the primary interpreters of the Bible within the early woman's rights movement, but her interests had turned to metaphysics. Her decision not to participate was also consequential. Stanton ultimately had to proceed without the assistance of ordained clergywomen with expertise in biblical criticism.[31]

Perhaps prospective members were intimidated by the description of the committee's elaborate agenda, because many women cited their own scholarly incompetence in their refusals. Even Blackwell complained that "thirty five-years ago I knew something of Hebrew and Greek; but am hardly sure I should know the letters of the alphabet in either language. The disuse of thirty years is fatal." Julia Ward Howe also demurred: "My scholarship, which enables me to enjoy some Greek authors, is not sufficient for the critical comparison of texts." Harriet Robinson, Mary Livermore, Harriette Shattuck, and others all claimed linguistic limitations. Aggravated by the raft of seemingly hollow excuses, Stanton dryly complained to her Free-thinking colleague Sara Underwood: "The humility of the educated women is quite praise-worthy. . . . When we get the volume completed I hope they will have sufficient capacity to read and understand it."[32]

Most of the women Stanton invited to join the committee considered the *Woman's Bible* an unwise venture. Several attested to their continuing faith in the essential goodness of the Bible. The British suffrage leader Milicent Fawcett insisted that when you focused on the "direct teaching of Christ there is nothing which sanctions the subjection of women, and indirectly a good deal that supports the doctrine of equality of men and women." Harriette Shattuck agreed: "The New Testament . . . ought to be read in the light and under the guidance of Jesus' life or teachings. He will be found on the woman's side and all that is inconsistent with what he says [and] does is no fact of Christianity and will not endure. A committee of women (or men and women) which should in this spirit interpret the texts which trouble your committee would be helping the liberal churches in their work of preaching true Christianity." "The revision is evidently needed for this poor little sister," Stanton sighed.[33]

Suffragists raised other, more practical concerns as well. Stanton's colleagues cautioned her about the possible antisuffrage backlash the publication of such a text might create, especially within the churches. While initially sympathetic to the enterprise, Mary Livermore worried that it would only be met with "the mad-dog cry of 'atheist,' 'infidel' and 'reviler of holy things.'" Others feared that the *Woman's Bible* would alienate the clergy, many of whom supported woman's rights.[34] Fawcett put it most bluntly in her rejection of Stanton's plea. The proposed *Bible*, she maintained, would not only do no good, "it would do positive harm." Stanton was inviting "ridicule" of the woman's movement, and she should reconsider the project.[35] Other suffragists, some of whom shared Stanton's skepticism, no longer saw the urgency of battling the Bible in the 1880s. Stanton's cousin, Elizabeth Smith Miller, insisted that none of "your great reforms has been dependent on the Bible. The cause of Woman is rapidly advancing and in my opinion does not require the proposed work and would probably derive no benefit from it. It strikes me as quite needless."[36]

Finally, although none of the potential contributors admitted as much to Stanton, the prospect of writing for a volume she was editing may not have appealed to them. Only months before, women reformers had suffered her sometimes imperious editing of their contributions to the *History of Woman Suffrage*. Amelia Bloomer, for example, complained to a friend about Stanton's repeated requests for rewrites and broken promises. Hoping "no other writer has had as much trouble as I," Bloomer suspected, however, "from what Mrs. Stanton has written me . . . [that] others have suffered, and complained of unfairness and broken faith."[37] Perhaps in the wake of the "History" project, the prospect of once again submitting their work to Stanton held little appeal.

Stanton tried in vain to address the concerns of reluctant revisers. "All who have no time to give to the work," she promised somewhat prophetically, "can shine in . . . history as the critics."[38] She assured women who claimed deficiencies in foreign languages that she already had arranged with scholars for that aspect of the work. (She exaggerated.) And Stanton assumed that those who disagreed with the intent of her project simply misunderstood. "It is quite evident," she responded in frustration to Harriet Robinson, "that you do not understand what we propose to do in 'revising the Scriptures.' *Our work has never been done before.*"[39] And so she repeated herself, clarified her intentions, and offered to take on the burden of the work. Still she had only a handful of willing committee members. By the end of 1886, Stanton had resorted to pleading with women to let her use their names in exchange for excusing them from the actual work, complaining, "I have dozens of such ridiculous letters of protest that I blush for the stupidity . . . of my sex."[40]

Discouraged by the lack of support, Stanton traveled to England in November 1886 to rejoin her daughter Harriot. Frances Lord, whose assistance had been crucial in publicizing the project and in getting the analysis of the Pentateuch under way, remained in Chicago engrossed in the Mind Cure. By the spring of 1887 Stanton was lamenting that Lord had "gone over hook and line into mind cure" and in her "present mental bewilderment" could not be relied upon for further assistance. That fall Lord and a friend returned to England but remained (Stanton said) "complete victims of the delusion," and Stanton was left with only the assistance that Harriot reluctantly provided.[41] Mother and daughter pressed on, spending much of Stanton's visit so thoroughly engrossed in "biblical lore that we have but little time for novels."[42] Harriot, however, found the work depressing, and with the Pentateuch portion completed, she "declared she would go no farther, that it was the driest history she had ever read and most derogatory to woman."[43]

Now completely on her own, Stanton looked ahead to the upcoming International Council of Women (ICW) as an opportunity to drum up support for her Bible. From the inception of the Bible project, she had talked of holding a Bible convention immediately following the ICW.[44] As the meeting neared, she urged Sara Underwood to make arrangements to attend, promising: "We are to have one day to discuss the attitude of the Church, the Bible, the Christian religion toward woman, prepare yourself [and] be there by all means."[45]

The International Council of Women

In 1888, suffragists in the NWSA organized an International Council of Women held in Washington D.C. in honor of the fortieth anniversary of the Seneca Falls convention. Gathering women reformers from Western Europe and North America, NWSA members proposed the ICW to "devise new and more effective methods" for securing justice and equality for women "in the State, in the Church and in the Home." Male sovereignty transcended national differences, the organizers argued, as "the position of women anywhere affects their position everywhere."[46] Although the council was sponsored by suffragists, the scope of the meeting was to include the full range of women's varied concerns, not to be focused exclusively on political rights. Drawing together leaders in temperance organizations, literary clubs, labor unions, peace movements, missionary societies, moral purity campaigns, and charitable, professional, and educational societies, organizers hoped to amass "the ablest and most imposing body of women ever assembled."[47] Stanton felt confident that, from this group, she could draft an international committee of women to investigate and comment on the Bible.

Controversy on another topic engulfed Stanton even before the council convened. The British delegation to the ICW was up in arms over the participation of Margaret Dilke, who represented the Newcastle Liberal Women's Union. Dilke's brother-in-law, Sir Charles Dilke, had recently featured in a notorious adultery case, and although Margaret was not personally implicated in the scandal, some British delegates refused to appear on a public platform with her. Stanton not only supported Margaret Dilke's right to participate in the program, but she took the steamer to America with Dilke and castigated her British detractors in the press. Helen Taylor, the stepdaughter of John Stuart Mill, withdrew from the program and cited Stanton's support of Dilke as her reason. Stanton's actions embarrassed Anthony, who worried that the taint of sexual impropriety would discredit woman suffrage in the public eye. At the very least, the Dilke scandal threatened to take precedence in the press over the work of the council.[48]

Perhaps the Dilke issue also alerted delegates to Stanton's appetite for controversy and diminished support for the "Woman's Bible." The ICW did not launch the project in the way Stanton had hoped it would, and the "Bible Convention" never materialized. Face to face with Stanton, a handful of women attending the council agreed to work on the project, but a broadly based commitment from the movement was never forthcoming. When only four of her revisers turned in any work, Stanton wrote to a friend, "the project seemed so herculean that it was suspended."[49]

Although it did not inaugurate the "Woman's Bible" project, the International Council did point up the religious differences that divided and preoccupied the woman's movement over the next decade. Stanton accurately perceived a resurgence in religiously based arguments against woman's rights in this period, but the number of reformers who could potentially unify around this concern had dwindled. The movement had not become more "secular," however. Certainly Stanton and some of her colleagues were secular in their opposition to a "Christian state." But the majority of women in the movement, even those who called for a secular government, were passionately religious. In fact, the variety of religious beliefs and practices among women reformers had proliferated dramatically, as women drew upon new intellectual and spiritual challenges to orthodoxy. Differences went beyond counterpoising evangelicals against secularists. The woman's movement now included both Freethought rationalists and evangelicals; believers in spirit and believers in matter; and finally, a few believers who held that religion was no longer a significant factor in women's emancipation. It would be an immense task to find common ground.

At least three visible positions on religion emerged full-blown at the ICW. Believers in Freethought, New Thought, and a progressive Christian orthodoxy all infused their political visions with their respective faiths.[50]

Organized under the auspices of the National Woman Suffrage Association, the International Council of Women was convened in Washington, D.C., in March 1888. Women representing reform movements throughout North America and Western Europe attended the eight-day convention. Top row, left to right: Bessie Starr Keefer (Canada), Rachel Foster Avery (U.S.), Sophia Groth (Norway), Margaret Dilke (England), May Wright Sewall (U.S.), Alice Scatchered (England), Margaret Moore (Ireland). Bottom row, left to right: Laura O. Chant (Scotland), Susan B. Anthony (U.S.), Isabelle Bogelot (France), Elizabeth Cady Stanton (U.S.), Matilda Joslyn Gage (U.S.), Alexandra Gripenberg (Finland). State Historical Society of Wisconsin (X3) 2883

These reformers' political and religious views were intricately interwoven with their beliefs about science, the human body, and, ultimately, the physical superiority of white Anglo-Saxons. A closer look at the International Council of Women Convention of 1888 will throw into bold relief these three distinct belief systems, their respective proponents, and their convergence in an uneasy alliance within the woman's movement of the 1880s. Taken in succession, explorations of Freethought, New Thought, and progressive orthodoxy demonstrate how beliefs about religion and science shaped women's political strategies; why certain coalitions of women were viable and others doomed to fail; and, finally, why Stanton's anticlericalism proved so unpopular. This intellectual, religious, and political context is vitally important for understanding the evolution of Stanton's thought, the creation of the *Woman's Bible*, its hostile reception, and the political realignment of the woman suffrage movement in the wake of the Bible controversy. Stanton hoped the ICW would generate enthusiasm for her Bible project and identify willing contributors. It did neither; rather it pointed up two defining elements of her final years: her deepening isolation and the seemingly paradoxical racial conservatism that accompanied her religious radicalism.

The Faith of Freethought: Science, Scientific Racism, and "Educated Suffrage"

Women reformers at the International Council differed in their understanding of science and its role in the elaboration of a woman's rights agenda. While New Thought advocates and Christian Scientists believed that "true" science was spiritually based, Freethought suffragists placed their faith in the materiality of science and commandeered it as a useful weapon in the campaign for women's equality. Freethinkers wielded the tool of science to correct cultural perceptions of women's bodily "inferiority" and, more generally, to displace the cultural authority of religion. This point of view could not have departed more drastically from the worldview of New Thought, which placed both science and religion in the realm of the spiritual. Freethinkers rejected the New Thought reliance on the soul and based their arguments for women's equality on the body itself.

A telling example can be found in the work of Helen Hamilton Gardener, a collaborator on Stanton's Bible committee. Gardener had first come to Stanton's attention for her collection of essays, *Men, Women and Gods* (1884), in which she denounced Christianity's subordination of women. In 1887, Gardener captured Stanton's interest with a new campaign. In the pages of the *Popular Science Monthly*, Gardener had taken on a former U.S. surgeon general, William Hammond, and his lamentable views on women's brains and mental capacities.[51] Gardener was reputed to be "logical [and] at the same time amusing," and Stanton urged her participation in the International Council.[52]

While religion had for some time been the target of Stanton's assault, science had enjoyed a much more privileged status. It was, Stanton had believed, the "magic wand of science" that would dismantle theology and liberate women from their "religious superstitions." Gardener's research, however, began to persuade Stanton that science might prove no more impartial to women than religion. "The last stronghold of the enemy is scientific," Stanton claimed as she introduced Gardener to the audience at the ICW.[53] Gardener expanded on Stanton's critique of clergymen by linking them with physicians as the "two conservative molders of public opinion."[54] She also used the methods of scientific inquiry to debunk what she termed "pseudo-science."

According to Gardener, the climate of debate was changing, as "hell went out of fashion . . . Conservativism, Ignorance, and Egotism, in dismay and terror, took counsel together and called in medical science, still in its infancy, to aid in staying the march of progress . . . It was no longer her [woman's] soul, but her body, that needed saving from herself."[55] The former U.S. surgeon general had joined other physicians in emphasizing the measurable inferiority of women's brains. He testified to "numerous and striking" sex-based differences in the size and structure of male and female brains, which demonstrated women's mental incapacity. According to Hammond, women were incapable of accuracy, sustained or abstract thought, unbiased judgment, judicial fairness, and "the accomplishment of any really first-class or original work in the fields of science, art, politics, invention, or even literature."[56]

Gathering expert testimony, Gardener undermined Hammond's central assumption that women's mental capacity could necessarily be inferred from the size, weight, or structure of the brain. She challenged the reliability of the structural differences Hammond had measured. And she suggested that, where sex-linked differences did exist, they could be explained more persuasively by a contrast in environment than by a contrast in innate structure. In short, Gardener exposed the "hereditary bias" of male-dominated medical science and its efforts to reinforce a vision of women's inferiority.

Then Gardener offered a second and rather startling challenge to Hammond and to her audience at the ICW:

The brain of no remarkable woman has ever been examined! Woman is ticketed to fit the hospital subjects and tramps, the unfortunates whose brains fall into the hands of the profession, as it were, by mere accident;

while man is represented by the brains of the Cromwells, Cuviers, Byrons and Spurzheims. By this method the average of men's brains is carried to its highest level in the matter of weight and texture; while that of women is kept at its lowest, and even then there is only claimed 100 grammes difference! It is with such statistics as these, it is with such dissimilar material, that they and we are judged.[57]

Gardener contended that women's claims to equality were marred not only by the distortions of a false science but also by the lack of representative, or, indeed, superior specimens for investigation. She called upon women to assume an active role in offsetting the prejudices of science by taking "a hand in the future investigations and statements themselves." To counter the samples from women whom she categorized as insane, imbeciles, or prostitutes, the brains of "able" and "eminent" women should be measured. As she told the ICW, "I think I know where some of them can be found without a search-warrant—when Miss Anthony, Mrs. Stanton, and some others I have the honor to know, are done with theirs."[58]

Since medical science was routinely cited to justify women's exclusion from everything from higher education to competitive sports, it stands to reason that women attempting to erode those boundaries might locate their counterarguments in the body as well. But Gardener was considered unique by many of her suffrage colleagues for taking on the medical men in the confrontational style she did. Carrie Chapman Catt remembered that most suffragists who were angered at medical doctors' pronouncements of their physical inferiority to men countered by pleading for an opportunity to prove the science wrong by demonstrating women's intellectual achievements. "But it was not so with Helen Gardener . . . who responded: Let us see about that!"[59] Gardener, Catt remembered, was one of the first feminists to challenge scientists on their own ground by advocating more accurate scientific investigations. Nonetheless, when Gardener argued that the intellectual capacity of women could not be inferred from the *available* specimens, she implicitly accepted the connection between brain size and intelligence. Thus, although she began by challenging "male" science, she ultimately was co-opted by its central assumption that an individual's capacity could be deduced from physical measurements. The attention to structural differences in the brain, she insisted, should be shifted away from a male/female comparison to uncover the significant, measurable differences among members of the same sex.

Gardener made an impact on Stanton. Her work did not alter Stanton's basic faith in science, but it did raise her awareness that science was not entirely free of cultural contamination. True science, Stanton believed, would demonstrate women's essential equality with men. After Gardener's "Sex in

Brain" lecture at the ICW, Stanton summarized her argument for a reporter: "Dr. Hammond says the female brain is much inferior to that of the male. . . . Miss Helen Gardener, in reply to the doctor tells him that he has never seen the brain of a distinguished woman. He has examined the brains of imbeciles and insane women. . . . We want the scientists to analyze our brains and find out about this matter."[60]

Stanton's and Gardener's quest to document their physical superiority provides a telling insight into the race- and class-based assumptions of gender shaping the political rhetoric of the woman's rights movement in this era. The medical attack on women's equality prompted Freethinking suffragists to redraw the boundaries of gender to exclude women whom they perceived to be inferior. Not coincidentally, the "woman" to be salvaged from "false science" was white, elite, and educated—the very woman who suffragists began to argue should have the right to vote on the basis of educational qualifications. From the postwar period to 1920, the white suffrage movement was routinely indicted by black reformers for its racially exclusionary politics.

Why did a movement whose purpose was to expand the electorate come to define citizenship so narrowly? Particularly, how did women who saw themselves as the radical vanguard of the movement come to espouse these positions? The movement's racist attitudes cut across political and religious lines. Frequently—and vigorously—leading the charge were religious liberals and agnostics like Stanton who, in their attempts to dismantle a theological worldview, championed the class- and race-bound tenets of nineteenth-century science. Stanton herself attributed the class and racial "bigotry" of her more conservative colleagues to their evangelical religious views.[61] Nevertheless, from Reconstruction until her death in 1902, Stanton lobbied relentlessly for the passage of "educated suffrage," a proposal designed to enfranchise educated white women at the expense of blacks and immigrants.

Historians have offered various explanations for the movement's increasingly virulent racism. In a path-breaking book in the early 1960s, Aileen Kraditor explained the movement's racism as a mutual effort on the part of northern and southern suffragists to accommodate the peculiar prejudices of each region. Throughout this era, Kraditor explained, justice arguments took a back seat to more instrumental claims about what woman suffrage would do if achieved. Maintaining white supremacy in the South and overwhelming the "ignorant foreign vote" in the North were but two of the "expedient" rationales white suffragists employed to advance their agenda. Kraditor exposed the contradiction between the justice arguments and the calls for expediency, but acknowledged that the movement's racism was not openly discussed. "Most often," she wrote, "the reason for the hostility of suffragists to immigrant, Negro, or Indian voters was not mentioned. One may assume that the women knew that their intended audience would understand."[62] Dissenting views were effectively silenced. Kraditor sympathized in particular with Susan B. Anthony, who privately confided her discomfort with this stance toward immigrants and African Americans, but for reasons of expediency stifled her own opinions.

Stanton seldom refrained from expressing her views for reasons of expediency. On the contrary, as she aged, she came to be regarded as a perennial liability by younger suffragists for her outspoken positions—particularly regarding the Bible, which they perceived to be jeopardizing public acceptance of their movement. Perhaps the irony of her "educated suffrage" campaign was that for once, Stanton was actually leading a charge that others in the movement could follow. Her views on race had multiple, entangled roots.[63] She had grown up in a family that embraced slavery, a truth that she, even as an abolitionist, never fully confronted. As a young woman who rejected Christianity, she deeply inhaled the spirit of Comte's Positivism with its worship of science, a faith that by 1888 carried her to the altar of scientific racism. But even earlier, Stanton's embrace of the "feminine element" had undercut her radicalism on race issues.

To understand her position fully, we must briefly consider her reaction to the disappointments of Reconstruction. These memories continued to gnaw at Stanton decades later. Because the Fifteenth Amendment, the capstone of the Reconstruction platform, made no provision for women voting, Stanton and Anthony had vehemently opposed its passage, even though it enfranchised African American men, a political goal they had long supported. Stanton espoused a religiously inspired, millennial vision of Reconstruction and the opportunities it might provide. Buoyed by her Positivist faith in the anticipated dawning of a new era, a "true republic" that would be brought about by woman's moral force, she staunchly resisted what she saw as the narrowness of the Republican plan for Reconstruction. "The work of this hour is a broader one than the reconstruction of the rebellious states, it is the lifting of the entire nation into higher ideas of justice and equality. It is the realization of what the world has never yet seen, a genuine Republic."[64] If according to Comte's Positivism, the "feminine element" was the essential catalyst to the impending moral revolution, nothing would be altered merely by adding more men to the electorate. Stanton stated repeatedly that "with the black man we have no new element in government."[65] Contrary to the abolitionists' cry that this was the "Negroe's Hour," Stanton countered that "This is the nation's hour! This is the hour to settle what are the rights of a citizen of the Republic. This is the hour to settle whether this nation shall live or perish."

Furthermore, Stanton asked, on what grounds did the morally bankrupt men of the North justify taking on this higher calling? "Every thoughtful person," Stanton insisted, "must see the Northern Representatives are in no condition to reconstruct the Southern States until their constitutions are purged of all invidious distinctions among the citizens of their own states."[66] It was time, she urged, "to bury the woman and the negro in the citizen."[67] But instead of living up to this challenge, northern men intended to create an "Aristocracy of Sex" by extending the franchise only to black men. They abandoned the aspirations of slave women, and of the women of their own families as well. Stanton chided Terry Greene Phillips, whose husband, Wendell Phillips, was a Radical Republican abolitionist, saying: "Of course they would rather see the experiment of equality tried in a Southern plantation than at their own firesides, in their own beds!"[68] Republicans' intransigence and open refusal to lift "the entire nation into higher ideas of justice and equality" through the enfranchisement of women outraged Stanton. Black men became the target of her misguided wrath. She wrote of the African American man: "As long as he was lowest in the scale of being, we were willing to press his claims; but now, as the celestial gate to civil rights is slowly moving on its hinges, it becomes a serious question whether we had better stand aside and see 'Sambo' walk into the kingdom first."[69]

Stanton's position on the Fifteenth Amendment divided the woman's rights movement for twenty years and cast a perpetual shadow over her politics. Her position had been uncompromising, her rhetoric virulently racist, and in the decades since 1865, she had not softened much. Reconstruction still represented to her a failed opportunity to open up the electorate to "all ostracized classes." According to Stanton's account, the Republican architects of Reconstruction had not simply postponed fulfillment of the constitutional aspirations of northern white women; rather, they had extinguished all possibility for women's emancipation by introducing "the word 'male' into the national Constitution."[70] This had been, for Stanton, a humiliating slap in the face. The sting lingered.

Even in the 1890s, when Stanton no longer believed in the unqualified power of the ballot to emancipate women, she continued to point a finger at white male "Republicans of the East." They had betrayed her personally, as well as her vision of a moral revolution. She vented her residual hostility first at African American men, and later at immigrant men, whom she perceived as having passed white women in the race for political equality. Once Stanton committed herself to this position, she never recanted. Rather, she revisited that humiliation anew as waves of new immigrants entered the country in the 1890s, greeting their arrival with language that was hauntingly familiar in tone. In fact, she perceived the enfranchisement of immigrant men as part and parcel of the failures of Reconstruction: "We can not make men see that women feel the humiliation of their petty distinctions of sex, precisely as the black man feels those of color," she wrote. "That all or-

ders of foreigners rank politically above the most intelligent, highly educated women—native born Americans—is indeed the most bitter drop in
the cup of grief, that we are compelled to swallow."[71] Stanton's statement,
written in 1893, did not acknowledge the ultimate failure of Reconstruction
in achieving black male suffrage. She held on to the belief that black men
had gained citizenship rights at the expense of white women, despite the fact
that African American men had by then been systematically eliminated from
the electorate by literacy tests, poll taxes, and intimidation.

Yet, although the tone of humiliation carried through from Stanton's earlier position, her argument had shifted dramatically. Women were no longer
viewed as the missing "element" whose difference from men was so significant that its mere inclusion in the electorate would lift "the entire nation
into higher ideas of justice and equality." Rather, by the 1890s, women's difference from men had been reduced, in Stanton's estimation, to "petty distinctions of sex." White men and women were not so profoundly different
from each other, Stanton argued, at least not when compared to the vast differences that separated whites from their "social inferiors." She had been
willing to overlook those differences when the revolution seemed near and
all of the "ostracized" stood together on the threshold of citizenship. She
was even willing to lend "the Negro" a hand, "as long as he was lowest in the
scale of being." But when black men entered the kingdom first, the revolutionary moment had been lost. The coalition of the ostracized had broken
down. If white men were going to ignore obvious racial hierarchies at the
expense of the feminine element, Stanton planned on exposing them.

Whether or not Stanton paused to consider the potential consequences of
her statements is unclear; they were politically catastrophic. She alienated
black reformers, particularly Frederick Douglass, and she severed her ties
with black women, as well as with the many white reformers who were committed to racial justice. By separating white women's political destiny from
that of African Americans, Stanton helped to cast postwar feminism in a
particular mold, which replaced the call for universal suffrage for all with
the demand for "educated suffrage" for some.[72]

In analyzing that transition from universal to educated suffrage, scholars
since Kraditor have emphasized the extent to which white suffragists' racist
policies were based on their ability to downplay their own class and race
privilege. White women, according to the historian Nancy Cott, have been
able to exercise "the privilege—or self-deception" of "gloss[ing] over their
class, racial, and other status identifications because those are culturally
dominant and therefore relatively invisible." Similarly, the historical sociol-
ogist Steven Buechler points out that white suffragists structured their
movement from a perspective of "class and race unconsciousness." Although
"unconscious," suffragists were implicitly racist and classist, Buechler ar-

Titled "American Woman and Her Political Peers," this postcard from 1893 illus-trates the racial stereotyping underlying Stanton's call for "educated suffrage." Frances Willard, the renowned leader of the Woman's Christian Temperance Union, represents virtuous white womanhood who despite her education lacked the right to vote. Joining her in this iconography of the disfranchised were (clock-wise from upper left): an "idiot," a "criminal," a pauper, and an Indian. State His-torical Society of Wisconsin (X3) 31379 gues, in "denying the importance of any status other than gender in shaping the situation of women." This unconsciousness spurred a critique among black suffragists, as the historian Rosalyn Terborg-Penn has shown, for whom "unconsciousness" was simply not an option. "Black feminists could not overlook the reality of racism and class conflict as determining factors in the lives of women of their race. . . . These feminists could not afford to dismiss class or race in favor of sex as the major cause of oppression among black women."[73]

Paradoxically, white suffragists were also in some ways highly self-conscious about race. When it came to understanding their own privilege, suffragists were unconscious of the power they exercised and the place they occupied as elite white women. It was this "unconsciousness" that allowed them to see gender as the source of all oppression, and that allowed Stanton to see religion as the key ingredient of gender oppression. This unconsciousness of other relevant identities also permitted suffragists to see gender and race as analogous, when they saw race at all. But when they felt oppressed and ostracized, white women became explicitly conscious of the racial differences that separated them from others who occupied subordinate positions. As the historian Louise Newman has demonstrated, white woman's rights activists were highly self-conscious of their race and class position when they needed to rely on those elements to distinguish themselves from the rest of the dispossessed. While turn-of-the-century suffragists continually frustrated black reformers by strategically defining race issues as "irrelevant" to the woman question, Newman maintains, they self-consciously constructed a woman's movement that had pronounced class and racial delimitations.[74] Stanton's position on race in this era sheds light on a more general pattern. In calling for "educated suffrage," Stanton was neither accommodating political expediency nor oblivious to her own race and class privilege. Rather, her position on the race issue was directly linked to the lingering "humiliation" of Reconstruction and bolstered by her growing faith in the power of science to triumph over Christianity.

Led by Stanton, the primary architects of educated suffrage were the same religious radicals who invoked science to establish their equality with white men and their superiority over other women. In both their private and public writings, several of Stanton's colleagues on the *Woman's Bible* project also advocated qualified suffrage to solve "social problems." The Reverend Olympia Brown, for example, warned that American women were being dominated by "all the riff-raff of Europe that is poured upon our shores." In a speech titled "Where Is the Mistake?" delivered to the NAWSA convention in 1890, Brown reignited the conflict over the country's Reconstruction "mistake" of enfranchising African American men and not white women. Helen Gardener turned her attention in the 1890s not only to educated suffrage but also to "race progress," "national purity," and the fledgling field of eugenics.[75] And, as the WCTU's scientific temperance campaign clearly demonstrates, scientific views might reinforce Christian beliefs. Conviction of the moral superiority of Protestant Christianity over competing religions claimed enthusiastic evangelical adherents for educated suffrage as well.[76] In fact, the few advocates of woman's rights who resisted "educated suffrage" did not draw on either scientific or religious justifications. Charlotte Perkins Gilman and Harriot Stanton Blatch critiqued it as "class legislation"; Ida B. Wells rejected it as reflecting a racist stereotype that blacks were illiterate.[77] Those lone voices of resistance, however, were drowned out by the tidal wave of support for educated suffrage by the turn of the twentieth century.

Categorizing themselves as "native born Americans," white suffrage leaders increasingly resisted throwing in their lot with "women" as a group. Educated suffrage was explicitly intended to exclude from the polls many of the groups whom Helen Gardener had hoped to displace from the scientific sample—people who were poor, black, or immigrant. "We must put up some barrier to hold this mighty multitude at bay," Stanton repeatedly cautioned.[78] The barrier, moreover, must be specifically drawn to protect the electorate from the ignorant votes of both men and women. Reacting to the argument that woman suffrage would "double the ignorant vote," Stanton and others insisted that the ballot be extended only to educated women. In both scientific and political contexts, late-nineteenth-century feminists argued for narrowing the margins of womanhood to exclude certain women whom they perceived to be retarding the emancipation of white "eminent" women. But constructing their political position as "educated women" was also useful and necessary to counter the voting power of men of other class and ethnic groups. Many suffragists' acceptance of evolutionary theory encouraged them to see the exclusions of "educated suffrage" as, to varying degrees, temporary. Stanton estimated that five years would be needed to evolve an intelligent electorate from among the dispossessed. Another suffragist suggested that, depending on the ethnic group in question, "it will surely require generations to make them enlightened citizens."[79]

In a movement of women for whom "the mind" was such an awesome weapon, wielding the power to heal the body and to transform the world, it is perhaps not surprising that Gardener and Stanton slipped so easily between brain or mind and heredity, between intelligence and education. In their view, the evidence of ignorance was lodged in the brain, manifest in political and cultural behavior, replicated through reproduction, and ultimately confirmed and quantified after death in the form of a brain specimen. For Freethinking suffragists, their superior political qualifications were situated in the body. As scientific subjects misrepresented in the samples, as would-be voters dominated by a "foreign element," white suffragists expended considerable energy defining their identities in opposition to these "other" women and men.

In their critical use of science, as in the educated suffrage campaigns, feminists deflated the dominant paradigm of the nineteenth century: the binary oppositions of sexual difference. In so doing, however, they conserved as much as they challenged. Far from rejecting the "essential" female body constructed by Victorian medical men, Stanton, Helen Gardener, and their followers simply substituted a superior model and then downplayed its difference from man's. Calling for "not sex but intelligence" as the prime marker of a voter's fitness, suffragists attempted to degender the body politic.[80] Paralleling their more religious colleagues who championed New Thought and a sexless soul, Freethought feminists employed science with the goal of developing an androgynous alternative. A genderless brain harmonized nicely with a sexless soul. Each innovation skirted traditional male power and masculine categories. By substituting race and class variations among members of the same sex for the more prevalent notion of sexual difference, however, Freethought suffragists left the body intact as the primary site for inscribing difference and entitling privilege.

In the early twentieth century, the suffrage movement's race and class antagonisms reached new heights. Echoing the broader call for Jim Crow, southern suffragists argued for woman's ballot to maintain white supremacy in their state electorates. Northern suffragists, according to the historian Marjorie Spruill Wheeler, did not simply accommodate their southern colleagues, they sensed an opportunity and seized it. They funneled resources to the region and enthusiastically embraced the white supremacist rationale for woman suffrage.[81] The woman's rights movement had originated in the abolition campaign and then divided during Reconstruction. It is suggestive of the continuing change in America's political climate that during the late nineteenth century racial intolerance became tolerated *within*—in fact, became an indispensable feature of—the woman's rights movement. Political expediency fused with scientific racism, resulting in a woman's movement united in its self-conscious whiteness and seldom willing to debate the issue publicly. Rather, ideological, regional, generational, and personal tensions within the movement were fought out over religion, and most dramatically, over the Bible.

New Thought, Freethought, and the Religious Symposium

For New Thought leaders in the movement, several of whom were on the program of the ICW, it was not the body but rather the unseen power of mind, soul, and spirit that would propel the woman's movement to its political goals. New Thought participants worked to set the tone of the council. As the Illinois suffragist and New Thought advocate Elizabeth Harbert explained, "it was the silent meetings of the believers in harmony which preserved the wonderful harmony of the thousands of women" attending the ICW.[82] Of the New Thought proponents in the woman's movement, Harbert, Lucinda Chandler, and Clara Colby were the most prominent. Their religious views reinforced the political goals of the Social Purity wing of the woman's movement, an agenda focused on bringing about a revolution in morals by instituting a single standard of sexual purity among men and women. Moral inequality, they argued, lay at the heart of women's political degradation.[83]

The Social Purity cause, which was also popular among evangelicals, harmonized with New Thought belief because it endeavored to realign the body and soul into their proper relation. As Lucinda Chandler wrote to her colleagues at the ICW: "We have the important lesson to learn that purity, moral advancement, and the higher humanity, can not be evolved by statute. The key note of the new dispensation is spiritual truth. Man is a soul force, capable of becoming an agency of divine power, not chiefly an animal organism."[84]

Despite Chandler's ethereal language, a quest for power was essential to this conceptualization of the soul. Spirit offered women unmediated access to power, and exercising power began at a very basic level. "How shall woman be educated to know she has the right to control her own person?" Chandler asked. "By listening to the voice of her own soul." Exercising the power of the soul began as an individual act; many souls acting in concert had the power to change the world. Within marriage, an enlightened woman would "obey the light of the soul" and thus prevent the divine act of procreation from degenerating into unbridled lust. Individual efforts to end prostitution "inside of marriage" would effectively erase the social blight in the outside world as well.[85] Souls exercised a collective power that could be activated by concentrated thought, whether the target was the body or the body politic. When, for example, woman suffrage amendments were before several state legislatures in 1912, Clara Colby organized a "world rally of New Thought forces" to hasten their adoption.[86]

Seizing upon the concept of an immortal, sexless soul, New Thought feminists pioneered an ideological alternative to the two strategies propelling the nineteenth-century woman's movement: natural rights and woman's piety. The "rights" argument depended upon women to demonstrate their equality with men; the "piety" argument rested on assumptions of woman's moral superiority to men. According to New Thought, gender was transcended by the power of the soul. As Elizabeth Harbert put it, "We are souls, not bodies."[87] New Thought did not deny the body entirely, but assumed its inferiority to the soul. Hence the popularity of the Mind Cure and Christian Science healing, both of which harnessed the spiritual power of the soul and applied it to bodily weaknesses. The concept of the immortal, sexless soul as an agent of social change permeated the sessions of the ICW, particularly the discussions of religion that dominated the final day of the convention.

The week-long International Council of Women concluded the day after Helen Gardener's talk on "Sex in Brain." It was Easter Sunday, 1888. This day was earmarked in the program for speeches and discussion on women and the church and Bible, the day Elizabeth Cady Stanton had eagerly anticipated, the day to publicize her Bible project and drum up support for its fledgling committee. Stanton did not hear the stunning array of religious viewpoints offered up during the religious symposium, however, for she remained in her room writing her speech for the closing session. The duty of chairing this session fell to Susan B. Anthony, for whom religion was not a burning issue. Anthony did note, as she called women to the podium, that "one of the most encouraging signs of the times is the eagerness with which the ministers of Washington have seized upon our women to preach for them morning, afternoon, and evening. It wasn't so in the olden days!"[88]

The religious symposium of the ICW demonstrated the range of religious belief within the woman's movement of the Gilded Age.[89] Proponents of New Thought and Freethought followed on the heels of more traditional Christians, as each believer emphasized the links between her faith and women's emancipation. The session began with a prayer by Mrs. J. P. Newman, who said in closing that, on this Easter Sabbath, she regretted that her name was not Mary, "because Mary was the mother of our Lord." But all was not lost, Mrs. Newman continued, because as Jesus said, " 'Whosoever doeth the will of my Father which is in heaven, the same is my mother, and sister, and brother.' And to-day we are brought into that beautiful relationship with Christ."[90]

Mrs. Newman's invocation of "God the Father" prompted Matilda Joslyn Gage to blast her sister reformers for their refusal to pay homage to a female deity. The "Divine Motherhood of God" (and by implication, not Mary the mother of Christ) deserved recognition among the women delegates. "The almost total ignoring of the Divine Motherhood of God by those who have in any way referred to the Supreme Power, has been to me a subject of profound surprise and astonishment," Gage lamented. Since the degradation of women for eighteen hundred years could be attributed to a "masculine interpretation of the Bible" and a "masculine Deity," this ignorance of Divine Motherhood struck Gage as dangerous. The wholeness of God would be entirely lost "until the feminine again is recognized as a component part of the Divinity."[91]

Gage, who combined Positivism with Theosophy and Freethought, came closer to Stanton's beliefs than anyone else in the suffrage movement. In her speech she recounted the long, depressing history of the early church replete with second-century women prophets whose writings were lost, fifth-century women deacons who preached and baptized, the slow erosion of their power, and a concomitant rise of a purely masculine God. Had not the time come to do something about the contemporary church, Gage asked, in which "proclaiming the unity of God, had in reality passed over to idolatry in a worship of the masculine"? Had not the time come for woman "to interpret the Bible herself?" Drawing on the millennial promise of Positivism, Gage declared: "The world is full of vague unrest; the people, the church, the state all have premonition of some great crisis at hand; but neither church, state nor people see this crisis to be an entire revolution in religious thought regarding the feminine." The feminine principle would be restored "in religion as well as in law," Gage promised. And it would undoubtedly require a new breed of teacher to bring this about. Bold women trained in "science, history and the laws of evolution," who would be "fearless in preaching the truth as to the absolute and permanent equality of the feminine with the masculine, not alone in all material, but in all spiritual things," were desperately needed.[92]

The next speaker, the Reverend Antoinette Brown Blackwell, exemplified the religious and scientific erudition for which Gage called, although her speech was more didactic than bold. Widely revered as the first woman to be ordained in the ministry, Blackwell had become deeply interested in the philosophy of science and, particularly, the project of using science to prove the existence of a great creator, no easy task in the wake of evolutionary theory. In a lecture that must have seemed interminable to its listeners, the sixty-three-year-old cleric described in impressive detail the great scientific theories of the age, touching on the theories of motion, gravitation, the "rhythm" of atoms, the relation between matter and motion, vibration, magnetism, chemical combination, the distribution of heat, the changes of gases to liquids, and properties of static electricity, among others. Her point seemed to be the intrinsic connection between mind and matter, emotion and motion, which cumulatively demonstrated "the need of a rational Creator." With God established by physical science, evolution no longer need be threatening to Christians, Blackwell asserted, because, although it established man's connection to "four-footed and no-footed folk," it also made humans kin to "Omnipotent Power."[93]

The connection between science and spirit also animated the comments of proponents of New Thought and Christian Science at the religious symposium. Elizabeth Boynton Harbert offered a New Thought meditation on the theme "God is Love." Harbert shared Blackwell's belief in a creator, as well as her belief that the universe had not evolved by chance, but for her, the most compelling evidence of the creator lay not in the laws of science but rather in the "divine spark within." Freedom for women would result only from "the emancipation of the spirit from materialistic fears." Harbert acknowledged that some members of the audience would question her teaching and fear that it contradicted the Bible. "Let us not forget," she cautioned, "the statement that the letter killeth, but the spirit maketh alive. We were endowed with reason before we were enriched by Bibles."[94] Harbert's language reveals the conjunction of reason with spirit that animated proponents of New Thought.

An aging pioneer of the woman's rights movement, Isabella Beecher Hooker, a sister of Catharine Beecher, Henry Ward Beecher, and Harriet Beecher Stowe, introduced herself as a Christian Spiritualist whose basic premise was that "immortality is absolutely proved by science," a philosophy shared by "Occultism, Theosophy, Christian Science, Mind Cure and metaphysics." Like the women who preceded her, Hooker discussed the relationship of mind to matter and that of science to religion. She was struck by the commonalities underlying different traditions of faith. "In the God of the Hebrew and the Christian, the Buddhist and the Mahometan, alike, we may recognize the all-wise, tender, brooding Mother Spirit of the Universe, under whose providential discipline, called evolution by the scientists . . . all souls shall at last reach their culmination." In contrast to Harbert, who argued that the soul must overcome the body and its evil tendency toward materialism, Hooker maintained that "matter, not less than spirit, is permeated by the Divine presence." But the Divine cannot work alone, and so, according to Hooker, "we join hands and hearts with the disembodied souls who have fought the good fight" and do the work here on earth, "consecrated, whether we know it or not, by the great, Divine, Over-Soul whom we reverently call God."[95]

After all the invocations of the Over-Soul, Mother Spirit, and Divine Motherhood, one can almost imagine an ever-judicious Anthony desperately casting about for a traditional Christian to put behind the podium. "I want to call on Miss Willard," announced Anthony, despite the fact that she had just declared the session closed even though women on the platform were still clamoring to speak, and Willard was obviously unprepared. Willard came forward; she had listened to all the various speakers, she said, "reverently, sisterly, kindly." Comparing herself to a bee who goes "buzzing around under the bonnets of the prettiest flowers," Willard buzzed into the "garden of thought" that afternoon, gathered the honey from the speakers, and carried "it all home to my own Methodist hive." She would have to deny herself in her "inmost heart," Willard testified, "if I didn't, above all the teachings and all the voices, reverence the voice that calls to me from the pages of the Bible; if I didn't, above all things and always, in my mentality and spirituality, translate God into the term of Jesus Christ. I can not rest except there. And so frankly I tell you how it is with me this sweet Easter Day. The inmost voice, deep down in my heart says: 'Lord Jesus, receive my spirit! Receive it as I sit here listening to women whom I love and revere and honor for their loyalty to what they believe is the highest and best. . . . Lord Jesus, receive my spirit!' "[96]

The moment was richly symbolic. Anthony's discomfort with the other-worldly pronouncements of her religious colleagues compelled her to push Frances Willard to the fore. A political being at heart, Anthony no more embraced Willard's call to Jesus than she did Hooker's talk of a Mother Spirit, but she was keenly aware of what would resonate with the rank and file of her movement. And for her part, Willard, who in other venues openly expressed great interest in the spiritual aspects of Mind Cure, nevertheless came to Anthony's rescue with a straightforward call to Jesus. Willard's spontaneous participation in the religious symposium with her mesmerizing, Bible-based evangelism marked a broader pattern as well: the infusion of Christian temperance advocates into the leadership of the woman's rights movement.

The Progressive Christian Orthodoxy of the WCTU

The Woman's Christian Temperance Union (WCTU) had organized in 1874 as a nonpolitical, religious body committed solely to eradicating intemperance. By 1881, under Willard's leadership, conservative evangelical women were turning their energies to woman suffrage as a means of achieving their goal of total abstinence. On the national level, the WCTU enjoyed many political ties to both the National and the American woman suffrage organizations. Willard was a respected member of the AWSA. Anna Howard Shaw, a member of the AWSA, served as the superintendent of the WCTU franchise department between 1888 and 1892. Alice Stone Blackwell, also an AWSA member, authored suffrage pamphlets for the WCTU's franchise department. As early as 1885, the NWSA passed annual resolutions recognizing the work of the WCTU in petitioning Congress for the passage of a national suffrage amendment.[97]

Although the 1880s witnessed dramatic expansion in women's reform activities, membership in suffrage organizations lagged. The two rival suffrage groups together claimed approximately 10,000 members. The WCTU was not only the largest temperance organization, it was the largest women's organization, boasting a membership of over 200,000.[98] Many suffragists welcomed with open arms the additional personnel and resources the WCTU could bring to the suffrage movement. NWSA leaders such as Stanton, however, feared that the liberal, Freethinking character of their movement would be compromised if its ranks were swelled with conservative evangelical women. Although Stanton herself had served in the early 1850s as the president of the Women's New York State Temperance Society, she had been deposed because of her religious radicalism. By the 1880s she had come to associate the WCTU and Willard's particular brand of evangelical politics with the narrowing vision of the woman's movement. She wrote to Clara Colby: "We who understand the dangers threatened in the Prohibition movement . . . must not be dazzled by the promise of a sudden acquisition of members to our platform, with the wide spread influence of the church behind them, if with all this is coming a religious proscription, that will undermine the secular nature of our government."[99]

The danger posed by the WCTU for the movement, at least to Stanton, can best be understood through the powerful evangelical rhetoric that animated Willard and her movement. Many of the WCTU's political innovations can be attributed to Willard's unique and powerful leadership. Willard served as the Union's national president during the height of its success, from 1879 to her death in 1898. She was not only the prime mover of the largest women's organization in the country; she was a gifted politician, instigating the WCTU's transition from an evangelical crusade to a broadly based and powerful political movement. A single woman who found support within intense relationships with women, Willard politicized motherhood perhaps more than any other women's leader in the nineteenth century.[100]

Temperance agitation was steeped in evangelicalism. Christian revivalism dominated the postwar temperance movement, from its language to its rituals.[101] By adopting an evangelical model for their protest, temperance women gained legitimacy in their own eyes and in the eyes of the public. Believing that God sanctioned them to do temperance work, women wrapped themselves in a power greater than their own at the same time that they claimed to be intensifying rather than abandoning their domestic role.

Under the banner of "Home Protection," WCTU members confronted the public world on its own turf. Temperance work did not abandon the home; it simply enlarged its meaning. The national headquarters pioneered the concept of the parlor meeting, encouraging women to meet and organize in familiar territory and enabling them to feel at home in the world of politics. The WCTU formed its vast network of local chapters through neighborhood churches. Chapter meetings routinely included a time of worship. Temperance women sponsored prayer and gospel meetings for the public, proselytized inebriates, and adapted the lyrics of familiar hymns to the temperance message.[102] In Willard's words, woman's role as the guardian of domestic morality prompted her entrance into "that large home we call society." One of Willard's initiatives was the "Work Among Mothers Campaign," which enlisted women to protect their sons from the snares of drinking. Naming the saloonkeeper as a seducer and a threat to the family, Willard preached a "Gospel of Prevention," urging that "special efforts should be made to help the mother in her unequal warfare with the dram-shop for the preservation of her boy." The government "of the nation his mother taught him to love next to his home and God" had abdicated its responsibilities, Willard argued, throwing "its protective aegis around the dram-shop rather than the home."[103]

Calling on women to protect the home, Willard led the WCTU to an even more daring posture, advocating woman suffrage. She had become convinced that in suffrage lay the only real hope of achieving the WCTU's agenda of total abstinence. Her first "Home Protection" speech evoked hostility from senior WCTU members and clerical critics alike. Comparing the spontaneous temperance crusades of the early 1870s with the legislative and suffrage demands of her day, Willard claimed that voting "may be just as really Christian work as praying in saloons was in those other glorious days. Let us not limit God, whose modes of operation are so infinitely varied in nature and in grace."[104]

As the historian Carolyn De Swarte Gifford has noted, Willard popularized the call for suffrage not in terms of a woman's "right" but rather, as a divinely inspired "conversion" experience. Willard traced the origin of her pro-suffrage convictions to a conversion she had experienced in 1875.

> Upon my knees alone, in the room of my hostess, who was a veteran Crusader, there was borne in upon my mind, as I believe, from loftier regions, the declaration "you are to speak for woman's ballot as a weapon of protection to her home and tempted loved ones from the tyranny of drink," and then for the first and only time in my life, there flashed through my brain a complete line of argument and illustration—the same that I used a few months later before the Woman's Congress, in St. George's Hall, Philadelphia, when I first publicly avowed my faith in the enfranchisement of women.[105]

The WCTU leadership followed Willard's lead in appealing to members as Christian women, not as potential suffragists. The WCTU franchise department distributed suffrage pamphlets to the locals, including, "The Bible for Woman Suffrage" and "Jesus the Emancipator of Women."[106] Stanton, in contrast, dismissed Jesus' authority on the issue of woman's rights, arguing that "He never expressed any opinion on the question, as Republics did not exist in his day."[107] Despite Stanton's view, however, the WCTU's unique brand of evangelical appeal, buoyed by Christ's authority, accounted for the large-scale conversion of conservative, formerly apolitical women to the ranks of the suffrage movement.

While Willard was busily making suffrage converts among temperance women, Freethinkers including Stanton, Matilda Joslyn Gage, and their New Thought collaborator Clara Colby were just as eagerly working to safeguard their movement against these new evangelical members. Stanton's persistent anticlericalism during these years was in part a response to the impact of Willard and the WCTU on the direction of the suffrage movement and national politics. When the WCTU lobbied for a constitutional amendment recognizing Christ as the "author and head of government," Stanton launched a counterattack. In a letter to Clara Colby published in the *Woman's Tribune,* Stanton contended that "there is no reason why theological dogma should be recognized in our National Constitution. . . . As all shades of religious opinions are represented in the American people . . . our first duty is to see that each and all stand equal before the law; their rights of conscience and individual judgment fully protected."[108]

In the months following the International Council, Matilda Joslyn Gage was increasingly alarmed by the growing conservatism of national politics and its reflection in the woman's movement. She wrote to Stanton: "The great dangerous organization of the movement is the W.C.T.U.; and Frances Willard with her magnetic force, her power of leadership, her desire to introduce religious tests into the government, is the most dangerous person upon the American continent to-day. You and I must stand firm; we have a great tide to stem, a great battle yet before us. We must have no religious test for anything. Get ready for a strong fight."[109] Stanton agreed, sending Gage's letter to Clara Colby to publish at once in the *Woman's Tribune.*

With the presidential election of 1888 approaching, Gage's letter went on, she was disturbed by the lack of visible support for woman suffrage among male politicians. She remained unconvinced that Willard's Prohibition Party, dominated by "Methodist brethren, too holy to exist," was ever going to come around on the suffrage issue, despite the support it enjoyed from the WCTU. Several state Prohibition conventions had failed to put through suffrage planks. At the New York convention, in Gage's words, "a battle occurred over woman—who was defeated." Even more exasperating, the WCTU had, at its annual convention, officially declared its belief in Christ as " 'the author and head of government' who should be recognized in all political platforms." The Prohibition Party and the National Reform Association endorsed the WCTU and pledged themselves to similar measures. Willard lay at the heart of it all, Gage was convinced; seeing Willard at the International Council earlier that year "opened my eyes as never before." And what kind of leadership was Susan B. Anthony providing? Gage was skeptical. At least Anthony was not as far gone as Willard. "I am glad, oh so glad," Gage wrote, "that Susan does not favor the Prohibition party. I have some hope for her yet, although she does not see the real danger."

Stanton and Colby's decision to publish Gage's letter had the effect of allying Susan B. Anthony and Frances Willard in their mutual embarrassment. Just days before, Willard and Anthony had exchanged polite but firm words over their divergent party affiliations. Willard received no small amount of grief from the Prohibition Party when Anthony came out for the Republicans. "I only fear they [Prohibition Party] may throw us off," Willard wrote Anthony, "for the conservatives among them are very fond of saying, 'You see how little backing-up we get from the old liners.' . . . If I say a word in public on this subject," she warned Anthony, "I know you will not take it as personal, but simply as the expression of my great regret that you feel it incumbent openly to stand with the Republicans."[110] However, when the *Woman's Tribune* appeared pronouncing Willard "dangerous" and Anthony as lacking insight, the offended parties put their differences behind them. Anthony vented to Willard:

> I am more vexed than I can tell you, that Mrs. Stanton should send that nonethical scribble of Mrs. Gage's to her, to the Woman's Tribune, and I am chagrined that Mrs. Colby should publish it, even if Mrs. S. did send it to her. It is too idiotic for anything. It is complimentary to you, in comparison to its fling at "Susan," the vulgar way in which it calls me "Susan" and sites my lack of sight and insight!! Well you and I can stand it! But the National W.S.A. platform is not agnostic any more than it is Roman Catholic or Methodist. Women of all beliefs have perfectly equal rights upon it and is on this point that both Mrs. S. and Mrs. G are at fault.[111]

Anthony told Willard that the trouble with so many religious liberals is that they "are likely to become as bigoted and narrow as any other bigots of the narrow religions of the past or present."

Appealing to Willard to "stick together on this front," Anthony's letter foreshadowed many of the tensions of the coming decade in women's politics. Freethought feminists' persistent critique of the "Christian state" and women's hand in building it only served to isolate them and render them politically vulnerable. The political bond and personal friendship between Willard and Anthony reflected a new alliance in the woman's movement between evangelicals and the movement's true "secularists," women like Anthony for whom religion was no longer a particularly crucial issue. On the other side, Stanton and her sister infidels forged an alliance of "liberal women," joining forces with the more spiritually oriented New Thought suffragists. But Stanton's persistence in attacking all things clerical, which

Frances Willard, the long-time president of the Woman's Christian Temperance Union, forged a political alliance with Susan B. Anthony in 1888. Willard's leadership and her "conversion" to woman suffrage were credited with making the suffrage movement more popular among church-going women. However, Willard was bitterly derided for her Christian politics by Freethinking suffragists such as Matilda Joslyn Gage. State Historical Society of Wisconsin (X313) 2819

was tolerated in the early 1880s as a legitimate if controversial part of the woman's rights agenda, by the 1890s had so aggravated Anthony and the emerging younger leadership that they redoubled efforts to avoid religious debate. Stanton's anticlericalism was an especially sore point for many of the new WCTU suffrage converts, whose membership and resources were desperately needed to achieve Anthony's goal of bringing the movement into the mainstream of American politics.

Anthony confided to Willard that Stanton and Gage had accused her of "having become weak and truckling" to the church women, and to society women as well. "They say I am eaten up with desire to make our movement popular," Anthony complained.[112] What Stanton regarded as concessions to popularity, Anthony perceived as a way of broadening the movement's support. Given the increasingly conservative political climate, in which women faced a cool reception from the major political parties and outright hostility from the liquor interests, as well as a resurgence of religiously based arguments for woman's place, Anthony steered clear of controversy. On the basis of her extensive work in the field, she believed the woman's rights campaign could no longer survive as the vanguard movement it had been before the war. Rather than a visionary enterprise embodying the views of a small class of reformers, the suffrage movement needed to broaden its base and reflect the majority of white, Christian women's views. This meant abandoning any pretense of racial inclusiveness and stifling issues that might offend prospective members, especially Stanton's anticlericalism and the nontraditional spiritual pronouncements of her New Thought colleagues. Broadening the base would also require smoothing over the political divisions among suffragists that had fractured the movement organizationally in the 1870s and 1880s.

Stanton's efforts to rally a committee to produce a *Woman's Bible* in this context only served to exacerbate tensions among woman's rights leaders. Criticism of her ideas reached new heights over the project. The response among suffragists to the prospect of publishing a *Woman's Bible* testified to the pivotal role of religion in the transformation of the direction, leadership, and ideology of the nineteenth-century suffrage movement.

In a broad sense, women reformers struggled to define the place of religion in emancipating women in ways that promised to transform the world and to save their individual bodies and souls. For Christian reformers such as Frances Willard, belief not only empowered them morally; it offered a missionary uplift of "civilization" and the promise of everlasting life. For proponents of New Thought such as Lucinda Chandler and Elizabeth Harbert, belief made available boundless spiritual power to vanquish social evils and transcend the limitations of the body. Matilda Joslyn Gage, who combined Theosophy and Positivism, glimpsed in her faith the missing "feminine element" whose suppression kept the coming religious revolution at bay. As the suffrage movement and many of its radicals aged, the issue of immortality became increasingly central to how many of the movement's religious thinkers conceptualized women's emancipation. At the religious symposium, for example, Gage, Hooker, and Blackwell, all in their sixties, had

This famous photograph pictured Elizabeth Cady Stanton and Susan B. Anthony working together in the 1890s. In point of fact, their political careers diverged significantly at the end of their lives. State Historical Society of Wisconsin (X3) 22877

invoked the issue, suggesting that the elusive equality they struggled for in this world would be realized in the hereafter. Even for Freethinkers such as Stanton and Helen Gardener, belief in true science rescued white women from the ravages of false science and offered a hopeful, evolutionary vision for the future. Religion, then, was not just a litmus test for conservative or liberal politics, a secular or Christian state; it was a complex set of discourses that women drew upon to elaborate their place and power, to come to terms with their bodies as well as their souls. Stanton, in her concerted effort to liberate women from "religious superstition," had their power in mind as well. But the movement she had pioneered would never concede to her anticlerical position. Religion mattered too much to too many.

The Reunification of the Movement

Stanton's discomfort with the organized woman suffrage movement continued to increase during the 1890s. At Anthony's urging, the organization she and Stanton led, the National Woman Suffrage Association, called a truce with its long-time rival, the American Woman Suffrage Association. In 1890 the two organizations merged under a new umbrella, the National American Woman Suffrage Association (NAWSA). This rapprochement was a painful adjustment for Stanton, dampening her hopes of forming a body of women committed to her vision of "religious liberty." Worse still, as far as she was concerned, the merger forced her into close quarters with Lucy Stone and Henry Blackwell.[113]

Just three years younger than Stanton, Lucy Stone was one of a handful of first-generation women college graduates who entered reform circles in the late 1840s. Stone had attended Oberlin College, where she became friends with Antoinette Brown. A gifted public speaker, Stone divided her time between antislavery and woman's rights in the 1840s and 1850s. Intimate friends and collaborators for woman's rights, Lucy Stone and Antoinette Brown became sisters-in-law when they married brothers from the remarkable Blackwell clan. In an iconoclastic move, Lucy Stone retained her name in her marriage to Henry Blackwell. Lucy Stone, Henry Blackwell, and Antoinette Brown Blackwell—and eventually, Stone and Blackwell's daughter, Alice Stone Blackwell—forged a formidable political alliance that endured throughout the woman's rights movement.

Stanton had worked amicably enough with the Stone/Blackwell triumvirate before their falling-out in 1869. But even during those years of cooperation, tensions foreshadowed future difficulties. As early as 1854, Stanton's anticlerical pronouncements worried Stone and Brown Blackwell. In her short tenure as president of the Women's New York State Temperance Society, Stanton tried unsuccessfully to convert the temperance women of the Empire State to woman suffrage. It was essential, she argued, that women not be held back by "religious scruples." Calling Paul's writings "human parchments in need of revision," Stanton wrote: "To any thinking mind, there is no difficulty in explaining those passages of the Apostle as applicable to the times in which they were written, as having no reference whatever to women of the nineteenth century."[114] While this argument would become increasingly accepted over the course of the century, in 1854 it courted disaster. Antoinette Brown, who had taken a similar position in a theological treatise on Paul's injunctions to women, was nevertheless alarmed by Stanton's political gaffe. "I am very sensitive about fastening theological questions upon the woman movement," Brown wrote to Stanton. "It is not that I am horrified at your calling St. Paul's writings human parchments; but because I think when it is done officially that it is really unjust to the cause." Lucy Stone agreed: "Nettie is right I think about Mrs. Stanton's appeal—which is good and grand in itself. . . . But it is a pity to raise any side issue. When you want to secure the right of suffrage dont clog that question with any thing else."[115]

Differences in political strategy separated Stanton from the Stone/Blackwell wing in the fatal falling-out of 1869. As collaborators in the American Equal Rights Association, all these reformers advocated "universal suffrage" for all citizens. When it became clear that the Republican sponsors of the Fifteenth Amendment were not going to revise the amendment to grant woman suffrage, Lucy Stone and Henry Blackwell reluctantly supported the Republicans and their amendment anyway. Stanton and Anthony formally separated from the Stone/Blackwell wing and formed their own organization, the National Woman Suffrage Association, which would be led by women exclusively and would focus on obtaining a constitutional amendment for woman suffrage. Stone and Blackwell, who formed the American Woman Suffrage Association, attempted not to compete with the Fifteenth Amendment and advocated woman suffrage on a state-by-state basis. From this 1869 schism until 1890, the movement for woman's rights was led by two rival organizations with two hierarchies, two newspapers, two annual conventions, and two strategies for achieving their common goal. Despite their political differences, Stanton and Antoinette Brown Blackwell had maintained a connection and frequently corresponded in their latter years. But Stanton would never be completely at ease with Lucy Stone and Henry Blackwell.

By 1890, Susan B. Anthony and Lucy Stone were determined to reconcile their organizations. Stanton, who "led" the NWSA in a more or less honorary capacity, was extremely resistant to the reorganization. No doubt part of her reluctance stemmed from the fact that the Stone/Blackwell wing had never fully supported her critique of religion. At Anthony's urging, she put on a good front, publicly decrying the antagonisms that had been "distracting forces in our cause for the last twenty years" and insisting on "the necessity of our union." Privately, however, she was not so sure.[116] Stanton seriously considered joining Matilda Joslyn Gage in defecting to a new organization of "liberal-thinking" women in which she would be free to continue her attack on organized religion. The suffrage movement had become timid, she argued. "We are just in the position of the churches, dead. You cannot arouse enthusiasm any longer on the old lines, hence they are revising their bibles, Prayer Books, catechism, creeds and discipline, and we must consider some onward steps."[117] Stanton was convinced that her "onward steps" would be blocked by the union with her long-time rivals. But despite Stanton's misgivings, the union proceeded as planned.

Out of a sense of personal loyalty, Anthony maneuvered Stanton's election as president of the newly merged NAWSA by declining the nomination herself and insisting that

> I will say to every woman who is a National, and who has any love for the old association or for Susan B. Anthony, that I hope you will not vote for her for President. . . . I have letters accusing me of trying to put Mrs. Stanton out. Now what I want to say is, don't you vote for any human being but Mrs. Stanton. There are other reasons why I want her elected, but I have these personal ones. When the division was made 22 years ago, it was because our platform was too broad, because Mrs. Stanton was too radical. A more conservative association was wanted. And now if we divide and Mrs. Stanton shall be deposed from the presidency you virtually degrade her. If you have any regared for the National from the beginning, that has stood like a rock without regard to creed or politics . . . that every woman should be allowed to come on our platfrom to plead for her freedom; if you have any regard for that grand old principle, vote for Mrs. Stanton.[118]

Anthony felt compelled to address her appeal in such a manner, urging former NWSA members to vote for Stanton, because the AWSA had already instructed its membership to vote for Anthony. Stanton made only a brief appearance at the first of the merged annual conventions. After delivering the opening address, she promptly set sail for England. Still, she was dying to know how the meeting had gone, and wrote to Clara Colby for a full report "of the true inwardness of the convention[;] the unwritten history [is] always the most interesting. How did Mr. Blackwell disport himself? I trust you have not made him president. . . . I am afraid we shall always have trouble with Blackwell and Lucy. You see they make a point of contradicting what I say."[119]

Stanton's position in the NWSA had been fairly comfortable. Although she had relinquished most of the organizational work to Anthony, she continued to use the National as a venue for honing her critique of organized religion. Anthony was not always in accord with Stanton's priorities, but she was grateful to have her lend her occasional presence and considerable talents to the organization. The possibility that union with the Stone/Blackwell wing might just be enough to propel Stanton out of the movement for good must have at least been in Anthony's mind when she engineered Stanton's unlikely election as president of the NAWSA. Stanton remained deeply suspicious and kept her distance. As she wrote to Colby: "The first thing to get absolute control is to kill me & then whoever else dares to differ. But we shall see in due time I am afraid we made a mistake when we welcomed them in as even partners."[120]

After decades of tension, division, and mutual distrust, the Stone/Blackwell wing had certainly earned Stanton's harshest criticism. Yet, in keeping with Stanton's instinctive protectiveness of the past, Stone and Blackwell appeared only fleetingly in any of Stanton's writings. The duo made an eleventh-hour appearance in the *History of Woman Suffrage*, and then only because Stanton's daughter Harriot insisted on their inclusion and wrote the chapter herself.[121] But Harriot did not exercise the same editorial control over her mother's autobiography, at least not while Stanton was still alive. In Stanton's memoir, Henry Blackwell merits a single sentence. In that passage, readers learn that in the Kansas campaign of 1867, Blackwell and Stone "preceded us and opened the campaign with large meetings in all the chief cities."[122] Demoted in the story to a warm-up act for Stanton and Anthony's main billing, Henry Blackwell and Lucy Stone are miscast as bit players, written out of the leading roles they played in the political dramas of Stanton's career. Indeed, one of those dramas was still unfolding as Stanton prepared her autobiography for publication: Henry Blackwell publicly opposed the *Woman's Bible* in 1896.[123] When Stanton shaped her life into a story, however, Blackwell was effectively muted. She accomplished in print what she could not always manage in real life.

The merger put the politics of the woman's rights movement back into the hands of Stanton's former rivals: Stone, Blackwell, and their younger protégés Alice Stone Blackwell and Anna Howard Shaw. Support for Stanton's religious agenda was waning in the last days of the NWSA; in the newly united movement, it virtually disappeared. Although Stanton commanded the respect of many suffragists for her stature and experience, she no longer served as the ideological leader of the movement. The political discord of Reconstruction, resurrected again in the merger of 1890, had made Stanton wary of organizations, coalitions, and politics in general as a means of achieving her goals. While she continued to work within the structures she and Anthony created, her enthusiasm for politics dimmed. Though the nominal president of the new organization, she spent much of her tenure in England where, among family and Freethinking friends, she continued writing and speaking on religious questions. On the eve of the merger, Gage, Helen Gardener, and other radical suffragists had attempted a defection to form what they called a "Liberal Suffrage League." Stanton, for the time being had elected to stay put, complaining that she was "sick of all organizations. . . . Once out of my present post in the suffrage movement I am a free lance to do and say what I choose and shock people as much as I please."[124] Several years later, when a comparable organization did form, Stanton agreed to serve as an adviser. She ignored what seemed to many (especially Anthony) a major conflict of interest, serving as honorary president of one organization and as an adviser to its rival.

An illustration of how removed from the mainstream Stanton had become is the flap over the Sunday closing of the World's Fair, the Columbian Exhibition, in 1893. Although she wrote speeches that Anthony read at the Fair and at the World Parliament of Religions, Stanton exerted most of her energy in protesting the Fair's Sunday closing policy and urged the NAWSA to respond to the issue in its official platform. Her extreme anticlericalism became even more public when the editor of the *Woman's Journal* chastised her, arguing that the Sunday closing issue had no place on the woman suffrage platform. Stanton's response revealed her growing desire to rid the woman's movement of evangelical influence. "There is an intimate connection between their [women's] subject condition and popular theology," Stanton wrote, arguing that women "have a far deeper reason than man has for striving to preserve the secular nature of our government."[125] But to the younger suffragists, Stanton appeared to be out of step when she pressed this issue.[126]

In an exchange with the editor of the *Woman's Journal*, Stanton tried to link the Sunday closing controversy to women's long-standing need to root out invidious religious influences. Women's oppression, she insisted, has always been traceable to religious superstition, dogmatic theology, and church discipline—all of which "teach the dignity of man and the degradation of woman." The editor's response, reflecting the younger and more moderate voices within the woman's movement, wondered aloud about Stanton's seemingly obsessive attack on the Sabbath observance and claimed that Sunday closing "involves no discrimination between the sexes." According to the editorial, "a perverted theology" was not, as Stanton had claimed, the " 'most powerful influence against women's emancipation.' " In fact, religious sensibilities had proved helpful, not hurtful, to the cause, the editor contended. "To-day I believe you would find fully as large a proportion of suffragists among church members as among the unchurched."[127]

Stanton would surely have agreed that the movement was, in fact, overrun with church members. In her mind, the merger with her former AWSA rivals had cost the movement its ideological integrity. With the influx of members from the AWSA and the WCTU, and in response to the lack of visible gains won by the suffrage movement in state and national politics, more emphasis was placed on unity for a single goal, the ballot. Dissent on controversial issues of the day—particularly religion—was increasingly considered a political liability.[128]

Stanton's increasing alienation from the organization that she at least nominally still led prompted her to direct her considerable energies elsewhere. Believing that "each mortal stands alone," a theme she captured in her "Solitude of Self" speech delivered to the House Judiciary Committee in 1892, Stanton made peace with her place as a "free lance." Much of her time and energy in the early 1890s was devoted to more solitary, less political endeavors. She continued to visit her children for long periods and began sketching her "Reminiscences" for a weekly column in the *Woman's Tribune*. As she told its editor, her friend Clara Colby: "I cannot work in the old ruts any longer. I have said all I have to say on the subject of suffrage. As to the Bible, I thought the moral effect of a committee of women to revise the Scriptures in council . . . would be very great. But I could not get a committee of leading English and American women. For me to do it as an individual would not have the same effect in dignity. And now I prefer to use my eyes for more pleasant occupations. . . . There is such a thing as being too active, living too outward a life."[129]

Stanton would return to the *Woman's Bible* project three years later and once again brace herself for "too outward a life."

4

"A Great Feature of the General Uprising": The Revising Committee and the *Woman's Bible*

> If we could get twenty-five intelligent well educated good common sense women we could make "The Woman's Bible" a great feature of the general uprising in this nineteenth century.
>
> ELIZABETH CADY STANTON
> to Elizabeth Morrison Boynton Harbert, 13 September, 1886

Stanton resumed full-time work on the *Woman's Bible* in 1895. As with the impetus for so much of her work over the years, it was the comments of a Baptist minister that caused her to resurrect her nearly moribund project.[1] During the NAWSA's annual convention in Atlanta, the first-ever held in the South, a Reverend Hawthorne denounced all suffragists (and their feeble-minded husbands) from his pulpit, causing quite an uproar. Several Atlanta newspapers carried his sermon. Suffragists felt compelled to reply to Hawthorne publicly. The Reverend Anna Howard Shaw, one of the rising stars of the movement, led the charge, addressing the convention and ostensibly urging the women not to respond. Hawthorne's sermon had been "ungentlemanly, uncalled [for] and unmanly." No lady, Shaw announced would "descend to that plane." Hawthorne's "dictatorial manner" showed plainly that "he has more dogma in him than reason." At that remark, a reporter noted, the crowd roared out of control, "the floor of the convention seemed to be swept by a storm."[2]

Stanton was not in attendance at the convention. But, she told a reporter, "when I read of the ferocious attack of the Baptist clergymen on woman . . . it seemed to me the time had come."[3] With renewed urgency, she returned to the Bible project, immersing herself in biblical criticism and church history in search of some explanation for "the degraded status of women under all religions, and in all the so-called 'Holy Books.' "[4] Within weeks, she had negotiated with Clara Colby for the serial publication of the Pentateuch section of the work to appear in the financially troubled *Woman's Tribune*.[5]

Excited by the prospect of publication, Stanton reveled in the conviction that her project would create quite a stir among the clergy, forcing "Priests and Bishops [to] open their eyes and say 'What will these women do next?'" The response in Atlanta to Reverend Hawthorne and the unanimity with which he was condemned by the convention contributed to Stanton's hope that, at long last, her colleagues would "awake" to the importance of the "Woman's Bible" and offer their services. The weekly appearance of parts of the "Woman's Bible" in the columns of the *Woman's Tribune*, Stanton naively assumed, would generate the necessary support to sustain the project. "The Woman's Bible will create great interest," she promised Colby, "and after we get fairly started we shall have no trouble in getting such names as we desire on the committee."[6]

Stanton could not have been more wrong. Almost immediately, the "Woman's Bible" generated not interest but acrimony. Without securing permission, Stanton published in the New York *World* the names of her phantom revising committee, which included political rivals Frances Willard, Isabel Somerset, and Mary Livermore, all of whom strenuously objected.[7] Stanton had envisioned the serial publication of the "Woman's Bible" not as a finished product, but as a means of conducting the work. Her plan involved using the *Tribune* as a clearinghouse for committee members' commentaries and responses. Each week a new commentary would be published; Colby would send copies to the members, who were free to respond in print in the next *Tribune*. The final version of the "Woman's Bible," for book publication, would then be settled by committee. (At this point Stanton had secured the serivces of three genuine committee members: Phebe Hanaford, Frances Ellen Burr, and Helen Gardener.) She began in March 1895 to publish her commentaries on the Pentateuch week by week. But the plan backfired. Although she signed each of her commentaries, committee members feared the public would mistakenly assume that Stanton's individual comments had the committee's sanction, a situation they found exasperating.[8]

Before publishing volume one of the book edition, Stanton attempted to mend fences. The work was essentially finished, but the problem of the committee persisted. Trying to muster support, Stanton wrote to each woman on her list from 1886 and asked permission for the continued use of her name. Temperance leaders Isabel Somerset and Frances Willard had to refuse, Somerset explained, owing to the company Stanton had assembled. There was no diversity of viewpoints among the Freethought radicals on Stanton's committee, Somerset complained, "as almost everyone held the same view, and that was not one that found acceptance with the women for whom we work." If Stanton had managed to recruit "women of conservative opinions" to work on the project, then "it would make the scheme much easier for us." But not only would she and Willard have to decline; Somerset was unable to suggest a single replacement. "People do not understand how they can come into a revision[,] a portion of which is already accomplished," she explained.[9] Willard and Somerset had their temperance constituencies to worry about. Susan B. Anthony, had a related problem, her male opponents in the liquor business. "*No*—I don't want my name on that Bible committee—you fight that battle—and leave me to fight the secular, the political fellows," she insisted. Anthony readily admitted that the religious question had never been her priority. But particularly at this juncture in the state campaign for woman suffrage in California, she would not risk her opponents "scoring me for belief one way or the other about the Bible . . . the men who hold me in durance vile—won't care a dime what the Bible says. All they care about is what the saloon says."[10]

In the midst of yet another wave of criticism and rejection, Stanton struggled to keep her project afloat. Using the pages of the *Tribune* as her forum, she addressed her critics in June 1895. Nearly three months' worth of "Woman's Bible" installments had appeared in the paper, but those columns had failed to quell the misgivings her colleagues had raised from the beginning. Readers rehearsed all the familiar objections: women should not revise the Scriptures; it was impolitic to "arouse religious opposition"; the commentaries were irreverent; the Bible was not worth this expenditure of energy; and, finally, the committee was too monolithic in its radicalism. Tirelessly, Stanton addressed each issue. Women were as entitled to revise the Scriptures as men; and Scriptures were as susceptible to revision as constitutions. Furthermore, opposition had always accompanied important reforms, Stanton argued. "Forty years ago it seemed as ridiculous to timid, timeserving and retrograde folk for women to demand an expurgated edition of the laws, as it now does to demand an expurgated edition of the Liturgies and Scriptures." To avoid arousing religious opposition, was in her mind, "but another word for cowardice." And if she had treated the Bible irreverently, Stanton explained, perhaps it was justified. While she reserved much reverence for the "great Creator of the universe of matter and mind," the "God of the Hebrews" deserved harsh words.[11]

Perhaps in response to Isabel Somerset's complaint that the committee was stacked with Freethought radicals—or anticipating Anthony's advice that Stanton should recruit at least a few members "who have even read the Bible once through, consecutively, in their lives"—Stanton published an open letter to the revising committee and again challenged conservative women to join the enterprise.[12] "It has all along been my idea to have all phases of thought represented in this work, Protestant, Catholic, Jew, Gentile, Evangelical, and Liberal," she wrote in the *Woman's Tribune*. "Our liberal women will be quite willing to have their commentaries bound up with those more conservative. If these have the greater truth, they should be willing, yea anxious, for our enlightenment, to antidote our errors with their more exalted inspirations."[13] Stanton also tried to involve Jewish women in the project. It seemed she had found a promising avenue in Elvira Solis, who assured Stanton that while she herself lacked the training to participate, she would find "someone competent to do this work." A Jewish member for the committee never emerged, however.[14] In addition, Stanton pursued a number of international members, again promising little or no work in exchange for names and influence. She wrote to her son Theodore in France seeking his help in recruiting women from the Continent.[15]

Stanton finally assembled a group of collaborators comprising women ministers from liberal denominations, radical suffragists, Freethinkers, New Thought advocates, and personal friends, an original list of twenty-three in all. The actual group of contributors to the two volumes was much smaller.[16] The committee Stanton assembled in 1895 differed significantly from the committee she had attempted to recruit in 1886. The changes reflected the shifting locus of power and influence in the woman's movement.

The *Woman's Bible* Revising Committee

Any discussion of the "revising committee" must proceed cautiously. After all, none of Stanton's elaborate plans for the committee and its work came to fruition. The committee per se never engaged in debate over the Bible, never worked collaboratively, and, in fact, never even met. Stanton's insistence on the "moral effect of a committee of women" in undertaking a "Woman's Bible" helps to explain her embellishment of the actual events. While she conveyed privately to Colby and others her disappointment in the lack of support she received, publicly she continued to maintain the existence of a committee. In the preface to the 1895 published volume, for example, Stanton reprinted her 1886 description of a three-part committee—concentrating on ancient languages, biblical history and "plain English" commentaries—although clearly this committee, or this level of scholarly enterprise, had never materialized. For twentieth-century readers, however, the committee has had an important legacy. Contemporary feminists have looked to Stanton and her committee as an inspiring precedent for collective work in feminist hermeneutics.[17] In her effort to give her sometimes solo effort the appearance of a movement, did Stanton essentially dupe her readers then and now into assuming a revising committee when none existed?[18] While they may never have functioned formally as a committee, these twenty-three women reflected the multiple and overlapping networks of those who played a critical, but overlooked, role in the suffrage movement of the nineteenth century.

Perhaps it says enough that most of these women were willing to lend Stanton their names and reputations when so many others would not risk it. Indeed, the initial list of revisers published in volume one underwent its own revision by the time volume two was off the press in 1898. Martha R. Almy, Cornelia Collins Hussey, and M. Louise Thomas, as well as the movement heavyweights Mary Livermore and Carrie Chapman Catt all managed to have their names deleted from future editions. As Frances Willard and Isabel Somerset had discovered earlier in 1895, Stanton was not beyond granting her "wish list" of revisers a more formal status. One wonders how many of the women who withdrew from the committee before 1898 had ever agreed to serve. Certainly none of the five just named contributed commentaries. Stanton solicited some women's names with an eye to their effect on readers. The inclusion of Mrs. Robert Ingersoll, for example, the wife of the notorious agnostic—and the only member listed in her husband's name—doubtless was intended to raise a few eyebrows in conservative circles. Likewise, the presence of Charlotte Beebe Wilbour, the famed Spiritualist lecturer of the 1850s, would have brought a touch of celebrity to the committee, at least for readers of Stanton's generation. Those readers would have been disappointed, however, if they had searched the book for either woman's commentary. For volume one, Stanton was resigned to citing women as committee members, even if they could not make a contribution to the text. Yet, she did not include her daughter Harriot or Frances Lord as "revisers" although both women had actually worked on the project in its earliest stages. Similarly, though the comments of Susan H. Wixon appeared in the serial version of the "Woman's Bible" run in the *Woman's Tribune,* her name never materialized on a committee list and, furthermore, her contributions were not included in the published volumes.[19] Presumably Harriot, Lord, and Wixon declined the honor of serving on the committee, but Carrie Chapmen Catt and Mary Livermore had done as much and still found themselves formally acknowledged as participants.

When Stanton's revised and final committee list appeared with volume two in 1898, it consisted of twenty American women and five "foreign members." Of the complete ensemble, only seven, besides Stanton, actually contributed to the text of the first volume. Furthermore, Stanton herself authored well over half of the passages. The level of committee participation in the second volume increased slightly, eight women in addition to Stanton contributed to the final version.[20] Yet, despite her overriding influence on the project, the committee itself deserves further discussion. These women were actively engaged in many of the battles—personal, political, and theological—that Stanton waged. Some of them—Clara Colby, Matilda Joslyn Gage, Helen Gardener, Lillie Devereux Blake—were among Stanton's closest friends and political allies. Others on the committee rounded out an intellectual community of radical women that Stanton so desperately craved in her elder years. Sara Underwood, Ursula Bright, Josephine K. Henry, Olympia Brown, and Frances E. Burr all corresponded with Stanton on religious topics throughout the 1880s and 1890s. But just as these women honored their ties to Stanton by agreeing to serve on her controversial Bible committee, they had vital connections to each other as well.

As a group the committee was composed of white women in their middle to later years. Stanton was the senior member, aged eighty when volume one appeared in 1895. Helen Gardener was the youngest member at age forty-two. All but one of the women were or had been married, although several frequently lived apart from their husbands, as had Stanton. Regionally, the committee was fairly diverse, but generally reflective of the pockets of women's activism around the country. Several of the members hailed from New England. Even more had roots in New York State, the home base of Stanton's political career. Blake, Ellen Dietrick, and Gardener were all transplanted Southerners. Josephine K. Henry, the lone Southerner in residence, made her home in Kentucky. Clara Colby and Olympia Brown represented the westernmost borders of the committee from their adopted states of Nebraska and Wisconsin.[21] A number of the committee members had ties to Chicago: Lucinda Chandler, Augusta Chapin, Gage, Ursula Gestefeld, Catherine Stebbins, Underwood, and an original contributor who later defected, Frances Lord. The foreign members, at least three of whom were recruited from the ranks of the International Council of Women in 1888, included Irma von Troll-Borostyani of Austria; Ursula Bright, a friend Stanton had made in England; Alexandra Gripenberg from Finland; Isabelle Bogelot of France; and Priscilla Bright-McLaren of Scotland. These names gave the volume at least the appearance of an international effort.[22]

Regional diversity and age span aside, the women of the revising committee had much in common. First and most obvious, almost all members had ties to the national suffrage movement and served in leadership capacities in state and local suffrage organizations, points to be explored later in the chapter. Second, virtually all the members—despite their diffidence in the pages of Stanton's Bible—were prolific writers. Lillie Devereux Blake and Helen Gardener had both earned national reputations as authors before the publication of the *Woman's Bible*. For many of the women, writing provided a source of much needed income. Blake, in particular, owing to a dwindling family income and a first husband's suicide, had been left perpetually reliant on her own talents for subsistence. Occasionally adopting pseudonyms, she published a number of popular books and hundreds of magazine articles. Her feminist novel *Fettered for Life, Or Lord and Master: A Story of Today* (1874) chronicled her heroine's search for an egalitarian marriage in a tale that included, among other plot twists, the unmasking of a transgendered character.[23] Transgression was also a theme in *A Daring Experiment* (1892), which probed the worthiness of cross-class love through the sad tale of Jack Burns, the village blacksmith, who pined—and ultimately sacrificed his life—for Miss Maud Maitland, the daughter of a millionaire. Blake's feminist fiction was credited with making the suffrage movement more popular in the eyes of the reading public. But Blake, like her mentor Stanton, was not one to shrink from controversy. She gained the respect of many of her colleagues for her courage in challenging clerical misogyny. Her book *Woman's Place Today* (1883) was the published version of a lecture series she delivered in response to the Reverend Morgan Dix's Lenten lectures on "woman's sphere."

Gardener—who legally changed her birth name, Alice Chenoweth, to her pseudonym Helen Hamilton Gardener—moved easily between fiction and nonfiction in her writing. Like Blake, Gardener was concerned about issues of sexual inequality as they affected women's private lives and found fiction a fitting vehicle for her views. Her most widely read popular novel, *Is This Your Son, My Lord?* (1890), took on the low age of consent laws, a target of Social Purity reformers. This novel, along with *Pray You, Sir, Whose Daughter?* (1892), attempted, in Stanton's words, to "do for her sex what Mrs. Stowe did for the black race in 'Uncle Tom's Cabin.'"[24] While Gardener published three other novels, her feminist nonfiction gained her the greatest publicity. Her first set of essays, inspired by her friendship with Robert Ingersoll, *Men, Women and Gods and Other Lectures* (1885), brought her to Stanton's attention as a sister infidel. In *Facts and Fictions of Life* (1893), Gardener included her much lauded speech "Sex in Brain," which had made such an impact at the ICW.

Science and religion were also topics of passionate conviction for Matilda Joslyn Gage, who published her mammoth *Woman, Church and State*, a trenchant indictment of organized religion, in 1893. Gage had suspended work on this project to edit the *History of Woman Suffrage* with Stanton and Anthony in 1882, and she included an abbreviated version of her religious treatise as an appendix to volume one of the history project. But in the final years of her life, Gage finished a longer version of her book; she also wrote pamphlets on metaphysical topics, including: "The Occult Science of Numbers" and the "Esotericism of the National Flag." Not unlike Gage who found her authorial voice late in life, Ellen Battelle Dietrick was prevented (in her case by an early death) from seeing much of her written work—including her contributions to the *Woman's Bible*—in published form. Dietrick's feminist analysis of Christian origins, *Women in the Early Christian Ministry*, was printed posthumously.

Ursula N. Gestefeld, like Gage, Blake, Gardener, and others, was interested both in spiritual life and in women's subjugation in this world. And like Blake and Gardener, Gestefeld published both fiction and nonfiction. Many of her writings were a result of her conversion to and ultimate defection from Christian Science and its popularizer, Mary Baker Eddy. When Gestefeld published her own treatise on Christian Science, Eddy expelled her from the Chicago Christian Science Church and thus launched Gestefeld's independent career as a New Thought leader and writer.[25] Most of Gestefeld's ten books and pamphlets published in the last two decades of the nineteenth century were metaphysical guides and manuals. Her one novel, *The Woman Who Dares* (1892), condemned the burden of male sexual demands accompanying marriage.[26]

A shade more conventional than Gestefeld, the Universalist minister Phebe Hanaford wrote with a foot still loosely planted in the Protestant tradition. But she was no less prolific, publishing fourteen books by the end of her career. Hanaford had also devoted a few years to editing denominational and women's newspapers, a credential shared by many of the committee members. Stanton edited the *Revolution*. Gage spent three years as editor of the radical suffrage paper the *National Citizen and Ballot Box*. Sara Underwood, author of *Heroines of Freethought* and several other works, coedited with her husband Benjamin a number of Freethought magazines in the 1880s and 1890s, including the *Index* and the *Open Court*. Underwood was also a regular contributor to the *Index*, and the *Arena*. Josephine K. Henry, author of numerous pamphlets, joined Gardener, Stanton and Underwood in the 1890s as a regular contributor to H. L. Green's *Free Thought Magazine*.

By far the most tireless of editors, Clara Colby single-handedly wrote and published the *Woman's Tribune* for over twenty-five years. One of several women on the revising committee with a college degree, Colby had made history at the University of Wisconsin by being one of the first women to take the "male" curriculum. This act of defiance nearly cost her her diploma, but ultimately Colby graduated valedictorian and Phi Beta Kappa.[27] Although a devoted worker on the National side of the movement, Colby had a reputation for being a freelance, which explains in part the mutual affection between her and Stanton. Her newspaper, while wholly a partisan of the NWSA, reflected her eclectic interests. When Colby and her husband adopted a Lakota Indian baby that Leonard Colby—then a brigadier general in the Nebraska National Guard—had allegedly rescued from the battle of Wounded Knee, stories about Native Americans and a column named for the daughter became regular features in the *Tribune*.[28] Similarly, Colby's personal religious quest, which ultimately led to her career as a New Thought leader, figured prominently in the paper, as she introduced her readership to the practices of mysticism and Eastern religions.

Clara Bewick Colby, editor of the liberal suffrage paper *Woman's Tribune*, served as a member of Stanton's *Woman's Bible* revising committee. A believer in the spiritual practices of New Thought, Colby sometimes clashed with Stanton's agnosticism. Still, she remained a loyal friend and political colleague of Stanton's from the 1880s until Stanton's death in 1902. Colby, like several of the other *Woman's Bible* contributors, was marginalized by the conservative leadership of the new National American Woman Suffrage Association. State Historical Society of Wisconsin (X3) 49506

Over the years, Colby's paper featured the contributions of Freethinkers and her sister Spiritualist and New Thought believers, Charlotte Beebe Wilbour, Olympia Brown and Lucinda Chandler, as well as Stanton.

As a rehearsal of the members' writings and editorial affiliations clearly demonstrates, an interest in New Thought connected many of the women on the revising committee. Indeed, the interest in and practice of alternative religions provided the conceptual glue of this geographically dispersed group. The members of the committee serve as a vivid illustration of the religious diversity among women who sought to protect the secular nature of the government.[29] These women were not "secular," at least not as we have come to understand the term in the twenty-first century. Rather, they expended considerable energy articulating religious alternatives to orthodox Christianity.

The religious backgrounds of the committee members reveal the centrality of Freethought and New Thought alternatives to mainstream religion, and at times their coexistence with it. Gage and Colby, for example, both maintained lifelong memberships in their families' denominations, Baptist and Congregationalist, despite their respective commitments to Theosophy and New Thought. As an indication of the overall tenor of the committee, the most theologically traditional members were the Universalists, all three clergy: Olympia Brown, Phebe Hanaford, and Augusta Chapin. But, as Brown put it, "half of the Universalist ministers are Spiritualists and make no secret about it."[30] Other members were already "out" as Spiritualists, including Lucinda Chandler, Catherine Stebbins and Charlotte Wilbour. As the historian Ann Braude has noted, Spiritualism attracted the most radical of the early woman's rights advocates because of its antiauthoritarianism and its extreme individualism.[31] Placing final and absolute authority in the individual soul, Spiritualists censured all institutions, including church and state, that infringed upon the soul's autonomy. New Thought and Freethought feminists would perpetuate this legacy in the pages of the *Woman's Bible*, criticizing biblical peoples for their obedience to external authorities and their neglect of the "inner truth of the individual soul" (*Woman's Bible*, 2:16).[32]

The notion of an autonomous soul comforted feminists spiritually and politically, but the practices of harmonial religions also provided relief for their aging and ill bodies. Several of the committee members pursued Christian Science or Mind Cure healing for a physical ailment. Frances Lord, who so frustrated Stanton in the summer of 1886 by abandoning the Bible project for her "Mind Cure" studies, saw the urgency of her situation a little differently. Troubled by ailments of her ear, eye, and leg, Lord felt she had no choice but to postpone her political work in favor of her training as a healer. Because she experienced some improvement, the Mind Cure

Olympia Brown was a Universalist minister and a suffragist from the Kansas Campaign of 1867 through the passage of the Nineteenth Amendment. Brown was a member of the *Woman's Bible* Revising Committee and a radical suffragist who defected from the conservative National American Woman Suffrage Movement and with Clara Colby formed a radical splinter group, the Woman's Federal Equality Association, in 1902. Ultimately Brown joined with the Congressional Union and the National Woman's Party and as an octogenarian picketed the White House and burned Woodrow Wilson's speeches. State Historical Society of Wisconsin (X3) 32702 struck her as "a Great Social Reform," perhaps even more crucial than Stanton's Bible or the WCTU. Lord was determined to proselytize: "The only way to know a subject is to use it, teach and heal, so I am doing both and intensely interested in it. Without experience of it for myself active and passive, I could not go about proclaiming it a true thing," she wrote to the Illinois suffragist Elizabeth Boynton Harbert.[33]

Lord, like many of the committee members, sought out Harbert, a devoted colleague and friend of Stanton, whose informal network of suffragists was built, at least in part, around her practice of New Thought healing. Six months after her initial enthusiasm, Lord wrote to Harbert from San Francisco to say that she suspected she had "chemicalized" under Harbert's treatments—a stage in which the mortal mind resists healing and the body weakens; her leg had in any case gotten worse. But although she admitted "a great deal of pain and inconvenience," Lord had not lost hope in the cure: "I can only suppose that the cure will come quite suddenly. Certainly it does not come partially."[34] By 1888, Lord had returned to Chicago where she continued to teach, edit her paper, *Woman's World*, and prepare a book titled *Christian Science Healing*. Harbert lived in nearby Evanston; from her home, armed with the healing powers of her mind, she treated sister suffragists from afar, a practice known as "absent healing." Louisa Southworth, a revising committee member and Cleveland resident, was one such patient. Writing to Harbert that she had been too busy to give much thought to her treatments, Southworth nevertheless noticed that her health had improved significantly: "Feeling certain that I owe this gain to you I think that if you are not weary of the work we had better continue it."[35]

Lord, Harbert, and others were drawn to the Chicago area as it emerged as a center for Christian Science and New Thought activity. Part of Chicago's appeal was the home and school of Emma Curtis Hopkins, a New Thought faith healer who made a point of affiliating with the woman's movement. Hopkins trained several *Woman's Bible* committee members as healers.[36] Chicago was also the site of Ursula Gestefeld's conversion to Christian Science. Gestefeld read Eddy's *Science and Health* and from its pages healed herself of several chronic illnesses. Her ill-fated tutorial with Eddy began in 1884. Two years later, Gestefeld advertised to Chicagoans her services as a "metaphysician." Eventually she institutionalized her metaphysical approach, "The Science of Being," by establishing first a club, and ultimately a church and college.[37] Sara Underwood moved to Chicago in the mid-1880s to edit the *Open Court*, pursued the Mind Cure, and published a book on a related topic, *Automatic or Spirit Writing* (1896).[38] Lucinda Chandler, another friend of Harbert's and a subscriber to Lord's *Woman's World*, also lived and worked in the city, where she participated in temperance, suffrage, and Social Purity campaigns. Chandler, whose only child had drowned as a toddler, made a career of politicizing "enlightened parenthood" in which she helped to popularize the Social Purity belief that a pregnant mother's exposure to "wine, strong drink, and unclean food" (and, she implied, sexual activity) threatened the integrity of the infant's body and soul.[39] Having founded a similar organization in Boston, Chandler served as the first president of the Chicago Moral Education Society, a vehicle for her motherhood and Social Purity campaigns. Like many New Thought disciples, Chandler grounded her theology in the belief that the eventual perfection of the race required honoring the soul over the imperatives of the body. So driven, she worked for "an equal and high standard of purity for both sexes."[40]

With so many of her friends and colleagues pioneering new avenues of reform, Stanton thought Chicago "a good field for liberal opinions."[41] As Frances Lord explored the Mind Cure, however, Stanton looked on with a mixture of amusement and frustration.[42] Before long, Stanton had not only lost Lord from the ranks of her revising committee; the "epidemic" had also claimed her most liberal woman correspondent, Sara Underwood. Worried that Underwood too had fallen victim, Stanton adopted a superior tone: "Have you been swept from your moorings, or are you still safely anchored on the rock of common sense in the harbor of calm waters, satisfied with securing what lies in your own horizon[?]"[43]

Despite her own occasional forays into faith healing, Stanton, grounded by what she termed her "too solid flesh," declared the practice of Mind Cure a fantasy. To be fair, Stanton had relatively little need for alternative therapies because she was blessed most of her long life with excellent health. It became a matter of pride with her.[44] A devoted homeopath, she routinely and successfully treated her own illnesses. When her eyesight and her legs began to fail her, she occasionally submitted to the ministrations of faith healers. On one such occasion, Stanton recorded the treatment of a healer who "placed her hands on my hands and knees alternately, and prayed aloud, suggesting to the Lord that I was a worthy child." But, Stanton reported, "the next morning I did not see nor did I skip about." She ultimately found relief from "beef tea, glycerine and whisky."[45] In general, she had little patience with sickness. Once when Harriot suffered a cold, Stanton joked to her son-in-law, "We must begin to treat sick people as criminals and administer reproof rather than sympathy."[46]

Many of Stanton's colleagues on the revising committee were not so fortunate in their health. A surprising number of Freethought and New Thought committee members battled recurring illnesses. In addition to Gestefeld, Southworth, and Lord, whose treatments have been mentioned, Ellen Battelle Dietrick, Lucinda Chandler, Matilda Joslyn Gage, Helen Gardener, Josephine Henry, and Catherine Stebbins all encountered health barriers to their political work that were publicly acknowledged and privately lamented.[47] Lucinda Chandler wrote to Elizabeth Harbert of being too weak to deliver her paper on Social Purity to the International Council of Women in 1888. Over the years, she kept Harbert posted on the ebb and flow of her health. As she approached the close of her seventy-fourth year, Chandler wrote to Harbert that she would be content to know the year "would usher me into the beyond where I might enjoy a satisfactory activity and be free from the needs of mortal body."[48] Gage too was reported, like Chandler, to have suffered from debilitating illnesses and "recurring periods of invalidism." When Gage died, Susan B. Anthony consoled her son, saying, "Had she been possessed of a strong constitution . . . she would have done more for the emancipation of women than all the rest of us put together. With her feeble health she accomplished wonders."[49]

The slower pace of her later years brought even Stanton to think more purposefully about metaphysical issues, she readily admitted. She wrote to Sara Underwood, upon reading Underwood's book of "psychical experiences," that "As I near the goal immortal I have an increasing interest in all that lies beyond."[50] In a similar vein, Lucinda Chandler noted that recurring periods of illness intensified Matilda Joslyn Gage's interest in "psychical studies."[51] Chandler spoke from personal experience because she too spent her periods of recovery engaged in the study of spirituality and political economy.[52] The appeal of immortality, the occult, and New Thought healing operated on several levels for *Woman's Bible* contributors. As an exploration of the text of their *Woman's Bible* passages will illustrate, New Thought provided its adherents an alternative theology of gender equality. But on a more deeply personal level, New Thought, like more traditional faiths, offered sustenance to body and soul.

Religious beliefs took on tangible dimensions in the political work of the committee members. The web of connections linking the group extended across the woman's movement. Committee members shared common allegiances and participated in mainstream women's reform campaigns. Hanaford and Wilbour had pioneered the New York–based woman's club Sorosis in the 1870s and were joined in membership by Clara Neyman, Augusta Chapin, and two *Woman's Bible* defectors, Mary Livermore and M. Louise Thomas. Similarly, assorted committee members were active in the Association for the Advancement of Women, the International Council of Women, the World Parliament of Religions, the Women's Suffrage Press Association and the Society for Political Study of New York City; a handful even belonged to the WCTU.[53]

The National Woman Suffrage Association, however, provided a common political thread weaving committee members together. The leadership of the NWSA in the 1880s prefigured the revising committee organized in

1895. In addition to Stanton, Matilda Joslyn Gage briefly served the organization as president in 1875–1876. Both Clara Colby and Olympia Brown enjoyed terms as vice presidents at large. Many of the women—Lillie Devereux Blake, Clara Neyman, Colby, Gage, and Brown—regularly gave speeches at NWSA conventions or joined colleagues in appearing before Congress. Other members had less visible positions, but participated in the organization as representatives of their state and local areas, including Catherine Stebbins, Lucinda Chandler, and Frances Burr. In fact, an impressive number of the revising committee were active suffrage leaders on the state and regional level. Brown, Gage, Colby, and Blake all had prior experience as presidents of their state associations. Blake spent 1886–1890 as president of both the New York State and New York City Suffrage Associations. Other committee members held posts in state or city suffrage societies, including Josephine Henry in Kentucky, Louisa Southworth in Ohio, Sara Underwood in Massachusetts, Catherine Stebbins in Detroit, Mary Seymour Howell in Albany, and Frances Burr in Hartford.[54] But the New York State Association, in Stanton and Anthony's home territory, provided the most direct pipeline for NWSA leadership. Gage, Blake, Neyman, and Mary Seymour Howell all rotated executive posts in the New York State Association between 1878 and 1890. Not only did NWSA participation engender a shared political perspective among future Bible revisers; it also provided important opportunities for shared work and the roots of long-term friendships and political alliances.[55]

In an alliance that would become even more pronounced in the wake of the *Woman's Bible* controversy, Freethought and New Thought feminists worked for the maintenance of a broad platform of woman's rights in an era when the movement's momentum pulled in the opposite direction. Consequently, virtually all the committee members had experienced both political marginalization and what they often bitterly protested as a devaluing of their contributions to the movement. A fuller discussion of the political fallout of the *Woman's Bible* is reserved for the next chapter, but important allegiances had already been formed by the time the "Woman's Bible" began to appear in serial form and influenced the composition of the revising committee.

In comparison, it is notable how few of these former NWSA luminaries and *Woman's Bible* collaborators assumed positions in the merged National American Suffrage Association in 1890 and afterward.[56] Tied too closely to Stanton, these women with their radical politics and alternative religious views were not in keeping with the comparatively narrow focus of the new association. Gage, Brown, Burr, Gardener, Chandler, Blake, and others began a series of defections to form rival associations explicitly for liberal women.[57] But others remained within the NAWSA, and their religious views would prove to be just as annoying to the new leadership as their politics. Colby, next to Stanton, was the most troublesome of the lot because she freely expressed her religious and political views in her paper. Anthony complained that Colby's paper strayed too far from the suffrage issue. "She won't abate one jot or trifle of her own personality—on Ghandi [*sic*] or Coxey," Anthony lamented.[58]

In the end, serving together on the revising committee of the *Woman's Bible* may have been mainly about risking a posture, but it was no less about standing by a friend. The list of names reflected the outlines and intersections of a community of like-minded women. Honoring a diversity of religious views and a common political orientation, these working relationships were cemented by years of friendship, starting with Elizabeth Cady Stanton and Catherine Stebbins at Seneca Falls in 1848. Stanton was at the center of the orbit, but the constellation of relationships extended far beyond her. Over the years, committee members would visit, heal one another, correspond, review each other's books, and write each other's obituaries. The *Woman's Bible* committee may have been Stanton's invention, but the community it represented thrived.[59]

Methods and Tools of Biblical Commentary

Initially, the *Woman's Bible* may appear like a rather straightforward march of women through the Bible. On page after page, biblical passages in which women appear are followed by commentary composed by Stanton and other committee members. Despite this superficial unity, however, the *Woman's Bible* resembles more an improvisation spun out of control than a melody sung in unison. While Stanton's voice dominates, the countervailing voices of the Old Testament authors, their translators, and her colleagues create a virtual cacophony. Part of the disjointedness resulted because Stanton, as both the book's primary author and its editor, filled two conflicting roles. As an author, she developed in the *Woman's Bible* her most elaborate indictment of the Bible, the clergy, and the Judaic-Christian tradition. As an editor, however, she put together a volume that contained a diversity of views, including harsh criticism of Stanton herself. Ultimately, she achieved her goal of juxtaposing numerous women's readings of the Bible and generating debate over the Bible's meaning. Commentators took issue with Stanton's irreverent readings; Stanton eyed her colleagues' more sacred interpretations suspiciously. This strategy rendered the volume ideologically incoherent and somewhat diluted Stanton's own anticlerical message. But in her mind, the debate itself and the "moral effect of a committee of women" engaged in the work was worth the price.[60]

As the overseeing editor, Stanton challenged her committee to focus on the passages of the Bible that were "degrading" to women. Believing that "two distinct lines of argument can be woven out of those pages on any subject," she desired her contributors, wherever possible, to reread the Bible in ways that reflected positively upon women.[61] Passages that could not be redeemed in women's favor needed to be exposed as corrupt. As an author, Stanton took a less gentle approach. Her own commentaries constituted one tireless effort, to "take note of these discriminations of sex, and reiterate them again and again to call the attention of women to the real source of their multiplied disabilities" (1:79). To that end, Stanton would employ virtually any manner of reading and interpretation available to her.

"Not being versed in scriptural metaphors and symbols," Stanton claimed she merely commented on the meanings of biblical texts as they appeared in "plain English."[62] Although all the commentaries were essentially imaginative impositions on the biblical texts, the committee distinguished between "plain English" interpretations and "esoteric" readings, interpretations that revealed the Bible's hidden or esoteric meaning. The "esoteric" interpretations were written by her New Thought colleagues, Clara Colby, Ursula Gestefeld, and Lucinda Chandler, and by Freethinkers Matilda Joslyn Gage, Frances Burr, and Clara Neyman; Stanton's own passages fused social commentary with critical analyses informed by her understanding of science, history, and biblical criticism. Stanton did not distinguish among these different strategies for assigning meaning to the biblical texts; they were all simply "plain English" commentaries. Yet the concept of "plain English" more accurately conveyed Stanton's political aspirations for the work than her actual strategies of reading and interpreting. Using the models of interpretation developed in feminist biblical hermeneutics as a guide, I have further differentiated Stanton's "plain English" commentaries into two categories: historical-critical and dialogical. In Stanton's work, historical-critical readings draw on the insights of science, history, biblical criticism, and Positivism to steer the interpretation of the text. Dialogical readings offer political, social, or even personal analysis of biblical passages and reflect an interaction between the text, the reader, and the interpretive community. The same distinction in interpretive strategies can be applied to the "esoteric" readings of Stanton's New Thought colleagues, although most of these passages fall into the "dialogical" category as the interpreters attempt to reveal the Bible's hidden meaning.[63]

Not only did her project draw on the interpretive conventions of more traditional biblical exegesis, the *Woman's Bible* also resembled more conventional Bible commentaries. In its layout, for example, it followed the common practice of dividing the text into discrete units for interpretation.[64] Stanton made a point of inverting one convention, however; she instructed the printer to typeset the commentaries larger than the Scripture. In general, however, the women commentators borrowed freely from among the available approaches to their work. In her sabbatical at the Convent de la Sagesse in Toulouse in 1882, Stanton had first read Voltaire's biblical exegesis and commented favorably on both its organization and its entertainment value. Now, Voltaire provided a model.

Stanton aimed the project at average women who, she lamented, "worship the Bible as a kind of fetish."[65] Trying to ease women out of that "superstition," she and her collaborators summoned a wide range of authorities, including scientific theory, comparative religion, occultism, contemporary politics, and "common sense." Not surprisingly, Darwin graced the pages of their commentary, but so too did discussions regarding the American Protective Association, Mormon polygamy, and astrology. Stanton found the Bible rich in parallels between past and present. Often these were gratuitous associations, as when she used the passage where Abraham paid for Sarah's burial place in silver as an occasion to plug the Free Silver movement, a Populist cause popular among Freethinkers in the 1890s (1:41). Similarly, a passage in the Book of Numbers detailing the provisions to be made for priests elicited from Stanton a typical anticlerical response. The Mosaic code, in her opinion, was to blame for contemporary abuses by the clergy, who lived off the largess of others. "Our Levites have their homes free, and good salaries from funds principally contributed by women, for preaching denunciatory sermons on women and their sphere. They travel for half fare, the lawyer pleads their cases for nothing, the physician medicates their families for nothing, and generally in the world of work they are served at half price" (1:110). Still, if the Bible were at times to blame for contemporary problems, at other times it could prove instructive, Stanton conceded. One of her favorite examples in the Pentateuch came from the Book of Numbers, in which the daughters of Zelophehad appealed to Moses for the right to inherit their father's estate. In view of her own history of agitation for the Married Woman's Property Act in New York, it is little wonder that this passage held great appeal for her. In fact, wrote Stanton, "It would have been commendable if the members of the late Constitutional Convention in New York had, like Moses, asked the guidance of the Lord in deciding the rights of the daughters of the Van Rensselaers, the Stuyvesants, the Livingstons and the Knickerbockers" (1:108).[66]

Like most of her dialogical commentary, the analysis of the daughters of Zelophehad illustrated Stanton's effort to analogize biblical precedents and current realities. An opposite tendency was at work in the historical-critical commentaries. In these passages, Stanton and her collaborators used history, biblical criticism, and science to reduce the universalizing nature of the Bible. The thrust of historical criticism was to demonstrate that passages in the Bible believed to be divinely inspired were, in actuality, unique to the culture that produced the text. The insights of the new field of comparative religions were invoked, for example, to show that the second creation account in which Eve was formed from Adam's rib was an allegory found in "some different form in the religions of all nations" (1:20). God's communication with Moses on Mount Sinai was also suspect, Stanton argued, as ancient Hebrews had no written language at that time. "Why should the customs and opinions of this ignorant people, who lived centuries ago, have any influence in the religious thought of this generation?" Stanton wondered (1:71).[67] Historical criticism seemed particularly useful in questioning the authenticity of various Old Testament miracles. Borrowing from the work of the Anglican skeptic John William Colenso, Stanton raised doubts about the viability of Noah's ark. How would it have been possible to gather two of every animal from multiple continents, keep them all fed and watered, and survive dramatic changes in climate? For Stanton, the authenticity of Noah's ark was "hedged with impossibilities . . . but if we make up our minds to believe in miracles then it is plain sailing from Genesis to the end of Deuteronomy" (1:120).

Biblical criticism was another tool of analysis for women interpreters, but they used it cautiously. Although an avid reader of the more popular works, Stanton remained skeptical about the ultimate value of biblical criticism for women's cause. Commentators through the ages had interpreted the Bible as "a collection of symbols and allegories, but none of them are complimentary to our unfortunate sex" (1:70). Certainly Stanton, for one, was consistently disappointed with the work of male revisers and critics who despite going "over these documents so often" still "adhered so closely to such gross translation" (1:60–61). The usefulness of biblical criticism was also limited, according to Stanton, because of its inaccessibility to general readers (1:56).

Still it seems obvious from the commentaries that Stanton and her colleagues gained momentum from critical studies of the Bible. Where they could apply information to the discussion of women, the contributors translated the findings of historical and biblical criticism into "plain English." The most basic questions raised by the new scholarship—the multiple authorship of the Pentateuch, for example—undermined the Bible's unassailable status (1:140). The *Woman's Bible* commentators were familiar with the scholarly work on this issue and discussed it approvingly in their commentaries. They were also not beyond hazarding an occasional guess about a book's authorship. Chapter 12 of the Book of Numbers was one whose Mosaic authorship Stanton questioned, owing to the phrase: "(Now the man Moses was very meek, and above all the men which were upon the face of the earth.)" It was remarkable, Stanton thought, "if Moses was as meek as he is represented . . . that he should have penned that strong assertion of his own innate modesty" (1:101).

If a case could be made for the mistaken identity of Old Testament authors, what of their many translators? At points, translation figured prominently in the *Woman's Bible* when its interpreters believed they could
demonstrate that the Bible's misogyny had been imposed by the translators.
According to Clara Colby, the translators were clearly not inspired, even if
the original Bible had been. "We have strong presumptive proof that prejudice of education was in some instances stronger than the grammatical context, in translating . . . contested points," she maintained (1:37). Particularly
vexing for feminist commentators was the translation, or imposition, of the
word "obey" in biblical discussions of marital relations. The word translated
as "obey" when used between husbands and wives was in other contexts
translated as "defer," a term less offensive to the women commentators.
Colby argued that, in fact, "You cannot find a direct command of God or
Christ for the wife to obey the husband." She took it as further proof that on
the two occasions where Sarah presumably "obeyed" Abraham, God "had to
interfere with a miracle to save them from the result of that obedience"
(1:37).

Among the Freethought commentators, tentative reliance on biblical
criticism stemmed from a distrust both of the underlying text and of the enterprise of redeeming it. This was particularly true for Stanton, who mar-
veled, "Those who can make these foul facts illustrate beautiful symbols
must have a genius of a high order" (1:129).[68] In contrast, the New Thought
commentators maintained that the Bible like many other "Oriental" texts
was spiritually inspired and esoterically encoded. They believed, however,
that the authority to decipher the code emanated from their study of the
Kabbalah, a Jewish mystical text, Christian Science, New Thought, and
Eastern religions, not from Western schools of biblical criticism. In both
cases, women revisers applauded critical analyses of the Bible and appropriated them when possible, but never embraced this approach with the certainty they would bring to other strategies of reading.

Science, in particular, seemed to offer Stanton and others a truth that was
as empirical and unassailable as the Bible was to many of its readers. A faith
in science brought together proponents of "plain English" and esoteric interpretive styles. *Woman's Bible* commentators envisioned "science" in the
broadest possible terms, from geology to numerology. Seemingly the only
criterion necessary to qualify an idea as "science" was its origin outside the
biblical text. But despite its broad definition, science worked in one direction in these texts: to show the progress of modernity over the world described in the Bible. In some cases, that progress was reflected in the superior understanding that modern science brought to a biblical event. Lillie
Devereux Blake used evidence from geology and archaeology to connect the
great flood of the Old Testament to the melting of the glaciers (1:38). Simi-

larly, the eugenic "laws of heredity" were invoked to explain the persistence of "petty deceptions handed down from generation to generation" among Old Testament patriarchs and matriarchs (1:52). Usually, however, Stanton simply stepped aside and pointed with wonder to the triumph of science and technology. The curses of Adam and Cain, for example, to till the ground which would bring forth weeds, had been neutralized by modern technology that not only decimated weed populations, but rendered the cultivation of the soil "a recreation and amusement." The farmer was not the lone beneficiary of modernity, for "the time is at hand when the heavy burdens of the laborer will all be shifted on the shoulders of these tireless machines" (1:30).[69] Women too were freed from their Old Testament fate through the use of anesthetics in childbirth (1:31). The historical-critical analyses drawing on science were somewhat limited by their authors' lack of formal training in either ancient languages or contemporary science. Yet, from the revisers' perspective, advanced scholarship was hardly necessary, the virtues of science over the Bible were so patently obvious.

In contrast to these historical-critical readings that challenged the Bible's claim to truth, symbolic or esoteric interpretations provided Bible readers a way to continue cherishing the Bible and to defend its spiritual truth. Esoteric readings stemmed from the belief that the Bible was an "occult" book encoded with hidden messages (2:106). Occultism appealed to many of Stanton's New Thought and Freethought colleagues on the committee because it allowed the Bible to become, in the words of Frances Burr, "something more than the old battle ground of controversy for warring religions" (2:106). The New Thought healer Ursula Gestefeld concurred. Rather than being seen as a historical document whose truth was impossible to verify, the Bible needed to be studied "as a record of the present," of present individuals and their quest for "perfect actualization" (1:143). Gestefeld explained the New Thought belief, reminiscent of Transcendentalism, that the Bible has both an exterior, the letter, and an interior, the spirit. Failing to recognize this dichotomy, traditional religions had misread the letter for the spirit. To derive the true and esoteric meanings from the texts, New Thought and Freethought writers turned to nontraditional sources: the Kabbalah, Native American legends, Egyptian lore, comparative religions, and the "internal evidence of the book itself" (1:147).[70]

Rereading Genesis

The *Woman's Bible's* commentary on Genesis, comprising fifty-four pages of volume one, constitutes its most in-depth treatment of any section of either Testament. Sensing the interpretative weight given to the Genesis account of the first woman, the commentators went to great lengths to supplant traditional doctrinal readings of these texts. Drawing support for their arguments variously from science, the occult and their own "common sense," Stanton and her colleagues attempted to establish the simultaneous creation of men and women, prove the existence of a "Holy Mother," reinterpret the "rib" story, and otherwise redeem Eve's behavior and disprove her curse (1:14–67).

In their rereading of Genesis, *Woman's Bible* commentators relied heavily upon the eighteenth-century findings of the French scientist Jean Astruc, who posited the existence of two separately authored creation accounts in Genesis. The two could be distinguished in the original Hebrew by the precise word each author used to refer to God. More was at stake here than word choice, however, because the two accounts offered contradictory explanations of woman's creation. In the first, man and woman were created simultaneously to share dominion over the earth. In the second account, however, man was created third, preceded only by land and water and followed by the other animals. Woman was created sixth and from a rib of man. Feminist commentators seized upon this contradiction. They correctly pointed out that many clergymen ignored the first account in favor of the second in which, as Stanton liked to say, woman was created "as an afterthought" (1:17–18). The *Woman's Bible* commentators showed no interest in reconciling these disparate stories. Some were determined to disprove the second, more popular, and comparatively misogynist account. Others sought out its metaphorical possibilities, maintaining the rib symbolized the positive values of monogamy and androgyny.

Just as male commentators had imposed the extra-textual discourse of "natural spheres" to prop up biblical infallibility, women commentators drew support from science and historical criticism to tear it down. Stanton, for one, explained that the second account, in which Eve emerged from Adam's rib, "a petty surgical operation," was not in keeping with the spirit of the grand evolution of the cosmos (1:20). In the same terms that she would frequently use to assert the existence of a Heavenly Mother in the Trinity, Stanton relied upon scientific theories of Positivism to justify the simultaneous creation of woman and man. With the paraphrase, "God created man in his *own image, male and female*," she contended that Scripture, science, and philosophy all mutually supported "the eternity and equality of sex—the philosophical fact, without which there could have been no perpetuation of creation, no growth or development in the animal, vegetable or mineral kingdoms, no awakening nor progressing in the world of thought" (1:15). Combining tenets of Positivism with a Darwinian model of development that linked evolutionary progress in both nature and culture, Stanton maintained the necessity of the simultaneous existence of male and female "elements" to assure the perpetuation of "creation." Once more, she resurrected the Positivist principle of masculine and feminine elements as central to and defining of the universe. Bound by the laws of attraction, the elements maintained "the equilibrium of the universe as positive and negative electricity, the centripetal and centrifugal forces . . . which bind together all we know of this planet" (1:15). Stanton's use of the immutable law of Positivism is revealing. Bearing no overt reference to the scriptural narrative, it is wholly imposed on the text.

The Positivist elements took the place of the customarily invoked "natural spheres." Spheres were separate, complementary, and rarely overlapping; Stanton's model posed elements "exactly equal and balancing each other"—not identical, but not hierarchical, either. Instead, they stood opposed yet interdependent, defining each other. Religious discourse had relegated women to a separate and at times irrelevant sphere; science, Stanton assumed, provided a superior arrangement that like "positive and negative electricity" guaranteed an equality essential to the universe (1:20). Her application of male and female elements, also prevalent in Spiritualist discourse, nicely harmonized with New Thought conceptions of the soul balancing its male and female qualities. However, Stanton's conception of elements—bound in attraction to each other and responsible for perpetuating creation—suggested a more kinetic, explicitly heterosexual dynamic than her New Thought colleagues attempted with the notion of the "sexless soul."[71]

In contrast, the second creation account, the rib story, lacked a scientific premise and could be dismissed easily. "It is evident," Stanton wrote, "that some wily writer, seeing the perfect equality of man and woman in the first chapter, felt it important for the dignity and dominion of man to effect woman's subordination in some way" (1:21).

Stanton's application of Positivism to her reading of the competing creation accounts was fairly abstract. Readers may have been more convinced by the committee's other efforts at historical criticism. The orthodox belief that Moses, inspired by God, authored the entire Pentateuch had been duly challenged in schools of higher criticism. "No Christian theologian of today," Ellen Battelle Dietrick asserted, "with any pretensions to scholarship, claims that Genesis was written by Moses" (1:16). Using evidence in the Apocrypha, a collection of noncanonical scriptural texts, Dietrick argued that the original Scriptures were lost in the destruction of Jerusalem in approximately 588 B.C. Not until three to four hundred years later was there "any record of a collection of literature in the re-built Jerusalem." According to Dietrick, contradictions like the competing creation accounts might easily be explained by the use of "uncritical copyists, who altered passages greatly, and did not always even pretend to understand what they were copying." Dietrick concluded, however, that the secondary creation of woman was no mere slip of the pen: "the second story was manipulated by some Jew, in an endeavor to give 'heavenly authority' for requiring a woman to obey the man she married" (1:16). As in several other passages of the *Woman's Bible*, "historical criticism" lapsed here into a thinly veiled anti-Semitic attack on the Hebrew Bible. Yet, for her readers, Dietrick's point about the imposition of a historical context onto the writing of "sacred" texts added another challenge to the Bible's authority. It was one that Stanton shared; at several points in her exegesis she too referred to a "highly imaginative editor" and "some wily writer" who essentially penciled in women's secondary status.

The use of a variety of exegetical tools seemed to improve woman's biblical position. In sum, woman's equality with man in the moment of creation was established by science, reinforced by historical criticism, and substantiated by the divine wisdom of alternative religions. Frances Burr claimed that the Kabbalah placed "women on a perfect equality in the Godhead." As Burr put it, "For better authority than that one can hardly ask" (2:112; 1:144).

But demonstrating women's equality in creation solved only half of the problem in Genesis. Women revisers still had to contend with Eve's troubling legacy. Her conduct in the Garden of Eden, many male commentators insisted, destined women to second-class status. Science, however, could be enlisted to challenge the parameters of truth in this chapter of Genesis as well. Invoking the biblical scholar Adam Clarke and the shadow of Darwin, Stanton proposed that the serpent may have, in fact, been an ape. The apple was also problematic, according to Stanton's brother-in-law, a professor of botany at Yale University, and was more than likely not an apple at all, but a quince. "If the serpent and the apple are to be withdrawn thus recklessly from the tableaux," she argued, "it is feared that with advancing civilization the whole drama may fall into discredit" (1:24).[72]

Despite these jabs, the *Woman's Bible* collaborators were far more interested in rescuing the Garden of Eden drama than in dismissing it as false. Regarding Eve, Stanton wrote, "we are equally pleased with her attitude, whether as a myth in an allegory, or as the heroine of an historical occurrence" (1:24). Taking the allegorical approach, Lucinda Chandler pointed out the "symbiology signifies a deeper meaning than a material garden, a material apple, a tree and a snake." It is, rather, the relation of the soul to the senses that is worked out in the drama, Chandler argued, an interpretation popularized by the Christian Scientist Mary Baker Eddy (2:166).

Stanton, writing a "plain English" dialogical commentary, found plenty to discuss as well. In contrast to male commentators who considered Eve only in terms of her sin and punishment, Stanton and her colleagues assigned a higher, nobler motivation to Eve's behavior. Rather than because of "worldly luxuries," they maintained, Eve had "fallen" as a result of woman's "natural" instinct for knowledge. "The unprejudiced reader must be impressed with the courage, the dignity, and the lofty ambition of the woman. The tempter evidently had found a profound knowledge of human nature, and saw at a glance the high character of the person. . . . Compared with Adam she appears to great advantage through the entire drama" (1:24).[73]

Stanton repeatedly claimed to have rejected the concept of "natural spheres" for the sexes; and yet she viewed the Bible, and Eve in particular, through her own Positivist filter of "woman's nature." Woman was not to be saved by religion or childbearing, but by her own "intense thirst for knowledge" (1:25). Knowledge for Stanton was a positive good; it was the key to woman's self-development and power. Male biblical commentators, however, had warned of the subversive dangers of knowledge: "See how destructive is the desire of unnecessary knowledge, under the mistaken notion of wisdom," wrote one clergyman regarding Adam and Eve. "Our first parents, who knew so much, did not know this, that they knew enough."[74] While in Stanton's interpretation, Eve sought knowledge to quench her intellectual appetite, "that the simple pleasures of picking flowers and talking with Adam did not satisfy," male clergymen imposed sexual analogies, admonishing that "the desire of knowledge is as liable to exorbitancy, as the sensual appetites; and, when not restricted by the Word of God, it degenerates into bold curiosity, skepticism and infidelity."[75] Uncontrolled appetites for intellectual or sexual knowledge would doom an entire society, one male commentator contended, arguing that knowledge without religion "does but increase a power . . . which may be ruinous . . . though knowledge be power, yet it is not virtue."[76]

For Stanton and the *Woman's Bible* commentators, however, knowledge was both power and virtue. In her esoteric commentary, Lucinda Chandler argued that Eve's quest for a special kind of knowledge actually curbed uncontrolled sexuality. "Knowledge, through intellect alone, is of the limitation of flesh and sense," Chandler conceded. But this was not the knowledge Eve pursued. Rather, Eve sought "Intuition, the feminine part of reason . . . the higher light" (2:167). Womanly intuition guiding the soul saved humanity from licentiousness. Eve's quest for knowledge, condemned as unregulated appetite by male commentators, elevated her in women's estimation.

In fact, the women revisers focused not on Eve's failings but on Adam's. If Eve's Old Testament conduct set the precedent for future generations of women, they asked, what could be said of the fate of men? Taking on male commentators who blamed Adam's fall on Eve, Chandler pointed out the irony that the man "who was 'first formed,' and therefore superior . . . not only was susceptible to the temptation to acquire knowledge, but should have been the weak creature who was 'overcome by the allurements of his wife' " (2:166). Adam had reneged on his responsibilities, argued Lillie Devereux Blake: "Had he been the representative of the divinely appointed head in married life, he assuredly would have taken upon himself the burden of the discussion with the serpent, but no, he is silent in this crisis of their fate" (1:26). Repeatedly *Woman's Bible* collaborators made strategic use of a "separate spheres" concept in their dialogic analyses. Blake selectively applied the social standards of "natural spheres"—namely, the husband's responsibility to protect his wife in public—to Adam's behavior. "The subsequent conduct of Adam was to the last degree dastardly," Blake inveighed. When his sin is discovered by God, Adam "endeavors to shield himself behind the gentle being he has declared to be so dear. 'The woman thou gavest to be with me, she gave me and I did eat,' he whines—trying to shield himself at his wife's expense!" Blake expressed amazement "that upon such a story men have built up a theory of their superiority" (1:27).

Woman's Bible commentators inverted many of the conventions of the doctrinal reading. Male-authored commentaries made Eve a supporting character, the agent of Adam's sin, or the victim of a corrupting serpent. In the *Woman's Bible*, in contrast, Eve was the uncontested subject of the Garden saga. In the male readings, her motivations were dubious at best, she was hapless and unwitting but, ultimately, sinful. For the *Woman's Bible* writers, Eve was virtuous, spiritually inclined, and unrelenting in the pursuit of knowledge; Adam's behavior, however, called for judgment.

Even Eve's curse could be reversed—not as male readers had suggested, by the Virgin Mary's giving birth to a Messiah, but simply by following sound medical advice. In league with liberal clergy, Stanton contended that "the supposed curse can be easily transformed into a blessing." Science was the catalyst. "With obedience to the laws of health, diet, dress, and exercise," Stanton advised, "the period of maternity should be one of added vigor in both body and mind, a perfectly natural operation [that] should not be attended with suffering" (1:25). Chandler agreed. Indulging in a bit of amateur anthropology, she asserted that women "of our aboriginal tribes, whose living was natural and healthful" simply were "not subject to the sufferings of civilized women." The apparent ease of childbirth among these "natural" women disproved Paul's contention that woman's curse was literal (2:167).

For conservative male clergy, there was no revision of Genesis. Eve's indictment and her resulting subjection to her husband were so commonly accepted that the reference to chapter and verse needed only to be cited in the margin of New Testament passages. The *Woman's Bible* commentators, on the other hand, offered a radical reinterpretation. They endowed Eve with the very qualities they valued in themselves: a rebellious spirit and a desire for knowledge of the soul. They rescued Eve by rereading her.[77]

Taking on Paul

Revising Eve's moral status served the additional purpose of disrupting Paul's easy formulas. Repeating their strategy from Genesis, *Woman's Bible* commentators brought a blend of historical-critical and dialogical analysis to their readings of Paul. By establishing woman's equality in creation and Eve's moral superiority over Adam, the writers had largely depleted Paul's antiwoman arsenal. For good measure, Freethought and New Thought women took issue with Paul on other fronts as well.

As early as the 1850s, Stanton had claimed that Paul's passages concerning women reflected the time in which they were written and should be viewed, "as having no reference whatever to women of the nineteenth century."[78] If these pronouncements could be dismissed as archaic, they could also be challenged on the basis of the Apostle's flawed character. As one woman wrote to a suffrage paper, women "should take comfort when they read what Paul wrote of himself," noting that he had confessed to the various sins of dishonesty, robbery, and boastfulness.[79] The Freethinker Helen Gardener put a related point bluntly: "What did he know about women anyway? He was a brilliant but erratic old bachelor who fought on whichever side he happened to find himself."[80]

Moreover, Paul was not alone, according to Ellen Dietrick, who laid blame on the Catholic Church. To Dietrick it seemed clear that the problematic passages in Pauline doctrine "are bare-faced forgeries, interpolated by unscrupulous bishops, during the early period in which a combined and determined effort was made to reduce women to silent submission, not only in the Church, but also in the home and in the state" (2:150).[81] And not just in "the early period," as Dietrick suggested, but "down these nineteen centuries," Lucinda Chandler exclaimed, "the contempt for woman which Paul projected into Christianity has been perpetuated" (2:165). Indeed it was Paul's persistent influence in the contemporary world that necessitated a total overhaul of the Bible.

At the same time, some *Woman's Bible* interpreters dismissed Paul's importance as a thinker. Stanton only briefly commented on the antiwoman pronouncements in Corinthians and Timothy. The brevity of her comment is striking; after all, these were the key passages used to delimit woman's rights in the nineteenth century, and Stanton wrote exactly four sentences in response. In her exegesis, she adopted wholesale the notion—an idea woman's rights activists had used in the 1840s—that the women of Corinth who were instructed to "keep silence" in the churches were not just speaking, but rather were asking "troublesome questions."[82] She then went on to challenge Paul's assumption that "men were wise enough" to answer women's questions. Women would be better off, Stanton insisted, "guided by their own unassisted common sense" (2:159).

The issue of women's public speech was taken up more extensively by Lucinda Chandler. As was customary, Chandler first commented on Paul in terms of contemporary notions about "woman's nature" and "natural spheres."

> Could Paul have looked down to the nineteenth century with clairvoyant vision and beheld the good works of a Lucretia Mott, a Florence Nightingale, a Dorothea Dix and Clara Barton, not to mention a host of faithful mothers, he might, perhaps, have been less anxious about the apparel and manners of his converts. . . . Or could he have had a vision of the public school system of this Republic, and witnessed the fact that a large proportion of the teachers are women, it is possible that he might have hesitated to utter so tyrannical an edict: "But I suffer not a woman to teach." (2:162)

Chandler offered a traditional view of woman's nature in which her capacity for teaching was essential. In her words, teaching was simply "the most necessary qualification of motherhood." But unlike more devout Christians who gave Paul the benefit of the doubt on women's teaching, Chandler made no effort to stretch his pronouncements to square with contemporary notions of woman's nature. Rather, she argued, Paul was clearly not "inspired by infinite wisdom." For Chandler and other collaborators, Paul's attempts to subvert women's natural instincts for knowledge cost him his "inspired" status. "This was evidently the unilluminated utterance of Paul, the man, biased by prejudice," she wrote. "Jesus is not recorded as having uttered any similar claim that woman should be subject to man, or that in teaching she would be a usurper" (2:163–164).[83]

While Jesus had not retreated to Old Testament law, according to Chandler, Paul had done so with a vengeance. She held Paul personally responsible for infecting the New Testament with what she perceived as the misogynist spirit of the Talmud (2:165). Like clergymen, Chandler commented on the connection between the Pauline dictates and the gendered hierarchy of the creation story, although she and the other *Woman's Bible* contributors found the linkage suspect. "The doctrine of woman the origin of sin, and her subjection in consequence, planted in the early Christian Church by Paul, has been a poisonous stream in Church and State," she wrote: "It has debased marriage and made both Canon and Civil law a monstrous oppression to woman" (2:164). Chandler bolstered her argument with examples from history; but the present conditions of women illustrated their oppression as well. Basing her comments on a case in the Court of Appeals in New York in 1890, she reminded her readers that a married woman could not collect damages for injury to her person. Legally, her husband owned her

(2:164). Paul's "poisonous stream" continued to pollute the lives of contemporary women.

Competing Readings in the *Woman's Bible*

Although Stanton had failed to entice evangelical or Jewish women to join the revising committee, her hope to engage women of different beliefs in a debate over the meanings of biblical texts bore ample fruit. Many of the colleagues she had managed to recruit overtly rejected her overall position on the Bible as well as her interpretations of specific passages. Despite Frances Willard and Isabel Somerset's complaint that Stanton had recruited women who all "held the same view," profound differences of opinion leapt off the pages of the *Woman's Bible*.

For example, much of Stanton's "plain English" commentary amounted to character assassination of the various women of the Hebrew Bible. Some of her colleagues found this tack offensive. In Jewish and Christian commentary, writers had continually pointed to women of the Hebrew Bible as "examples worthy of imitation" (1:53). In other words, Stanton was taking on not just the Bible, but a large literature of female scriptural biography that had popularized Old Testament figures such as Sarah, Rebekah, and Rachel as contemporary heroines and showcased them in handsome volumes with elaborate illustrations.[84] For Stanton, however, "the only significance of dwelling on these women . . . is to show the absurdity of pointing the women of the nineteenth century to these as examples of virtue." Any one of several Old Testament heroines—"all untruthful, and one a kleptomaniac"—would illustrate Stanton's point, but her disdain for Sarah set the tone for much of her commentary (1:53).

In the pages of nineteenth-century popular literature, Sarah, "mother of the Jewish nation," was considered in the words of Harriet Beecher Stowe, "an object of traditional respect and homage in the Christian Church."[85] Lauded for her beauty and the quiet power it gave her over her husband Abraham, Sarah served as a perfect model for nineteenth-century "true womanhood." She achieved great stature through her beauty and power, but still she "wanted what every woman of antiquity considered the crowning glory of womanhood. She was childless."[86] When her slave Hagar, at Sarah's urging, bore Abraham a much wanted son, the domestic tranquillity of this ancient story was disrupted. Complicating the plot even more, at long last and in the ripeness of old age, Sarah bore Abraham an heir, Isaac. Eventually, Sarah insisted that Hagar and her son be banished. Abraham agreed. With visions of Hagar and Ishmael wandering in the wilderness, how were readers to interpret Sarah's behavior? Not with the "undue harshness" that a superficial reading of the Bible might produce, cautioned one of her nine-teenth-century popularizers.[87] Rather than turning a blind eye to Sarah's less regal moments, H. B. Stowe instead insisted that Sarah, with these "few touches, [was] made as real flesh and blood as any woman in the pages of Shakespeare,—not a saint, but an average mortal, with all the foibles, weak-nesses, and variabilities that pertain to womanhood."[88] Indeed, another writer concurred, "If she had her faults, she had her virtues likewise; and those virtues seem to heighten, by contrast[,] her frailties."[89]

Sarah's frailties, according to Stanton's reading, were unforgivable and deserved little space in print, as Sarah "did not possess any of the heroic virtues, worthy our imitation." Or perhaps Sarah's story required just enough commentary to point out that in the experience of motherhood, the "divine awakening of a new affection does not seem to have softened Sarah's heart towards her unfortunate slave Hagar" (1:36). Stanton seemed to de-rive some satisfaction from Sarah's subversive efforts to dominate Abraham. But on balance, Stanton concluded, "we cannot recommend her as an exam-ple to the young women of our day, as she lacked several of the cardinal virtues. She was undignified, untruthful, and unkind to Hagar" (1:41).

Clara Colby countered Stanton's "plain English" interpretation with an "esoteric" one and reproached Stanton for dismissing Sarah so lightly.[90] "Wherever she is mentioned the reader is made to feel that she is an impor-tant part of the narrative and not merely a connecting link between two generations. In this story she carries her point, and Abraham follows her in-structions implicitly, nay is even commanded by God to do so" (1:42). Fur-thermore, Stanton had taken the story of Hagar's banishment out of con-text, Colby pointed out. When establishing Sarah and Abraham's motives for banishing Hagar, it was essential to "remember that it had been promised to Abraham that of Ishmael a great nation should be born." More important, the true meaning of this story was not apparent in its literal ren-dering, a point lost upon many "Western thinkers [who] are so matter-of-fact in their speech and thought" (1:43). Rather, the mystical significance of this allegory set a crucial precedent for women of the nineteenth century. According to Colby, the story of Hagar's banishment should be read as a censure of the "double standard." A woman should not have to compete for her husband's affection in her own home. Her personal dignity depended on it. "It is an inspiration to woman to-day to stand for her liberty. The bondswoman must be cast out. All that makes for industrial bondage, for sex slavery and humiliation, for dwarfing of individuality . . . must be cast out from our home, from society, and from our lives. The woman who does not claim her birthright of freedom will remain in the wilderness with the chil-dren that she has born in degradation . . . only to find they are Ishmaels, with their hand against every man" (1:43–44).[91] Only by casting out the internalized slave, and her sexual exploitation, could women experience authentic personal liberty, Colby argued. Women were better off accepting this moral truth of the allegory than expending much energy scrutinizing the behavior of its cast of characters.

In Stanton's analysis, women of the Pentateuch were not so much allegorical symbols as they were "members of an oppressed class" (1:36). Her criticisms of Sarah were echoed in passages on Rebekah, who lacked "a nice sense of honor," and Rachel, who was tragically marred by a penchant "for theft and deception" (1:47, 49). Miriam, in contrast, warranted much praise, but less ink. Impressed with Miriam's "prophetic genius," her judgment and diplomacy, Stanton declared: "If Miriam had helped to plan the journey to Canaan, it would no doubt have been accomplished in forty days instead of forty years." But the very fact that Miriam's leadership talents were overshadowed by Moses' was evidence in "plain English" of woman's degraded position in the Bible (1:101, 103).

In contrast, many of Stanton's committee members, particularly those with a Theosophical or New Thought allegiance, believed that woman's true relationship to man in the Bible was visible only in the esoteric realm.[92] A failure to view the Bible from this angle would explain why Stanton could see biblical women only as "degraded." As Frances Burr pointed out in her essay on the Kabbalah, these "Hebrew esoteric doctrines" demonstrated the essential equality of the sexes by proving that God was simultaneously female and male. Stanton and other religious radicals had long called for the recognition of a Heavenly Mother in the Trinity, an idea Stanton first acquired from Theodore Parker. The Kabbalah, according to Burr, proved the Heavenly Mother's existence by recognizing the Holy Spirit as feminine. Subsequent translators, however, had successfully masked all references to the female aspects of the deity (2:107). But this rediscovered truth was the potentially radical news of the *Woman's Bible*. Indeed, a Moses was needed, Ursula Gestefeld urged, "to see and declare this promised land" of gender equality to women whose "religious nature is warped and twisted through generations of denominational conservatism" (1:143).

Unlike Stanton, who devoted her energies to dissuading women of the Bible's power and authority, her more spiritual colleagues resituated the "esoteric" Bible as a new source of women's power. Theosophists and New Thought practitioners used the Bible's esoteric insights to conceptualize a notion of spiritual androgyny, a sexless soul that was at once external, as a spiritual presence, and internal, as a divine part of each woman and man. For some believers, the androgynous soul was premised on an absence of gender: the soul was, in fact, sex-neutral. Evidence from Occult teachings even suggested that it was not the soul alone that was androgynous. The true meaning of the "rib story," Frances Burr explained, was a symbolic reference to a time past, "before man was differentiated into sexes—that is, when he was androgynous" (2:110). Sometimes even Jesus was invoked on the side of spiritual androgyny: "He spoke to the individual soul, not recognizing sex as a quality of spiritual life" (2:165). For other believers, however, the soul contained elements of both sexes held in tension. The soul, according to Lucinda Chandler, was the internal, feminine part of man, "his living mother," his intuition, and stood in opposition to the physical, "external man of sense" and reason (2:167). While the soul derived its life from spirit, "the eternal substance, God," the external sense was sustained through intellect and flesh. Intuition, the feminine part of reason, was, of course, "the higher light." If the soul, Chandler wrote, "the feminine part of man, is turned toward God, humanity is saved from the dissipations and perversions of sensuality" (2:167). Just as God was both male and female, every soul searched to balance its dual sexes. Gestefeld concurred that "man" as he appears in the Bible was in actuality not gendered male, but rather a "generic man." "The exterior or male half is outermost, the interior or female half is covered by the outer. One is seen, the other has to be discerned," she explained (1:144).

As Chandler's vision of the soul triumphing over the perversion of sensuality illustrated, the esoteric Bible resonated with advice to women on how to balance the demands of the soul and the body. New Thought readers decoded the ancient texts to sound a repeated call: freedom from sexual demands. Hagar's banishment was a metaphor for rejecting woman's sexual slavery. Conversely, Sarah's prerogative to banish Hagar established woman's right to purity and monogamy within her marriage. Even the dreaded "rib story" had a redemptive possibility in esoteric analysis. One New Thought commentator pointed out that this story—one man, one rib, one woman—established the divine plan of monogamy, "a true and progressive idea established with the foundation of the Christian Church" (2:169).

New Thought commentators drew upon the clergy's traditional respect for motherhood, considered woman's redemptive role (or more pessimistically, her curse), but reinterpreted that familiar role within their own frame of reference. No longer just motherhood, but "enlightened motherhood" was the divine mandate. "Enlightened motherhood" for its New Thought and Social Purity advocates was a coded discourse on sexuality. Enlightened mothers resisted sexual contact except when instructed by the inner light of the soul that divine procreation might proceed. A passage by Lucinda Chandler explained that enlightened motherhood required a "new man" to accompany the "new woman" into marriage. "He is inspired by the Divine truth that woman is to contribute to the redemption of the race by free and enlightened motherhood. He is proving his fitness to be her companion by achieving the greatest of all victories—victory over himself" (2:163).

No one championed the individual soul more than Elizabeth Cady Stanton. But these New Thought readings with their allegiance to the Bible, albeit an esoteric one, did not sit well with her straightforward analysis of women's oppression in the Old and New Testaments. Still this was a debate that she, as the editor of the volumes, facilitated. New Thought contributors' greatest departure from Stanton's agenda lay in offering readers an entirely spiritual alternative to the traditional Bible. Even Theosophists and Freethinkers on the committee were more committed than Stanton to finding a strategy by which the Bible could be saved. Matilda Joslyn Gage agreed with the New Thought contributors that the Bible was "a record of ancient mysteries hidden to all but initiates." The Bible should be placed, according to Frances Burr, a Theosophist, "where a spiritually enlightened people can see it in its true light"—a book whose "bright jewels" were buried under "some rubbish, perhaps, as well as under many symbolisms and mystic language." Restoring the Bible's true symbolism heralded, Burr concluded, a new "dispensation" (2:112).

New Thought healer Ursula Gestefeld was Stanton's most explicit critic in the pages of the *Woman's Bible*. The creation of a "woman's" Bible should not merely repeat the mistakes of men by separating the sexes, Gestefeld warned. The soul, being both masculine and feminine, required the wisdom of both sexes: "This would be an attempt to separate what is intensely joined together and defeat the end desired" (1:147). Gestefeld also chastised Stanton for her overly intellectual approach to the Bible. Woman's intellectual path to agnosticism may have begun as "liberal," Gestefeld conceded, but it soon deteriorated into "dogmatic materialism," that is, a blatant denial of the spiritual. Women caught up in the "exhilaration of intellectual activity," presumably like Stanton, were no more liberated than their sisters bound to conservative religious creeds. The dogma of materialism was "sensuous" and implicitly male; intellectual women needed to take stock of their journey and to seek balance, to "be brought in again" to "see that religion is of the soul" (1:146).

Far from presenting one seamless theory, the *Woman's Bible* rather confronted its readers with several parallel possibilities: "plain English" and esoteric readings; critical and dialogical strategies; rational and spiritual approaches; and a variety of faiths. The various threads of analysis were woven together into a common blanket of disapproval for traditional forms of Christianity. Yet, despite its internal contradictions, the *Woman's Bible* represented a quest for new ideological grounds for gender equality.

Stanton, for her part, hoped to dislodge women's faith in the Bible and to expose it as the source of their oppression. In some ways, however, Stanton's irreverent passages offered readers a rather limited argument for women's emancipation. Her time-worn Positivist balancing of male and female elements established the feminine principle as essential to the laws of the universe. For Stanton, science had the power to trump the Bible and establish woman's equality with absolute certainty. But while scientific evidence might persuade women that their equality with men was "natural," it did not provide a spiritually empowering alternative. Stanton's collaborators did. New Thought commentators plying their esoteric biblical interpretations offered women readers a valuable alternative to the tried and tired arguments for equality based on either "natural rights" or "woman's piety." Rather than asserting a natural rights argument for *equality with* men, rather than assuming a piety argument for women's moral *superiority over* men, these passages in the *Woman's Bible* articulated a position that was self-consciously gender-neutral. Transcending the limits of gender, the sexless soul offered women a position that was both politically and spiritually powerful. And the Bible held the key to its destiny. As Gestefeld put it, "The book is the soul's guide in the fulfilling of its destiny—that destiny which is involved in its origin; and the soul, in sleep, is sexless" (1:147). Contradictions abounded, but the effort to advance a new theoretical position complicates our earlier understanding of the prevailing ideological strategies in the woman's rights movement of this period.

More polemical than scholarly, the *Woman's Bible* was at once a Bible commentary, a spiritual guidebook, and a political treatise. It was also a commentary on its times. Laced throughout the passages on ancient texts were feminist critiques of contemporary issues in religion, politics, and gender relations. But the passages were also riddled with commentators' elitist and ethnocentric assumptions about the nature of the world—though these followed no simple formula. Attitudes toward Judaism provide an apt illustration. Stanton, joined by Dietrick and others, harshly criticized the Jews of the Bible for their treatment of women. Her censure of these ancient figures, however, evoked contemporary ethnic stereotypes and were frequently anti-Semitic. Jewish patriarchs were "cunning" and "wily" (1:190). Jewish men and women—and their God—are portrayed as morally lax, greedy, and materialistic. The history of the Jews, Stanton wrote, was marked by "corruption, violence, lust and petty falsehood. . . . The only value of these records to us is to show the character of the Jewish nation, and make it easy for us to reject their ideas as to the true status of woman, and their pretension of being guided by the hand of God, in all their devious wanderings" (1:72). Not all her colleagues agreed, however. Clara Colby took issue with Stanton's interpretation of ancient Judaism, pointing out that the "Jewish women were treated with greater politeness than the daughters of neighboring peoples" (1:48). Frances Burr's tribute to the Kabbalah and Jewish mysticism further disrupted Stanton's attack on Judaism as the taproot of all sexism.

The classist and racist ideas infusing the *Woman's Bible* situate it in its historical context, an era that witnessed "radical" suffragists calling for "educated suffrage," legislation restricting immigration, unchecked enthusiasm for American imperialism, and an epidemic of lynchings of African Americans. The commentaries demonstrate the multiple and conflicting possibilities of languages of faith in the 1890s. These women found within their religion an oppositional discourse of gender equality, even as they deployed it to establish their own social and racial superiority. In that sense the *Woman's Bible* collaborators were not far from their Christian opponents whose belief in the supremacy of Christian civilization stoked the fires of cultural imperialism.

The elitism that surfaces in the pages of the *Woman's Bible* is just one indication that, despite its heretical tendencies, Stanton's radical Bible conserved a great deal. By focusing on the individual as the agent for change, the *Woman's Bible* drew upon the assumptions of traditional Protestantism. According to Stanton's model, individual women would read the *Woman's Bible*, experience a conversion to a rationalist worldview, and thereby accelerate their own emancipation. The role of the *Woman's Bible* in the liberation of women as a whole depended on the salvation of individual women, a strategy that by its very nature undermined more broad-based, collective approaches to social change. Stanton herself was deeply interested in more "co-operative" strategies, as evidenced by her attraction to socialism in these years. Before collective strategies could bear fruit, however, more preparatory work had to focus on uprooting the religious faith of individual women.

Publishing the *Woman's Bible*

When volume one of the *Woman's Bible* was published in 1895, Stanton believed she had finally brought to fruition what for so long had been desperately needed in the woman's rights struggle: a forceful solution to women's degraded condition. On the eve of publication, she had high hopes for redirecting the woman's movement. "The importance of this work cannot be over estimated," she wrote to Colby. "Religious ideas are everywhere the strongest motive power of the race," and "the Bible is the Magna Charta of woman's freedom when rightly interpreted." Once it emerges in book form, Stanton declared, "it will be the crowning achievement of the nineteenth century . . . the emancipation of women."[93]

Despite these great expectations, and notwithstanding the strength of friendship and political camaraderie that bolstered the revising committee, the book's publication was marred by a private but painful controversy. Stanton apparently reneged on a promise to share the book's copyright with her friend and colleague Matilda Joslyn Gage. To add insult to injury, Stanton did not inform Gage about deleting her from the copyright. Gage learned the truth when she inquired of Clara Colby, the person responsible for filing the copyright with the Library of Congress. Gage fired off a letter to Stanton demanding to know at once "the reason why the copyright of 'The Woman's Bible' was not taken out in *my* name as well as your own." She also included instructions to Stanton about how to remedy the copyright "mistake" by filing a new application. Stanton's response to Gage has not survived. It is clear, however, that copyrighting the *Woman's Bible* solely in her own name was not an oversight on Stanton's part. Despite her frequent laments about lack of support, at least when it came to Gage, Stanton appeared to have chosen to proceed alone. In fact, the application was filed on June 4, 1895, exactly one week after Gage posted her letter of complaint. Stanton never offered an explanation, informing Colby simply, "No matter about Mrs. Gage, I have written her that I shall have the book copyrighted in my name alone."[94] In recompense, Stanton offered Gage $100 to assist her in finishing the analysis of the Old Testament.

In the pages of her autobiography, Stanton made amends to Gage, in a curious, round-about way. She pleaded guilty to a lesser charge. Accused for decades of having appropriated from Gage the phrase "There is a word sweeter than Mother, Home or Heaven; that word is Liberty," Stanton owned up to the plagiarism in her memoir and, at least in her mind, put the issue to rest. She asked her "autograph admirers, from New York to San Francisco" that whenever they saw the phrase in question "to remember it belongs to Matilda Joslyn Gage."[95] For Gage, this long-awaited acknowledgment may have come a bit too late. She died just weeks after the book's publication. Stanton could nonetheless take comfort in knowing she had "made the *amende honorable*." It was true that over the course of their decades of collaboration, Gage begrudged Stanton the use of her original inscription. She never forgot it.[96] But while Gage had been miffed by the autograph issue—she assumed, probably accurately, that when readers saw the phrase, they would naturally attribute it to her more famous colleague—she was completely outraged about the *Woman's Bible* fiasco.

Although more of Gage's side of this argument has survived than Stanton's, it seems that Stanton struggled to compensate Gage in a fashion. But in confessing to usurping the autograph phrase but not the copyright, Stanton revealed no hint of moral ambiguity. She had set things right with Gage, she wrote, "as I always strive to do when friends feel they have not been fairly treated."[97] The larger irony, of course, is that amid the stream of rejections associated with the "Woman's Bible" project, Gage stood steady as a rock, always supportive of Stanton's venture. Moreover, Gage was one of the few women who brought a deep intellectual background to the work.

Once Stanton had assembled the commentators, received their various texts, and handled the copyright issue, finding a suitable publisher proved to be yet another problem. Although the idea of a "Woman's Bible" had piqued the interest of at least one potential publisher who, according to Stanton, "thought it would have a great sale," Stanton, with the help of her sons, was finally obliged to front the publication costs herself.[98] Financing the publication of the *Woman's Bible* and, several years later, of her autobiography as well put her in the awkward position of having to promote their sale. Although the initial controversies surrounding the *Woman's Bible* generated a demand for available copies, before long Stanton found herself with a lot of books on her hands. For years she wrote countless letters to friends and reformers across the country offering discounts for bulk sales. "The retail price is fifty cents," read a typical letter; "if you take one or two dozen you get them for thirty cents. Thus in a large number you could make a good profit. If you take a package of twenty-five or over you get them for 25 cents a piece."[99] Out of loyalty, Susan B. Anthony took Stanton up on the deal, purchasing twenty copies for ten dollars, but confided she had no hope of selling them. She would attempt to give them away, she explained to Colby, "when I find a person whom I think will read [them]." In the meantime, Anthony was aghast to learn that Stanton's reported "twenty-five dollar contribution" to Colby's flagging newspaper the *Woman's Tribune* "was simply 50 copies of the Bible!!"[100]

The publication of the *Woman's Bible* sparked neither the emancipation of women as a group nor the emergence of Freethought individualism among its readers. Rather, its appearance signaled Stanton's diminishing impact on the woman's movement. Her difficulty finding willing collaborators, a willing publisher, and willing buyers was perhaps only fitting. By this time most of her colleagues found her radical views more dangerous to the woman's movement than was the religion she was so busy attacking.

Ironically, the *Bible* would increase Stanton's notoriety and, at least for a generation, diminish her historical legacy. But living on the radical edge had never particularly worried Stanton. By 1895 she was eighty years old and more committed than ever to finishing the work she had started. She was an outsider, but it was a position with which she had grown familiar: "I am out of all official connection with women's organizations," she told a reporter. "I want nothing. I have no sails to trim to catch the favor of men or women. I have no offices to aspire to. I am beyond all that now, and regard it [the *Woman's Bible*] as the culminating work of my life."[101]

In the following months, Stanton needed to summon the strength of that conviction. The Bible as a source of inspiration may have long lost its power for her, but it found ardent defenders among clergy, women reformers, and the public.

"The Bigots Promote the Sale": Responses to the *Woman's Bible*

If this is the way in which the wives and mothers of this land are being trained to look and speak of God's word, how long will it be before we are ready for the utter collapse and corruption of organized society?

From "A Striking Sign of the Times: A Chapter from the Woman's Bible," *Our Hope* 2 (August 1896)

Just two weeks before the first volume of the *Woman's Bible* appeared, Elizabeth Cady Stanton stood, with assistance, before an audience of 8,000 assembled in New York's Metropolitan Opera House to commemorate her eightieth birthday. For a year reformers had been planning the extravaganza sponsored by the National Council of Women. Women had united for the affair, over twenty different organizations in all, making it, in Susan B. Anthony's words, "the greatest event of the year . . . and, I think, of all the years." To Anthony, the celebration marked a new epoch of cooperation and understanding among women of vastly different commitments. That all these women and their societies, "the majority of them differing seriously and painfully from Mrs. Stanton in her theological notions, should combine together in the Council and extend to her this great ovation as the leader of the pioneers and of the movement itself," was cooperation of grand proportions.[1] Just months later, Stanton would again be the center of national attention, not as the beloved mother of the movement, but as an infidel whose *Woman's Bible* had damaged the cause of woman suffrage.

Critics and Reviewers, Male and Female

In the weeks and months following the *Woman's Bible*'s publication, newspapers and magazines announced its arrival with fanfare. Some accounts invested Stanton with the status of a biblical scholar, comparing her favorably with the commentators Albert Barnes, George Whitfield Clark, and Matthew Henry. Other notices treated her Bible more lightly, including the *Hartford Seminary Record*, which dubbed it "The most humorous book of the year." While most journalists predicted that the clergy would oppose the *Woman's Bible*, they disagreed as to its long-term impact on the emancipation of women. The *Albany Evening Journal* named the *Woman's Bible* the "most serious labor undertaken by the woman's rights leaders." A Trenton, New Jersey, paper, on the other hand, failed to see that "the prospects of woman will be at all improved by this new version of the Bible."[2]

Disagreement over the impact of Stanton's Bible on the prospects of women divided readers as well. As Stanton had anticipated all along, many male clergymen denounced the work. Her most vitriolic exchange was with a minister who insisted, "It is the work of women, and the devil." "This is a grave mistake," Stanton replied; his "Satanic Majesty" had not been invited to join the all-woman revising committee. Besides, she wrote, he had been so busy working the floors of denominational conventions in order "to prevent the recognition of women delegates, that he has no time to study the languages and 'higher criticism.' "[3]

As their sensitivity to the *Woman's Bible* made clear, the clergy stood to lose the most in the circulation of Stanton's controversial new book. As a group, their continued livelihood depended on the support of largely female congregations, who looked to them as spiritual advisers who provided guidance in biblical interpretation. The *Woman's Bible* threatened to intrude upon this relationship. By offering women a key to their own spiritual autonomy, unmediated by the church or clergy, Stanton provoked censure and derision. A Southern Presbyterian, a Bishop Haygood, warned of the possible consequences: "Such trifling with the Holy Scripture makes infidels by the thousand. Better establish a society to sow down the land with infidel tracts than to have women who claim leadership in all manner of reform movements, changing the Word of God to suit their whims and conceits."[4] Another clergyman, writing in a religious weekly, called the *Woman's Bible* "a pernicious and dangerous book, which will tend to weaken the virtue of faith, and undermine respect for God and revealed truth." The women behind the project, this minister explained, disregarded the basic truth that the Bible was the source, not of their oppression, but of their emancipation. The word of God had saved women from the "degradation" that came with paganism. "The spectacle of woman to-day hurling insult and ridicule at the divine word, because it seems not to harmonize with her advanced notions, is not without a touch of sadness," he concluded. "Such a course is suicidal. It cannot but result in positive evil. It is a movement backward. For the world in general and for women in particular, it were better the Woman's Bible had been left unwritten."[5]

"Hurling ridicule at the divine word" was particularly transgressive when women attempted it. One minister inquired whether their gender alone qualified women to make such pronouncements on the Scripture. The familiar notion of woman's "natural" piety was challenged by clergy such as Bishop Haygood, who questioned the legitimacy of women examiners: "Do they monopolize the scholarship of godliness? Are women, because women, the best critics, philologists, exegetes? Have they, because of sex, spiritual insight? Do they know what inspiration might to [*sic*] be?"[6] Indeed, spiritual infidelity among women seemed particularly dangerous because woman's vaunted piety stabilized the family and the society at large. Ministers apparently did not even need to read the book to perceive this peril. A Father Cleary supposed that in the *Woman's Bible*, "man will be assigned to the inferior place for which they [the revisers] claim nature intended him."[7] Indeed, the fear that the *Woman's Bible* would disrupt the gendered hierarchy of the family caused genuine alarm among clergy and the religious press. The editors of *Our Hope* warned readers of the social anarchy that would result from women reading the book: "if woman saps the foundation of the family, how can society and the state continue to stand? The pillar of the church is the headship of Christ. The pillar of the family is the headship of man. Truly perilous times are upon us."[8]

The religious papers and their Freethought rivals concurred that "the ministers are unanimous against the revision." According to one Freethinker, the emergence of the *Woman's Bible* proved to be nothing less than "a bomb in the camp of ecclesiasticism."[9] But Stanton was not without her clerical defenders. Clara Colby dutifully logged each one in the pages of the *Woman's Tribune*. A Universalist minister from Rochester, N.Y., the Reverend D. M. Kirkpatrick, flew in the face of clerical opinion and preached a sermon praising the *Woman's Bible*. According to the *Tribune*, Kirkpatrick agreed with the volume's central message that the Bible and its priestly interpreters had reinforced ideas of women's inferiority. The *Woman's Bible* was needed as a weapon to enable women "to think religiously, for herself, and to defend herself against religious opinion."[10]

Stanton and the *Woman's Bible* had no more eloquent defender than the Reverend Alexander Kent, a Universalist minister in Washington, D.C. In a sermon delivered just days before the 1896 NAWSA convention opened in his city, Kent expounded on the book's attributes and documented its occasional flaws. His careful preparation indicated that he, unlike the vast majority of Stanton's critics, had actually read the text and found it worthy of serious discussion.

Casting his vote with an overwhelming majority of readers, Kent objected to the title: "Not merely because it conveys the impression that the book is written in a polemical spirit; and like the old one, under the influence of sex prejudice; nor because it would needlessly offend many who hold the Bible as the word of God," although these were certainly legitimate concerns. The appellation *Woman's Bible* was regrettable because the finished product would never "justify the title." It was not a Bible, nor even a commentary on the Bible, but a "collection of comments on a few detached passages that refer in some way to woman." Kent lodged other minor criticisms as well, suggesting that the quality of the book was uneven. He was, however, particularly impressed with Stanton's voice, unburdened by "any inheritance of orthodoxy"; her commentaries were "vigorous, fearless and plainspeaking." Stanton wielded a "sharp, incisive pen" and did "not scruple to use ridicule or sarcasm when occasion requires," Kent noted approvingly. The other commentators approached the Bible with a "higher estimate of its general content." Yet, Mrs. Stanton was the most logical and consistent of the commentators as she directed the "shafts of her wit and argument and ridicule" at the Bible's status as the word of God.[11]

In sympathy with the spirit of the undertaking, Kent announced that "if the church has cause to mourn the publication of this work, it has only itself to blame." With the authority of the Bible invoked so regularly to limit woman to her "sphere," it was no wonder that women reformers perceived a need for "some power outside of the church to break the grip of this old belief," he wrote. "There are some weak passages in the 'Woman's Bible,' but there is nothing there that is morally and philosophically so stupid and senile" as the orthodox arguments for woman's timeless and universal subjection to man.

Perhaps most important, Kent compared the *Woman's Bible* favorably to male-authored biblical commentaries. He found Stanton's critical analysis of Genesis, in which she argued the scientific basis of the first creation account, to be inspired. Quoting at length her Positivist argument for masculine and feminine elements "essential to the maintenance of the equilibrium of the universe," Kent applauded the scholarship. "Now, I venture to say that you will search in vain in any orthodox commentary for the thought which Mrs. Stanton has here so clearly developed, and yet which lies on the very face of the passage," he wrote.

As to the ridicule heaped upon Stanton and her colleagues, Kent reminded his congregation that the orthodox clergy who had revised the Testaments ten years earlier had also suffered painful rebuke. "The fools are not all among the women," he wrote. "The religious press of the country teemed with articles arguing the wickedness even of any attempt on the part of uninspired men to revise the word of God." The trustees of libraries had limited the circulation of the *Woman's Bible*; religious book concerns had refused to carry it; all of which, Kent suspected, would only add to the curiosity surrounding it.

Many of Stanton's targeted readers, average church-going women, were less than curious about the contents of the *Woman's Bible*, however. Some were quite explicit in stating, as the Christian author Margaret Sangster did, that they had no need of a woman's Bible and "no interest in any variety of unorthodox statements."[12] The evangelical journal the *Truth* quoted an anonymous "Christian lady" who in response to the *Woman's Bible* "indignantly exclaimed, 'What fools women are, when they leave their proper place: they have no more sense than hens!' Her daughter replied, 'They have as much sense as roosters.' This is certainly true; the Higher Critic roosters led off, and the cackling hens followed."[13] Stanton claimed that her Bible was indeed intended for the average "Christian lady" and her daughter, like these readers of the *Truth*. Such readers, however, were firmly rooted in their devotion to the traditional Bible.[14] As individuals and as members of women's organizations, church-going women joined their clergy in publicly denouncing Stanton's text. Some stressed that the Bible had been a vital support for them. In dismissing Stanton's Bible, one newspaper editor no doubt expressed the view of many of her readers in declaring "the old Bible is plenty good enough for me, just as it has been for the majority of women for the past twenty centuries."[15] "At my side lies a Bible three hundred years old," Amelia Barr told the readers of *Ladies Home Journal*, "filled with the annotations and confirmations of my ancestors, who not only read it, but thought it worth their while to fight for the right to do so. I would do the same to-day, if occasion demanded it. I want no 'revised' Bible. I want no 'woman's' Bible. The Bible of the martyrs and confessors of our faith is sufficient. It has never deceived and never failed me."[16] In fact, many women objected to the *Woman's Bible* on the grounds that the Bible was directly responsible for the emancipation of women in particular, and for the rise of civilization in general. "No other agency," wrote Margaret Sangster, "has been so divine in its influence in uplifting the downtrodden, in encouraging the sad and in widening the intellectual and spiritual horizon of the world, for women as well as men."[17]

For many Christian women and their clergy, women revisers tampering with biblical texts was a sign of the perilous modern times. For a writer named Annie Bronson King, in contrast, the *Woman's Bible* was a hundred years behind the times, especially in its scholarship. Writing in the pages of the *Critic*, King suggested that in a nation where atheism and agnosticism were in decline, the *Woman's Bible* was a throwback to an earlier, more primitive belief system. "How . . . are we to account for this spectacle of white-headed women, most of whom are grandmothers and many of whom have been devoted all their lives to good and great objects, posing in the role of the Deists of the last century?" King asked. The "profound significance" of the *Woman's Bible*, for this critic, was not that women had staked out new territory, or initiated a revolution in thought, or even threatened orthodox religion; but rather that the committee had revealed the depth of women's collective ignorance. Adopting language that Stanton herself might have applied to Christian women, King proposed that the ignorance should reflect "not so much upon the writers as upon the teaching they have received." She took issue with Stanton for failing to use the insights of science, anthropology, and biblical criticism to come to an understanding of the liberal Protestant notion of "progressive revelation." "Had these women received that better understanding of the Bible which the patient toil of the neteenth-century scholar has brought us, theirs had never been compiled," King concluded.[18]

Stanton took umbrage at King's comments and rushed off a letter to the *Critic* defending the reputation of the revising committee. King's ability to evaluate the capacity of the "thirty" members of the committee at such a quick glance testified to her "remarkable" critical abilities, Stanton wrote. Perhaps King would consider infusing "into our counsels the needed wisdom" to redeem the *Woman's Bible* project. "She need not be ashamed of such coadjutors." The committee included authors of books, public speakers, editors of papers and, of course, three ministers, all of whom graduated from theological programs with honors. It was fair to assume that they, at least, were well versed in biblical criticism. But in any case, the capacity of the committee was equal to the work, Stanton contended, which was simply "to comment, in plain English, on the few texts relating to woman, and to ascertain her status, as a factor, in the Scriptures."[19]

Reading the Bible with their own "unassisted common sense," Stanton went on, she and her collaborators hoped to free women from the superstition that "the great Spirit of the Universe" was in some way responsible for their oppression. That was the political goal of the work and it required little in the way of scholarly apparatus. "If the salvation of our souls depends on obedience to [the Bible's] commands, it is rank injustice to make scholars and scientists the only medium of communication between God and the mass of the people," Stanton argued. " 'The Woman's Bible' comes to the ordinary reader like a real benediction," offering women what scholars and clergy dare not:

> It tells her the good Lord did not write the Book; that the garden scene is a fable; that she is in no way responsible for the laws of the Universe. The Christian scholars and scientists will not tell her this, for they see she is the key to the situation. Take the snake, the fruit tree and the woman from the tableau, and we have no fall, nor frowning judge, no Inferno, no everlasting punishment—hence no need of a Savior. Thus the bottom falls out of the whole Christian theology. Here is the reason why in all the Biblical researches and higher criticisms, the scholars never touch the position of woman.[20]

Two months later an unsigned review of the *Woman's Bible* appeared in the *Critic*, and again the issue of the volume's scholarly credibility was raised. Stanton's "plain English," which she considered a political weapon, had backfired. "Their right course," the reviewer suggested, "would have been to point out, in a dispassionate, scientific manner, what elements of the Bible belonged to the temporary patriarchal conditions, and then to separate these accidents from the essential religion and ethics of the sacred writings." If the tone of the *Woman's Bible* was problematic, its organizing principle was no less so. The project might have been more effective had its compilers imposed an organizational framework on their task, the critic charged. The revisers, for example, might have selected all the passages in the Bible supporting woman's emancipation and commented on those. But as it stood, they followed "no discernible pattern of selection" and, like their clerical opponents, fell victim to "literalness."[21]

Moving beyond the sheer sensationalism attending a "woman's Bible," the review in the *Critic* was the most incisive criticism Stanton received. In addition to the volume's lack of scholarship and random organization, the reviewer noted that the *Woman's Bible* was conceptually flawed because its claims were grounded in an outmoded theory of individualism. As an instrument for social change, the reviewer implied, the text had limited use. A foundation in individualism, "a snare in this woman's movement," prevented solidarity among women and between women and men. Social progress, the reviewer argued, "will be accelerated only by the union, and not by the disunion, of the interests of woman and man." The attempt in the *Woman's Bible* to downplay the differences between men and women—recasting Genesis as a fable, for example—neatly skirted the "everlasting truth" that "physiologically, psychologically, and therefore socially and politically, 'male and female created He them.' " The woman's movement should simultaneously shake off notions of woman's inferiority, embrace the differences between the sexes, and join the reviewer in admitting "that in the modern process of social revolution, woman has not yet found her exact place." The *Woman's Bible*, moreover, did not provide a map: "We beg leave respectfully to doubt that 'The Woman's Bible,' with its calm ignoring of Biblical scholarship, of fundamental economic and social problems, of the history of the evolution of the race and, above all, of that foundation of all individual, social and political rights—to wit, duty—will help much in the adjustment of woman in her proper social relations and true functions."

Reviewers and readers who espoused such a position differed both from Stanton and from her evangelical adversaries. These women agreed with Freethinkers that the church had not always accelerated women's emancipation; but like the progressive orthodox of the woman's movement, they were ultimately committed to a liberating Christian theology and the role of the church in implementing its message.

The writer Jeannette Gilder was one such reader who believed that "very few texts in the Bible . . . if taken with the proverbial grain of salt and served with common sense, will not prove sufficiently wise, just and helpful for the most progressive of her sex." Far from championing woman's special piety, Gilder too seemed disturbed by the separatist nature of the *Woman's Bible*: "I do not see why women should set about to kick against the pricks. There are some pretty harsh strictures on the conduct of the masculine congregations addressed by St. Paul and men are not foolish enough to waste their time writing a 'Man's Bible' to prove their exalted worth. They work to prove their superior merit." Gilder, a single woman who forged a successful career as the literary editor of the *New York Herald* and later as editor of the *Critic*, had little time for either empty claims of women's piety or weighty analyses of women's oppression. Rather, she seemed to agree with Annie Bronson King that the *Woman's Bible* was antiquated, an archaic weapon ineffective in contemporary battles. "Above all things," she wrote, "it is necessary to understand that woman's progress is today an established thing. No word of either a religious or secular nature could retard her advancement at this stage of the game."[22]

Even some of Stanton's liberal friends and colleagues agreed with Gilder's position. Over the years, Stanton tried to entice her cousin Elizabeth Smith Miller into joining the Bible enterprise, urging her to read the controversial writings of John William Colenso, which had wielded such influence in Stanton's own analysis. But Miller considered Stanton's Bible work an unnecessary reform and "very unworthy of [Stanton's] great powers."[23] Susan B. Anthony privately concurred. "Your experience with Mrs. Stanton's 'Bible' is about like mine," she wrote a friend. "I invested in twenty for the sake of helping her son, Robert, along a little, but the thing seemed to fall flat."[24] Anthony's response is not surprising given her waning tolerance for Stanton's attack on religion. Yet politics aside, Anthony, like Stanton's harshest critics, considered the *Woman's Bible* vastly inferior to her previous literary efforts:

> Contrast it . . . with her "Solitude of Self" [speech] given before the House Judiciary Committee in 1892 just four years ago. That is masterly—noble, and I always keep a pile on my desk, and enclose a copy to each stranger I write. . . . Of that [and] of all her great speeches I am always very proud, but of her Bibel [*sic*] Commentaries, I am not proud—either of their spirit or letter. But on the other hand, I could cry a heap, every time I read or think of them, if it would *undo* them—or do anybody or myself or our cause or Mrs. Stanton any good. They are so entirely unlike her former

self—so flippant and superficial. But she thinks I have gone over to the enemy, so counts my judgment worth nothing more than that of any other
narrow souled body. Perhaps I am shriveled up in body [and] soul, [and]
she expanded in both beyond my comprehension. But I shall love [and]
honor her to the end, whether her Bible pleases me or not.[25]

Anthony had her own reasons for regretting the publication of the *Woman's Bible*. But her criticism of the "flippant and superficial" quality of the analysis resonated with other readers.[26]

For many, the most flippant aspect of Stanton's project was its title. Friends and enemies agreed on this one issue: the title, they charged, created a misapprehension about the nature of the book (*Woman's Bible* 2:7). To her nineteenth-century audiences, the title "Woman's" Bible suggested something even more dangerous than the text bearing its name. Newspaper reports repeatedly pointed out, "the new Bible does not change the old, but simply embodies the revisers' idea of how the book should read."[27] "Had it been called 'A Woman's Bible Commentary,'" a journalist commented, "it would have been taken for what it is; simply a criticism on the attitude of the Hebrews who wrote the various books toward the position of woman, and in large measure it is justified and a good thing to have; but its title misrepresents it."[28] Stanton, however, liked the ambiguity the title created. Comparing herself favorably to John Stuart Mill, she wrote to Clara Colby:

The Woman's Bible is the most happy title that could have been selected. I am sure of that. Woman's Commentaries on what the Bible says of woman would have been too lumbering. When John Stuart Mill gave his little book the title "The Subjection of Woman" everybody carped at it. Men said it made them appear like tyrants and suggested to women that they were victims. Although they were victims, they did not like to be published as such. Mill said he knew he had hit the right title because everybody was down on it. I am sure our title is the true one for the same reason.[29]

Many found the title misleading because it advertised the book as a Bible rather than as a more pedestrian volume, a Bible commentary. But the "woman" in the title was also an overstatement claiming the volume spoke to women, and for womanhood. Both clergy and the press rushed to point out that many women themselves repudiated the *Woman's Bible*. The committee that created such a work was obviously "so feeble in numbers and influence," one reviewer speculated, "that its presumption in claiming to speak for the entire sex provokes scorn rather than serious attention."[30]

The conflict around the title encapsulates the controversial nature of the *Woman's Bible*. From Stanton's perspective, such concepts as "woman's sphere" and "domesticity" were traceable to the Bible and its misreading by women and men alike. Yet, was not the creation of a "woman's" Bible a natural extension of a "woman's" sphere? No; and that was what made the *Woman's Bible* so jarring. In nineteenth-century parlance, the possessive noun "woman's" could be joined to any number of other nouns without provoking alarm, for example: woman's sphere, woman's piety, and woman's work. The possessive marked the noun it possessed in certain acceptable ways. That is, "woman's work" was gendered and therefore implicitly different from "work" itself, which was also gendered, but invisibly so. "Work" was understood as "man's work," but it was not essential to say so. It was assumed. "Woman's work" was somehow segmented, partial, and less valued. Women could freely appropriate "woman's work" because no one else claimed it. The Bible, however, was not eligible for appropriation. It carried too much power and authority. Its wholeness (and, we might infer, its implicit maleness) was sacred. It was not woman's to appropriate, compartmentalize, or comment upon. So when readers saw the title "Woman's Bible," it was at once a familiar construction, and upon closer inspection, a deeply disturbing one.

With the publication of the *Woman's Bible*, Stanton managed to transcend her immediate audience of suffrage reformers, in large part because her text exposed the social tensions knotted beneath the surface of "woman's sphere." The public response indicated that this flexible and overused rhetoric could not be stretched far enough for the comfort of most readers, of whatever stamp. The broad base of Stanton's opposition—uniting evangelicals and liberals, women and men—testified to the centrality of the fears and anxieties this failure provoked. In the debates surrounding its publication, the *Woman's Bible* was no longer simply a book; it had become a symbol freighted with both the fears of its detractors and the hopes of its advocates.[31]

The NAWSA and the *Woman's Bible* Debate

Elizabeth Cady Stanton pinned her last hopes of mobilizing a movement to reverse the NAWSA's conservative drift on the publication and open discussion of the *Woman's Bible*. Yet from the barrage of negative response the publication of her Bible had elicited, Stanton might have anticipated the controversy to come.

On an overcast Thursday morning, January 23, 1896, the National American Woman Suffrage Association gathered in the Church of Our Father in Washington, D.C. for the opening session of its twenty-eighth annual convention. Despite the weather, an article in the press reported, several hundred "bright-faced women" filled the "cozy little church." The delegates, this reporter continued, were "all animated by the same motive, the desire to secure equal rights before the law for women."[32]

As the proceedings got underway, however, tension among the delegates overshadowed shared motives. Rachel Foster Avery, NAWSA's corresponding secretary, submitted an annual report that concluded:

> During the latter part of this year, the work of our Association has been in several directions much hindered by the general misconception of the relation of the organization to the so-called "Woman's Bible." As an association we have been held responsible for the action of an individual (an action which many of our members, far from sympathizing with, feel to be unwise) in issuing a volume with a pretentious title, covering a jumble of comment (not translation, as the title would indicate) without either scholarship or literary value, set forth in a spirit which is neither that of reverence or inquiry. If the organization were not in so many quarters held responsible for this work, I should feel it out of place to mention it here; but I should be untrue to my duties as secretary of the Association did I fail to report the fact that our work is being damaged.[33]

The report concluded with a call for a convention resolution denouncing the individual action of this officer. The unnamed but hardly unknown "officer" was, of course, Stanton, who despite her retirement from the association retained the title of honorary president. She was not in attendance at the convention. But two of her *Woman's Bible* collaborators were. Clara Colby and Lillie Devereux Blake rushed to the defense.

Colby immediately objected to the report, called for the paragraph on the *Woman's Bible* to be expunged, and offered a defense of Stanton and free speech.[34] Colby was countered by other speakers who, according to the reporter from a Washington paper, the *Evening Star*, handled the book "pretty roughly." Blake took a different tack, insisting that much of the criticism rose from sheer ignorance about the book. She asked the audience for an indication of how many had actually read the *Woman's Bible*. Reporters counted a total of eight hands.[35]

Several delegates attempted to dodge the issue, suggesting that the national convention was an inappropriate forum for a debate so clearly outside the boundaries of the suffrage movement. Influential officers, however, insisted that the book had a direct and damaging impact on suffrage work. Laura Clay of Kentucky, widely recognized as the leader of the suffrage movement in the South, spoke from experience: the *Woman's Bible* "belittled the grandeur of the Scriptures and jarred painfully upon the feelings of all devout Christians." The NAWSA treasurer, Harriet Taylor Upton of Ohio, concurred: the secretary's denunciation "voiced the sentiments of the rank and file of the party in every portion of the Union."[36] Worried that this discussion would dominate the convention, Anthony as the NAWSA president succeeded in tabling the report and at the same time chastised the younger officers for using the convention's time in this manner. If "the association should take to criticizing and repudiating the views of individual members," Anthony warned, "it would have very little time left to do anything else." A head-on collision between the *Woman's Bible*'s opponents and advocates was temporarily averted.[37]

News of Avery's attack on the "literary style" of the *Woman's Bible* reached Stanton in New York immediately. Although annoyed, Stanton did not appear particularly worried at first. "Perhaps we can induce Mrs. Avery to write one chapter to give us a lesson in style," she scoffed to Colby. Avery was not a worthy adversary, she assured her: "Mrs. Avery knows nothing about style. I never saw anything from her pen that was not very commonplace." It was clear to Stanton that the attack was a personal one, and she regretted that Avery spoke "so slightingly of all the writers of the Bible in order to belabor me." By the next day, however, Stanton was taking action. She had already fired off letters to Colby and Anthony. Now she sent a package of her speeches "to be scattered in the convention." Her son Bob was sending "Woman's Bible" newspaper articles "to the ends of the earth." Despite this flurry of activity, Stanton had begun to agonize. She wrote again to Colby, asking: "Did the Blackwells vote against [me?]"[38]

The controversies that erupted at the opening of the convention continued to seethe. Lillie Devereux Blake tried to use the meeting of the executive committee to make an end run around the larger convention. Attempting to eliminate all further public discussion of the *Woman's Bible*, Blake proposed that the NAWSA executive committee quietly accept the corresponding secretary's report dissociating the organization from the Bible project, but she also insisted on expunging from the report all the language critical of the *Woman's Bible*. Blake contended that this compromise would avert further public acrimony. Susan B. Anthony would hear nothing of it. She declared that the "first part of the clause," which assailed the book's literary value, was "just as objectionable as the last," which called for a resolution of censure. She would permit neither. Blake's compromise (intended to spare Stanton the humiliation of an official censure) struck Anthony as a capitulation to Avery and the other young leaders, her "nieces," as Anthony had dubbed them in a calmer moment. Anthony apparently had confidence that she could suppress this rebellion among her nieces. She underestimated their tenacity and organizational prowess.[39]

As the convention drew to a close, Stanton became genuinely alarmed.

Trying to rally support, she continued sending daily missives from New York to her colleagues at the meeting in Washington. Clara Colby, having published excerpts of the *Woman's Bible* in her newspaper, was no doubt quite familiar with Stanton's arguments. Still Stanton rehearsed them in detail: the only truly liberal association of women should not "cater to the religious bigotry of the age." The Bible is the "millstone round the neck of Christianity." The "best" men fear woman suffrage because "the influence [of women] would be against the secular nature of our government." Woman suffrage would be bought "at too dear price . . . in a union of church and state." And finally, Avery's attack on the "literary style" of the *Woman's Bible* was a ruse; the real fear was that the book had assailed the popular faith in the divine inspiration of the Bible. Such letter writing served a dual purpose. It fortified her and gave her the sense that she was doing something to avert this potential disaster. But the letters were not just therapeutic, they supplied Stanton's supporters with scripts, strong arguments and carefully honed words. No argument seemed more forceful to her than this: "a convention denouncing the *Woman's Bible* with Susan B. Anthony in the chair, would be a stain on Susan's honesty that would never be forgotten." Anthony would be compelled to resign the presidency, Stanton felt certain.[40]

Stanton's isolation and physical limitations pained her in this moment. "If I had had any idea of such a betrayal of principle[,] I should have gone to Washington to help strengthen the work . . . [and]oppose the bigots." As she reminded Colby, "I stood alone in demanding suffrage in the first convention but after prolonged discussion carried it unanimously at last." She stood truly alone now, dependent on others to carry her argument. "I trust that Susan will be able to stand firmly for religious equality after fifty years of education," she told Colby. "Make the speech of your life in favor of religious freedom," she urged her.[41]

Stanton's opponents were undeterred. In the final session of the convention, they presented a convention resolution on the *Woman's Bible*. Compared to the initial critique of the book in Avery's report, the resolution was relatively brief and to the point, stating simply: "That this Association is non-sectarian, being composed of persons of all shades of religious opinion, and that it has no official connection with the so-called 'Woman's Bible,' or any theological publication."[42]

In a debate that was "long and animated," opponents of the *Woman's Bible*, led by the influential NAWSA officers Carrie Chapman Catt, Rachel Foster Avery, Laura Clay, and Anna Howard Shaw, claimed that the book had driven potential suffragists from the movement.[43] Catt, who would ultimately assume Anthony's role as the organizational leader of the movement, strongly urged delegates to repudiate the *Woman's Bible*, which had been "seriously injurious to the work of organizing." She cited a district in southern Illinois where the publication of the *Woman's Bible* had effectively ended the suffrage campaign. "We had to withdraw," Catt said simply. "Every organizer has reported that [she] met the obstacle of the 'Woman's Bible' everywhere. No lecturer who has not been in the field since December 1 has any right to say that it has not injured us," she claimed. Moreover, now the reports of the Bible debate had "gone out all over the country." Without the repudiation, Catt insisted, "We shall be considered to have endorsed the 'Woman's Bible' and we shall be put back many years."[44]

Some anecdotal evidence bears out Catt's assertion that the *Woman's Bible* was harming the cause, particularly in the South. Catt served the NAWSA as the officer in charge of national organizing. In 1895, she had accompanied Susan B. Anthony on her extensive tour of the South and witnessed the situation firsthand. Even Anthony had been stunned by the religious conservatism of the region. From Wilmore, Kentucky, she wrote her sister Mary that she "had an old-fashion pious, cold & generally comfortless time" among the Methodists. At the college in Wilmore, the minister, his wife, and a faculty member "each labored to get my soul into rapport with Jesus." Anthony confided to Clara Colby that these Methodists in rural Kentucky reminded her of what she had encountered "forty years ago all through New York." She urged Colby to be careful in selecting promotional materials to send to this region, instructing her to "send only what might be called 'milk for babies'—but don't say it out loud—only words of cheer and encouragement must be sent to these people . . . especially don't send any anti church things."[45] According to several of the NAWSA national organizers, the clergy of the South posed the most vocal opposition to woman suffrage in their region, and the *Woman's Bible* gave them all the tangible proof they needed of the risks involved. Viola Neblett, vice president of the Equal Rights Association of South Carolina, sent Laura Clay, a NAWSA officer and Kentucky native, a newspaper clipping denouncing the *Woman's Bible*. "Whatever progress the woman suffragist idea may have made in this country," wrote A. B. Williams, the editor of the *Greenville Daily News*, "will probably be undone by this publication. The divorce of women and Christianity would be the most horrible and the most disastrous divorce in the world's history. We cannot imagine worse conditions than the Christian religion without women or women without religion."[46] "You will see how they use Mrs. Stanton's Bible against us," Neblett wrote.[47]

By the time of the 1896 convention, there could be little doubt that the *Woman's Bible* debate was generating publicity. The *Evening Star* ran a multicolumn background story on Stanton and the project. Other papers in Washington and New York headlined the Bible debate as the main event of the convention. Although Stanton had not appeared at the convention, a popular political cartoon placed her there. Drawn by G. Y. Coffin, the car-

Drawn by G. Y. Coffin and published in various newspapers during the National American Woman Suffrage Convention of 1896, this cartoon manipulated an image that would have been familiar to many Americans. Coffin reproduced the image of George Washington that graced the capitol rotunda, replacing the angels who normally flanked him with Stanton and Anthony. Stanton, the angel to the left of Washington, held a copy of the controversial *Woman's Bible*. Division of Prints and Photographs, Library of Congress

toon, captioned "The Apotheosis of Liberty," pictured Anthony and Stanton seated beside George Washington with the banner of the NAWSA convention draped behind them. The triumvirate had apparently ascended to heaven. Stanton was holding a copy of the *Woman's Bible*.[48]

This kind of publicity fanned the movement to censure the *Woman's Bible*. Stanton's adversaries at the convention never discussed the book's content. In fact, although Avery's report had leveled several trenchant criticisms at the book, by the convention's close, opponents had reduced their argument to a single but compelling factor: the *Woman's Bible* was damaging the cause.

Supporters of the *Woman's Bible* failed to present a united front. They included suffragists with personal loyalties to Stanton as well as delegates who opposed the resolution's spirit of censorship. Colby and Blake addressed the issue of the text's negative impact by arguing that even if the book had damaged the cause, a resolution would not fix it. Other Stanton supporters noted that in their organizing work they had not encountered opposition to the *Woman's Bible*. And if they did, offered one delegate, they should respond by saying, they "swore by Mrs. Stanton as a suffragist and not as a theologian." Still, it seemed nothing Stanton's supporters could offer countered the powerful image of doors slammed in the faces of organizers in the field. Behind those closed doors stood untold numbers of potential converts. As Laura Johns of Kansas put it: they were lost to the NAWSA as long as it "had anything to do with the Woman's Bible."[49]

Susan B. Anthony was conspicuously silent. Finally, at the urging of several representatives, she took the floor. Declaring herself a "heretic" since birth, Anthony conceded that she herself had told Mrs. Stanton repeatedly that it was a great waste of time to "descant on the barbarisms of 6,000 years ago." But the larger question at issue for the convention was whether "you will sit in judgment on a woman that has written views different from yours."

> Neither you nor I can tell but Mrs. Stanton's Woman's Bible will prove the greatest thing ever done for woman's cause. Lucretia Mott at first thought Mrs. Stanton had injured the cause of woman's rights by insisting on the demand for woman suffrage, but she had sense enough not to pass a resolution about it. . . . If you fail to teach women a broad catholic spirit, I would not give much for them after they are enfranchised. If they are going to do without thinking, they had better do without voting. . . . You had better organize one woman on a broad platform than 10,000 on a narrow platform of intolerance and bigotry.
>
> I pray you all, vote for religious liberty to each and all, without censorship, without inquisition. This resolution adopted will be a vote of censure. It cannot mean less.[50]

Anthony's image of a broad platform opposing a narrow one precisely captured the fundamental question of the direction of the suffrage movement and the specific role religion played within that struggle. Although in many respects Anthony had abandoned Stanton's campaign for a broad platform of woman's rights, her defense of Stanton before this body testified to their enduring alliance.

Despite Anthony's eloquence, several attempts to amend the resolution were made without success. Charlotte Perkins Gilman, sick with the mumps, rallied to drag herself to the meeting to "fight the resolution disavowing the 'Woman's Bible.' "[51] Gilman suggested that the resolution be

Susan B. Anthony did not approve of Stanton's focus on "religious bigotry" in the 1890s, but she staunchly defended her friend in the wake of the *Woman's Bible* denunciation. State Historical Society of Wisconsin (X3) 12220

passed simply omitting the phrase, "the so-called Woman's Bible." In this way, the organization could declare itself nonsectarian without specifically censuring Stanton. Gilman's amendment failed by only five votes, but the fact that it failed at all reveals how insistent the convention leaders were in their efforts to disgrace Stanton. Ironically, to discredit her they relied on the rhetoric she herself had championed as well as a tactic she had honed over the years. The call for a movement that was "non-sectarian" had long been part of Stanton's vision. (From her point of view, however, simply declaring the movement "non-sectarian" would not make it so.)[52] Moreover, Stanton had always placed a great deal of emphasis on the convention resolution as a tool for education and agitation.

When the unamended resolution repudiating the *Woman's Bible* finally came to a vote, it passed by a margin of 53 to 41, in Gilman's words, "hotly and closely contested."[53] Immediately obvious from the roll call vote is that the resolution drew its support from a combination of long-time Stanton rivals from the former AWSA, including Henry Blackwell, and the emerging cadre of young, conservative officers including Carrie Chapman Catt, Rachel Foster Avery, Anna Howard Shaw, Alice Stone Blackwell, Harriet Taylor Upton, and Laura Clay.[54] In fact, Susan B. Anthony was the only officer of the organization who voted against the resolution. The roll call did not reflect a detectable geographical voting pattern. Despite Catt's earlier charge that the *Woman's Bible* had caused the most damage in the South and West, delegates failed to vote as a region or even as a bloc within states.[55] Geography was not entirely irrelevant, however. The single largest source of opposition to the *Woman's Bible* came from women who had worked as organizers for the National in 1895. Led by Carrie Chapman Catt, who chaired the committee on organization, these women had traveled extensively into areas where state associations were either nonexistent or lagging. It was their perception that Stanton's antichurch campaign, and the *Woman's Bible* in particular, were damaging the work in the field. Or, as Kentuckian Laura Clay put it, "The South is ready for woman suffrage, but it must be woman suffrage and nothing else."[56] Of the sixteen women who had done national organizing work in 1895, eleven were voting delegates or officers at the 1896 convention. All but two voted for the resolution censuring the *Woman's Bible*. One of the two who opposed it was Susan B. Anthony.[57] Furthermore, the national organizers, and the NAWSA officers as well, were quite effective in mustering votes among the delegates of their home states. From Kentucky, where Laura Clay, a national organizer in 1895, ran the state association, five out of six delegates voted to censure Stanton. From Pennsylvania, where NAWSA officers Anna Howard Shaw and Rachel Foster Avery made their homes, all four delegates voted along with their leadership, delivering a total of six votes against Stanton's Bible. The enormously influential Blackwells, Henry and his daughter Alice, no doubt persuaded the Massachusetts delegates to vote in unison for the resolution.[58]

The state with the largest number of delegates, New York, was also among the most conflicted. From Stanton and Anthony's home territory, it stands to reason that most of the delegates would, out of a sense of personal

Pictured here in 1896, Carrie Chapman Catt led the National American Woman Suffrage Association's denunciation of the *Woman's Bible*. Ironically, twenty-four years later, when the Nineteenth Amendment stood before the Tennessee legislature for ratification, the *Woman's Bible* was advertised by antisuffragists as "Mrs. Catt's Bible." State Historical Society of Wisconsin (X3) 42030 and political loyalty, oppose the resolution. Eleven did. But New York was also the home of the rising politician of the next generation, Carrie Chapman Catt, and her presence and persuasiveness may have accounted for the four New York votes in favor of censure.

Despite their opposition to the *Woman's Bible*, Carrie Chapman Catt and the other young leaders were not, as Stanton insisted, religious "bigots." To varying degrees, they subscribed to the progressive orthodoxy position. Catt, for example, had written a speech titled "Women Suffrage and The Bible" in 1890 in which she took a position characteristic of liberal Protestantism. Catt conceded that "for spiritual life, the Bible is an ample guide." For "material" life—"political economy . . . governmental affairs, or social economics"—however, the Bible was a problematic teacher, owing to its "contradictory, ambiguous, [and] inexpedient" statements. Catt called upon "real Christians, to put the soul with justice and love of right on top and make the body with prejudice and selfishness bow in submission" when considering the "Word of God concerning women." Indeed, Catt argued, it was the fact that some so-called Christians had made the Bible "stand for so many abominable things"—slavery, polygamy, and prostitution—that accounted for the rise of unbelief in America. Read with "the soul on top," the Bible stood for the ideal of perfect equality, an equality promised in creation and guaranteed by Christ's redemption of the world. "Nothing in the Bible," Catt concluded, "could possibly indicate that God wished the women of America to remain in political bondage." This was the position that she and the other young leaders tended to espouse. The Bible was not literally true, but read in the spirit of Christian justice, it promised equal rights. Another NAWSA convention resolution aptly summed up the position of the new leadership. It maintained: "that the very essence of religion is just and exact justice for all women and men; therefore, the demand for woman suffrage is in the largest sense a moral and religious movement, and its advocacy is a moral and religious duty." This resolution was not adopted by the convention at large, but it did demonstrate that the leadership, even as it declared the organization "non-sectarian," embraced a religious justification for the movement that was at odds with Stanton's anticlericalism.[59]

Finally, Stanton's absence from the meeting was yet another critical factor in the outcome of the vote. Although she had with some difficulty attended her birthday celebration in November, she had not attended a NAWSA convention since 1892. As she put it in her diary, "I can still do good work with my pen. . . . But I cannot clamber up and down platforms, mount long staircases into halls and hotels, be squeezed in the crush at receptions, and do all the other things public life involves. That day is passed for me."[60] Anthony optimistically continued to advertise Stanton's appearance in the calls for each convention, and she personally rallied Stanton to attend each one.

But in point of fact, Stanton's absences had become routine. Anthony fumed with frustration over the situation. She realized how difficult travel had become for Stanton, and she knew full well that Stanton would not attend a convention without one of her sons to help her in and out of carriages. But the two children who grasped the political and historic significance of their mother's work—Harriot and Theodore—lived in Europe. The two who shared their mother's home—Bob and Maggie—could not be relied upon in this regard.

The difficulties surrounding Stanton's travel no doubt heightened the tensions at the convention on all sides. But, obviously, her absence dealt an immense advantage to the opponents of the *Woman's Bible*. It seems clear, from the accolades showered upon her at her birthday celebration only months before, that face to face with Stanton, many of the women would have thought long and hard before voting against her. She had, however, to rely on her surrogates to defend her position. And one of her most able advocates, Josephine K. Henry of Kentucky, an acclaimed public speaker who had electrified the Atlanta convention in 1895, was not in attendance. Henry's voice might have quelled some of the concern about the role of the *Woman's Bible* in the South. Stanton's available defenders, Anthony, Colby, and Blake, used every ounce of personal and political capital they commanded to squelch the resolution. They failed and then had to bear the news to Stanton and subsequently endure her disappointment and second-guessing. On the other hand, the young suffragists who planned to use the forum of the national convention to censure Stanton knew in advance they could do so with the honorary president in absentia.

Once the new leadership had achieved that aim, they were not about to allow a barrage of postmortem debates in the pages of the suffrage periodicals to further threaten harmony within their movement. Dissent from the action of the convention was effectively silenced. Anthony complained to Lillie Devereux Blake that Alice Stone Blackwell's "Woman's Journal of last week is here, and, tho this is the third issue since the convention, there is not the slightest intimation that either you or I dissented from the Woman's bible resolution."[61] Anthony feared that the official record might not fully and accurately report the debate, that Stanton's opponents might attempt to give the resolution the gloss of unanimity. She encouraged Blake to secure from Blackwell her "report of what you said on the Woman's Bible-matter—so that you may be sure to go down in history truthfully."[62]

Anthony's frustration with her young protégés continued in the months following the convention, as she attempted to balance the desires of the emerging leadership for damage control with her own issues: her friend's outrage, the vitality of her own leadership, and her genuine belief that the *Woman's Bible* vote and discussion "marks a great epoch in our movement."

Moreover, although she insisted on the need to record this history—for "all those who stood for religious freedom" to be given their due—Anthony nevertheless found her name invoked by the new leadership for the purpose of burying the *Woman's Bible* controversy. Stunned, she wrote to Clara Colby upon learning that Alice Stone Blackwell had received at least three written protests against the *Woman's Bible* resolution and had refused to publish them. In defending herself, Blackwell apparently argued that journalistic standards of fairness would have compelled her to publish not only the dissenting pieces but also a countervailing editorial, which "would hurt Miss Anthony's feelings more [and] they were quite enough hurt now."[63]

Playing off Colby's accusation to Stanton that "Miss Anthony is like putty in the hands of her young lieutenants," Anthony urged Colby to counter the new leadership's propagandizing with a full response in the pages of the *Woman's Tribune*, admitting she was putty in hands "none more willingly than Mrs. Colby's."[64] Anthony was caught in the changing of the guard. Her own belief about the necessary direction of the movement legitimated the new leadership she had hand chosen, their political conservatism, and their emphasis on pragmatic strategy at the expense of ideological boldness. And yet her personal ties to Stanton and Stanton's vision of religious liberty— which resonated in Anthony's own words as a "broad platform"—kept her with a foot in both worlds. She could not condone what she perceived as both disrespect and pure censorship on the part of her successors. Neither could she comply with Stanton's wish that Anthony respond to the "want of confidence" voted against her friend by resigning. She regretted the convention's actions, she conveyed to Colby; "for the time being the majority must have its way, but I greatly miscalculate if a year from now the vote won't be rescinded, for it cannot be possible that well-meaning women can escape seeing that their action this year was not only unjust, but in the largest sense inexpedient, for nothing unjust can in the end be expedient."[65] But despite her impassioned speeches on Stanton's behalf both before the convention and in the months that followed, Anthony ultimately joined the momentum of the new generation of suffrage leaders toward an exclusive focus on the ballot, lamenting that "at the time being, at any rate," censuring Stanton had "brought to the front the 'bible' question, making it take precedence of woman's enfranchisement in the public mind."[66] The momentum for the ballot above all else was, as the historian Ellen DuBois has pointed out, a momentum Anthony herself had done a great deal to get rolling. Her decision to concentrate on the ballot further reduced Stanton and her supporters to shadowy figures of an earlier, more radical movement.[67]

Despite their different visions, Anthony struggled somewhat futilely over the next several years to keep Stanton from disengaging entirely from the movement. In the days following the convention, Anthony conveyed to

Colby that she had gone immediately to visit Stanton and found her "as you may well understand, thoroughly indignant over the petty action of the convention."[68] During her visit, Anthony ordered Carrie Chapman Catt to appear at Stanton's home "for a show down after the convention." According to her biographer, Catt listened "pale and silent," as Anthony lit into her. Stanton took considerable satisfaction in the performance, reporting to Colby that Susan's outrage had produced some "hot scenes with her lieutenants." Chagrined, Catt left Stanton's home, in the words of her biographer, "with mingled exasperation and envy for Mrs. Stanton who had apparently managed to live eighty years without repressing any desires."[69]

Stanton pointed out to Anthony that this was not the first coup attempted by the lieutenants. Three years earlier, her resolution protesting the Sunday closing of the World's Fair had been defeated by the very same women, who argued that it was irrelevant to the suffrage convention. "Certainly, if the question of opening the gates of that World's Fair to the working men and women of the nation was irrelevant in our convention, this question of an individual member writing a book against the plenary inspiration of Joshua, Peter and Paul in the Bible must be quite as far from coming within the purview of . . . our association," Anthony agreed.[70]

Stanton maintained a stiff upper lip to the press, but privately she was stung by the convention's denunciation. She wrote to Charlotte Perkins Gilman that she was more upset by the action than she "would be willing to have our suffrage friends know. We have always organized to be the most liberal organization of women in the country & to have a majority pass such a resolution was indeed humiliating." Stanton was particularly offended by Avery's "rude and ignorant" denunciation and further galled by Alice Stone Blackwell's publication of it. Avery's report, with its long-winded indictment of the *Woman's Bible*, had, in Stanton's estimation, itself been "repudiated by the convention." Furthermore, Stanton reminded Gilman, she was not a lone wolf in this enterprise. The "learned suffrage critics' " charge that the *Woman's Bible* lacked in "either scholarship or literary value" was an insult to its several esteemed writers and their variety of literary styles.[71] But clearly, in Stanton's view, the resolution had been intended as a personal attack. Who was next? Stanton wondered—privately—whether Gilman might be a future target. After all, Stanton, indulging in a bit of gossip, jotted in the margin of a letter she had received; when Gilman's ex-husband married Grace Ellery Channing, Gilman actually attended the wedding and bequeathed their daughter to the new Mrs. Stetson. Perhaps the National Suffrage Association "should at its next convention bring in a resolution denouncing [Gilman's] lax ideas on the marriage & maternal relations!! They must clear their skirts of any responsibility for her action."[72]

Stanton was even more candid in her letters to Colby. They provide an insight into the depth of her pain and outrage. "I have written you pretty freely in regard to the situation," she told Colby, "but do not put one word I say to you in print." She was not yet ready to assess publicly the action of the convention, but she thought Colby had hit the mark when Colby identified spite as the primary motivation behind the censure. Again, Rachel Foster Avery was Stanton's favorite target. "If Rachel's grandfather had learned to wield a pen as well as a cleaver[,] she would have made a better literary critic," Stanton fumed to Colby. Worried that the cleaver reference would be too obscure, Stanton provided an explanatory footnote: Avery's grandfather "was a butcher in my native town[,] her mother [and] aunt were servants in our family, she knows that [and] thinks I talk down on her but I have no such feelings." Despite her disclaimer, Stanton insisted that if Avery "had the instincts of a lady," she would have framed her resolution more properly. "In trying to spite me she kills six other workers . . . and the fledglings all say amen," Stanton vented to Colby. In her most defensive moments, Stanton resorted to the gratuitous bigotry she so deplored in others. It stood to reason that Avery was incapable of understanding the importance of the *Woman's Bible* or judging its literary value, because, according to this logic, her grandfather was a butcher and her mother a servant for Stanton's own family. From Stanton's perspective, narrowed by rage, Avery had clearly stepped out of her place.[73]

Still nursing old wounds from the past, Stanton insisted that her opponents were out to reinjure her. She could not see that they held a viable political position. Theirs was a personal (and short-sighted) attack that would bring down the cause. "This is the most painful spectacle we have had since the inauguration of our movement," she told Colby. She predicted catastrophic results: "Susan will resign at the end of this year [and] then Mrs. Catt will no doubt take her place [and Henry] Blackwell will kill the association just as he did the American [Woman Suffrage Association]. Disintegration began when they joined the National, a few years more will do the work."[74]

While the Blackwells' paper *Woman's Journal* censored all dissenting voices in the *Woman's Bible* debate, the Freethought papers seized upon the episode and pursued it with abandon. Given her Bible's urgent message for women's emancipation, Stanton's Freethinking supporters found particularly galling the mistreatment she received from her sister suffragists. The NAWSA resolution was condemned, its supporters berated. "Elizabeth Cady Stanton Convicted of Heresy," headlined an editorial in *Free Thought Magazine* in the issue following the NAWSA convention. Casting Stanton's adversaries Carrie Chapman Catt and Henry Blackwell variously as bigots, "constantly on their knees begging favors of the church," and "mental Lilliputians, who had not the intellectual capacity to comprehend the great work that their convict was engaged in," the editor, Horace L. Green, restaged Stanton's "conviction" in epic proportions.[75]

Stanton's case was analogous to that of the great, misunderstood heretics of history, Green wrote, beginning with the "radical reformer" Jesus, and going on to the martyr Giordano Bruno, who, "like Mrs. Stanton . . . endeavored to put a more humane, scientific and reasonable construction on 'God's Word.' " Because Christians of Bruno's day were no more willing than modern ones to see changes to the Bible, "on the seventeenth day of February, 1600, the Blackwells and Catts and their bigoted associates of that ignorant day kindled a fire around the body of the brave and noble iconoclast and looked on with ecstasy as they saw his quivering flesh burn to embers." Cumulatively, the editor argued, "such trials and convictions prove the truth of the new Gospel of Evolution,—that progress is the eternal law of the universe and can not be prevented or stayed by persecution. The advocates of a great truth may be nailed to the cross, or burned at the stake, or resoluted out of 'respectable orthodox society,' but as it was with the martyr John Brown, their souls go marching on, and future generations are sure to do them justice."[76]

The magazine's trenchant critique of the NAWSA led readers, contributors, and editors to continue to debate the ultimate meanings of the *Woman's Bible*, the NAWSA censure, and even the Bible itself in the next several issues. The resolution was the focal point. Henry Blackwell politely responded to the editorial and its "unintentional" misrepresentation of the association's action. The resolution, according to Blackwell, was merely intended to silence suffrage critics who claimed that the suffrage association had officially circulated the controversial Bible—"quite at variance with the views of a large part of the American people." Furthermore, the resolution "casts no reflection whatever upon the 'Woman's Bible,' or upon its author. It applies equally to the original Bible itself, and to all theological works, no matter how orthodox. It disclaims all sectarianism, and recognizes the equal rights of all its members, Mrs. Stanton included, to hold their own opinions and to have them respected."[77]

Not surprisingly, Blackwell's position found little support in *Free Thought Magazine*. First of all, the editor inquired in rebuttal, what was Blackwell doing at the women's convention? "Would it not have been in better taste to have quietly held his peace and let the women run their own convention to suit themselves?" Green went on to charge that Blackwell had achieved national prominence only through his marriage to a distinguished woman, Lucy Stone. Obviously, however, the marriage had not engendered in Blackwell the capacity to understand the magnitude of Stanton's work, if he would so willingly sacrifice her "for the sole purpose of quieting the false apprehensions of a lot of orthodox bigots." Perhaps Blackwell had pecuniary motives, the editor speculated, exploiting Stanton's disgrace for the sake of selling more copies of the *Woman's Journal*. "We know nothing against the private character of Editor Blackwell," his Freethought rival concluded, "but we have never learned there was any blemish on the character of Judas before he betrayed Christ, or of Benedict Arnold before he betrayed his country."[78]

Jean Brooks Greenleaf, president of the New York State Woman Suffrage Association, wrote to the magazine to express her opposition to the NAWSA resolution, but also to defend Carrie Chapman Catt, whom she characterized not as a religious bigot, but rather as "a practical woman" who had encountered difficulties in her organizing work. Catt was "liberal-minded," but young and politically inexperienced. "Had these women borne the opposition that the pioneers of our cause encountered," Greenleaf suggested, "the roars of the present lion in the way would not have stricken them with such terror."[79] The agnostic Lucy Coleman agreed. Henry Blackwell harbored an old grudge against Stanton, Coleman explained, but she wondered "how many of this majority of women who cast that vote of condemnation knew what they were doing?" Stanton had labored for a half century for women's emancipation and now "these modern women, who have but recently espoused the cause of woman's enfranchisement . . . presume to reprehend her."[80] Josephine K. Henry published an article in the magazine that was even less generous in its interpretation. "The few women who recently condemned the 'Woman's Bible' in the national Suffrage Convention before they had read it, at once published to the world their mental limitations."[81] Helen Gardener, another of Stanton's committee members, concurred. The resolution was hypocritical. What was Stanton doing in the *Woman's Bible*, but simply commenting on the translated texts prepared by male scholars? "Surely no one not a hopeless fanatic can say that women have not the right to do this. Every time that Reverend Anna Shaw preaches *she* does it," Gardener argued. But more important, the women who passed the resolution were "unable to see that by so doing they are giving the strongest weapon possible against their own enfranchisement into the hands of men," who will then turn the tables and use women's religious "fanaticism" against them. Gardener believed the resolution would "set the cause back for years—as no other act could have done." She had expected as much from the WCTU, "but for the incoming leaders of Suffrage to have taken such a step will weaken the work done by those who made the younger leaders a possibility."[82]

Gardener, Henry, and other Stanton supporters hoped that the resolution would be rescinded. The editor of *Free Thought Magazine* provided a revised text: "Resolved: That this national Woman's Congress gratefully thanks our great leader, Elizabeth Cady Stanton, for the grand and noble work she is engaged in endeavoring to revise portions of the Bible that it shall not here-after continue to degrade our sex in the eyes of all civilized people as it has heretofore done."[83]It was the duty of the members of the association, the editor contended, to have endorsed Stanton's work—work that was, after all, done on their behalf. Instead they passed a "cowardly resolution to gain popularity with the orthodox church. With this resolution the National As-sociation struck their greatest leader and best friend a blow, for the sake of making friends with their direst enemies."[84]

Stanton deeply appreciated Green's support. She wrote her son Theodore that Green "has attacked the bigots. He handles them without gloves. I did not know he intended to do it. However, the action in Washington sold off the edition in a twinkling and we are getting ready for the second edition."[85]

The Political Fallout of the NAWSA Resolution

In the immediate aftermath of the NAWSA's repudiation, Anthony too felt that, in some fundamental sense, the censure had backfired. The publicized discussion of the Bible debate brought nationwide attention to the book and its author. "These short-sighted girls have precipitated the result which they declared they wished to avoid," Anthony noted.[86]

Yet the longer-range effects were very different. The *Woman's Bible* de-bate not only solidified Stanton's position as an outsider. The controversies were a crucial factor in the broader transformation of the suffrage move-ment at the turn of the century. As well as the resolution repudiating Stan-ton's Bible, the 1896 NAWSA convention witnessed subtle efforts on the part of both Stanton and Anthony's protégés to jockey for power. Stanton's supporters came up short every time. The leadership who triumphed in the Bible debate were positioning themselves to steer the movement into the twentieth century.

Stanton's treatment at the hands of the younger women ultimately served to convince her more firmly than ever that she had truly "outgrown" the movement, much to Anthony's distress. On the most basic level, this convic-tion exacerbated a labor crisis that Stanton's focus on religion had already precipitated for Anthony, whom Stanton once described as "afraid of a pen."[87] Anthony had indeed grown accustomed from their years together to relying on Stanton as her "Jimmy Grind" to crank out opinion and analy-sis.[88] Before the conventions in 1896 and 1898, she appealed to Clara Colby to "put on your thinking cap and prepare the resolutions," because Stanton would no longer "do a thing."[89] Colby seemed Stanton's logical heir appar-ent, her "Spiritual Undertaker," because of her progressive stances on polit-ical issues and her obvious literary ability.[90] But it was not at all clear that

Colby was comfortable with the arrangement. In response to a letter from Colby apparently questioning the policy of crediting her own writing to Anthony, Anthony wrote: "Of course [the editor] will want the article over my name—and it was to be thus placed—that I asked you to write it—because I thought you could sum up our present position better than Mrs. Stanton. . . . So if you cannot do it for me—I must grind it out by myself."[91] Perhaps Colby's resistance to this arrangement was the pivotal issue, but Anthony also complained to Stanton that Colby was too encumbered by "her house, hog, Indian, etc." to drop everything and become Anthony's ghost writer (a position ultimately filled by the journalist Ida Husted Harper).[92] In any case, it is unlikely, given Colby's antipathy to Anthony's other "lieutenants," that the partnership would have had a bright future. The difficulties of working with Colby magnified for Anthony her loss of Stanton and her reliable pen, for now "I know of no one to look to."[93]

But the problem was not just that religion, and in particular, the Bible debate occupied so much of Stanton's energy. Anthony also grew intolerant of what she perceived as the irrelevant and apolitical nature of the religion issue. Her impatience with "the Bible question" stemmed from her belief that it was an evasion of responsibility, "a way of seeking a 'refuge of lies,' " of blaming the past for the sins of the present.[94] She regretted that Stanton so rarely "centered [her] big brain on the crimes we ourselves as a people are responsible for" when her trenchant criticisms were so urgently needed on a wide array of topics.[95] Arguing that race and sex discrimination were the "false religion of this day," Anthony chided Stanton that contemporary "barbarism does not grow out of ancient Jewish Bibles—but out of our own sordid meanness!! . . . Nobody does right or wrong because St. Paul [told] them to—but because of their own *black 'true inwardness'*—The trouble is in *ourselves to day*—not in men or books of thousands of years ago."[96]

But at least Stanton's critique of the clergy, church, and Bible still had a political edge to it. Anthony had even less sympathy for the New Thought and "esoteric" influences imbuing the pages of the *Woman's Bible*. Anthony's traveling companion of these years, Anna Howard Shaw, related a telling incident that took place when she and Anthony visited the British Theosophist Annie Besant. Though impressed by Besant's intellect, Anthony was, according to Shaw, quite appalled by Besant's "flowing and picturesque white robes, . . . her bare feet, . . . her incessant cigarette smoking," but above all, the "other-worldliness" of her views. Anthony concluded her visit by urging Besant to "make that aura of yours do its gallivanting in this world, looking up the needs of the oppressed, and investigating the causes of present wrongs."[97] Anthony's pragmatic approach to politics left little room for speculation of the sort in which either Besant or even the more down-to-earth Stanton engaged.

In theory, Anthony championed a broad platform of woman's rights. In actuality, she had learned from a career of cumulative disappointments that only a narrow platform was politically viable. She allowed little in these years to disrupt her focus on building an institution, a suffrage movement equipped with the funds and leadership to survive her. That was her legacy. And it directed much of her action. When, for example, Stanton proposed spending the summer with Anthony in Rochester in 1897, Anthony panicked about the impact Stanton's presence would have on the work. "You know if Mrs. Stanton were here, the summer would have to be spent in catering and visiting."[98] Much as Anthony loved Stanton, and much as she tried to keep Stanton as an active presence in the movement, she would not permit even a visit from Stanton to derail her work.

Those she trained to follow her had already shown themselves politically able. By the late 1890s the young women whom Anthony had cultivated to be her loyal lieutenants were not only voting independently of her; they had virtually engineered the *Woman's Bible*'s repudiation. They also politically marginalized Stanton's leading loyalists and the principal defenders of the controversial Bible, Josephine K. Henry, Lillie Devereux Blake, and Clara Colby.

Stanton's primary supporter in the South met with ostracism in the wake of the *Woman's Bible* debacle. Josephine K. Henry had not attended the 1896 NAWSA convention; still, her work on the *Woman's Bible* and her defense of it and Stanton in the press essentially ended her career in suffrage politics. In a step maneuvered by Laura Clay, the newly elected auditor of the NAWSA, Henry was expelled from the Kentucky Equal Rights Association because of her participation in the *Woman's Bible* project. Differences of opinion on the Bible were significant enough to rend organizations and shatter friendships. "You may think the Bible is God's holy word," Henry wrote to Clay, "pure, instructive, elevating and consoling, and the charter of liberty. While I think with its cruelty [and] debauchery, its contradictions and absurdities, its nonsense and false reasoning, its lustfulness, polygamy, slavery, intemperance, cannibalism, murder, rapine, robbery, ruin, war and this curse upon woman, it is the worst of all books, but why should that mar friendship?" Apparently, Henry had attempted to resign "gracefully" before the state association took official action to eject her as an "undesirable member." Still, she claimed to have nothing but "the kindest feeling for every member mixed . . . with a little double distilled compassion for the narrowness and bigotry exhibited."[99]

At the national level, Henry, Blake, and Colby were essentially so hamstrung by the new leaders that they were unable to effect any change in the direction of the association. At the 1896 NAWSA convention, Blake and Colby, who between them had decades of office-holding and political experience, made several unsuccessful bids for national office, losing every time to one of Anthony's enormously popular "lieutenants." All three of Stanton's defenders were placed on the same NAWSA committee for 1896, the committee "on plan of work." This committee, which had once functioned broadly as a steering committee for the national organization, had been chaired in 1895 by Carrie Chapman Catt. However, Catt had funneled her personal energies and the focus of the national association into the newly formed committee on organization. This committee was granted a fundraising capacity and solicited donations to carry out its organizing work.[100] In the meantime, the plan of work committee, which had spawned the committee on organization, was entirely superseded by it. The plan of work committee continued to exist, but it had no budget and seemed to be composed of NAWSA members who were politically marginalized in the newly reorganized movement. In addition to Colby, Blake, and Henry, two other lone wolves were assigned to it: Lavinia Hatch, the one delegate from the old Massachusetts "National" association, and Abigail Scott Duniway, the western suffragist with a reputation for being a political maverick.[101]

Not only did Stanton's supporters lose convention elections and find themselves assigned to a politically visible but impotent committee; they looked on helplessly as Anthony's underlings solidified their power. At the convention, for example, Blake had proposed term limits for the position of the NAWSA president. Her proposal was defeated unanimously.[102] Clearly, Blake had reason to be concerned about the future direction of the organization. In the months following the Washington convention, both Colby and Blake discovered Anthony's lieutenants had replaced them as organizers in the statewide woman suffrage campaigns in California and Delaware.[103] Anthony tried to run interference, but to no avail. She had already conceded so much of her power to Anna Howard Shaw and, increasingly, to Carrie Chapman Catt, that, as Anthony put it to Blake, "I do not feel that I have a right to countermand her orders, or to give her orders."[104] When Blake was also displaced from representing the NAWSA at the Republican and Democratic national conventions later that year, she again appealed directly to Anthony to intervene. Anthony explained that she had appointed Catt "manager of the Republican and Democratic conventions," and in her own absence, and that of Vice President Anna Howard Shaw, she considered that Catt, as "the National Organizer should be the one to have the management. Therefore, I shall leave it absolutely to her to select the other members of the delegation."[105]

Their unconventional religious ideas and participation in the *Woman's Bible* were the major strikes against Blake and Colby as far the new leadership was concerned, but both women also brought other complications to the movement. In particular, both were handicapped by their precarious financial positions. Women who were wealthy as well as effective organizers, like Carrie Chapman Catt, seemed to get the nod over Blake, Colby, and other impoverished religious radicals. Blake, for example, had originally been asked to go to California to serve in the campaign there, but her work was consistently rerouted or canceled entirely by Catt. In February, Anthony wrote Blake to cancel her California appearance and explained that she and Catt had decided that Blake would be more appropriate for the Delaware campaign.[106] By April, Blake's husband had died. She was counting financially on the work in Delaware, but discovered that Catt had suddenly replaced her there too and taken over the Delaware campaign herself. Then in May, Blake learned that she would not be part of the delegation to the national political conventions. Anthony explained the bottom line; "the cash question is the one that hinders, or will hinder, large numbers of women. . . . If each woman could pay her own expenses, the question would be quite different. There is no money out of which such expenses can be paid save the organization fund, and I expect that Mrs. Catt has already calculated . . . to more than use up all that was pledged."[107]

Colby too suffered financially from the new leadership's control of the NAWSA funds and their willingness to sideline her. Anthony was more sympathetic to Colby than to Blake, but still seemed powerless to alter the situation. She wrote to Colby, "I feel the world—our cause especially—robbed because of the enslavement of poverty with its appalling burdens—that hold you away from the grand work you long to do."[108] In point of fact, had either Blake or Colby had the money to pay her own way, she could have stayed at the center of suffrage organizing. This was true of several of the "liberal" women who had contributed to the *Woman's Bible*. The Reverend Olympia Brown, for example, wrote to Colby lamenting, "It is painful to think of the things I would have done in the suffrage work had I had money." Still, Brown admitted, her financial sacrifices for the movement paled in comparison to Colby's.[109] Under Catt's (and later Anna Howard Shaw's) guarded leadership, what money was available to pay organizers went to the lieutenant-nieces. Anthony was left in the thankless position of making excuses to Blake and Colby. When Colby offered to go to California anyway and take up collections to pay her expenses, Anthony was skeptical; Anna Howard Shaw could barely command donations, and she was the most popular woman in California. Furthermore, the speaking positions paid for by the California Joint Campaign Committee were already being filled by Shaw and Catt, Anthony explained, "since it is pledged to pay them it will not engage to pay any other one . . . I am pulling every possible string to get as many places for non partisan women speakers as possible, and your name stands *first* on my list—after Shaw & Catt."[110]

Frozen out of the leadership and from organizing work, Colby, Blake, and

Henry attempted to use what little power was delegated to them as the heart of the plan of work committee. When this committee proposed significant changes in the focus and operations of the organization the following year at the 1897 convention, they were soundly rejected.[111] Anthony expressed her frustration to Colby who, as the committee chair, had erred in being so ideologically bold. Instead of trying to "make the entire revolution," Anthony reprimanded Colby, she would have been better off with a more modest goal, simply asking the "delegates to work for your election as the new auditor."

Anthony, confident in the leaders she had selected, with whom she shared great affection, did not want to look too carefully at these disagreements. In the wake of the Bible debacle, she had to admit the narrow vision of her lieutenant-nieces, but after that controversy had receded a bit, she more often explained the differences between Stanton's loyalists and her own as personal, not political or ideological, conflicts. Anthony particularly lamented the marginalization of Colby, whose talents she genuinely admired. But ultimately, the fault was Colby's, Anthony told Stanton: "I do wish she had the faculty of chiming in with the other young girls—and so become a helper—and not a mere criticiser!!"[112]

It would be easy to dismiss these controversies as personality conflicts. Certainly those abounded. But the political and religious differences among these groups of women had long-term political, financial, and even historical consequences. These women—Catt, Shaw, Avery, Blackwell, and, to a lesser extent, Clay—maintained control of the NAWSA for years to come.[113] And these leaders successfully managed to keep New Thought and Freethought feminists—particularly the perpetually destitute Colby and the "fair Lillie"—marginalized.[114] One expression of this hostility was the new leadership's critical stance toward Colby's newspaper, the *Woman's Tribune*. As Anthony tried to explain to Colby, "your espousal of the '*Woman's Bible*'—and the publication of it in your paper—has cut off all possibility of your gathering around you the majority of the suffrage women—Very many of them still cling to the Bible as a sacred book—and they will not have a paper that ridicules it—in their homes for their children to see."[115]

In addition to boycotting the *Tribune*, the new leadership, as a general policy, refused to entrust Stanton followers with responsibilities and minimized, whenever possible, their public exposure. Rachel Foster Avery, as the NAWSA corresponding secretary, was principally responsible for arranging the agendas of the convention programs as well as the bi-annual hearings before the Senate Select Committee on Woman Suffrage and the House Committee on the Judiciary.[116] The NAWSA, for example, planned a major "Jubilee" for 1898, celebrating fifty years of suffrage agitation. The historic nature of the event inclined many of the pioneers of the movement to anticipate a place on the program. Anthony agreed, in principle, that the women who had long been affiliated with the movement, and with herself and Stanton, should be given a place on the program, especially since many of them, Elizabeth Harbert, Olympia Brown, Matilda Joslyn Gage, Isabella Beecher Hooker, and Lillie Devereux Blake, had become virtual outsiders since the merger of 1890. Anthony's premier concern was, of course, to have Stanton present at the Jubilee, although all along Stanton expressed concern to Avery that she would be "unable to walk up the steps to the capitol."[117] Anthony had her work cut out for her, trying to convince Rachel Foster Avery, the program committee chair, of the importance of including these outsider women at the Jubilee. "I do so want Mrs. Stanton at my right hand at each hearing," Anthony wrote Avery, adding, "not that I do not love & value my right-hand girls each & all—but that [I] do long to have this last appearance of the 'old war horses' —before both [House and Senate] Committees." Avery was less than moved. She would, of course, make space for Stanton, but she wrote to Anthony, "when I hear that you have invited Mrs. Harbert, and that I must put Mrs. Blake, Mrs. Gage, Mrs. Seymour Howell and Mrs. Hooker on, it makes me want to be acting Chairman of the Program Committee another twenty years."[118]

While some of the older "war horses" were satisfied just to complain about their treatment at the hands of Avery and the other younger women, Blake—the youngest of the lot, but still a good twenty-five years older than Avery—was determined to do something about it. She burrowed her way onto the program. Blake argued that she had organized a union of all the suffrage societies in greater New York City and wished to address the House Judiciary Committee because she "had a new viewpoint to represent." Furthermore, she pointed out, she was a ranking veteran of the movement, "having come into active work in 1869," and she expected to be given a place.[119] When Blake was put off by Avery in her quest for a spot at the congressional hearings, she appealed to Stanton to intervene on her behalf. Circumventing the younger women, Stanton simply offered Blake her own time at the hearings and caused an uproar among Avery, Anthony, and the others.[120] Anthony conceded and demanded that Avery find a place for Blake on the program. But Anthony nonetheless tended to dismiss Blake as yet another difficult personality who could not manage to get along with her "nieces." Blake was even worse than Colby in this regard, Anthony felt, as "she has managed for the last six years to keep Mrs. Stanton in a discontented state of mind in regard to me and the business committee."[121]

It was little wonder that Blake and Stanton's other associates were discontented. Avery exercised iron control over speaking opportunities. To Stanton's supporters, known to be both religious and political radicals, Avery started assigning speech topics—selecting the most narrow, mind-numbing, dry, and lackluster—when she allowed them to speak at all. Anthony objected to the policy and instructed Avery to allow the women to name their topics, but Avery would not comply. She had two reasons: she hoped Stanton loyalists might refuse the honor of speaking on an assigned topic; and, if not, at least by assigning the narrow topics, Avery had a better chance of keeping "Mzoomdar and all the other Orientals" off the program.[122] She even attempted to alter the topics of Stanton's two addresses, which she would be sending on for someone else to read in the congressional hearings of 1898. Stanton had written speeches on "Educated Suffrage" and "Immigration Restriction," and Avery complained to Anthony that these themes were off the topic: "they cannot possibly have a place in the program of such a Hearing."[123]

The division between Stanton and Anthony's political protégés culminated in the NAWSA presidency contest of 1900, in which Blake ran unsuccessfully against Catt. Although Stanton was no longer active in the organization, she threw what weight she could still command to Blake's cause, praising her "splendid work for the last thirty years." Stanton also could not resist a jab at Catt: "I admire Mrs. Catt greatly. I think her a woman of wonderful ability—executive ability, I mean. She is younger than Mrs. Blake, she has a wealthy husband, who is willing to help her: she has what Susan B. Anthony has and I had not, the faculty of raising money. Susan was always a great beggar. I never was. Mrs. Catt is."[124] When it appeared Blake had little support in the upcoming election, Stanton consoled her younger protégé and urged her to "use your powers as a free lance, you can do better work with your pen than as an officer in an association with restricted limits—and so can I."[125] Blake, however, was not ready to heed that advice. By April 1900, Blake presided over a new suffrage organization she formed with Josephine K. Henry, the National Legislative League. She urged Elizabeth Harbert to join: "I know that you are familiar with the proceedings of the N.A.W.S.A. for some years past and will realize that after the election in Washington there would never again be any possibility of work within its lines for me or any of the other older workers."[126]

The new leadership minimized the role Stanton and her Freethought and New Thought colleagues had played in the late nineteenth-century movement. Even in their histories and private correspondence, they continued that trend. A virtual newcomer to the movement in the waning days of Stanton's public life, Carrie Chapman Catt simply never understood the older woman's appeal as a leader or as a person. As she wrote to Alice Stone Blackwell in 1930, "I never came in contact with Mrs. Stanton. I had barely met her and had taken lunch at her house once or twice. I never liked nor admired her, although I thought she had a real gift with her pen." Furthermore, Anthony's devotion to Stanton was puzzling to Catt, and she doubted aloud whether the relationship was one of "simple affection and devotion or if there were other reasons. I still wonder."[127] By 1930, Catt, who had in her youth invested considerable energy in censuring Stanton, could barely remember her. What she managed to remember was the inexplicable mystery of Anthony's devotion to Stanton, an attachment so perplexing it could only be explained by some "other reason"—Catt's insinuation of a hidden perversion. The memory of Stanton seemed to fade with other women of Catt's generation as well who (with less bitterness) blurred the boundaries between Stanton and Anthony. The historians Elisabeth Griffith and Ellen DuBois have demonstrated that the younger women sanctified Anthony and ignored Stanton, even crediting Anthony with the Seneca Falls convention that she did not attend. Similarly, in her autobiography, Anna Howard Shaw constructed Anthony as the sole mover and shaker in the Married Woman's Property Act agitation in New York State, a campaign Stanton and Anthony had labored on together.[128]

It was precisely the rising influence of these young, conservative leaders within the suffrage movement that Stanton most feared. For years she had argued that their narrowing political focus endangered the movement's traditional vision of a broadly based emancipation of women, one that insisted on women's simultaneous liberation in the state, the church, and the family. In publishing her Bible, Stanton hoped at best to radicalize the conservative elements within the NAWSA and at least to counteract them. Her efforts backfired. Little did she expect that the Bible debate would actually cement the unlikely alliance of religiously liberal, but politically pragmatic, figures like Catt, Avery, and Alice Stone Blackwell with more conservative religious women like Anna Howard Shaw and Laura Clay.

Historians have associated the emergence of this more conservative leadership with the "mainstreaming" of the suffrage movement—the simultaneous broadening of the constituency and narrowing of the political agenda. With Stanton censured and her supporters virtually ostracized, the NAWSA experienced little dissension in solidifying a pragmatic reform strategy that focused almost exclusively on the ballot as the means of redressing women's social and political inequities. It was a strategy that catered to the most conservative elements in the movement. With Stanton no longer physically able or personally willing to lead a revolution, the younger women who had been her colleagues were left with little more than their individual ideas and talents. They forged yet another liberal alternative to the NAWSA in 1902, an organization that became the Federal Woman's Equality Association, but its leaders suffered the fate of being a splinter group. They lacked the funds and visibility of the NAWSA. As Olympia Brown put it to Clara Colby: "They have the money & the machine. . . . We can only work here & there as we can without their knowledge."[129]

The *Woman's Bible* and the Public Discourse on Womanhood

In the two years following the NAWSA "Bible" convention, the aftershocks of the repudiation continued to register in women's organizations around the country. The NAWSA's public response to Stanton's Bible transformed the book's status from a political fracas among suffragists to an issue of public debate. Stanton's visibility within the NAWSA and the negative impact of her Bible on suffrage organizing had formed the NAWSA's official rationale for denouncing her work. The responses among the broader public suggest the extent to which Stanton challenged social values beyond suffrage circles. For many of her readers, she had dangerously undermined the Bible, organized religion, and women's claims to piety—the very moral fiber of American society. National and local women's organizations, private citizens, and clergymen making efforts to discredit the *Woman's Bible* could now use the condemnation of Stanton's own suffrage organization to bolster their views. The evangelical editors of the *Watchman* breathed a collective sigh of relief when news of the NAWSA's repudiation hit the papers, reassuring their readers: "The women can be trusted to deal with the so-called Woman's Bible as it deserves."[130]

In response to the public uproar, the Woman's Christian Temperance Union, like the NAWSA, felt compelled to denounce the *Woman's Bible* at its annual convention in 1896. Rumors of Frances Willard's involvement in the project—dispensed somewhat carelessly owing to Stanton's loose definition of her "committee"—threatened harmony within the Union. Although Stanton insisted that Willard had initially allowed her name to be published as an adviser to the project, the national WCTU convention rushed to assure its membership of Willard's innocence.[131] Like other critics, the women of the WCTU took issue with Stanton's title, stating: "While we recognize the right of women to make commentaries on the Bible, as men have done from the beginning until now, we regret the name 'Woman's Bible' to any volume, and we further deplore the misapprehension of the press, secular and religious, in styling this commentary on those parts of the Bible only relating to woman as a new version of the Scriptures."[132]

Both the NAWSA's and the WCTU's repudiation of the *Woman's Bible* resulted from the association of their national leadership with the Bible controversy. However, local women's organizations without direct ties to Stanton or her Bible also denounced it in their meetings. Almost two years after the NAWSA's condemnation, the Board of Censors of the Topeka, Kansas, Federation of Woman's Clubs voted to exclude the *Woman's Bible* from its library on the grounds that it was "written in a flippant, coarse and inelegant style."[133] Similarly, a convention of women in Richmond, Virginia, passed a resolution denouncing the *Woman's Bible* and reportedly sent a copy of its action to every newspaper in the country. The fact that none of the Virginians had ever seen or read the book was of little consequence. They admitted as much, yet pressed on in their condemnation. Their action reflected a striking tendency in the public response to the *Woman's Bible*: people did not have to read it to know they did not like it. These women, Stanton retorted, manifested "the same spirit of religious bigotry that burned, drowned and tortured witches in the seventeenth century."[134]

Jewish women too found the work less than persuasive and the attack on the Pentateuch particularly troubling. The Jewish *Messenger* predicted that no Jewess would be found in America supporting Stanton's Bible. At least one contingent of Jewish women openly expressed their disappointment in the *Woman's Bible*. A group visited Stanton to convey in person their dismay at her distortion of their religious traditions. Stanton reported the visit to Elizabeth Smith Miller:

> They said Jewish women were reverenced in their religion, that the wife and mother was considered the most exalted position a human being could fill; that their men thought it would be a desecration to their holy office to tax them with public affairs, they worship their women. Why, then, if they really do consider them so exalted, do they say in their synagogues every Sunday "I thank thee, O Lord, that I was not born a woman!" "That," they say, "is an interpolation in our service and was not originally there." If the church does not approve of it why is it not expunged? "It is not meant in an unfriendly spirit to degrade or humiliate women." "But it does," said I, "nevertheless. Suppose they said, I thank thee, O Lord; that I was not born a jackass." Oh no, ladies, the Jews accord no more honor than the Gentiles.[135]

Stanton shared this anecdote with Miller, presumably, to illustrate the superiority of her own position. Stanton's tone, her cultural insensitivity in assuming a Sunday Sabbath, her use of the Christian term "the church" to refer to organized Judaism all indicate that she was simply not open to a new interpretation of Judaism based on the lived experiences of her readers. Her anecdote permits but a brief glimpse into the reactions of Jewish women to the *Woman's Bible*. Still, it suggests they would have found a great deal of the text objectionable. Stanton's harsh reading of the lives and characters of the Jewish matriarchs, as well as her conviction that the patriarchal culture of the Hebrew Bible was responsible for the flawed state of contemporary gender relations, no doubt prompted the visit. But the women's effort to convey to Stanton that "the wife and mother was considered the most exalted position" in their religious practice fell on deaf ears.[136]

Although Stanton continually pointed to contemporary Jews who had in-spired her—Ernestine Rose and Felix Adler, in particular—she participated in the anti-Semitism that was a defining element in the Freethought move-ment. Yet she had trouble understanding why she might be labeled a "Jew hater," an appellation she vigorously denied.[137] In Stanton's way of thinking, Jews were no worse than Christians in terms of their historical record on woman's rights, but anyone who rose to defend biblical misogyny provoked her harsh judgment. Her colleagues and supporters in the Freethought movement accentuated these tensions. When, for example, the woman's clubs of Topeka removed copies of the *Woman's Bible* from the schools and libraries of their area, *Free Thought Magazine* admonished "these little fe-male bigots . . . [who] can swallow all the nastiness in the old Jew book with-out wincing, [yet] are horrified at the 'coarseness' and 'inelegance' of the *Woman's Bible*."[138]

Freethinkers were, it seems, equally committed to discrediting Christians and Jews; and the *Woman's Bible* provided an irresistible opportunity to vent hostility in several directions at once. In fact, the Freethought press kept Stanton's book in the public eye during these years and continued to gener-ate a discussion about the relationship of religion to women's emancipation. Dubbing Stanton the "Thomas Paine of her day and generation" and "the female Voltaire of the last years of the nineteenth century," Freethinkers celebrated the *Woman's Bible* as "the best and most important work that has ever been done in behalf of the rights of woman."[139]

Delighted by the antagonism the *Woman's Bible* generated among the clergy, Freethought leaders applauded Stanton's efforts to emancipate women "from the thralldom of pietistic pretension and priestly falsehood in regard to woman's indebtedness to the Bible." The wrath of orthodox clergy was not surprising: "the new work appeals especially to women; and women, the clergy have been accustomed to regard generally as beyond the reach of radical, free thought influence."[140] Women's unqualified respect for the clergy had been a persistent obstacle to their emancipation, wrote H. L. Green, the editor of *Free Thought Magazine*, but the *Woman's Bible* threat-ened to undermine that relationship. Stanton's strike at the "taproot of [woman's] slavery" was a justifiable cause for alarm among clergy, Stanton's collaborator Josephine K. Henry agreed, because it would further encour-age women to interpret the Bible for themselves:

The clergy are finding out that they have a heavy contract in their hands to keep women in the church pasture. Those who escape into the high-road of investigation find such rich mental browsing that they refuse [any] longer to listen to the mildewed pulpit platitudes from the Mosaic and Pauline codes, which teach that woman is the cause of all evil in the world, that she is inferior to man, as man is to God, and that her highest privilege is to confess to her priest, and live in obedience to her lord and master. If there were nothing wrong in this system, surely the ecclesiastics should hail with joy the fact that women are studying the Bible.[141]

But would women even read the *Woman's Bible*, critics commonly asked? "Not if the clergy can prevent them," Henry responded. Without reading it themselves, Henry pointed out, clergy were warning women against it and using their influence to ban it from libraries, but "happily their influence is not what it once was."

Freethinkers' vigorous defense of Stanton's Bible went beyond the concern for women as theological victims, having been "duped, driven, browbeaten and hoodwinked by priestcraft for ages."[142] This anxiety was frequently expressed, but a fear of a more acute nature underlay it. As their own interpretations of the Bible revealed, Freethinkers were particularly concerned about the relationship between the Bible, the church, and women's sexual vulnerability. The Bible itself contained many passages of such an obscene and disturbing nature that Freethinkers wondered aloud why the Book had not been banned under the Comstock Law, a law named for its chief proponent Anthony Comstock that declared illegal the use of the U.S. postal system for the distribution of "obscene materials."[143] Parker Pillsbury, Stanton's former coeditor of the *Revolution*, warned readers against the fifth chapter of Numbers, for example, in which instructions for a purification ritual to be administered to the unfortunate wife of a jealous husband are elaborated. "Let any one attempt to read to his family, or even to himself aloud . . . [this passage] and then see if he can get the loathsome taste out of his mouth for at least one whole day! Is there another book in all the languages and literatures of the world, that . . . tolerates such filthiness?" Pillsbury asked.[144]

The early years of the Christian church provided no safe haven for women either, an editor wrote in a thinly veiled attack on the Catholic Church, as "husbands by thousands fled from their wives, and multitudes contracted no marital relations but swarmed in monasteries," which, he insisted, destroyed "manliness" and resulted in a thousand years of "mental and moral darkness."[145] The church of the nineteenth century was no better; women were discovering "the cold, hard fact that Bible Christianity is the one drunken religion that is debauching the nations of the earth." In fact, according to Josephine Henry's article, the hypocrisy of the church was directly implicated in the rise in crime against women. Christian America boasted its moral supremacy and its "millions of Bibles," but it was in this devout nation where "young college men who will soon seize the reins of church and state, mob in the streets of our cities helpless girls, while they rend the air with yells of hyena laughter, and the ribaldry of satyr lust as they pursue to disgrace and death their helpless victims." Still, Henry argued, "not a preacher throughout our broad land utters a word of protest." The double standard that perpetuated sexual violence was encoded in the Bible, but it was disseminated unchecked because of the clergy's refusal to act boldly as moral guides. The Bible, the guide for American civilization, was at the root of the social problem because it gave divine sanction to the practices of incest, murder of women, rape of little girls and maidens, and "filthy stories of concubinage."[146]

Women, Henry urged, ought to grow tired of "hearing the church called 'She' when in reality it is a 'He' institution, with a He God, He Christ, He priesthood, He Bible, and only He angels in heaven." For women to embrace the *Woman's Bible* was the only way clear. "When a truth once gets abroad in the world no power on earth can imprison it," Henry concluded. "The 'Woman's Bible,' whatever its defects, is heralding truth."[147]

Responding to Her Critics

In December 1896, Stanton read Andrew Dickson White's *A History of the Warfare of Science with Theology in Christendom* (1896). Or more likely, White's treatise was read to her by the young woman whom she had hired for that purpose, two hours a day, since July. Stanton was on fire, she wrote to Elizabeth Smith Miller. She would be too busy to spend Christmas with Miller in Geneva, she would be working every day, as she put it, on "my Bible and Reminiscences." White's book had reawakened her to the Bible's "dangerous influence." "I will work now more than ever on the Woman's Bible. I do hope I shall live to finish it."[148] With renewed zeal, Stanton set about the publication of the second volume. She began by responding to the host of criticisms generated by volume one.

Patiently, but relentlessly, Stanton defended her work and attempted to help readers interpret its importance. As to the obvious misunderstanding about its purpose, she explained that the *Woman's Bible* had never been intended as a translation of the Bible. "We accept what the wise men of various revising committees have given us." And just in case, the committee had a literal translation by a woman, Julia Smith, for comparative purposes. The main focus of the work, moreover, was to "lift women out of their superstitious reverence for the word of God." When in one moment, woman is told she owes all of her progress to the Bible, and in the next, is told the Bible is opposed to her claims for larger liberty, someone needs to sort out the contradiction, Stanton argued. How could woman's emancipation and subjection be legitimated by the same book? Stanton applied her rationalist critique to the Bible in an effort to expose that central contradiction. Did such an analysis require scholarly credentials, as her critics insisted? Not according to Stanton, who repeated her belief that "no liberal translation, nor mysterious symbolizing can make that book exalt [and] honor woman." Furthermore, if a reader needed Greek and Hebrew to understand the Bible's philosophy, "then why give it to the multitude to read?"[149]

For reasons that remain somewhat unclear, Stanton sought out a new venue for the serial publication of volume two. Clara Colby's *Woman's Tribune* was apparently no longer an option. Stanton had written to Colby repeatedly in January of 1896 asking her to commit to the second volume. "Perhaps it injures rather than helps you," she worried.[150] Canceled subscriptions and constant criticism had been Colby's reward for running volume one. Her own family had condemned her for working on the *Woman's Bible*. Edwin Mauger, a wealthy relative who occasionally had lent Colby money, was "compelled in loyalty to my Lord" to ask her to stop sending the *Woman's Tribune* to his home and cited her "personal participation in and publication of the 'Woman's Bible' " as the reason. "Our prayers will not cease to ascend for your deliverance from Satan's snare," he assured her.[151] Given her perpetual poverty, Colby may have considered the second volume of the *Woman's Bible* too great a financial risk. Susan B. Anthony, in fact, repeatedly pointed to "that old Bible business [blistering] over all its pages," as the reason for the paper's chronically precarious financial state.[152] Colby clearly felt pressure to back away from the *Woman's Bible* project.

Another factor that no doubt played into her decision was that Stanton and Colby had become increasingly aware of their differences of opinion regarding religion. As their antagonistic views of the Jewish matriarch Sarah, published in volume one of the *Woman's Bible*, had vividly illustrated, Colby had much more faith in religion and, particularly, in the power of New Thought esoteric interpretations of the Bible to redeem it as a text supportive of women's liberty. From the mid-1880s forward, the pages of Colby's *Woman's Tribune* had been at Stanton's disposal. Even when Anthony complained to Colby that Mrs. Stanton was rushing articles to print without letting anyone else read them first, Colby never censored Stanton.[153] After the NAWSA censure, her position toward Stanton changed, however, at least in part because of their religious differences. When, for example, Stanton submitted an article to the *Woman's Tribune* praising the agnostic Robert Ingersoll, Colby refused to print it.[154] Their disparate positions on Ingersoll pointed to a profound difference in Stanton and Colby's basic faith in religion's potential for liberating women. As Colby became increasingly involved in the practices of New Thought, she more than ever embraced the possibilities of women's spiritual emancipation. Stanton, for her part, felt just as strongly that she had investigated all the alternative religions and had yet to find one that made woman man's equal.

So, for a combination of reasons, Stanton sought out other publishing options. When she floated the idea of running volume two in the *Boston Investigator*, a Freethought paper, and threatened the same fate for her other writings as well, Anthony bemoaned the decision: "No don't go to the Investigator—that would be *carrying coals to New Castle.*"[155] Anthony, though no doubt relieved that volume two would not be blistering the pages of Colby's suffrage paper, did not want Stanton's work to be hidden away in a journal that few Americans read. She desperately wanted Stanton to remain in the public eye and urged her to publish her writings—even on the tiresome religion question—in one of the daily papers with a massive circulation. Over Anthony's objections, however, Stanton launched the project with the serial publication of the commentaries in Ernest Mendum's *Boston Investigator*.

No doubt with a sense of déjà vu, Stanton again wrote countless letters to women urging their participation. To those who had refused her previous requests to serve on the committee, she offered an eleventh-hour invitation to appear in the volume, albeit in the appendix. She invited contributors to submit "your opinion as to whether the Bible elevates or degrades the mother of the race, whether it has advanced or retarded women's progress to equality."[156] Women on all sides of the issue complied. For many, it offered an occasion to state publicly their opposition to the enterprise without having to risk an association with the committee. For others, it was simply an opportunity to express their support of Stanton and the project. In the appendix, as in the volumes themselves, rationalist critiques shared the pages with esoteric interpretations and liberal and evangelical defenses of the Bible.

Taken as a whole, this set of letters reveals the complexity of women's responses to the *Woman's Bible*. Critics charged Stanton and her collaborators with various offenses. Rather than reading the Bible in the "light of its times," the Reverend Antoinette Brown Blackwell suggested, the committee had misdirected the "fast, increasing" searchlight of the present back onto the ancient texts. "Turn on the light and so change the point of view," Blackwell cautioned (2:186). Warning Stanton that she "cannot say anything that you will wish to print," the reformer Ednah Cheney also disputed Stanton's treatment of the Bible. Cheney believed the Bible to be great literature and "one of the best educators of the common people" (2:189). The pioneering woman physician Elizabeth Blackwell agreed; the Bible served as "the most wonderful record of the evolution of spiritual life which our race possesses" (2:193). Echoing the perspective of her aunts, Alice Stone Blackwell, who had quietly worked behind the scenes to force the NAWSA repudiation of

Stanton's book, contended that, with the exception of Paul's passages, "the general principles of righteousness and justice laid down in the Bible have elevated the race in general, the mothers included, and have aided in securing reforms for women, as well as for other classes" (2:212). Frances Willard, respected leader of the WCTU, put it boldly: "No such woman as Mrs. Elizabeth Cady Stanton, with her heart aflame against all forms of injustice and of cruelty, with her intellect illumed and her tongue quickened into eloquence, has ever been produced in a country where the Bible was not incorporated into the thoughts and the affectations of the people and had not been so during many generations." But the Bible not only prepared women for a public life like Stanton's, Willard wrote; it also served as "the dear and sacred home book which makes a hallowed motherhood possible because it raises woman up, and with her lifts toward heaven the world." Reiterating a position that inspired missionary societies and American imperialism as well, Willard attested to the role of the Bible and Christianity in "civilizing" the world. Christianity's respect for women marked the height of a civilization:

> The nations which treat women with the most consideration are all Christian nations; the countries in which women have open to them all the opportunities for education which men possess are Christian countries; coeducation originated in Christian colleges; the professions and the trades are closed to us in all except Christian lands; and woman's ballot is unknown except where the Gospel of Christ has mellowed the hearts of men until they became willing to do women justice. Wherever we find an institution for the care and the comfort of the defective or the dependent classes, that institution was founded by men and women who were Christians by heredity and by training. (2:200)

Sarah Perkins agreed with Willard and argued that to see the advantages of Christianity over "heathenism," one needed to look no further than the Indian Territory in the United States. "Under the influence of Christian missionaries the Indian woman is an important factor in Church and State," Perkins contended. "Where the Gospel of Christ is not preached the women are slaves to the men. In their long tramps they do not even walk beside their husbands but follow behind like dogs" (2:213).

Stanton's rationalist colleagues took issue with these pious defenses of the Bible, Christianity, and "Civilization." Women's progress throughout Christendom, Sara Underwood wrote, occurred only in places where biblical doctrines had been "modified through the influence of science, of skepticism, and of liberal thought." In fact, the Bible had worked directly against the elevation of women, as well as the abolition of slavery, "because of the infallibility and the Divine authority with which the teachings of the Bible have been invested" (2:191).[157] "If the Bible had elevated woman to her present status," Josephine K. Henry maintained, "it would seem that the fact could be demonstrated beyond question; yet to-day the whole Christian world is on the defensive, trying to prove the validity of this claim." Evidence against the assertion could be found in the frightening statistics of wife abuse and "the carnival of wife murder which reigns throughout Christendom." Ecclesiastical history was "fetid with the records of crime against women," but "what of the history which Christianity is making today?" Henry asked: "Answer, ye victims of domestic warfare who crowd the divorce courts of Bible lands. Answer, ye wretched offspring of involuntary motherhood. Answer, ye five hundred thousand outcast women of Christian America, who should have been five hundred thousand blessings, bearing humanity in your unvitiated blood down the streams of time. Answer, ye mental dwarfs and moral monstrosities, and tell what the Holy Bible has done for you." Henry was convinced that Christianity was incompatible with women's freedom from domestic abuse, unwanted pregnancy, prostitution, venereal disease, and physically and morally diseased, that is, "illegitimate," offspring. "If the priest, with the Holy Bible in his hands, can show just cause why woman should not look to reason and to science rather than to Scripture for deliverance, 'let him speak *now*, or forever after hold his peace' " (2:194–198). In attributing women's sexual exploitation to the failures of Christian morality, Freethinkers like Stanton and Henry applied a critique common in the Freethought movement—a frank moral assessment of Christian cultures—to the specific issues of women's status.

New Thought readers, however, used a very different strategy in their analysis. A literal reading of the Bible—either by Christian apologists or Freethought detractors—naturally degraded women and men, the New Thought healer Ursula Gestefeld maintained. In a literal reading, one woman in the Bible—"portrayed as the mother of the Savior of the world"—is exalted "and the sex has been crucified. This one woman has been lifted above her place; and all women have fallen correspondingly below it." But when the inner light of the soul unlocks the Bible's esoteric meanings, woman's "spiritual motherhood of the race" will be discerned and woman will be elevated to her true place. "Men and women will clasp hands as comrades with a common destiny" (2:187–188). Ursula Bright agreed implicitly with Gestefeld that the degradation of women to be found in the Bible was derived only from its literal meaning, its "exoteric" interpretation, "the weak points of which have been so mercilessly exposed in Part I of 'The Woman's Bible.' " Since the Bible was misleading to anyone "ignorant of its esotericism," Bright questioned the ultimate value of the *Woman's Bible*. In her judgment, the project as conceived was futile. Hoping for a future revision of the Bible that would usefully reveal its inner, esoteric meanings, Bright was, in the meantime, "doubtful of the wisdom of laying too much stress on passages whose meaning is entirely misunderstood by the vast majority of Christians" (2:188–189).

Stanton rounded out the dialogue with her own concluding statement. Again she expressed dismay at the tenacity of women's faith and the "difficulty of substituting reason for superstition in minds once perverted by a false faith." She had little more tolerance for the beliefs of her New Thought allies, who denied the Bible's degrading messages and sheltered "themselves under false translation, interpretations and symbolic meanings." The tools of analysis were all equally useless—biblical research, higher criticism, Egyptian hieroglyphics, astronomy, astrology—for the Bible's varied interpreters still could not "twist out of the Old or New Testaments a message of justice, liberty or equality from God to the women of the nineteenth century!" (2:213–214).

Stanton's decision to incorporate both a critique and a defense of the *Woman's Bible* within its covers is a remarkable one. On one level, these letters finally achieved one of Stanton's long-held goals for the project: to bring together the diverse views of women reformers on the Bible. Then too, the marketability of such a controversial volume was not lost upon her, or apparently, some of her contributors. Including the text of the NAWSA resolution condemning the project as well as these critical letters within the covers of volume two served both to preserve the debate and to contain it, to reduce its power. Stanton did not, after all, elect to archive *all* the criticism her book generated. (The more scholarly critiques that appeared in the *Critic* were not included in this appendix to volume two.) It was a certain political and religious response in defense of the Bible that legitimized her work. She appropriated it for her own purposes, published it, dwarfed it with her own lengthy commentary, and always had the last word.

On Christmas Eve, 1897, Stanton expressed in her diary her elation that "The Woman's Bible and my reminiscences are now in print, and I am as much relieved as if I had given birth to twins."[158] With the publication of volume two, the book's title was still the greatest point of controversy. The *Chicago Inter Ocean* reported that for the time being "the authors have apparently exhausted their spleen" with this final volume. But the damage had been done, "for the bitterest enemy of womankind, were he gifted with the malice of Satan himself, could not have invented anything to bring such disrepute upon the sex as to call this ignorant and blasphemous tirade against the scriptures 'The Woman's Bible.' "[159]

Stanton delighted in her self-appointed role of religious heretic, the controversies she instigated, and their impact on sales. After the WCTU had repudiated the *Woman's Bible* in 1896, a midwestern newspaper editor expressed shock that Stanton failed to apologize for the religious heresies she had committed in her Bible. In fact, Stanton replied, the WCTU's censure would provide a "fine advertisement" for the book, leading the editor to believe that her primary concerns were entrepreneurial.[160] In September 1898 she was able to write to her son Theodore: "My books are selling pretty well. Whenever there is a lull in the sale of the *Woman's Bible,* some convention denounces it or some library throws it out, then there is immediately a fresh demand for it. So the bigots promote the sale every time. . . . They buy the book and then advertise it free of all expense to us. The Western papers have given columns to the discussion of removing it from the libraries. It is a tempest in a teapot."[161]

Stanton's life had long been marked by public controversy; she did not shrink from it in her final years. To her, public repudiation meant only that people were taking her ideas seriously. "All are howling on my track," she wrote to a friend regarding the *Woman's Bible* in 1898, "I have stirred up a regular hornet's nest. Discretion perhaps had better keep you out of it, if you have other important irons in the fire. There is no use courting ostracism unless one is impelled by stern principle, and then one needs to be sure that the motive is principle and not mere obstinacy or love of notoriety."[162] Through her persistent and public display of religious dissent, Stanton laid a fair claim to her share of "love of notoriety." But she also spent the last four years of her life relentlessly defending the *Woman's Bible* and her call for a new public discourse on women's roles.

In the wake of volume two, Stanton continued to use the columns of the Freethought press to expound her anti-Bible critique of American society. After the journal's staunch defense of her and her Bible, she agreed to serve as a regular contributor to *Free Thought Magazine,* condensing in its pages many of the arguments from the *Woman's Bible.* In 1898, for example, she wrote to persuade readers that an "expurgated" Bible was urgently needed for use in the public schools. Like many of her Freethought colleagues, Stanton was offended by the multitude of passages in the Bible which she described as obscene and "unfit to place in the hands of the youth of our nation."[163]

This series of articles in *Free Thought Magazine* from 1898 to her death in 1902 served as her last stand on the religious questions that had absorbed her attention for well over fifty years. These writings also demonstrated once again the class and ethnic tensions at work in the *Woman's Bible,* which had led Stanton to ascribe the timeless subordination of "women" to the Jews of the Old Testament. In these articles, she no longer just interrogated the "morality" of biblical Jews; occasionally she questioned their very existence in the ancient world. "What history, except their own, gives to us any account of them so far back as the days of the prophets?" she asked. "If such

"A leader of thought not numbers," Elizabeth Cady Stanton spent her later years engaged in writing and increasingly isolated from the woman's rights movement. State Historical Society of Wisconsin (X3) 26158

an extraordinary people existed as the Bible gives to us an account of, is it not strange that they should have been unknown to all the other nations in the then civilized world?"[164] In Stanton's last writings, the gateway to an emancipated womanhood—freed from the rub of organized religion—often hinged on narrow assumptions of middle-class, Anglo supremacy.

In April 1902, Stanton wrote in *Free Thought Magazine* of her conviction that grew stronger each year that "the canon law, with all the subtle influences that grow out of it, is more responsible for woman's slavery today than the civil code." She called for hearings to be held in the ecclesiastical bodies, comparable to those held before Congress over the past forty years, in which women could advocate their rights. Again, an expurgated Bible would be an essential part of this reform campaign, so that women would no longer be exposed to notions of their sinfulness and inferiority when attending church. In Stanton's eyes, the power of the state paled in comparison to the ideological power of the church in sustaining women's subordination. For women to choose their own emancipation, the "doctrine of original sin" needed to be dislodged permanently from theology and from women's self-perceptions. "To change the position of woman in dogmatic theology, where she is represented as the central figure in Paradise lost and regained, the medium alike for rebellion and redemption, is to revolutionize the system," she wrote.[165]

No part of the system called for greater change than prostitution and its everyday equivalent, women's sexual exploitation in the home. Stanton joined her Freethought feminist colleagues in arguing that the Bible makes "woman the mere victim of man's lust." But, not following Josephine K. Henry's critique of the hypocrisy of middle- and upper-class men's sexual exploitation of lower-class women, Stanton asserted a different class analysis. "The sentiments of men in high places are responsible for the outrages on woman in the haunts of vice and on the highways," she charged. Men of standing and power authored the theory of woman's sexual degradation, even if men of the lower class, in imitation, enacted it. Young men of the "masses" must be taught to revere the "Mother of the Race" much as they have been taught to respect the material culture of holiness: "cathedrals, altars, symbols and sacraments." "You can not go so low down in the scale of being," Stanton wrote, "as to find men who would enter our churches, to desecrate the altars." If this respect could only be extended to women, "these problems would be speedily solved." On this issue, the Catholic Church, by teaching love and respect for the Virgin Mary, had done the institution of motherhood a service and had "mitigated, in a measure, the contemptuous teachings of Protestantism in her Biblical literature."[166]

Stanton felt untold frustration with women's resistance to change on these points that she had belabored for over twenty years. In the summer of

1902, she wrote to Josephine K. Henry: "As most women are the devoutest believers, and accept as law and gospel everything bound up in 'The Holy Bible,' though hopelessly degraded by many of its declarations, I think the time has come for liberal men and women to meet in a grand international convention, review the Scriptures and give mankind a consistent version, in harmony with science and philosophy, and worthy the reverence and belief of intelligent human beings."[167] Her call for an international convention echoed her plan of 1888 for a world-wide forum to discuss the proposed *Woman's Bible*. She believed to the end that real change in woman's condition could be made only by educating the culture to think differently about women. The Bible was once again her starting point because, as she frequently said, "So long as tens of thousands of Bibles are printed every year, and circulated over the whole habitable globe, and the masses in all English-speaking nations revere it as the word of God, it is vain to belittle its influence" (1:11).

Stanton felt free to speculate about the limitations of all the "fragmentary reforms" of her day—"woman suffrage, temperance, social purity, peace, rigid Sunday laws, physical culture and higher education"—in search of a grand theory to solidify the fragments.[168] Increasingly concerned with the conditions of the poor as well as religious tyranny, she relinquished her faith in free market principles and embraced the promises of socialism to "realize in co-operation the true principle in government, religion, industrial and social life."[169] "Miss Anthony complains that I give less time to the Woman Suffrage Movement," Stanton wrote in 1898, "But surely I have served that cause sufficiently long."[170]

"Sowing Winter Wheat"

In 1853, a famous phrenologist, a nineteenth-century medical practitioner whose work involved assessing character traits by feeling the skull to detect the exact shape and position of the brain, determined that Elizabeth Cady Stanton's faith was weak when compared to her reason. "You are governed by what you can understand and comprehend," the phrenological report informed her, "more than by faith."[171] The phrenologist confirmed what Stanton already knew. It was a diagnosis that placed her at odds with her colleagues and the larger culture. But with her unassailable faith in what she could see and comprehend, Stanton grew comfortable with the perpetual conflict that characterized her career. In point of fact, she relished controversy. After reading her autobiography in 1898, Theodore Tilton wrote to her to say that he remembered well her appetite for conflict: "You always had some anecdote or sarcasm wherewith a woman's wit could successfully torture a masculine mind! I think the form of wrangle you most piously en-joyed was with deacons, elders and other 'theologs' . . . who ventured to the front with the Biblical and pre-Adamic proofs of the exact shape of 'woman's sphere!' "[172] From taking on the well-known clergy of her day, to pressuring the woman's movement to take a stand against the church and Bible, to chal-lenging individual women to abandon their religious superstitions, Stanton thrived on agitation and controversy. For her, provoking debate was an im-portant kind of political work. Yet there was no question in her mind that she had been misunderstood and had paid a price for her views. As she wrote to her younger colleague Lillie Devereux Blake in 1899:

> You have not been treated by our young co-adjutors with less considera-tion than I have been. They refused to read my letters and resolutions to the conventions; They have denounced the 'Woman's Bible' unsparingly; not one of them has ever reviewed or expressed the least appreciation of 'Eighty Years and More.' Not one of my suffrage friends has ever thought it worth a complimentary notice in any of the metropolitan journals, or even in the woman's papers. . . . For all this I make no public protest,—I propose no revenge. Because of this hostile feeling I renounced the Presi dency and quietly accept the situation and publish what I have to say in the liberal papers. I do not cultivate any feelings of revenge or hostility but quietly do my work in other ways that are open to me.[173]

After a lifetime of failed coalitions, Stanton had made peace with her role as a political maverick, a freelance, a leader of thought, not numbers. She spoke candidly of having "outgrown" the woman suffrage association as the "ultimation of human endeavor." Only from her position beyond "that field, with its limitations" could she continue to make an impact.[174] Wielding the *Woman's Bible* as her weapon, Stanton challenged not only the direction and limitations of the suffrage movement, but also the broader construction of women's social, religious, and political roles during this period. Repeatedly, she talked in her last years of the fragmented condition of American reform. Workers labored in their own separate corners but lacked a larger vision. It no longer took courage to "talk suffrage," Stanton argued; women needed to "demand equality everywhere."[175] According to her thinking, a grand, over-arching critique was needed to bring about all the changes that individual reformers in discrete fields could never effect on their own. Denouncing or-thodox Christianity and its limited vision of womanhood supplied Stanton with a grand theory, and the *Woman's Bible* supplied her with the means of provoking this essential debate.

Stanton felt, as she wrote in her diary near the close of her life, a pro-found transformation: "as my eyes grow dimmer and dimmer from day to day, my intellectual vision grows clearer." What she saw through the cataracts of age and experience was a brilliant vision of the future. Women, emancipated from blinding faith, were freed to stand equal to men in the church, the state, and the family. But, as she aged and her vision clarified, others questioned it. Seeing only eyes dulled by cataracts and a body slowed by the years, even Susan B. Anthony found Stanton "very far from being her old self either in bodily or intellectual strength."[176] Yet, "though denounced by our co-adjutors," Stanton never faltered. She maintained her resilient faith in her work and in the future. "I never forget that we are sowing winter wheat," she wrote, "when the coming Spring will see sprout and when other hands than ours will reap and enjoy."[177]

Archival Abbreviations

DLC   Library of Congress
CSmH   Huntington Library, San Marino, California
KyU   University of Kentucky Libraries, Lexington
MCR-S   Schlesinger Library, Radcliffe Institute, Cambridge, Massachusetts
MoSHi   Missouri Historical Society, St. Louis
N-Ar   New York State Archives, Albany
NjR   Rutgers University Libraries, New Brunswick, New Jersey
NN   New York Public Library
NPV   Vassar College Library, Poughkeepsie, New York
NRU   University of Rochester Library, Rochester, New York
PHi   Historical Society of Pennsylvania, Philadelphia
WHi   State Historical Society of Wisconsin, Madison

Notes

Introduction

1. Important work has been done on Elizabeth Cady Stanton beginning with Eleanor Flexner, *Century of Struggle: The Woman's Rights Movement in the United States* (1959; rpt. Cambridge: Harvard University Press, 1966); Aileen Kraditor, *The Ideas of the Woman Suffrage Movement, 1890–1920* (1965; rpt. New York: W.W. Norton, 1981); Ellen Carol DuBois, *Feminism and Suffrage: The Emergence of an Independent Women's Movement in America, 1848–1869* (Ithaca: Cornell University Press, 1978); DuBois, ed., *The Elizabeth Cady Stanton–Susan B. Anthony Reader: Correspondence, Writings, Speeches* (1981; rev. ed., Boston: Northeastern University Press, 1992); and DuBois, *Woman Suffrage and Women's Rights* (New York: New York University Press, 1998). Biographies include Alma Lutz, *Created Equal: A Biography of Elizabeth Cady Stanton, 1815–1902* (New York: John Day, 1940); Mary Ann B. Oakley, *Elizabeth Cady Stanton* (Old Westbury, N.Y.: Feminist Press, 1972); Lois Banner, *Elizabeth Cady Stanton: A Radical for Woman's Rights* (Boston: Little, Brown, 1980); and Elisabeth Griffith, *In Her Own Right: The Life of Elizabeth Cady Stanton* (New York: Oxford University Press, 1984). The Seneca Falls convention is generally considered to be the first American woman's rights meeting. However, the historian Nancy Isenberg has challenged that claim, arguing that the Seneca Falls meeting was not a national convention and that it followed closely on the heels of, and resembled in tone and purpose, the Boston anti-Sabbath convention of 1848. According to Isenberg, the Worcester convention of 1850 was the first national woman's rights meeting. Nancy Isenberg, *Sex and Citizenship in Antebellum America* (Chapel Hill: University of North Carolina Press, 1998), 2–6, 87.

2. Stanton to Equal Rights Club of Hartford, Conn., as quoted in *Boston Investigator,* 4 April 1886. All of Stanton's (as well as Susan B. Anthony's) papers—including correspondence, manuscript writings, coverage of lectures and meetings, testimony, interviews, and legal papers—are now published and commercially available in microfilm in Patricia G. Holland and Ann D. Gordon, eds., *Papers of Elizabeth Cady Stanton and Susan B. Anthony* (Wilmington, Del.: Scholarly Resources Inc., 1991, microfilm), series 3. Many of the texts quoted in this book are now published in that collection. Permission to quote unpublished materials has been granted by the Schlesinger Library, the Huntington Library and the University of Kentucky Special Collections and Archives.

3. Stanton to Olympia Brown, 8 May 1889, Olympia Brown Papers, Schlesinger Library, Radcliffe Institute, Cambridge, Mass. (hereafter MCR-S).

4. Stanton to Clara Dorothy Bewick Colby, 8 December 1892, Clara Colby Papers, State Historical Society of Wisconsin, Madison (hereafter WHi). Stanton, *The Woman's Bible*, Parts I and II (New York: European Publishing Co., 1895, 1898; rpt. New York: Arno, 1972). Later reprints include: *The Original Feminist Attack on the Bible*, introd. Barbara Welter (New York: Arno, 1974); Stanton and the Revising Committee, *The Woman's Bible* (Seattle: Coalition Task Force on Women and Religion, 1974); and Stanton, *The Woman's Bible*, foreword Maureen Fitzgerald (Boston: Northeastern University Press, 1993). As I will discuss more fully in Chapter 4, Stanton was both the book's editor and its primary author. She organized and compiled the volume and wrote well over half of its commentaries. Because of Stanton's close identification with the project and her sometimes solo efforts to keep it afloat, I will frequently refer to the *Woman's Bible* as "her" book and to Stanton as the book's "author."

5. *Des Moines Leader*, n.d., as quoted in "Press Comments," "The Woman's Bible" circular, Stanton to Margaret Olivia Slocum Sage, 20 April 1899, enclosure. Margaret Olivia Slocum Sage Collection, Emma Willard School Archives, Troy, N.Y.

6. For example, Stanton, "Bible and Church Degrade Woman," pamphlet, (Chicago: H. L. Green, n.d.), Elizabeth Cady Stanton Papers, Library of Congress (hereafter Stanton Papers, DLC).

7. Stanton to Clara Colby, quoted in *Woman's Tribune*, 23 February 1895.

8. *Springfield (Missouri) Republican*, 6 December 1896.

9. Stanton, *Eighty Years and More: Reminiscences, 1815–1897*, introd. Ellen DuBois, afterword Ann D. Gordon (1898; rpt. Boston: Northeastern University Press, 1993), 453.

10. Barbara Welter, "The Cult of True Womanhood, 1829–1860," *American Quarterly* 18 (1966): 151–174; Kathryn Kish Sklar, *Catharine Beecher: A Study in American Domesticity* (New Haven: Yale University Press, 1973); Frances B. Cogan, *All-American Girl: The Ideal of Real Womanhood in Mid-Nineteenth-Century America* (Athens: University of Georgia Press 1989); Nancy F. Cott, *The Bonds of Womanhood: "Woman's Sphere" in New England, 1780–1835* (New Haven: Yale University Press, 1977).

11. Ann D. Gordon makes this point in the most recent edition of Stanton's autobiography. See Stanton, *Eighty Years*, 480–481. For an excellent discussion of daughter Harriot's efforts to restore her mother's historical importance, see Ellen DuBois, *Harriot Stanton Blatch and the Winning of Woman Suffrage* (New Haven: Yale University Press, 1997), 246–261.

12. Olympia Brown to Clara Colby, 19 June 1909, Clara Colby Collection, Huntington Library, San Marino, Calif. (hereafter CSmH); Harriot Stanton Blatch to Alma Lutz, n.d., Alma Lutz Papers, Vassar College, Poughkeepsie, N.Y., as quoted in DuBois, *Harriot Stanton Blatch*, 338, n.28.

13. See Griffith, *In Her Own Right*, xv; DuBois, "Making Women's History: Historian-Activists of Women's Rights, 1880–1940," in *Woman Suffrage and Women's Rights*, 215, 223–226.

14. Anna Howard Shaw, *The Story of a Pioneer*, with Elizabeth Jordan, ed. Rowena Keith Keyes (1915; rpt. New York: Harper and Brothers, 1929), 274–275.

15. Griffith, *In Her Own Right*, xv.

16. Important work has been done on Stanton and Anthony's partnership beginning with DuBois, ed., *Stanton-Anthony Reader*; Banner, *Elizabeth Cady Stanton*; Griffith, *In Her Own Right*; Kathleen Barry, *Susan B. Anthony, A Biography of a Singular Feminist* (New York: New York University Press, 1988); and Ken Burns's film and the accompanying volume by Geoffrey C. Ward, *Not for Ourselves Alone: The Story of Elizabeth Cady Stanton and Susan B. Anthony, an Illustrated History* (New York: A. A. Knopf, 1999).

17. "The Woman's Bible," Woman's Bible Subject File, National American Woman Suffrage Association Papers (hereafter NAWSA Papers), container 77, DLC; J. C. McQuiddy, "Mrs. Catt and Woman-Suffrage Leaders Repudiate the Bible," Anti-Suffrage–Tennessee Subject File, NAWSA Papers, container 41, DLC. See also "The Dark and Dangerous Side of Woman Suffrage," Anti-Suffrage–Tennessee Subject File, container 41, NAWSA Papers, DLC.

18. Abbey Crawford Milton, oral history, 3 August 1983, interview by Marilyn Bell, Tennessee State Library. My thanks to Elisabeth Perry for this citation.

19. Stanton's process of drafting a committee and the troubles she encountered are detailed in Chapter 4.

20. For a lively account of the ratification battle in Tennessee, see Marjorie Spruill Wheeler, *New Women of the New South: The Leaders of the Woman Suffrage Movement in the Southern States* (New York: Oxford University Press, 1993), 31–36; also Anastatia Sims, "Armageddon in Tennessee: The Final Battle over the Nineteenth Amendment" in Marjorie Spruill Wheeler, ed., *One Woman, One Vote: Rediscovering the Woman Suffrage Movement* (Troutdale, Ore.: NewSage Press, 1995), 333–352.

21. Ann Loades, ed., *Feminist Theology: A Reader* (London: Westminster/John Knox Press, 1990), 13. Loades refers to Stanton as "the doyenne of the present movement."

22. Historians' neglect of Stanton's religious views has been particularly consequential. Zillah Eisenstein, for example, has argued that Stanton's radical feminist critique of women's oppression was undercut by her inadequate "liberal-legal political strategy" to combat that oppression. Such an analysis is only possible if one ignores Stanton's major religious writings, especially the *Woman's Bible*. There and elsewhere Stanton put forth her argument that women's inclusion in the electorate would prove meaningless without a simultaneous revolution in the cultural ideas about womanhood. See Zillah R. Eisenstein, *The Radical Future of Liberal Feminism* (New York: Longman, 1981), 146, 160. Historians who have addressed Stanton's religious views include Aileen S. Kraditor, Barbara Welter, Ellen DuBois, and Maureen Fitzgerald. In her 1965 book, *Ideas of the Woman Suffrage Movement*, Kraditor devoted a chapter to religious ideas in which Stanton figured prominently. Barbara Welter added an excellent introduction to the 1974 Arno press edition of *The Woman's Bible*. DuBois's views on Stanton's religious thought can be found in "The Limitations of Sisterhood: Elizabeth Cady Stanton and Division in the American Suffrage Movement, 1875–1902," in *Woman Suffrage and Women's Rights*, 160–175; and also DuBois, ed., *Stanton-Anthony Reader*, 182–193. Maureen Fitzgerald provided a "Foreword" to the latest edition of the *Woman's Bible* (1993) in which she argues for the "religious roots" of Stanton's thought, see Stanton, *The Woman's Bible*, foreword Fitzgerald, vii–xxix.

23. See Kraditor, *Ideas of the Woman Suffrage Movement*, 163–218; Angela Y. Davis, *Women, Race, and Class* (New York: Vintage, Random House, 1983), 110–126; Rosalyn Terborg-Penn, *African American Women in the Struggle for the Vote, 1850–1920* (Bloomington: Indiana University Press, 1998), 14–15, 21, 22–23, 27–28 ; Steven M. Buechler, *Women's Movements in the United States* (New Brunswick: Rutgers University Press, 1990), 135; and Louise Michele Newman, *White Women's Rights: The Racial Origins of Feminism in the United States* (New York: Oxford University Press, 1999), 63–65.

24. Jane T. Walker to Sisters, n.d., in Stanton and the Revising Committee, *The Woman's Bible*, v.

25. Eleanor D. Bilimoria, Shirlie Kaplan, Jessie Kinnear, "Commentaries by Members of the Coalition Task Force on Women and Religion," in Stanton and the Revising Committee, *The Woman's Bible*, vii, xiii, xviii.

26. Eleanor D. Bilimoria, "Editor's Preface," in *ibid.*, viii.

27. For a discussion of the state of feminist hermeneutics in the 1970s and 1980s, see Cullen Murphy, "Women and the Bible," *The Atlantic*, August 1993, 39–64. The historian Gerda Lerner has argued that the invisibility of women's prior exegetical work on the Bible is what has allowed the *Woman's Bible* to ascend to its symbolic position as the "beginning" of a feminist hermeneutical tradition. Lerner points out that even Stanton seemed not to have realized that one of the abolitionists she admired, Sarah Grimké, had published her own biblical exegesis, *Letters on the Equality of the Sexes*. Lerner writes, "Over and over again, individual women criticized and re-interpreted the core biblical texts not knowing that other women before them had already done so." See Gerda Lerner, *The Creation of Feminist Consciousness* (New York: Oxford University Press, 1993), 165.

28. Elisabeth Schüssler Fiorenza, *In Memory of Her: A Feminist Theological Reconstruction of Christian Origins* (New York: Crossroad, 1983), 11. Early work on Stanton's Bible by religious studies scholars include Elaine C. Huber, "They weren't prepared to Hear: A Closer Look at the *Woman's Bible*," *Andover Newton Quarterly* 16 (1976): 271–276; James Smylie, "*The Woman's*

Bible and the Spiritual Crisis," *Soundings* 59 (1976): 305–328; Anne McGrew Bennett, et al., "*The Woman's Bible*: Reviews and Perspectives," *Women and Religion: 1973 Proceedings* (Tallahassee: American Academy of Religion, 1973), 39–78.

29. Fiorenza, *In Memory of Her*, 11, 21.

30. Elisabeth Schüssler Fiorenza, ed., *Searching the Scriptures*, Vol. 1: *A Feminist Introduction* (New York: Crossroad, 1993), 12. Fiorenza's use of the term "kyriarchal" designates elite power differences (presumably of class, race, nationality, etc.) that would have divided women and complicated the universalizing construct of "woman."

31. Ibid., 3, 18. See also Carol A. Newsome and Sharon H. Ringe, eds., *The Women's Bible Commentary* (Louisville: Westminster/John Knox Press, 1992), xv. *The Women's Bible Commentary* was so titled to commemorate Stanton's volume, but the collaborators chose the plural "women's" rather than Stanton's singular "woman's" to "recognize the diversity among women who read the Bible and study it. There is no single 'woman's perspective' but a rich variety of insight that comes from the different ways in which women's experience is shaped by culture, class, ethnicity, religious community, and other aspects of social identity."

32. Fiorenza, ed., *Searching the Scriptures*, 15. Fiorenza notes another important distinction: unlike the *Woman's Bible*, "which on the whole was not able to attract women schooled in higher criticism, *Searching the Scriptures* brings together the best scholarship in contemporary feminist biblical and historical studies not only from the United States but from around the world."

33. Ibid., 13.

34. Ibid., 9.

35. Ibid., 8–9. See Chapter 4 for an in-depth analysis of the diversity of the revising committee. I mention just a few of the differences among the women here to complicate Fiorenza's generalizations about the *Woman's Bible* and its approach. Among other flaws in the *Woman's Bible* that Fiorenza points out is that Stanton and her colleagues "did not break through their canonical limitations and theological frameworks . . . [and] they reinscribed canonical authority." But as a textual analysis of the *Woman's Bible* makes clear, the members of Stanton's committee, none of whom were formally trained as biblical exegetes, used the Apocrypha and the Kabbalah to challenge canonical texts. Fiorenza also criticizes the *Woman's Bible* because "it does not sufficiently appreciate that the Bible is a cacophony of interested historical voices and a field of rhetorical struggles in which questions of truth and meaning are being negotiated." In fact, this was precisely what the *Woman's Bible* collaborators attempted in their volumes. Feminists working in history and religious studies have different intellectual priorities and disciplinary expectations, which accounts for these different "readings" of the *Woman's Bible*. A historically informed textual analysis of the *Woman's Bible* was beyond the scope of *Searching the Scriptures*, which emphasized the multivocal, multicultural state of contemporary feminist analysis of Scriptures. But the absence of such an analysis inadvertently conflates the different points of view represented in the *Woman's Bible*. *Searching the Scriptures* includes a fine historical account of Stanton's project. See Carolyn De Swarte Gifford, "Politicizing the Sacred Texts: Elizabeth Cady Stanton and *The Woman's Bible*," 52–63.

36. DuBois, "The Radicalism of the Woman Suffrage Movement: Notes toward the Reconstruction of Nineteenth-Century Feminism," *Feminist Studies* 3, no. 1/2 (1975): 65; DuBois, ed., *Stanton-Anthony Reader*, xiii–xiv, 182–193; DuBois, *Feminism and Suffrage*, 21–52; DuBois, "The Limitations of Sisterhood: Elizabeth Cady Stanton and Division in the American Suffrage Movement," in *Woman Suffrage and Women's Rights*, 160–171; DuBois, "The Last Suffragist," in *Woman Suffrage and Women's Rights*, 3.

37. Since DuBois's earliest work, *Feminism and Suffrage*, scholarship on the nineteenth-century woman's movement has stressed the multiple and conflicting role of religious rhetoric in articulating woman's rights. The antebellum period is particularly well documented. Nancy Hewitt, for example, in her study of women's activism in Rochester, found that many forms of religiously inspired activism did not lead to woman's rights activism, while the most radical, particularly Quakerism, did. Lori Ginzburg extended her study into the postwar period and found, like Hewitt, that both religious rhetoric and electoral politics held contradictory possibilities for women's activism. Ann Braude in *Radical Spirits* explored the intersections of Spiri-

tualism and woman's rights and located within these circles some of the most radical of women's activists. Nancy Isenberg argues that church politics was one of the primary venues in which feminists articulated "rights" in antebellum political culture. Additionally, a sampling of dissertations and other works appearing since about 1985 establishes the intersections of religion and the woman's rights movement as a new focus of inquiry in the disciplines of history, religious studies, and American literature. Works by Patricia Ash, Elizabeth Clark, Maureen Fitzgerald, Carolyn De Swarte Gifford, Carolyn Haynes, Nancy Isenberg, Kathi Kern, Evelyn Kirkley, Beryl Satter, and others investigate the "religion question" and woman's rights from a variety of angles. See Lori D. Ginzberg, *Women and the Work of Benevolence: Morality, Politics, and Class in the Nineteenth-Century United States* (New Haven: Yale University Press, 1990); Nancy A. Hewitt, *Women's Activism and Social Change: Rochester, New York, 1822–1872* (Ithaca: Cornell University Press, 1984); Ann Braude, *Radical Spirits: Spiritualism and Women's Rights in Nineteenth-Century America* (Boston: Beacon, 1989); Nancy Isenberg, *Sex and Citizenship in Antebellum America* (Chapel Hill: University of North Carolina Press, 1998); Beryl Satter, *Each Mind a Kingdom: American Women, Sexual Purity, and the New Thought Movement, 1875–1920* (Berkeley: University of California Press, 1999); Evelyn A. Kirkley, *Rational Mothers and Infidel Gentlemen: Gender and American Atheism, 1865–1915* (Syracuse: Syracuse University Press, 2000); Patricia Ash, "The Quest for Harmony: Religion in the Origin of the Antebellum Woman's Rights Movement" (Ph.D. diss., Claremont Graduate University, 1998); Elizabeth Battelle Clark, "The Politics of God and the Woman's Vote: Religion and the American Woman Suffrage Movement, 1848–1895" (Ph.D. diss., Princeton University, 1989); Maureen Anne Fitzgerald, "Religion and Feminism in Elizabeth Cady Stanton's Life and Thought" (M.A. thesis, University of Wisconsin–Madison, 1985); Carolyn Haynes, "Women in a Divine Republic: Feminism and Protestantism in Late-Nineteenth-Century America" (Ph.D. diss., University of California, San Diego, 1993); Nancy Gale Isenberg, " 'Co-Equality of the Sexes': The Feminist Discourse of the Antebellum Women's Rights Movement in America" (Ph.D. diss., University of Wisconsin–Madison, 1990); Kathi Kern, "*The Woman's Bible*: Gender, Religion and Ideology in the Work of Elizabeth Cady Stanton, 1854–1902" (Ph.D. diss., University of Pennsylvania, 1991); Evelyn Anne Kirkley, " 'The Female Peril': The Construction of Gender in American Freethought, 1865–1915" (Ph.D. diss., Duke University, 1993); and Beryl Satter, "New Thought and the Era of Woman" (Ph.D. diss., Yale University, 1992).

38. Anne Firor Scott and Andrew Mackay Scott, *One Half the People: The Fight for Woman Suffrage* (Urbana: University of Illinois Press, 1975), 24; Flexner, *Century of Struggle*, 262.

39. In an article in which she addresses "Gilded Age suffragism's conservative turn," DuBois writes that, "influenced by the rise of the Moral Majority and other fundamentalist-based conservative politics in the 1980s, I linked sexual conservatism and the Protestant Christian revival in the Gilded Age, especially as manifest in the success of the WCTU in joining suffragism." See DuBois, "The Last Suffragist," in *Woman Suffrage and Women's Rights*, 15.

40. Kraditor's central argument is that in the period she covers, 1890–1920, "justice" arguments took a back seat to "expediency" arguments. See Kraditor, *Ideas of the Woman Suffrage Movement*, 43–74.

41. DuBois, "The Last Suffragist, " in *Woman's Suffrage and Women's Rights*, 16.

42. On the WCTU, see, for example, Ruth Bordin, *Women and Temperance: The Quest for Power and Liberty, 1873–1900* (Philadelphia: Temple University Press, 1984); and Barbara Leslie Epstein, *The Politics of Domesticity: Women, Evangelism, and Temperance in Nineteenth Century America* (Middletown, Conn.: Wesleyan University Press, 1981). For a critique of the interpretation of Stanton and her wing of the suffrage movement as "secularist," see Maureen Fitzgerald's essay in Stanton, *The Woman's Bible*, foreword Fitzgerald, ix, xix–xx. Nancy Isenberg counters what she has termed the "secularization argument" of the woman's rights movement in *Sex and Citizenship*, xvi–xvii, 207, n. 7.

43. Stanton, "To the Women of the State of New York," 11 December 1854, as printed in *Lily* (Seneca Falls, N.Y.) 1 January 1855.

44. Stanton, *Woman's Bible*, 1: 8.

45. Stanton to Equal Rights Club of Hartford, Conn.

46. Ibid.

47. On the violence of the 1890s, see Nell Irvin Painter, *Standing at Armageddon: The United States, 1877–1919* (New York: W. W. Norton, 1987), and Mark Wahlgren Summers, *The Gilded Age, Or the Hazard of New Functions* (Upper Saddle River, N.J.: Prentice Hall, 1997).

1. "The Sunset of Life": Elizabeth Cady Stanton and the Polemics of Autobiography

1. Elizabeth Cady Stanton to Theodore Weld Stanton, 26 January 1898, Theodore Stanton Collection, Elizabeth Cady Stanton Papers, Mabel Smith Douglas Library, Rutgers–The State University of New Jersey, New Brunswick, N.J. (hereafter NjR). After the death of her husband, Henry Stanton, in 1887, Stanton sold their home in Tenafly, N.J., and eventually settled in New York City, living in a series of apartments that she shared with two of her adult children, Robert, an unmarried lawyer, and Margaret, a widowed daughter who, according to Stanton's biographer Lois Banner, became a professor of physical education at Columbia Teacher's College. See Lois Banner, *Elizabeth Cady Stanton: A Radical for Woman's Rights* (Boston: Little, Brown, 1980), 171.

2. Stanton to Victoria Claflin Woodhull Martin, 4 October 1898, Martin Papers, Special Collections, Morris Library, Southern Illinois University, Carbondale.

3. Elizabeth Cady Stanton, *Eighty Years and More: Reminiscences, 1815–1897*, introd. Ellen Carol DuBois, afterword Ann D. Gordon (1898; rpt. Boston: Northeastern University Press, 1993) (hereafter: *Eighty Years*, with page references appearing in my text), 456.

4. Ann Gordon argues in the afterword to *Eighty Years* that readers in the nineteenth century would have been much more familiar with the outlines of Stanton's public career than are readers today. See Gordon, "Afterword," in *Eighty Years*, 469–470.

5. Despite their familial ties to Gerrit Smith, a prominent abolitionist, the Cady family and particularly Daniel Cady objected to Elizabeth's marrying an abolitionist. Her father was also concerned about Henry Stanton's ability to support a family financially.

6. Meeting Lucretia Mott in London is just one of many pivotal events in Stanton's memoir that may not have occurred the way Stanton remembered and described it. Later in the chapter I will explore some of Stanton's problematic memories. On her meeting with Lucretia Mott, see Nancy Isenberg, *Sex and Citizenship in Antebellum America* (Chapel Hill: University of North Carolina Press, 1998), 4; also Keith Melder, *The Beginnings of Sisterhood: The American Woman's Rights Movement, 1800–1850* (New York: Schocken, 1977), 118.

7. Isenberg has offered a compelling critique of this narrative of the origins of the woman's rights movement in America; her analysis suggests that both Seneca Falls and Stanton's ideological leadership have been overemphasized. My purpose here is not to reinscribe "Stanton's master narrative" but rather to summarize her story as she told it in her autobiography. See Isenberg, *Sex and Citizenship in Antebellum America*, xvi, 2–6; see also Judith Wellman, "The Seneca Falls Woman's Rights Convention: A Study of Social Networks," *Journal of Women's History* 3(Spring 1991): 9–37.

8. Because of slavery and its legacy, African American women's rights were more circumscribed than those of white women. Slavery persisted in New York State until 1827. According to the historian Edgar McManus, slaves in New York State were permitted to own private property as early as the eighteenth century. This right was codified in a law passed in 1809 which recognized the right of slaves to own and transfer property. Another law passed in the same year gave legal recognition to slave marriages, but how this law may have affected enslaved women's property rights McManus does not elaborate. See Joan Hoff, *Law, Gender, and Injustice: A Legal History of U.S. Women* (New York: New York University Press, 1991), 130; Edgar J. McManus, *A History of Negro Slavery in New York* (Syracuse: Syracuse University Press, 1966), 63, 178.

9. The reference to Stanton's "decapitation" comes from Susan B. Anthony. See Anthony to Stanton, 2 December 1898, Anthony Family Papers, Huntington Library, San Marino, Calif. (hereafter CSmH).

10. Lincoln's Emancipation Proclamation freed slaves in Confederate states. Stanton, An-

thony, and others called for the immediate abolition of slavery everywhere in the United States.

11. Those with whom Stanton and Anthony parted company included their woman's rights colleagues Lucy Stone, Henry Blackwell, and Frederick Douglass. Although Blackwell endorsed black male suffrage and the Fifteenth Amendment, it is difficult to classify him as a progressive on racial issues. He was the earliest exponent of the theory that woman suffrage in the South could preserve white supremacy. I return to this topic in more detail in Chapter 3. See Ellen Carol DuBois, *Feminism and Suffrage: The Emergence of an Independent Women's Movement in America, 1848–1869* (Ithaca: Cornell University Press, 1978), 193–202; also Majorie Spruill Wheeler, *New Women of the New South: The Leaders of the Woman Suffrage Movement in the Southern States* (New York: Oxford University Press, 1993), 114.

12. See Ellen Carol DuBois, "Outgrowing the Compact of the Fathers: Equal Rights, Woman Suffrage, and the United States Constitution, 1820–1878," in DuBois, *Woman Suffrage and Women's Rights* (New York: New York University Press, 1998), 103.

13. Stanton to Maria Louise Palmer Thomas, 19 February 1898, Elizabeth Cady Stanton Papers, Vassar College Library, Poughkeepsie, N.Y. (hereafter NPV).

14. Stanton to Olivia Bigelow Hall, 30 January 1899, Hall Papers, Library of Congress (hereafter DLC). Stanton had campaigned in the Michigan state suffrage campaign in 1874 and devotes several pages of *Eighty Years* to her visit to the University of Michigan: see pp. 268–270.

15. See Elisabeth Griffith, *In Her Own Right: The Life of Elizabeth Cady Stanton* (New York: Oxford University Press, 1984), 207. Ann Gordon, in the afterword to the 1993 reprint of *Eighty Years*, develops an extended critique of Stanton's memory, demonstrating that Stanton frequently changed the order in which events in her life transpired and that she sometimes collapsed many different events and experiences into a single homogenized, prototypical narrative. See, for example, her chapter "Lyceums and Lectures," in which, Gordon argues, Stanton constructed an archetypal year.

16. Jacquelyn Dowd Hall, " 'You Must Remember This': Autobiography as Social Critique," *Journal of American History* 85 (1998): 440. Carolyn Heilbrun has written that stories made of memories actually constitute the past: "We tell ourselves stories of our past, make fictions or stories of it, and these narrations *become* the past, the only part of it that is not submerged." See Carolyn G. Heilbrun, *Writing a Woman's Life* (New York: Ballantine, 1988), 51.

17. Isenberg, *Sex and Citizenship in Antebellum America*, 1–6, 11–13. One of Isenberg's central arguments is that church politics provided early feminists with an important "religious public" in which to articulate "rights."

18. Ibid., 4. Isenberg quotes Ellen DuBois, *Feminism and Suffrage*, which maintains that the vote was "the cornerstone of the women's rights program." See DuBois, *Feminism and Suffrage*, 41.

19. Stanton, *Elizabeth Cady Stanton as Revealed in Her Letters, Diary and Reminiscences*, ed. Theodore Stanton and Harriot Stanton Blatch, 2 vols. (New York: Harper, 1922), 1: xvi (hereafter *Elizabeth Cady Stanton as Revealed*).

20. Susan B. Anthony to Clara Colby, 3 May 1897, Clara Colby Collection, CSmH.

21. Stanton interview with *Cincinnati Daily Enquirer,* "An American Stateswoman," 15 October 1869, published New York *World* 15 October 1869 (hereafter, Stanton, interview, "American Stateswoman").

22. Stanton to Marietta Holley, 9 May 1898, Marietta Holley Papers, Jefferson County Historical Society, Watertown, N.Y.

23. The four plots I have developed for investigation—unacceptable ghosts, the problem of boyhood, the suffocation of religion, and the limits of politics—are based on my assessment of the major themes that run through Stanton's memoir. With the exception of "unacceptable ghosts," which focuses on stories Stanton repressed, these plots align with four events that Stanton claimed "decided the whole trend of my life." These she enumerated: (1) the death of her brother; (2) the influence of the Presbyterian clergyman; (3) the marriage of her sister Tryphena to Edward Bayard; and (4) her experience in her father's law office. The only event I do not cover among these is her sister's marriage to Bayard, but I do cover the major "effect" of

that marriage, which was Stanton's youthful conversion to science and reason during the trip to Niagara Falls. See Stanton, "Reminiscences of Elizabeth Cady Stanton," Political Equality Club of Minneapolis Papers, Minnesota Historical Society (hereafter Stanton, "Reminiscences"). The phrase "unacceptable ghosts" is from Hall, " 'You Must Remember This,' " 440.

24. Hall, " 'You Must Remember This,' " 440.

25. Ellen DuBois maintains that Margaret Cady, Stanton's mother, was not the cold, distant figure she appears to be in Stanton's memoir. DuBois bases her assessment on the considerable insight she gained into Margaret Cady through Cady's relationship with her granddaughter, Harriot Stanton Blatch. See Ellen Carol DuBois, *Harriot Stanton Blatch and the Winning of Woman Suffrage* (New Haven: Yale University Press, 1997), 16–17.

26. Records of the U.S. Census Bureau, Fourth Census of the United States (1820), New York, Population Schedules, 2: 358. The New York census for Johnstown, Montgomery County, accurately reflects the status of the Cady household between the end of January (as it reflects the birth of Catherine Cady as one of the four free white females under age 10) and the middle of September (when the sixteenth birthday of Tryphena Cady would have placed her in the next category, free white females, aged 16–24. Similarly, the tenth birthday of Harriet Cady on October 5 would have placed her in the next age grouping, free white females, aged 10–14). For geneological data on the Cady family, see Patricia G. Holland and Ann D. Gordon eds., *The Papers of Elizabeth Cady Stanton and Susan B. Anthony, Guide and Index to the Microfilm Edition* (Wilimgton, Del.: Scholarly Resources, 1992), 52–55. Given the property laws of the time, slaves in the Cady family would have technically belonged to Daniel Cady. It is quite possible, however, that the slave might have come into the marriage through Margaret Livingston's family, which was considerably more affluent than Daniel Cady's. In 1800, the year prior to Daniel Cady and Margaret Livingston's marriage, James Livingston, Margaret Livingston Cady's father, is listed as the "head of family" of a household of nine that included two slaves. See Records of the U.S. Census Bureau, Second Census of the United States (1800), New York, Population Schedules, 3: 68–69.

27. Lois Banner identified the "Peter" from Stanton's memoir as Peter Teabout. Since the manuscript census lists only the names of heads of households, it is impossible to say with absolute certainty that Peter Teabout was the male slave aged 26–44 listed at the Cady household in 1820, but it seems likely. Reflecting the abolition of slavery in 1827, Teabout, a free man of color, aged 36–55, appears on the manuscript census of 1830 and on the Fulton County Censuses of 1845, 1855, and 1860. See Banner, *Elizabeth Cady Stanton*, 6; see also Records of the U.S. Census Bureau, Fifth Census of the United States (1830), New York, Population Schedules, 12: 186; and Fulton County Census Records, 1845: 255; 1855: 295; 1860: 47, Fulton County Clerk's Office, Johnstown, N.Y.

28. For an excellent analysis of the practice of "historical amnesia" regarding northern slavery, see Joanne Pope Melish, *Disowning Slavery* (Ithaca: Cornell University Press, 1998). Melish contends that the erasure of slavery from northern history created a particularly devastating form of racism. Rather than explaining the economic and political disadvantages that black people inherited as a result of a particular historical experience (i.e., slavery), those disadvantages were understood to be "natural" and rooted in the body as racial difference.

29. See Shane White, *Somewhat More Independent: The End of Slavery in New York City, 1770–1810* (Athens: University of Georgia Press, 1991), 11, 38, 54; see also Arthur Zilversmit, *The First Emancipation: The Abolition of Slavery in the North* (Chicago and London: The University of Chicago Press, 1967), 213–214. Zilversmit estimates that 10, 000 slaves were emancipated in New York State in 1827. Fourth Census of the United States (1820); totals for Johnstown, N.Y., appear on sheet 381. The census recorded 66 slaves and 86 Free People of Color, a total of 152 African Americans in households in Johnstown in 1820. It bears noting, however, that historians who work extensively with the manuscript census have found errors in the computations of the totals.

30. In many northern towns, under the legal rubric of gradual manumission, slave owners were prohibited from emancipating older slaves (fifty or older) because the towns feared that aged, destitute slaves would become a drain on the public purse. Even after the enactment of Final Abolition, the prior condition of slavery implied an obligation on the part of owners to

continue to provide materially for elderly, infirm, or destitute slaves. The legal obligation of supporting former slaves had been undone by the 1817 law, but a moral obligation remained. McManus, *A History of Negro Slavery in New York*, 142; Zilversmit, *The First Emancipation*, 213.

31. See Fulton County Census Records, 1845: 255; 1855: 295; 1860: 47.

32. Peter was not the only slave held by Elizabeth Cady's extended family; he was, however, the one she knew best. In her memoir Stanton mentions in passing two other black "menservants" who served her family. These men, Jacob and Abraham, may have been slaves in residence at the homes of relatives or neighbors. In addition to her father, several other men in Elizabeth Cady's life variously owned slaves and employed free people of color in their homes: her grandfather James Livingston (two slaves, 1800); her minister Simon Hosack (one slave, two free people of color, 1810; one male free person of color under age 10, 1830); and her brother-in-law Edward Bayard (one male free person of color, aged 10–24, and one female free person of color, aged 24–36, 1830). See Second Census of the United States (1800), New York, Population Schedules, 3: 58, 68–69; Third Census of the United States (1810), New York, Population Schedules, 4:32–33; Fourth Census of the United States (1820), New York, Population Schedules, 2: 358, 364; Fifth Census of the United States (1830), Population Schedules, New York, 12: 185, 186, 188.

33. Mary P. Ryan, *Women in Public: Between Banners and Ballots, 1825–1880* (Baltimore: Johns Hopkins University Press, 1990), 22.

34. Graham Hodges, "New York," in Paul Finkelman and Joseph C. Miller, eds., *Macmillan Encyclopedia of World Slavery*, vol. 2 (New York: Macmillan, 1998), 641. For a discussion of celebrations among slaves and free people of color in the antebellum North, see Shane White, " 'It Was a Proud Day': African Americans, Festivals, and Parades in the North, 1741–1834" *Journal of American History* 81 (1994): 13–50. White maintains (p. 38) that the Fourth of July was traditionally a "white" holiday and that the choice of this date for the final abolition "posed some awkward questions for African Americans." Some chose to celebrate the Final Abolition on the following day, July 5; others chose to reclaim July 4 as the "Jubilee of Emancipation from Domestic Slavery."

35. White, " 'It Was A Proud Day,' " 22. White has reconstructed a rich tradition of African American festivals that punctuated the calendar year in upstate New York. Especially prominent was the "Pinkster" festival, held in honor of the Dutch celebration of Pentecost. Other festivals included "Election Day" or "Negro Election Day" in which blacks elected a king or governor. Training Day was typically held in June in a break in the agricultural calendar after the crops were planted. White contends that these events were originally "white" holidays that African Americans gradually appropriated and infused "with new life and meanings."

36. Stanton's portrayal of Peter is in keeping with the dominant white culture's feminization of black male servants, although she might not have seen it as such. She remembered his playfulness and domesticity with fondness and, particularly as a grandparent, interacted with her own grandchildren in similar ways. When her grandchildren were little, she was "impressed into their service to dress dolls and tell stories" just as she had been when her own children were young. Stanton, a generation older, used to get very tired and "sometimes, when I heard the little feet coming, I would hide, but they would hunt until they found me" (428). On the feminization of black male servants, see Jan Nederveen Pieterse, *White on Black: Images of Africa and Blacks in Western Popular Culture* (New Haven: Yale University Press, 1992), 154.

37. Stanton's reference to Peter as "a prince" and "the grandest specimen of manhood" served explicitly to counter the hegemonic discourse of "civilization" that linked whiteness, manhood, and power in the 1890s, a decade that witnessed the construction of the "Negro rapist" as the primary threat to civilized white manhood (and womanhood). For an excellent analysis of this discourse, see Gail Bederman, *Manliness and Civilization: A Cultural History of Gender and Race in the United States, 1880–1917* (Chicago: University of Chicago Press, 1995), 45–76.

38. Stanton quotes "Uncle Ned," a famous nineteenth-century minstrel song. The figure of "Uncle" in American culture—popularized in part by Harriet Beecher Stowe's *Uncle Tom's Cabin*—referenced an older black male, stereotypically faithful and satisfied with life under slavery. Invoked by white people, the term "Uncle" "might be [a term] of affection, which indi-

cated that the blacks were regarded as 'family.' " For this analysis, see Pieterse, *White on Black*, 154; see also Marlon Riggs's film *Ethnic Notions*. Peter Teabout's death is recorded as 12 December 1862. See "Peter Teabout," obituary card file, Johnstown Public Library, Johnstown, N.Y. (hereafter NJost).

39. Stanton's biographer Elisabeth Griffith does not mention Peter. Alma Lutz writes, "A Negro to her was a friend—just as Peter had been in her childhood. She had never thought of his color. . . . She could not bear to think of him as a slave, sold perhaps to a cruel master. But at home abolition was never discussed and Abolitionists were regarded as fanatics stirring up trouble." Lois Banner makes a similar point: "Witnessing prejudice against Peter predisposed her toward her later abolitionism." See Griffith, *In Her Own Right*; Alma Lutz, *Created Equal* (New York: John Day, 1940), 13–14; Banner, *Elizabeth Cady Stanton*, 6.

40. Stanton was in certain respects quite private and particularly protective of the memory and reputation of her family. Elisabeth Griffith, for example, writes about a Custom House scandal in 1863 that implicated both her husband and her son Daniel, both of whom lost their positions. Stanton chose not to write about it, although surely it must have augmented her feelings of "betrayal" by the Republican Party, a theme she did write about repeatedly. On the scandal, see Griffith, *In Her Own Right*, 113–115.

41. This is a chronological stretch, as Cady was elected to Congress in 1814.

42. Stanton seemed to have contradictory memories of her brother's death. In at least two versions of this story (1889, 1898) Stanton remembers her father having been present at Eleazer's death: "Well do I remember how tenderly he watched my brother in his last illness, his sighs and tears as he slowly walked up and down the hall" (20). In a 1894 version, in contrast, Stanton remembers her father having been away and returned to find his son "in a coffin." See Stanton, "Reminiscences: Church and Parsonage," *Woman's Tribune*, 20 April 1889; Stanton, *Eighty Years*, 20; Stanton, "Reminiscences"; Stanton, "Reminiscences of Elizabeth Cady Stanton," *Mail and Express* (New York) 15 December 1894, clipping, Stanton Papers, DLC.

43. In another version, Stanton wrote that "I went to bed that night thinking what I would do. I decided that I would learn to ride my pony." See Stanton, "Reminiscences," 1.

44. Stanton, "Reminiscences: Church and Parsonage," *Woman's Tribune*, 20 April 1889.

45. In another version Stanton credits her brother-in-law Edward Bayard with teaching her to ride, but the intended result was the same: to please her father. See Stanton, "Reminiscences," 2.

46. Stanton, "Reminiscences," 2. Daniel Cady's suggestion to delegate the sewing to a "strong Irish girl," presumably a servant, adds a class and ethnic dimension to this particular vision of "boyhood." Irish girls might, like boys, be strong, but their strength should be directed to household tasks. The strength of his young daughter, on the other hand, could be applied to more leisurely pursuits.

47. The historian Anthony Rotundo has demonstrated that in nineteenth-century small towns, "the neighboring orchards, fields, and forests provided a natural habitat for boy culture." See E. Anthony Rotundo, *American Manhood: Transformations in Masculinity from the Revolution to the Modern Era* (New York: Basic Books, 1993), 33.

48. On the values of boyhood in the nineteenth century, see Rotundo, *American Manhood*, 41–46. Navigating one's own vessel was a metaphor Stanton used in her famous "Solitude of Self" speech in 1892: "To guide our own craft, we must be captain, pilot, engineer; with chart and compass to stand at the wheel; to watch the winds and waves, and know when to take in the sail. . . . It matters not whether the solitary voyager is man or woman; nature, having endowed them equally, leaves them to their own skill and judgment in the hour of danger, and, if not equal to the occasion, alike they perish." See Stanton, "The Solitude of Self" in Ellen Carol DuBois, ed., *The Elizabeth Cady Stanton–Susan B. Anthony Reader: Correspondence, Writings, Speeches* (1981; rev. ed., Boston: Northeastern University Press, 1992), 248 (hereafter *Stanton-Anthony Reader*).

49. Stanton, "Reminiscences," 2. While Stanton constructs the Reverend Hosack primarily as a foil for her father, like Peter he also functions as a surrogate mother. In this case his maternal shoulder provides comfort from the sting of her father's harsh indictment: "you should have been a boy."

50. See Stanton, "Reminiscences," 1. Stanton makes several references to Hosack's poverty, explaining his indigence by "the six negroes who ate him out of house and home." When Stanton's children published a highly edited version of her autobiography in 1922, the language of slavery had become explicit: the neighbor endured "a family of slaves who ate them out of house and home." See Stanton, *Elizabeth Cady Stanton as Revealed*, 1: 19. In the 1820 census, the household headed by Simon Hosack included only one other person. In 1810, however, Hosack's household included one slave and two free people of color. In 1830, Hosack's household included one free person of color, a male child under the age of ten. None of the manuscript censuses from 1800 to 1830 recorded the "six negroes" whom Stanton described in her writings. Hosack owned real estate valued at $800, but apparently had difficulty maintaining it. In 1826 the village government ordered Hosack to repave the area opposite his lot. When he failed to comply, the village board authorized their attorney to prosecute Hosack. A year later, the board ordered Hosack to install a sewer. See Records of the U.S. Census Bureau, Second Census (1800), Population Schedules, New York, 3: 68–69; Third Census (1810), Population Schedules, New York, 4: 32; Fourth Census (1820), Population Schedules, New York, 2: 364; Fifth Census (1830), Population Schedules, New York, 12: 188. Information on Simon Hosack's property values, tax liabilities, and difficulties with the village government can be found in Johnstown Village Minute Book, 1808–1836, microfilm 76-27-1, Manuscripts and Special Collections, New York State Archives, Albany (hereafter N-Ar). See entries dated 2 June 1826, 5 August 1826, and 21 June 1827.

51. Stanton, "Reminiscences," 3. Another question one might ask: what was Hosack's investment in his young neighbor? Stanton provided one clue in her "Reminiscences." For four or five years, Elizabeth drove the Reverend's carriage "while he sat reading the *Edinburgh Review*."

52. Register, Troy Female Seminary, 2 January 1831, 2 March 1831, 21 September 1831, Emma Willard School Archives, Troy, N.Y.

53. Stanton, "Reminiscences," 5.

54. Rotundo, *American Manhood*, 39. Rotundo writes, "Indeed, the consideration of loyalty was so important in the competitive milieu of boy culture that these youthful relationships often took on the qualities of an alliance."

55. Rotundo, *American Manhood*, 43.

56. Stanton to Victoria Clafin Woodhull Martin, 4 October 1898.

57. As quoted in *Proceedings of the First Anniversary of the American Equal Rights Association, Held at the Church of the Puritans, New York, May 9 and 10, 1867* (New York: Robert J. Johnson, 1867), 47.

58. Judith Butler has developed a "performative" theory of gender that has deeply influenced the way historians of gender conceptualize men's and women's roles, behaviors, and identities in the past. Butler goes beyond arguing for a "socially constructed" as opposed to a "natural" ontological status for gender; she maintains, rather, that gender categories attain their status as "natural" only through constant imitation and performance. I am using Butler's theory to suggest that Stanton's "womanly performance" actually permitted her a wider range of transgressive behaviors and views. See Judith Butler, *Gender Trouble: Feminism and the Subversion of Identity* (New York: Routledge, 1990); and "Imitation and Gender Subordination," in Henry Abelove et al., eds., *The Lesbian and Gay Studies Reader* (New York: Routledge, 1993), 307–320.

59. Stanton, "Solitude of Self," in *Stanton-Anthony Reader*, 253–254. This same passage can be found in earlier speeches as well. See, for example, her 1881 address to the Free Religions Association printed in *Free Religions Index*, 23 June 1881.

60. Stanton interview, "An American Stateswoman." Evidence of boyhood aspirations abounds in this scene. According to Anthony Rotundo, an important aspect of nineteenth-century boy culture was the practice of imitating the work of one's father. See Rotundo, *American Manhood*, 37.

61. In an earlier version of this story, Stanton makes the point that the laws regarding property are particularly cruel to married women: "A woman who had a child out of marriage could own it." See Stanton, "Reminiscences," 3. While Stanton's analysis relies on anecdotal evidence and suggests that at least part of the fault of women's economic dependence lies in lap of un-

grateful sons, her observations are reflective of a larger pattern. The postrevolutionary period witnessed the decline of women's dower rights (entitlement to lifetime use of one third of the husband's estate upon his death) in virtually every state. Although dower rights had not been abolished, new restrictions were placed upon them, making it increasingly difficult for women to sustain themselves in widowhood. See Hoff, *Law, Gender, and Injustice,* 106–116.

62. Stanton, interview, "An American Stateswoman."

63. In the version of this story Stanton tells in the autobiography, she does not even indicate that Flora Campbell has a legal problem. Stanton says simply: "However, this mutilation of his volumes was never accomplished, for dear old Flora Campbell, to whom I confided my plan for the amelioration of the wrongs of my unhappy sex, warned my father of what I proposed to do." In another version, Stanton plants more evidence of her childhood anticlericalism, contending that the attack on the law books was planned for a Sunday morning "when they are all in church." See Stanton, "Reminiscences," 3.

64. Stanton, "Reminiscences," 4.

65. This is a curious omission, especially as every biography relies on the same source, Stanton's autobiography, the principal writing in which she details the story of the coral jewelry and the law books. Yet virtually every interpretation of Stanton—from the first biography of her written by Alma Lutz in 1940 to Ken Burns's 1999 film—makes the same omission. Separated by four decades, the biographies by Alma Lutz and Elisabeth Griffith both omit the coral jewelry episode. See Lutz, *Created Equal,* 3–5; Banner, *Elizabeth Cady Stanton,* 8; and Griffith, *In Her Own Right,* 11. Lesser-known works also eliminate this part of the story. See, for example, Alice Hubbard, *Life Lessons: Truths Concerning People Who Have Lived* (East Aurora, N.Y.: Roycrofters, 1909), 155; and Mary Ann B. Oakley, *Elizabeth Cady Stanton* (Old Westbury, N.Y.: Feminist Press, 1972), 19. See also Barbara Goldsmith, *Other Powers: The Age of Suffrage, Spiritualism, and the Scandalous Victoria Woodhull* (New York: Knopf, 1998), 42.

66. Emphasis added. The text is almost identical in the column in the *Woman's Tribune.* Stanton deleted the story about the jewelry in only one version. See Stanton, "Reminiscences," 3.

67. Stanton, "Reminiscences," 3; Elisabeth Griffith makes this point in *In Her Own Right,* 11.

68. There is some confusion over the actual date of this speech. In the autobiography, Stanton places the speech in 1854 (p. 187). Ann Gordon points out, however, that in other versions of her "Reminiscences," Stanton dated the speech as 1840, 1846, and 1848, but never as 1854. Furthermore, Gordon notes that the legislators only received a printed copy of the 1854 speech, as Stanton had not been invited to appear before them. See Gordon, "Afterword," in *Eighty Years,* 475–476.

69. Stanton to Equal Rights Club of Hartford, Conn., *Boston Investigator,* 4 April 1886.

70. I return to the "limits of politics" theme in Chapter 3, where I examine Stanton's political career in the 1880s–1890s.

71. Stanton remembered Peter as "the only colored member of the church" (17). However, the Parish Register of the Church enumerated five baptisms, three marriages, and two burials of African American members between 1818–1834. Town lore and local histories confirm Stanton's account that, in the words of one popular writer, "The Cadys were Presbyterians but Black Peter went to the Episcopal Church." However, Peter Teabout does not appear in local church records until he joined the First Methodist Episcopal Church with his wife Mariah in 1847. In 1823, however, the attorney for the Episcopal Church was authorized to pursue Daniel Cady for "immediate payment for all back [pew] rent," raising the possibility that Cady was expected to underwrite Peter Teabout's pew costs at the Episcopal Church. See St. John's Episcopal Church, Parish Register, 1815–1862, compiled by Mildred Rothburn, NJost; Catherine Bryant Rowles, *Tomahawks to Hatpins* (Lakemont, N.Y.: North Country Books, 1975), 135; Peter Teabout, Obituary Card File, NJost; St. John's Episcopal Church (Johnstown, N.Y.) Vestry Records, 1809–1863, 17 February 1823, p. 135, microfilm #76-28-1, N-AR.

72. See, for example, Mary P. Ryan, *Cradle of the Middle Class: The Family in Oneida County, New York, 1790–1835* (Cambridge: Cambridge University Press, 1981); Whitney R. Cross, *The Burned-Over District: The Social and Intellectual History of Enthusiastic Religion in Western New York* (Ithaca: Cornell University Press, 1950).

73. Stanton's negative reaction to Finney reflected her foundational belief that clergy too often inspired fear and subverted the power of individual conscience. However, Finney's historical legacy has been much more positive. Finney has earned a reputation as a great democratizer of American Christianity. Finney was noted for his use of the vernacular, his audience-centered worship style, and his belief that salvation rested with the individual, not with the arbitrary grace of God. See, for example, Charles Grandison Finney, *Lectures on Revivals of Religion*, ed. William G. McLoughlin (Cambridge, Mass.: Belknap, 1960), viii–xi; also Nathan O. Hatch, *The Democratization of American Christianity* (New Haven and London: Yale University Press, 1989), 196–201.

74. To track Finney's whereabouts in 1831–1832, I used correspondence, newspaper accounts, and Finney's memoir. No contemporary accounts place Finney in Troy at the revival of 1830–1831. On two occasions during Stanton's tenure at the seminary, Finney appeared in Troy for several days—in July 1831 and December 1832—but never for a stretch of six weeks as Stanton remembered and never coinciding with a revival. For coverage of the Troy revival (1830–1831), see *New York Evangelist*, 8 January 1831, 161; 15 January 1831, 167; 22 January 1831, 171; 12 February 1831, 183; 19 February 1831, 185. For evidence of Finney's presence (and subsequent illness) in Rochester during the time of the Troy revival, see *New York Evangelist*, 15 January 1831, 167; 12 February 1831, 183; see also "Chronology of Charles G. Finney's Life," 7–8, Charles G. Finney Papers, Oberlin College Archives, Oberlin, Ohio; and *The Memoirs of Charles G. Finney*, ed. Garth M. Rosell and Richard Dupuis (Grand Rapids: Academie Books, 1989), 328–330. On Finney's brief visits to Troy, see *Memoirs of Charles G. Finney*, 340, n.61; Charles G. Finney to Theodore D. Weld, 21 July 1831, Weld-Grimké Family Papers, Clements Library, University of Michigan, Ann Arbor; and "Chronology of Charles G. Finney's Life," 8, 10. On the timing of Elizabeth Cady's arrival at Miss Willard's School, see Register, Troy Female Seminary, for term beginning September 15, 1830, Emma Willard School, Troy, N.Y., Archives. The name "Elizabeth Cadey" appears out of alphabetical order on the third page of "Boarders" under the date January 2, 1831.

75. Stanton, "Fear," n.d., 8–9, Stanton Papers, DLC.

76. According to Bernard Weisberger, Beman was not entirely popular in Troy. He was, like Finney, a proponent of the lively "new methods" of salvation that many traditional Presbyterians, clergy and lay people, resented. See Weisberger, *They Gathered at the River: The Story of the Great Revivalists and Their Impact upon Religion in America* (New York: Quadrangle, 1958), 115–117.

77. Josephus Brockway, *A Delineation of the Characteristic Features of a Revival of Religion in Troy, in 1826 and 1827. By J. Brockway, Lay Member of the Congregational Church in Middlebury, Vt., Now a Citizen of Troy* (Troy, 1827), 40, as quoted in Weisberger, *They Gathered at the River*, 115.

78. Beman faced a heresy trial in 1826. See Weisberger, *They Gathered at the River*, 114–115.

79. Gordon, "Afterword," in *Eighty Years*, 476.

80. In thinking about historicizing "experience," I have been influenced by Joan W. Scott's "The Evidence of Experience," in Abelove et al., eds., *The Lesbian and Gay Studies Reader*, 397–415.

81. Perhaps not coincidentally, Niagara Falls is often cited in delineating nineteenth-century agnostics' belief in the "religion of nature." In his novel *Esther*, Henry Adams places his heroine at Niagara Falls, "that huge church which was thundering its gospel under her eyes." For this analysis, see James Turner, *Without God, without Creed: The Origins of Unbelief in America* (Baltimore: Johns Hopkins University Press, 1985), 255.

82. In this passage, Stanton portrayed the Mormons as Bible-based Christians; however, many traditional Christians saw the Mormons as heretics, in part because of their practice of polygamy.

83. Maureen Fitzgerald has argued the importance of the religious roots of Stanton's thought, particularly her concept of the soul, which was "far more encompassing than the concept of political citizenry." See Stanton, *The Woman's Bible*, foreword Maureen Fitzgerald (Boston: Northeastern University Press, 1993), ix.

84. Carroll Smith-Rosenberg, "The Female World of Love and Ritual," *Signs: Journal of Women in Culture and Society* 1: 1 (1975): 1–29.

85. Stanton, "About the Woman's Bible," *Woman's Tribune,* 15 June 1895.
86. Heilbrun, *Writing a Woman's Life,* 17–31. Heilbrun discusses the various "plots" available (and more often unavailable) through which women wrote their lives in the nineteenth century; a religious calling was virtually mandatory.
87. Ibid., 25.
88. Ibid., 23.
89. On Frances Willard's conversion see Carolyn De Swarte Gifford, "Frances Willard and the Woman's Christian Temperance Union's Conversion to Woman Suffrage," in Marjorie Spruill Wheeler, ed., *One Woman, One Vote: Rediscovering the Woman Suffrage Movement* (Troutdale, Ore.: NewSage Press, 1995), 117–134.
90. Stanton, "Bible and Church Degrade Woman," (Chicago: H.L. Green, n.d.), Stanton Papers, DLC.
91. Stanton to Clara D. Bewick Colby, 16 February 1895, Clara Colby Papers, State Historical Society of Wisconsin, Madison; Stanton, "Reminiscences," *Women's Tribune,* 5 September 1891.

2. The "Emasculated Gospel": New Religions, New Bibles, and the Battle for Cultural Authority

1. Harriot Stanton Blatch and Alma Lutz, *Challenging Years: The Memoirs of Harriot Stanton Blatch* (New York. G. P. Putnam, 1940), 63, 61; Elizabeth Cady Stanton, *Eighty Years and More: Reminiscences, 1815–1897,* introd. Ellen Carol DuBois, afterword Ann D. Gordon (1898; rpt. Boston: Northeastern University Press, 1993), 337 (hereafter: *Eighty Years*); Elizabeth Cady Stanton, *Elizabeth Cady Stanton as Revealed in Her Letters, Diary, and Reminiscences,* ed. Theodore Stanton and Harriot Stanton Blatch, 2 vols. (New York: Harper, 1922), 2:192, 193, 195 (hereafter, Stanton, *Elizabeth Cady Stanton as Revealed*); Ellen Carol DuBois, *Harriot Stanton Blatch and the Winning of Woman Suffrage* (New Haven: Yale University Press, 1997), 47–51.
2. Stanton, *Elizabeth Cady Stanton as Revealed,* 2: 191.
3. Susan B. Anthony to Rachel Foster Avery, 29 December 1897, and 17 December 1897, Susan B. Anthony–Rachel Foster Avery Papers, University of Rochester Library, Rochester, N.Y. (hereafter NRU).
4. William R. Hutchinson to Paul A. Carter, 31 March 1969, as quoted in Paul A. Carter, *The Spiritual Crisis of the Gilded Age* (DeKalb: Northern Illinois University Press, 1971), viii. See also William R. Hutchinson, *The Modernist Impulse in American Protestantism* (Cambridge, Mass.: Harvard University Press, 1976).
5. R. Laurence Moore, *Selling God: American Religion in the Marketplace of Culture* (New York: Oxford University Press, 1994), 209.
6. Bernard A. Weisberger, *They Gathered at the River: The Story of the Great Revivalists and Their Impact upon Religion in America* (New York: Quadrangle, 1958), 177; James F. Findlay, Jr., *Dwight L. Moody: American Evangelist 1837–1899* (Chicago: University of Chicago Press, 1969), 198–199.
7. Moore, *Selling God,* 146.
8. Peter J. Wosh, *Spreading the Word: The Bible Business in Nineteenth-Century America* (Ithaca: Cornell University Press, 1994), 241.
9. Robert David Thomas, *"With Bleeding Footsteps": Mary Baker Eddy's Path to Religious Leadership* (New York: Knopf, 1994); Beryl Satter, *Each Mind a Kingdom: American Women, Sexual Purity, and the New Thought Movement, 1875–1920* (Berkeley: University of California Press, 1999), 57–70.
10. Stanton to Elizabeth Morrison Boynton Harbert, 9 December 1883, Harbert Papers, Box 7, Folder 102, Huntington Library, San Marino, Calif. (hereafter CSmH).
11. Stanton to Susan B. Anthony, 31 August 1883, Theodore Stanton Collection, Elizabeth Cady Stanton Papers, Rutgers University Libraries, New Brunswick, N.J. (hereafter NjR); Stanton, *Eighty Years,* 356; "Manuscript of Address by Elizabeth Cady Stanton at Prince's Hall, London, England, June 25, 1883," p 70, Elizabeth Cady Stanton Papers, Library of Congress (hereafter DLC). This address is indexed in the Stanton and Anthony Papers as "for National Society for Women's Suffrage meeting." A later version of this speech appeared as "Has Chris-

tianity Benefited Woman?" *North American Review* 140 (May 1885): 389–399. South Place Chapel was Moncure Conway's radical church.

12. Priscilla Bright McLaren to Stanton, 17 July 1883, Theodore Stanton Collection, Elizabeth Cady Stanton Papers, NjR.

13. Stanton to Antoinette Louisa Brown Blackwell, 27 April 1886, Blackwell Family Papers, Schlesinger Library, Radcliffe Institute, Cambridge Mass. (hereafter MCR-S). For a detailed treatment of this dynamic, see Chapter 3.

14. Stanton, *Elizabeth Cady Stantons as Revealed*, 2:264 ; Ellen Carol DuBois, ed., *The Elizabeth Cady Stanton–Susan B. Anthony Reader: Correspondence, Writings, Speeches*, (1981; rev. ed., Boston: Northeastern University Press, 1992), 183–184, (hereafter *Stanton-Anthony Reader*); Barbara Taylor, *Eve and the New Jerusalem: Socialism and Feminism in the Nineteenth Century* (New York: Pantheon, 1983), 284. Taylor has argued that in Britain, Secularism provided a space for feminist agitation and also had extensive ties to working-class radicalism. Besant eventually abandoned Secularism for Theosophy, a conversion that Stanton found lamentable.

15. Stanton, *Eighty Years*, 360.

16. Ellen DuBois's insight that Stanton applied, adapted, and diverted theories intended to apply exclusively to men holds true here as well. DuBois makes this point briefly in regard to Stanton's contributions to Secularism and more extensively in regard to her feminist appropriation of "natural rights" theory. See Ellen DuBois, "The Limitations of Sisterhood: Elizabeth Cady Stanton and Division in the American Woman Suffrage Movement, 1875–1902," in *Woman Suffrage and Women's Rights* (New York: New York University Press, 1998), 163; DuBois, ed., *Stanton-Anthony Reader*, xiii.

17. William Leach, *True Love and Perfect Union: The Feminist Reform of Sex and Society* (New York: Basic Books, 1980), 142. Lois Banner also discusses Stanton's Positivism. See Banner, *Elizabeth Cady Stanton, A Radical for Woman's Rights* (Boston: Little, Brown, 1980), 86.

18. Henry Edger, interview, New York *World*, 14 September 1867.

19. Stanton, "Rev. Henry Edgar [*sic*]," *Revolution*, 10 June 1869. I use the term "nineteenth-century feminist" with awareness of the debate among historians as to whether or not this usage is anachronistic. Though I use such language sparingly, I agree with those who argue that the history of "feminism" precedes the use of the term.

20. Auguste Comte, "Conclusion: The Religion of Humanity," in *Système de Politique Positive*, Gertrude Lenzer, ed., *Auguste Comte and Positivism: The Essential Writings* (New York: Harper, 1975), 383.

21. Comte, "Cours de Philosophie Positive" in *Auguste Comte and Positivism*, 204, 210.

22. Henry Edger, interview, New York *World*.

23. Stanton, "Rev. Henry Edgar [*sic*]" *Revolution*, 10 June 1869. See also Leach's argument for a feminist reformation of Positivism in *True Love and Perfect Union*, 153–157.

24. As quoted in Elizabeth Cady Stanton, et al., eds., *History of Woman Suffrage*, vol. 2 (Rochester: Susan B. Anthony, 1881), 186; see also *Proceedings of the First Anniversary of the American Equal Rights Association, Held at the Church of the Puritans, New York, May 9 and 10, 1867* (New York: Robert J. Johnson, 1867) (hereafter AERA *Proceedings*).

25. AERA *Proceedings*, 9–10.

26. For a treatment of Henry Edger's career, see Robert Edward Schneider, *Positivism in the United States: The Apostleship of Henry Edger* (Rosario, Argentina: Universidad Nacional, 1946).

27. As quoted in Stanton, "Rev. Henry Edgar [*sic*]," *Revolution*, 10 June 1869.

28. Stanton, "Rev. Henry Edgar [*sic*] (cont.)," *The Revolution*, 17 June 1869.

29. AERA *Proceedings*, 9–10.

30. Stanton, "Woman in the Bible," 6–11; Stanton Papers, DLC. References within the speech situate it within the 1867 Kansas campaign.

31. Stanton's untitled speech to the Free Religions Association was printed in *Free Religions Index*, 23 June 1881. Examples of her adaptations of Positivism in the 1880s can also be found in "Manuscript of Address by Elizabeth Cady Stanton at Prince's Hall," 38, 77; and "Has Christianity Benefitted Woman?" 393, 394.

32. Stanton, "Worship of God in Man," *Open Court* 7 (Oct 26, 1893): 3850–3852. Stanton did not attend the World Parliament of Religions, held in conjunction with the World's

Columbian Exposition in Chicago, 1893. Susan B. Anthony delivered Stanton's speech, "Worship of God in Man."

33. Anthony to Stanton, 24 July 1895, Anthony Family Papers, CSmH.

34. For an excellent study that demonstrates the centrality of Spiritualism to American culture and the woman's rights movement, see Ann Braude, *Radical Spirits: Spiritualism and Women's Rights in Nineteenth-Century America* (Boston: Beacon, 1989); also R. Laurence Moore, *In Search of White Crows: Spiritualism, Parapsychology, and American Culture* (New York: Oxford University Press, 1977).

35. Works on Eddy include Robert Peel, *Mary Baker Eddy: The Years of Discovery* (New York: Holt, Rinehart and Winston, 1966); Thomas, *"With Bleeding Footsteps"*; and Gillian Gill, *Mary Baker Eddy* (New York: Perseus Book, 1998).

36. Satter, *Each Mind a Kingdom*, 66–78. Satter convincingly demonstrates that the contested debates over the gendered nature of mind and matter were tied to a larger debate about "civilization" and whether it would be enhanced by women's virtue or men's passion.

37. Ibid., 57–78.

38. Ibid., 82, 84.

39. Emma Curtis Hopkins, "C.S. Ordination Address," *Christian Science* 1, no. 10 (June 1889): 272–273, quoted in Satter, *Each Mind a Kingdom*, 92.

40. Stanton to Elizabeth Smith Miller, 31 October 1886, Theodore Stanton Collection, Elizabeth Cady Stanton Papers, NjR.

41. Stanton, *Eighty Years*, 392.

42. Stanton to Rachel Foster Avery, 12 January 1887, Anthony-Avery Papers, NRU.

43. Stanton to Sara Underwood, n.d. August 1887, Elizabeth Cady Stanton Papers, Vassar College Library, Poughkeepsie, N.Y. (hereafter NPV); Stanton to Benjamin and Sara Underwood, 5 April 1887, Stanton Papers, NPV.

44. Stanton to Elizabeth Smith Miller, 29 May 1888, Theodore Stanton Collection, Elizabeth Cady Stanton Papers, NjR.

45. In Great Britain the older label "Freethought" gradually gave way to the more modern term "Secularism." In the United States, however, the term "Freethought" persisted, although in the postwar period it was used seemingly interchangeably with "Secularism." In London in 1869, Thomas Huxley coined the term "agnosticism," which was also used widely in America to connote a suspension in the belief in God.

46. These themes are developed in James Turner, *Without God, without Creed: The Origins of Unbelief in America* (Baltimore: Johns Hopkins University Press, 1985), 172.

47. See the *Index*, 28 September 1882; 12 October 1882; 4 January 1883.

48. Andrew Dickson White, *A History of the Warfare of Science with Theology in Christendom* (New York: D. Appleton, 1896). Robert Green Ingersoll, *The Lectures of Col. R. G. Ingersoll* (Chicago: Rhodes and McClure, 1898), 787.

49. Stanton read Andrew Dickson White's book, corresponded with him, and sent him a copy of the *Woman's Bible*. She nearly became his relative as well. For a brief period in the 1880s, Stanton's son Theodore was engaged to White's daughter, but the engagement was (amicably) broken. See DuBois, *Harriot Stanton Blatch*, 36.

50. Stanton to Harriot Stanton Blatch, 21 February 1895, Theodore Stanton Collection, Elizabeth Cady Stanton Papers, NjR. Stanton was deeply saddened at Ingersoll's death. On July 27, 1899, she wrote: "No other loss, outside of my own family could have filled me with such sorrow. The future historian will rank him as one of the heroes of the nineteenth century." See Stanton, *Elizabeth Cady Stanton as Revealed*, 2: 340.

51. Stanton to Sara Underwood, 11 July 1885, Special Collections, Chicago Public Library.

52. Stanton to Benjamin Franklin Underwood, 11 April 1885, Stanton Papers, MCR-S.

53. Stanton, untitled, *Free Religious Index*, 23 June 1881.

54. Benny Kraut, *From Reform Judaism to Ethical Culture: The Religious Evolution of Felix Adler* (Cincinnati: Hebrew Union College Press, 1979).

55. Stanton wrote about Adler in her diary on 25 November 1880, and 29 May 1881. See Stanton, *Elizabeth Cady Stanton as Revealed*, 2: 180, 184.

56. Stanton to Henry Brewster Stanton Jr., 2 August 1880, in *Elizabeth Cady Stantons as Re-*

vealed, 2: 171. Stanton wrote this letter in reference to her reading of William Lecky's *History of Rationalism in Europe*.

57. On the connections between gender, equality, and Freethought, see Taylor, *Eve and the New Jerusalem*, 123. Taylor argues that in the 1830s–1840s, English Owenite feminist infidels determined that sexual emancipation depended upon dismantling patriarchal, Christian orthodoxy. Lori Ginzberg has found a different tendency among Freethinkers of the antebellum United States: a resistance among male Freethinkers to women's full equality. Lori D Ginzberg, " 'The Hearts of Your Readers Will Shudder': Fanny Wright, Infidelity, and American Freethought," *American Quarterly* 46 (1994): 195–226.

58. Tensions between Stanton and Gage erupted over the copyrighting of the *Woman's Bible* in 1895. See Chapter 4. On Gage's career, see Mary E. Paddock Corey, "Matilda Joslyn Gage: Woman Suffrage Historian, 1852–1898" (Ph.D. diss., University of Rochester, 1995); Leila Rae Brammer, "The Exclusionary Politics of Social Movements: Matilda Joslyn Gage and the National American Woman Suffrage Association (Ph.D. diss., University of Minnesota, 1995).

59. Stanton, "Has Christianity Benefited Woman?", 397.

60. Stanton to Benjamin Franklin Underwood, 19 October 1885, Stanton Papers, NPV.

61. Stanton, "The Clergy and the Woman's Cause," *Index* (Boston), 5 March 1885.

62. Matilda Joslyn Gage, *Woman, Church and State* (1893; rpt. New York: Arno, 1972), 533.

63. Thomas DeWitt Talmadge, "Downfall of Christianity," *Christian Herald and Sign of Our Times*, 12 February 1885. For an analysis of women's response to this literature, see Joan Jacobs Brumberg, "Zenanas and Girlless Villages: The Ethnology of American Evangelical Women, 1870–1910" *Journal of American History* 69 (1982): 347–371. See also a fascinating discussion of this debate in Louise Michele Newman, *White Women's Rights: The Racial Origins of Feminism in the United States* (New York: Oxford University Press, 1999), 22–55.

64. Stanton to Sara Underwood, 11 July 1885.

65. Stanton to Sara Underwood, n.d. August 1887.

66. T.B.W. [Thaddeus B. Wakeman], "Elizabeth Cady Stanton's Life and Liberalism," *Woman's Tribune*, 30 April 1898, 36.

67. William Leach suggests in *True Love and Perfect Union* that Stanton, because of her Positivism, was a collectivist rather than an individualist and that historians have essentially miscast her. I argue instead that Stanton found plenty of support within Positivism for her commitment to the individual conscience. For example, Comte argued that the "organic state" would first emerge in the minds of individuals and eventually become embodied in institutions. It seems to me that as Stanton aged, her commitment to the individual conscience became more pronounced, although she never stopped searching for more collective solutions to social problems. She believed that large scale social change had to begin at the level of the individual conscience. See Leach, *True Love and Perfect Union*, 143–152.

68. Diary entry, 25 November 1882 in Stanton, *Elizabeth Cady Stanton as Revealed*, 2: 198.

69. Stanton to Elizabeth Smith Miller, 5 March 1887, Theodore Stanton Collection, Elizabeth Cady Stanton Papers, NjR.

70. On the impact of Darwin, see Lewis Perry, *Intellectual Life in America: A History* (New York: F. Watts, 1984), 292. "To be sure," writes Perry, "one die-hard Princeton theologian, Charles Hodge, wrote *What is Darwinism?* (1874) and gave the answer, 'It is Atheism.' " But Hodge's significance has "often been exaggerated." See also Bruce Kuklick, *Churchmen and Philosophers: From Jonathan Edwards to John Dewey* (New Haven: Yale University Press, 1985), 78. Kuklick has maintained that secularists who were inspired by Darwin, such as John Dewey, made a practice of translating older religious values into a modern scientific discourse, rather than replacing those values with new "scientific" ones. See also Charles E. Rosenberg, *No Other Gods: On Science and American Social Thought* (Baltimore: Johns Hopkins University Press, 1962), 3; Cynthia Russett, *Darwin in America: The Intellectual Response, 1865–1912* (San Francisco: W. H. Freeman, 1976), 25–26; and Philip Appleman, ed., *Darwin, Norton Critical Edition* (New York: Norton, 1979).

71. Turner, *Without God, without Creed*, 122, 185.

72. Sydney E. Ahlstrom, *A Religious History of the American People*, vol. 2 (New York: Doubleday, 1975), 224–249.

73. T. J. Jackson Lears, *No Place of Grace: Antimodernism and the Transformation of American Culture, 1880–1920* (1981; rpt. Chicago: University of Chicago Press, 1994), 41, 22–23.

74. Turner, *Without God, without Creed*, 182.

75. For a discussion of the impact of Colenso in America, see Ira V. Brown, "The Higher Criticism Comes to America, 1880–1900," *Journal of the Presbyterian Historical Society* 38 (1960): 193–212.

76. For a discussion of the impact of David F. Strauss, see Jerry Wayne Brown, *The Rise of Biblical Criticism in America, 1800–1870: The New England Scholars* (Middletown, Conn.: Wesleyan University Press, 1969), 140–152; also Turner, *Without God, without Creed*, 147. In the antebellum period, Brown argues, Bible scholars had divided into liberal and conservative camps. Centered at Harvard, New England liberals used higher criticism not to invalidate the Bible but to deflate orthodox Calvinism. Conservatives, anchored at Andover Theological Seminary, taught biblical criticism from a perspective that preserved the doctrines of inspiration and infallibility. After the Civil War, the "progressive orthodox" at Andover Seminary abandoned their conservative origins and pioneered a new, highly secularized approach to the Bible. On Andover liberals and their progressive orthodoxy, see Kuklick, *Churchmen and Philosophers*, 216–225.

77. Stanton and the Revising Committee, *The Woman's Bible*. (New York: European Publishing Co., 1895; rpt. Seattle: Coalition Task Force on Women and Religion, 1974), 1: 56 (hereafter *Woman's Bible*).

78. Philip Schaff, *Historical Account of the Work of the American Committee of Revision* (New York: Charles Scribner and Sons, 1885), 3.

79. Philip Schaff, "The Old Version and the New," *North American Review* 132 (1881): 428.

80. A proposed alteration failing to earn a two-thirds vote was relegated to the margins of the revised text. So were changes proposed by the American committee, but rejected by the even more cautious British committee with whom the Americans collaborated on the revision.

81. Philip Schaff points out in his *Historical Account* that the clergy were not paid a fee for the revision. They raised funds for the work through subscriptions sales to patrons. However, virtually all committee members were employed by divinity schools or denominations that would have certain expectations of their revising work.

82. *New York Herald*, 21 May 1881; *New York Tribune*, 21 May 1881; *New York Times*, 22 May 1881; *New York Independent*, 26 May 1881.

83. *New York Herald*, 21 May 1881.

84. *New York Herald*, 21 May 1881; *New York Tribune*, 21 May 1881; *New York Times*, 23 May 1881.

85. *New York Times*, 20 May 1881; 23 May 1881. Reporters found one pastor who heralded the revision as "the greatest event that has happened in the religious world in 300 years."

86. F. F. Bruce, *The English Bible: A History of Translations from the Earliest Versions to the New English Bible* (New York: Oxford University Press, 1970), 138.

87. W. C. Doane, "The Revision of the New Testament," *American Catholic Review* 36 (1881): 63. See also James A. Concoran, "The Latest of the Revisions," *American Catholic Quarterly Review* 6 (1881): 150–168; Edward F. X. McSweeny, "The Scholars and the Bible," *American Catholic Quarterly Review* 6 (1881): 300–315; and J. J. Steward Perowine, "The Revised Version of the New Testament," *Contemporary Review* 40 (1881): 150–168.

88. Thomas A. Becker, "The New Version of a Protestant New Testament," *Catholic World* 33 (1881): 568.

89. Doane, "The Revision of the New Testament," 63–64.

90. As quoted in *New York Times*, 6 June 1881.

91. O. D. Miller, "The Revised Version," *The Universalist Quarterly and General Review*, New Series, 18 (1881): 467; G. Vance Smith, "A Reviser on the New Revision," *Nineteenth Century* 9 (1881): 919.

92. Reviewers had mixed reactions to the committee's decision to piece together a hybrid Greek text. Some clergymen believed the committee should have based the revision on just one of the existing Greek translations.

93. Having promised to "introduce as few alterations as possible into the text of the Autho-

rized Version," Doane noted, "they have introduced, and state it with a sort of boast, between eight and nine changes in every two verses." Doane, "The Revision of the New Testament," 63–64.

94. Smith, "A Reviser on the New Revision," 933; *Edinburgh Review* 154 (1881): 179. Those alterations with the greatest theological import centered around issues of salvation and damnation. Was it appropriate, for example, for the revisers to replace "evil" in the Lord's Prayer—"deliver us from evil"—with the new phrase, "the evil one," thus reinforcing the concept of a satanic being? As Smith suggested, this choice in translation reflected a theological interpretation. "Satan was a personage of supreme importance with the old Church Fathers, as indeed he still is with no small number of modern theologians. They saw him and his bad influence everywhere, as they are still seen by multitudes."

95. *New York Times* 23 May 1881.

96. T. DeWitt Talmadge as quoted in *New York Times*, 6 June 1881.

97. Schaff, "The Old Version and the New," 434.

98. *New York Times*, 21 November 1881 and 28 October 1881.

99. Talmadge as quoted in *New York Times*, 6 June 1881. Other clergy defended the Americans on the revising team, but blamed the "literary botch" on the English. The American Baptist Union, for example, announced yet a newer edition of the revision that would adopt the American changes and place those of the British in the margins. See *New York Times*, 21 June 1881.

100. *Edinburgh Review* 154 (July 1881): 188. One reviewer, for example, disparaged the process of revising the New Testament as "laying it on the table of the anatomist and dissecting it," as quoted in Smith, "A Reviser on the New Revision," 919; another reviewer charged that the number of minute changes showed that the "microscope has been used too much and the telescope too little." See Doane, "The Revision of the New Testament," 82.

101. *New York Times*, 23 May 1881 and 28 October 1881.

102. The *New York Times*, 28 October 1881, reported: "It was the child of the nineteenth century—scientific, but not poetic; accurate, but not spiritual. . . . It could never be the Bible of the people."

103. *Woman's Bible*, 1: 12.

104. Stanton, interview, New York *World*, 17 March 1895.

105. Stanton, "Bible and Church Degrade Woman," pamphlet (Chicago: H.L. Green, n.d.), 5, Elizabeth Cady Stanton Papers, DLC.

106. For discussions of the growth of the religious publishing market in the nineteenth century, see Moore, *Selling God*, and Wosh, *Spreading the Word*.

107. Stanton to Robert Livingston Stanton, 3 August 1895, Theodore Stanton Collection, Elizabeth Cady Stanton Papers, NjR.

108. Robert Jamieson, A. R. Fausset, and David Brown, *A Commentary Critical and Explanatory on the Old and New Testaments*, vol. 1 (Cincinnati: National Publishing Co., 1871), 1.

109. George P. Fisher, "The Revised New Testament," *Scribner's Monthly* 22 (1881): 300.

110. Becker, "The New Version," 559.

111. *Watchman*, 7 March 1895, 5.

112. Stanton, *Woman's Tribune*, 1 June 1895, 85.

113. Ingersoll, *The Lectures*, 789.

114. *Watchman*, 23 May 1895, 27.

115. Frances E. Willard, *Woman in the Pulpit* (Chicago: Woman's Temperance Publication Assoc., 1889; rpt. Washington, D.C.: Zenger, 1978), 23.

116. The discussion of Bible reading in this chapter has been informed by the work of literary critics and cultural historians who collectively have challenged the idea of a text having a fixed and singular meaning. The contribution of reader-oriented criticism has been to shift the focus away from the text per se to explore the process by which readers assign meanings to the works they read. For an introduction to the theoretical arguments for reader-based criticism, see Stanley Fish, *Is There A Text in This Class?: The Authority of Interpretive Communities* (Cambridge: Harvard University Press, 1980); Jane Tompkins, *Reader-Response Criticism: From Formalism to Postructuralism* (Baltimore: Johns Hopkins University Press, 1980); and Janice Rad-

way, *Reading the Romance: Women, Patriarchy, and Popular Literature* (Chapel Hill: University of North Carolina Press, 1984). For a discussion of the uses of reading within a historical context, see, for example, Nina Baym, *Novels, Readers, and Reviewers: Responses to Fiction in Antebellum America* (Ithaca: Cornell University Press, 1984); Cathy Davidson, ed., *Reading in America: Literature and Social History* (Baltimore: Johns Hopkins University Press, 1989); Helen Horowitz, " 'Nous Autres:' Reading, Passion, and the Creation of M. Carey Thomas," *Journal of American History* 79 (1992): 68–95; Barbara Sicherman, "Reading and Ambition: M. Carey Thomas and Female Heroism," *American Quarterly* 45 (1993): 73–103; and Louise Stevenson, *The Victorian Homefront: American Thought and Culture, 1860–1880* (Boston: Twayne, 1991).

117. *Religious Outlook* (Columbia, S.C.) 1 October 1897, 232.

118. Lears, *No Place of Grace*, 4–5.

119. Gail Bederman, " 'The Women Have Had Charge of the Church Work Long Enough': The Men and Religion Forward Movement of 1911–1912 and the Masculinization of Middle-Class Protestantism," *American Quarterly* 41 (1989): 432–465; see especially the discussion of "muscular Christianity," 435–440. It is important to point out that Protestants who lamented an "emasculated Gospel" and advocated muscular Christianity were also responding to a critique of their religious practice made by Catholic thinkers. Protestants, whose path to salvation had become "convenient and comfortable" lacked the tough aceticism of Catholics. The Reverend M. J. Spalding, Archbishop of Baltimore, offered the following observation of the soft side of Protestantism: "What does Protestantism enjoin or recommend that is particularly painful to the senses? . . . Does it not place the married above the unmarried life, in direct opposition to St. Paul? Does it often breathe a syllable about mental prayer, about entire abstraction from the world, about mortification of our carnal appetites, about love of solitude?" See M. J. Spalding, *Miscellanea: Comprising Reviews, Lectures, and Essays on Historical, Theological, and Miscellaneous Subjects*, 2 vols., (Baltimore: John Murphy, 1895) 1:426–427.

120. Philip Schaff, ed., *Popular Commentary on The New Testament by English and American Scholars of Various Evangelical Denominations*, vol. 3 (New York: Scribners, 1882), 219.

121. Jamieson, Fausset, and Brown, *Commentary Critical*, 19; see also Thomas Scott as quoted in William Jenks, ed., *The Comprehensive Commentary on the Holy Bible* 5 vols. (Philadelphia: American Publishing House, 1891) 5:29.

122. Jenks, *Comprehensive Commentary*, 1:31, 5:467.

123. John Robert Dummelow, *A Commentary on the Holy Bible by Various Writers* (New York: Macmillan, 1908), 9.

124. Biblical commentators debated Eve's intentionality. Matthew Henry argued "Probably he [Adam] was not with her when she was tempted, or he would have interposed to prevent the sin." Some commentators, like Dummelow, were quite generous in their assessment, believing that Eve behaved honorably toward her husband persuading him to eat the apple "with a sincere view as to his advantage." Others, like Scott, and this was the predominate view, took a dimmer view of Eve's acts, noting, "those that have themselves done ill, are commonly willing to draw in others to do the same." Eve may have begun in innocence, however, "entangled in unbelief she suspected divine veracity and goodness, conceived hopes of impunity in transgression, and expected vast gratification both of ambition and the sensual appetite." Matthew Henry as quoted in Jenks, ed., *Comprehensive Commentary*, 1:33; Dummelow, *A Commentary on the Holy Bible*, 9; see also Scott quoted in Jenks, ed., *Comprehensive Commentary* 1:32.

125. Matthew Henry's analysis in Jenks, ed., *Comprehensive Commentary*, 1:37.

126. Ingram Cobbin, *Cobbin's Commentary on the Bible for Young and Old*, 2 vols., ed. E. J. Goodspeed (New York: S. Hess, 1876), 1:23.

127. Dummelow, *A Commentary on the Holy Bible*, 10.

128. Scott as quoted in Jenks, ed., *Comprehensive Commentary*, 5:468. The editor of this particular volume of commentaries, William Jenks, took issue with Scott's generous interpretation, however, pointing out that salvation for women through childbirth is problematic, as "not being confined to Christian or even virtuous women."

129. W. J. Conybeare and J. S. Howson, *The Life and Epistles of St. Paul*, vol. 1 (New York: Charles Scribner's Sons, 1890), 60. In biblical commentaries, male clergy freely substituted "public" for "church" in Paul's doctrine. In this 1890 translation of Paul's letter to the

Corinthians, for example, the passage traditionally translated, "Let your women keep silence in the churches; for it is not permitted unto them to speak" was newly translated, "In your congregations, *as in all the congregations of Christ's people*, the women must keep silence; for they are not permitted to speak *in public*." (emphasis added).

130. Schaff, ed., *Popular Commentary*, 219. See also Scott as quoted in Jenks, ed., *Comprehensive Commentary*, 5:306–307; Dummelow, *A Commentary on the Holy Bible*, 916; Charles James Bloomfield as quoted in Jenks, ed., *Comprehensive Commentary*, 5:307.

131. As quoted in Willard, *Woman in the Pulpit*, 126–127.

132. Schaff, ed., *Popular Commentary*, 219. Brown's single concession to women's contemporary role in the church was simply to acknowledge that in Paul's dictums, like all things, "doubtless there are exceptional cases."

133. See Jenks, ed., *Comprehensive Commentary*, 5:307. So potentially troubling was this questioning of the universal application of Paul's dictum, that this editor actually interjected, with brackets, numerous references to verses that would contradict the commentator and shore up Paul's universality.

134. See Scott as quoted in ibid., 467. See also the *Watchman*, 7 February 1895, 19.

135. Matthew Henry as quoted in Jenks, ed., *Comprehensive Commentary*, 5:306–307.

136. Bederman, " 'The Women Have Had Charge,' " 432–465.

137. Sara Underwood, "The Pioneers of the Woman's Movement, and Its Opponents," *Index*, 31 May 1883, 568.

138. Evelyn Brooks Higginbotham, *Righteous Discontent: The Women's Movement in the Black Baptist Church* (Cambridge: Harvard University Press, 1993), 147.

139. See, for example, Nancy F. Cott, *The Bonds of Womanhood: "Woman's Sphere" in New England, 1780–1835* (New Haven: Yale University Press, 1977); Mary P. Ryan, *Cradle of the Middle Class: The Family in Oneida County, New York, 1790–1865* (New York: Cambridge University Press, 1981); and Barbara Welter, "The Cult of True Womanhood, 1829–1860," *American Quarterly* 18 (1966): 151–174.

140. Elizabeth Blackwell to Stanton, 4 July 1883, Stanton Papers, DLC.

141. Writings abounded instructing women on the particulars of her "sphere." Examples include: A. W. Chase, *Dr. Chase's Third, Last and Complete Receipt Book and Household Physician* (Detroit: Dickerson, 1889); and *The Mother's Magazine* 13 (1845). Scholarly treatments of this literature include: Kathryn Kish Sklar, *Catharine Beecher: A Study in American Domesticity* (New Haven: Yale University Press, 1973); Frances B. Cogan, *All-American Girl: The Ideal of Real Womanhood in Mid-Nineteenth-Century America* (Athens: University of Georgia Press, 1989); and Cott, *Bonds of Womanhood*. For critiques of historians' use of the "woman's sphere" paradigm, see Nancy Hewitt, "Beyond the Search for Sisterhood: American Women's History in the 1980s," *Social History* 10 (1985): 299–321; and Linda K. Kerber, "Separate Spheres, Female Worlds, Woman's Place: The Rhetoric of Women's History," *Journal of American History* 75 (1988): 9–39.

142. Stanton as quoted in the *Woman's Tribune*, 23 November 1895.

143. See, for example, Sheila M. Rothman, *Woman's Proper Place: A History of Changing Ideals and Practices, 1870 to the Present* (New York: Basic Books, 1978); also, Steven M. Buechler, "Elizabeth Boynton Harbert and the Woman Suffrage Movement, 1870–1896," *Signs: A Journal of Women in Culture and Society* 13 (1987): 78–97. Rothman argues that the doctrine of "separate spheres" was redefined in three ways during this period. An emphasis on maternal love replaced earlier notions of parental discipline that centered on "breaking the will" of a disobedient child. A woman's responsibilities within marriage increased with the added role of civilizing her "untamed" husband. Finally, woman's role as moral guardian expanded to include not only her family and immediate community but also the world at large. The popularization of the call to social housekeeping in the advice literature accounted for the renewed commitment to "separate spheres" among many of its middle-class adherents. In a slightly different vein, Buechler argues that a distinctively middle-class domesticity—stressing social control above social housekeeping—developed in response to immigration, urbanization, and class conflict in the late nineteenth century.

144. Daniel Scott Smith, "Family Limitation, Sexual Control, and Domestic Feminism in

Victorian America," *Feminist Studies* 1 (1973): 40–57; Robert V. Wells, "Family History and the Demographic Transition," *Journal of Social History* 9 (Fall 1975): 1–20.

145. *Woman's Tribune*, 28 January 1888.

146. See Barbara Miller Solomon, *In the Company of Educated Women: A History of Women and Higher Education in America* (New Haven: Yale University Press, 1985). Catherine Clinton discusses the banning of women doctors from medical practice and the closing of medical schools to women in *The Other Civil War: American Women in the Nineteenth Century* (New York: Hill and Wang, 1984), 144–145. Women in other fields struggled for professional recognition during this period, including battling for ordination in Protestant denominations. See, for example Carolyn De Swarte Gifford, ed., *The Defense of Women's Rights to Ordination in the Methodist Episcopal Church: Women in American Protestant Religion, 1800–1930* (New York: Garland, 1987). Women journalists, numbering as high as twenty in the congressional press gallery in 1870, had all but disappeared by 1890.

147. Walter F. Wilcox, "Statistics of Marriage and Divorce in the United States" (1909): 4; "Statistics of Divorce," Ninth Annual Report of the National Divorce Reform League (1889) in *History of Women Microfilm Series*, 9262 (Woodbridge, Conn.: Research Publications, 1983).

148. *Woman's Tribune*, 6 June 1886.

149. Arthur T. Pierson, "God's Word to Woman," *Northfield Echoes* 3 (1896): 262, 253.

150. "The Ministry of Woman," *Truth* 21 (March 1895): 92.

151. *Truth* 21 (March 1895): 121.; see also *Watchman*, 7 March 1895, 1–2.

152. T. DeWitt Talmadge, "The Choice of a Wife," *Christian Herald and Sign of Our Times*, 14 January 1888, 21.

153. Alexander Kent, "The Woman's Bible," sermon reprinted in *Woman's Tribune*, 7 March 1896, 27.

154. Matthew Henry as quoted in Jenks, ed., *Comprehensive Commentary*, 1:30.

155. Ibid., 467.

156. As quoted in Willard, ed., *Woman in the Pulpit*, 88–89, 85, 74–75.

157. Ibid., 162, 90.

158. See, for example, Scott quoted in Jenks, ed., *Comprehensive Commentary*, 5:306–307; Bloome quoted in Jenks, ed., *Comprehensive Commentary*, 5:307; Dummelow, *A Commentary on the Holy Bible*, 916; see also Willard, ed., *Woman in the Pulpit*, 84, 159, 163.

159. Willard, *Woman in the Pulpit*, 159, 93.

160. Paul's contradictions could be exploited, but so too could the tarnished reputations of the other "apostles," thus casting a shadow on their collective credibility. Coaching women to counter conservative ministers, T. L. Townsend urged reformers to point out passages in the New Testament where an apostle (usually Peter) disagreed with Jesus, thereby showing that "the individual opinions of the writers of the Bible need not be regarded as infallible." Ibid., 79, 156.

161. Anna Howard Shaw, "Heavenly Vision," in Susan B. Anthony and Ida Husted Harper, eds., *History of Woman Suffrage*, vol. 4 (Rochester: Susan B. Anthony, 1902), 131. It is striking how many different constituencies attempted to appropriate Paul for their own purposes. Catholics located in Paul's writings the foundation for the practice of celibacy among the priesthood. Protestants rejecting celibacy as "unmanly," recuperated Paul's masculinity by emphasizing his subordination of women. Similarly, in the woman's rights movement, Paul was understood in opposing ways: as the great reformer who guaranteed women's equality and as the great betrayer who delivered women into perpetual oppression.

162. The term "progressive orthodox" originated at Andover Theological Seminary in the 1880s, but historians have applied it more generally to designate a category of "evangelical liberals," Christians who used new methodologies to maintain the Bible's sacred status and to find within it progressive strategies for social change. *Women's Penny Paper*, (London) 27 October 1888; Higginbotham, *Righteous Discontent*, 120–149, 266 n. 47; Kuklick, *Churchmen and Philosophers*, 216–225.

163. Julia Ward Howe, speech, as quoted in Elizabeth Cady Stanton et al., eds. *History of Woman Suffrage*, vol. 2 (Rochester: Susan B. Anthony, 1881), 293.

164. Mary Baker Eddy, *Science and Health with Key to Scriptures*, (1875; rpt. Boston: First

Church of Christ Scientist, 1994), 533–534. For this interpretation, see Satter, *Each Mind a Kingdom*, 67.

165. Willard, ed., *Woman in the Pulpit*, 46–47.

166. Higginbotham, *Righteous Discontent*, 120–49; quotations on 133, 123, 125.

167. Ibid., 131; Willard, ed., *Woman in the Pulpit*, 40, 48. This type of analysis—using Jesus to contradict Paul—is known as a textual-hermeneutical approach. See Elisabeth Schüssler Fiorenza's discussion of this Neo-Orthodox model of feminist biblical criticism in *In Memory of Her: A Feminist Theological Reconstruction of Christian Origins* (New York: Crossroad, 1983), 14–21.

168. 1 Timothy 2: 8–9.

169. Willard, ed., *Woman in the Pulpit*, 18, 23, 21; see also Carolyn De Swarte Gifford, "American Women and the Bible: The Nature of Woman as a Hermeneutical Issue," in Adela Yarbro Collins, ed., *Feminist Perspectives on Biblical Scholarship* (Chico, Calif.: Scholars Press, 1985), 11–33.

170. Stanton, "Woman in the Bible," 5.

171. Stanton, "Manuscript of Address by Elizabeth Cady Stanton at Prince's Hall," 65.

172. Stanton to Sara Underwood, 31 March 1889, Stanton Papers, NPV.

173. Turner, *Without God, without Creed*, 143.

3. Sacred Politics: Religion, Race, and the Transformation of the Woman's Suffrage Movement in the Gilded Age

A portion of this chapter appeared in Kathi L. Kern, "Gray Matters: Brains, Identities and Natural Rights," in Theodore R. Schatzki and Wolfgang Natter eds., *The Social and Political Body* (New York: Guilford Press, 1996).

1. Elizabeth Cady Stanton, *Elizabeth Cady Stanton as Revealed in Her Letters, Diary and Reminiscences*, ed. Theodore Stanton and Harriot Stanton Blatch, 2 vols. (New York: Harper, 1922) 2: 212–213; Stanton, *Eighty Years and More: Reminiscences 1815–1897*, introd. Ellen Carol DuBois, afterword Ann D. Gordon (1898; rpt. Boston: Northeastern University Press, 1993), 375–376.

2. Stanton, *Elizabeth Cady Stanton as Revealed*, 2: 208; Stanton, *Eighty Years*, 374.

3. Stanton, *Elizabeth Cady Stanton as Revealed*, 2: 213–214; Stanton, *Eighty Years*, 375–376.

4. H. P. Blavatsky, *The Secret Doctrine*, 3 vols. (New York: 1893–1895) 1: 42–45, 27, 559–561, as quoted in Sydney E. Ahlstrom, *A Religious History of the American People*, 2 vols. (New York: Doubleday, 1975), 2: 551–552; Stanton, *Elizabeth Cady Stanton as Revealed*, 2: 254.

5. Stanton, *Eighty Years*, 377. Later Stanton changed her views on Theosophy. In 1890, when she again met Annie Besant, Besant had abandoned Freethought and Fabian Socialism for Theosophy. Stanton challenged her: " 'The Fabian Society can do more for the amelioration of humanity than the Theosophical Society,' . . . But I saw this pained her, so I let her go on in her enthusiasm for Mme. Blavatsky, 'of whom I am a devoted pupil,' she said." See Stanton, *Elizabeth Cady Stanton as Revealed*, 2: 264.

6. Stanton, *Elizabeth Cady Stanton as Revealed*, 2: 217.

7. For example, in response to an NWSA convention resolution of 1886 which identified the church as "the greatest barrier to woman's emancipation," a younger suffragist maintained: "I don't think the churches are our greatest enemies. They might have been so in Mrs. Stanton's early days, but today if she went over the United States as I do she would find the [church] membership our best helpers." See Sarah Perkins's comments in *Woman's Tribune*, n.d. April 1886.

8. Susan B. Anthony to Harriet Taylor Upton, 23 December 1895, Anthony Papers, Manuscript Division, New York Public Library.

9. Mari Jo Buhle and Paul Buhle, eds., *The Concise History of Woman Suffrage: Selections from the Classic Work of Stanton, Anthony, Gage, and Harper* (Urbana: University of Illinois, 1978), 96.

10. Elizabeth Cady Stanton, Susan B. Anthony, and Matilda Joslyn Gage, eds. *History of Woman Suffrage*, vol. 1 (1881; rpt. Rochester, N.Y.: Charles Mann, 1889), 365, 532, 381 (hereafter *History of Woman Suffrage*).

11. Ibid., 539, 536.

12. Nancy Isenberg, *Sex and Citizenship in Antebellum America* (Chapel Hill: University of North Carolina Press, 1998), 66–77.

13. Stanton to Anthony, 31 December 1884, Theodore Stanton Collection, Elizabeth Cady Stanton Papers, Rutgers University Libraries, New Brunswick, N.J. (hereafter, NjR).

14. Francis E. Abbot to Stanton, 10 January 1877, as quoted in the *Index*, 6 August 1885, 69. The letter was addressed and read to the NWSA Convention of 1877. A comprehensive study of the role of religion in the regional NWSA meetings is beyond the scope of this study. However, the rich source material suggests that religious arguments for woman suffrage (and to a much lesser extent anti-church appeals) were points of frequent discussion in regional meetings. When, for example, the Methodist Episcopal Church voted to exclude women as lay delegates to their General Conference in 1888, the topic was widely discussed in local and regional meetings. See, for example, the following coverage of an NWSA meeing in Massachusetts: "Get Out of that Church: Susan B. Anthony Tells the Women how to Treat the Methodists," *Boston Globe*, 30 May 1888; and the coverage of the Kansas Equal Suffrage Association's resolution against the Methodists in *Woman's Tribune*, 8 December 1888. To see how Stanton's anticlericalism played out in a local organization, see the rich exchange between Stanton and Frances Ellen Burr, the secretary of the Hartford Connecticut Equal Rights Club and a writer for the *Hartford Times*. See "Equal Rights Club," unidentified clippings, *Hartford Times*, 10 April 1886, Susan B. Anthony Clippings Scrapbooks, Rare Books, CSmH.

15. Washington (D.C.) *National Republican*, 22 January 1885. Robinson-Shattuck Papers, Scrapbook #55, Schlesinger Library, Radcliffe Institute, Cambridge, Mass. (hereafter MCR-S). The text of the 1885 resolution was strikingly anti-Semitic: "Whereas the dogmas incorporated in religious creeds derived from Judaism, teaching that woman was an afterthought in creation, her sex a misfortune, marriage a condition of subordination, and maternity a curse, are contrary to the law of God as revealed in nature and the precepts of Christ; and whereas these dogmas are an insidious poison sapping the vitality of our civilization . . ." Later Stanton wrote in her autobiography that members of the resolution committee had substituted the above text for her anti-Christian resolution, "handing over to the Jews what I had laid at the door of the Christians." See Stanton, *Eighty Years*, 382.

16. As quoted in Stanton interview, *Washington Post*, 26 January 1885, clipping in Susan B. Anthony Scrapbook, no. 11, Library of Congress (hereafter DLC).

17. Ibid.

18. Olympia Brown, "Woman and Skepticism," *Alpha*, 1 March 1885, 1–9, in Olympia Willis Brown Papers, MCR-S. Talmadge's sermon was preached two Sundays after the Patton/Brown sermons, 8 February 1885. For Talmadge's text, see Thomas DeWitt Talmadge, "Downfall of Christianity," *Christian Herald and Sign of Our Times*, 12 February 1885.

19. Stanton to Benjamin Franklin Underwood, 27 March 1885, Elizabeth Cady Stanton Papers, Vassar College Library, Poughkeepsie, N.Y. (hereafter NPV).

20. As quoted in Buhle and Buhle, eds., *Concise History of Woman Suffrage*, 317.

21. *Woman's Tribune*, n.d. April 1886, 2–4.

22. Stanton, *Eighty Years*, 390.

23. Stanton to Clara D. Bewick Colby, 16 February 1895, Clara Colby Papers, State Historical Society of Wisconsin, Madison (hereafter WHi); Stanton, "Reminiscences," *Woman's Tribune*, 5 September 1891. The original manuscript version of the *Woman's Bible* is housed in the Elizabeth Cady Stanton Papers, DLC.

24. *Index*, 19 August 1886, reprinted in Stanton, *The Woman's Bible, Part I* (New York: European Publishing Co., 1895), 7.

25. *Woman's Tribune*, 12 September 1891.

26. Stanton to Antoinette Brown Blackwell, 27 April 1886, Blackwell Family Papers, MCR-S.

27. Stanton, *Elizabeth Cady Stanton as Revealed*, 2: 209.

28. *Index*, 19 August 1886, 86–87; and 21 October 1886, 197. The *Index* was a liberal, Freethought paper. Stanton also advertised in the suffrage papers.

29. Frances Lord, "The Woman's Bible," *Index*, 26 August 1886, 103, 104.

30. Stanton to Elizabeth Boynton Harbert, 13 September 1886, Elizabeth Boynton Harbert

Collection, Box 7, Folder 102, Huntington Library, San Marino, Calif. (hereafter CSmH). See also Ellen Carol DuBois, "The Limitations of Sisterhood: Elizabeth Cady Stanton and the Division of the American Suffrage Movement, 1875–1902," in DuBois, *Woman Suffrage and Women's Rights* (New York: New York University Press, 1998), 160–175.

31. Antoinette Louisa Brown Blackwell to Stanton, 10 August 1886, and Julia Ward Howe to Stanton, 23 October 1886, both in Scrapbook no. 2, Elizabeth Cady Stanton Papers, NPV. Several ordained Universalist clergywomen endorsed the project and lent their names to Stanton's revising committee. They did not, however, prepare many commentaries. The Reverend Phebe Hanaford contributed one passage to volume two.

32. Blackwell to Stanton, 10 August 1886; Howe to Stanton, 23 October 1886; Harriet Jane Hanson Robinson to Stanton, 29 September 1886, Robinson-Shattuck Family Papers, MCR-S; Stanton to Sara Underwood, 18 November 1886, Elizabeth Cady Stanton Papers, NPV.

33. Milicent Fawcett to Frances Lord, 15 September 1886, Theodore Stanton Collection, Elizabeth Cady Stanton Papers, NjR; Harriette Lucy Robinson Shattuck to Stanton, 8 September 1886, with Stanton's marginalia, Robinson-Shattuck Family Papers, MCR-S.

34. Mary Livermore to Stanton, 1 September 1886, Elizabeth Cady Stanton Papers, DLC; Florence W. Harberton to Stanton, 24 December 1886, Theodore Stanton Collection, Elizabeth Cady Stanton Papers, NjR.

35. Fawcett to Lord, 15 September 1886. See also Harriet Jane Hanson Robinson to Stanton, 26 September 1886, Robinson-Shattuck Family Papers, MCR-S.

36. Elizabeth Smith Miller to Stanton, 29 August 1886, Theodore Stanton Collection, Elizabeth Cady Stanton Papers, NjR.

37. Amelia Bloomer to Elizabeth Morrison Boynton Harbert, 10 March 1886, Harbert Collection, Box 3, Folder 21, CSmH.

38. Stanton to May Wright Sewall, 10 October 1886, Harbert Collection, Box 7, Folder 102, CSmH.

39. Stanton to Harriet Jane Hanson Robinson, 30 September 1886, Robinson-Shattuck Family Papers, MCR-S.

40. Stanton to May Wright Sewall, 10 October 1886.

41. Stanton discussed Lord and the Mind Cure with her colleague Sara Underwood. See, for example, Stanton to Benjamin and Sara Underwood, 15 April 1887, and Stanton to Sara Underwood, 1 November 1887, Elizabeth Cady Stanton Papers, NPV.

42. Stanton to Elizabeth Smith Miller, 5 March 1887, Theodore Stanton Collection, Elizabeth Cady Stanton Papers, NjR.

43. Stanton, "Reminiscences: The Woman's Bible," *Woman's Tribune*, 5 September 1891.

44. Stanton to Harriet Jane Hanson Robinson, 30 September 1886. Stanton told Robinson to expect the Bible convention to be held in New York or London and to follow on the heels of the first International Council of Women in March 1888.

45. Stanton to Sara Underwood, 1 November 1887.

46. Susan B. Anthony to Frederick Douglass, 6 February 1888, enclosure, Frederick Douglass Papers, DLC.

47. Ibid. For an excellent study of the history of women's international organizing (including the ICW), see Leila J. Rupp, "Constructing Internationalism: The Case of Transnational Women's Organizations, 1888–1945," *American Historical Review* 99 (1994): 1571–1600; and Rupp, *Worlds of Women: The Making of an International Women's Movement* (Princeton: Princeton University Press, 1997); and Margaret H. McFadden, *Golden Cables of Sympathy: the Transatlantic Sources of Nineteenth-Century Feminism* (Lexington: University Press of Kentucky, 1999).

48. Helen Taylor to Susan B. Anthony, 7 March 1888, Ida Husted Harper Collection, CSmH. See also Stanton to Helen Taylor, 6 March 1888, Mills-Taylor Papers, British Library, London; Stanton, interview, 27 March 1888, New York *World*, n.d., National American Woman Suffrage Association Papers, DLC. Opponents of the woman's movement attempted to associate women reformers with sexual scandals to discredit the movement. In 1874, Stanton and Anthony were badgered by the press for information on the Henry Ward Beecher–Elizabeth Tilton adultery scandal, which Victoria Woodhull had publicized. See Stanton, interview, 26 July 1874, *Brooklyn Daily Argus*, Beecher-Tilton Scrapbook 7, p. 54, New York Public Li-

brary, Main Reading Room. See also Barbara Goldsmith, *Other Powers: The Age of Suffrage, Spiritualism, and the Scandalous Victoria Woodhull* (New York: Knopf, 1998). At other times, suffrage and temperance leaders were themselves falsely accused of sexual scandals. Helen Gougar, a suffragist from Indiana, had to go to court to defend herself against an accusation of sexual impropriety. See Helen Gougar to Elizabeth M. Boynton Harbert, 28 January 1883, Harbert Collection, Box 4, Folder 51, CSmH. Harbert's testimony provided Gougar's defense; see "Helen M. Gougar vs. Henry Maudler," portion of direct examination of Mrs. Elizabeth Boynton Harbert, n.d., Harbert Collection, Box 4, Folder 51, CSmH.

49. Stanton to Clara D. Bewick Colby, 16 February 1895, Clara Colby Papers, WHi.

50. As I noted in Chapter 2, I use the term "progressive orthodox" to denote those women who used the Bible and Christianity as a starting point for women's emancipation. See Evelyn Brooks Higginbotham, *Righteous Discontent: The Women's Movement in the Black Baptist Church* (Cambridge: Harvard University Press, 1993), 120–149.

51. See *Popular Science Monthly* 31 (June 1887): 266–268; (August 1887): 554–558; (September 1887): 698–701; (October 1887): 846. See also Cynthia Eagle Russett's treatment of the Gardener-Hammond debates in *Sexual Science: The Victorian Construction of Womanhood* (Cambridge: Harvard University Press, 1989), 35–39, 164–165.

52. Stanton to Rachel G. Foster, 27 January 1887, Susan B. Anthony–Rachel Foster Avery Papers, University of Rochester Library, Rochester, N.Y. (hereafter NRU). Stanton told Avery to secure Gardener for the program, for "one speech on our heads, as to their size and contents," would no doubt enliven the ICW.

53. As quoted in Helen Hamilton Gardener, "Sex in Brain," in *Facts and Fictions of Life* (Chicago: Kerr. 1893), 96.

54. Ibid., 97.

55. Ibid., 98.

56. As quoted in ibid., 110, 121.

57. Ibid., 122–123.

58. Ibid., 124. Gardener not only willed her own brain to Cornell University; she insisted that Stanton had done so as well. As it turned out, Gardener would have needed a search warrant to collect Stanton's brain. When Stanton died in 1902, Gardener was out of the country. Returning several weeks later, Gardener approached Stanton's family to collect the brain. They were aghast. As Anthony put it, "It would have been becoming in her to have talked *first* with the family before starting the talk about the brain." Probably, Anthony suggested, Stanton had listened intently to Gardener's request for the donation without actually ever acquiescing. In any case, Gardener had waited too long. According to Anthony, "The time was to have gone *immediately* to the family and seen about it," as "it was already beginning to return to mother nature for after being buried two weeks it must have de-composed." Helen Gardener published a humorous fictional account of the afterlife of Stanton's brain; housed in a specimen jar in the Cornell University Brain Collection, it still loudly advocated women's rights. See Susan B. Anthony to Clara Colby, 25 November 1902, Clara Colby Collection, CSmH; see also Last Will and Testament of Helen H. Gardener, p. 15, Helen Hamilton Gardener Papers, MCR-S; Gardener, "The Brains at Cornell," *Free Thought Magazine* 18 (1900): 94.

59. Carrie Chapman Catt, "Eulogy for Helen Gardener," Helen Hamilton Gardener Papers, MCR-S.

60. Stanton, interview, *Rochester Herald*, 3 August 1888, Susan B. Anthony Scrapbook no. 13, DLC. Woman's rights advocates rallied to Gardener's message. Her speech, "Sex in Brain," was highlighted in suffrage newspapers, reprinted in the Council proceedings, published in a collection of essays, and continued to provoke occasional letters to suffrage newspapers for the next several years. Gardener's popularity as a public speaker grew, and so did interest in her topic. On at least one occasion suffrage leaders rerouted their lecture tours to put in an appearance at the meeting of the American Association for the Advancement of Science. See, for example, "American News," *Women's Penny Paper* (London), 17 November 1888, 2; Gardener, *Facts and Fictions of Life*.

61. See for example Stanton to Clara Colby, 25 March 1898, Clara Colby Collection, CSmH; or Stanton's speech "The Degradation of Disfranchisement," in *History of Woman Suf-*

frage, 4: 176. Stanton, Gardener, Matilda Joslyn Gage, and other radical feminists of the 1880s were involved in the Freethought movement, whose agenda included challenging Christian theology using the latest developments in science, such as geology and evolutionary theory. Stanton and Gage frequently wrote of the virtues of science in liberating women. Consequently, these women came later to a critique of medical science than did either more conservative Christian suffragists in the United States or feminists in Western Europe. Stanton was a committed homeopath, so allopathic medical science was never very sacred to her, but "true science" was. Julia Ward Howe took on Dr. Edward Clarke in her edited collection *Sex and Education: A Reply to Dr. E. H. Clarke's "Sex in Education"* (Boston: Roberts Brothers, 1874). British and German feminists challenged medical opponents in the 1870s and early 1880s. On British suffragists, see "The Inferiority of Woman Established by Science," *English Woman's Review*, 15 October 1881, 449. For a discussion of this topic among German feminists, see James C. Albisetti, *Schooling German Girls and Women: Secondary and Higher Education in the Nineteenth Century* (Princeton: Princeton University Press, 1987), 126, 185–188.

62. Aileen S. Kraditor, *The Ideas of the Woman Suffrage Movement, 1890–1920* (1965; rpt. New York: W. W. Norton, 1981), 163–166, 173, 128.

63. My emphasis is on the connections between Stanton's religious views and her views on race. It seems only fair, however, to point out that Stanton's racism was inconsistent and contradictory. Certainly she did not consider herself prejudiced along racial and ethnic lines, and she frequently lamented the mistreatment of racial, ethnic and religious groups. For example, she told the Free Religious Association in 1881, "I never look a colored man, woman, or child in the face that my soul does not glow with an intense desire . . . to give them some sign of my recognition of their equal humanity, as their just due from every member of the Saxon race for all the wrongs they have suffered at our hands." At the height of American racism of the 1890s, she wrote in her diary, "I am much worked up over the infamous Geary bill against admission of the Chinese into the United States. How my blood boils over these persecutions of the Africans, the Jews, the Indians, and the Chinese. I suppose the Japanese will come next. I wonder if these fanatical Christians think that Christ died for these people, or confined his self-sacrifice to Saxons, French, Germans, Italians, etc.?" See *Free Religious Index*, 23 June 1881, and Stanton, *Elizabeth Cady Stanton as Revealed*, 2: 294.

64. Stanton, speech, "Reconstruction," Lecture in the Fraternity Course and Tour of New York State, 19 February 1867 and later, Elizabeth Cady Stanton Papers, DLC.

65. *Proceedings of the First Anniversary of the American Equal Rights Association, Held at the Church of the Puritans, New York, May 9 and 10, 1867* (New York: Robert J. Johnson, 1867), 13 (hereafter AERA *Proceedings*).

66. Stanton, "Reconstruction."

67. See for example, Stanton to Sojourner Truth, 24 March 1867, Post Family Papers, NRU; also Stanton's address to the First Anniversary Meeting of the American Equal Rights Association, AERA *Proceedings*, p. 8.

68. Stanton to Terry Greene Phillips, 1 May 1867, Wendell Phillips Papers, Massachusetts Historical Society, Boston.

69. Stanton to Editor of [American Anti-Slavery] Standard, 26 December 1865, as quoted in *History of Woman Suffrage*, 2: 94–95. Compare this quotation from 1865 with a similar passage from *Eighty Years*: "Women have stood with the negro, thus far, on equal ground as ostracized classes, outside the political paradise; and now, when the door is open, it is but fair that we both should enter and enjoy all the fruits of citizenship" (255).

70. Stanton, *Eighty Years*, 241, 242.

71. Stanton, "Immigration and Suffrage," *Wisconsin Citizen*, 28 February 1893.

72. See Ellen Carol DuBois, ed., *The Elizabeth Cady Stanton–Susan B. Anthony Reader: Correspondence, Writings, Speeches* (1981; rev. ed., Boston: Northeastern University Press, 1992), xvi; 88–92; Louise Michele Newman, *White Women's Rights: The Racial Origins of Feminism in the United States* (New York: Oxford University Press, 1999), 56–85.

73. Nancy F. Cott, *The Grounding of Modern Feminism* (New Haven: Yale University Press, 1987), 9; Steven M. Buechler, *Women's Movements in the United States* (New Brunswick: Rutgers University Press, 1990), 135, 138; Rosalyn Terborg-Penn, "Discontented Black Feminists:

Prelude and Postscript to the Passage of the Nineteenth Amendment," in Lois Scharf and Joan M. Jensen, eds., *Decades of Discontent: The Women's Movement* (Westport, Conn.: Greenwood Press, 1983), 261; see also Terborg-Penn, *African American Women in the Struggle for the Vote, 1850–1920* (Bloomington: Indiana University Press, 1998).

74. Newman, *White Women's Rights*, 7, 56–85.

75. Olympia Brown, "Foreign Rule," in *History of Woman Suffrage*, 4: 147–148; see also Lucinda Chandler's series in the *Woman's Tribune*, 1889. For coverage of Helen Gardener's work in the race purity movement, see Linda Gordon, *Woman's Body, Woman's Right: A Social History of Birth Control in America* (1976; rpt. New York: Penguin, 1990), 113, 127–129. Even New Thought contributors to the *Woman's Bible* could harmonize with their colleagues on class and race issues. Lucinda Chandler, for example, shared Brown's concerns about the "Catholic threat" to free institutions in America. Beryl Satter has argued that "whiteness" is central to the theology developed by New Thought advocates. See Satter, *Each Mind a Kingdom: American Women, Sexual Purity, and the New Thought Movement, 1875–1920* (Berkeley: University of California Press, 1999), 140.

76. For many Christian reformers, the understanding of sexual difference was in opposition to the Freethought formulations of Stanton and Helen Gardener. In short, the heightened differences between men and women were considered prime evidence of a highly evolved, Christian civilization. See Joan Jacobs Brumberg, "Zenanas and Girlless Villages: The Ethnology of American Evangelical Women, 1870–1910," *Journal of American History* 69 (1982): 347–371. On the relationship of evolutionary theory to reform, see Newman, *White Women's Rights*, 22–55, and Gail Bederman, *Manliness and Civilization: A Cultural History of Gender and Race in the United States, 1880–1917* (Chicago: University of Chicago Press, 1995). Beryl Satter has coined the phrase "evolutionary republicanism" to describe the belief that white Anglo-Saxon Protestants had inherited the skills needed for virtuous political participation. See Satter, *Each Mind a Kingdom*, 183–184.

77. Harriot Stanton Blatch to Stanton, *Woman's Journal*, 17 November 1894. Ida B. Wells's response to educational qualifications is discussed briefly in Vron Ware, *Beyond the Pale* (London: Verso, 1992), 200.

78. Stanton, "Immigration and Suffrage;" also *Woman's Journal*, 5 January 1895.

79. *Woman's Tribune*, 23 March 1889. See also Helen Gardener, *Pulpit, Pew and Cradle* (New York: The Truth Seeker Co., 1891), 22. Gardener was skeptical that education could improve over the course of generations. "Stupid mothers never did and stupid mothers never will furnish this world with brilliant sons," she charged.

80. *History of Woman Suffrage*, 5: 77.

81. Marjorie Spruill Wheeler, *New Women of the New South: The Leaders of the Woman Suffrage Movement in the Southern States* (New York: Oxford University Press, 1993), 101–102.

82. Elizabeth Boynton Harbert, "Health: Its Requisites for Continuance," *Christian Science* 1 (1889): 221–231, 206–208, as quoted in Satter, *Each Mind a Kingdom*, 275–276, n. 20.

83. David Pivar, *Purity Crusade: Sexual Morality and Social Control, 1868–1900* (Westport, Conn.: Greenwood Press, 1973).

84. *Report of the International Council of Women, March 25 to April 1, 1888* (Washington, D.C.: Rufus H. Darby, 1888), 285.

85. Ibid. Although Stanton opposed much of the Social Purity agenda—particularly its ties to organized Christianity—she was an early and radical proponent of voluntary motherhood.

86. Clara Colby to Elizabeth Morrison Boynton Harbert, 11 October 1912, Harbert Collection, Box 3, Folder 34, CSmH. The concentration of thought was apparently a fairly standard political practice among New Thought Feminists from the 1880s–1910s. For another example, see the message from Anna Howard Shaw to Elizabeth Harbert in which Shaw concludes: "I trust that you may have a successful conference together with that concentration of thought upon that third day of your meeting that will help to make the world feel at one with you and your purpose." Anna Howard Shaw to Harbert, 8 March 1904, Harbert Collection, Box 7, folder 98, CSmH.

87. *Report of the International Council of Women*, 416.

88. Ibid., 418.

89. That is: the range of belief among Protestants and those who practiced "new religions." Catholics and Jews and, consequently, their religious beliefs were not yet represented in the council's religious symposium.

90. *Report of the International Council of Women*, 400. Newman's church affiliation was the Metropolitan Church of Washington, D.C.

91. Ibid., 400–401.

92. Ibid., 405–407.

93. Ibid., 407–415.

94. Ibid., 415–418. Beryl Satter has noted that this debate over mind and matter was the major cultural obsession of the period and was closely linked to a debate over idealized masculinity and femininity. See Satter, *Each Mind a Kingdom*, 9–19.

95. *Report of the International Council of Women*, 418–420.

96. Ibid., 423–424. Frances Willard was theologically eclectic. As we saw in Chapter 2, she embraced a liberal Protestant strategy for interpreting the Bible, yet she framed it in evangelical rhetoric. Hence, the term "progressive orthodoxy" seems an apt description of Willard's theological perspective.

97. Washington (D.C.) *National Republican*, 22 January 1885. For more information on the emergence of the WCTU, see Ruth Bordin, *Women and Temperance: The Quest for Power and Liberty, 1873–1900* (Philadelphia: Temple University Press, 1984); Ian Tyrell, *Woman's World, Woman's Empire: The Woman's Christian Temperance Union in International Perspective, 1880–1930* (Chapel Hill: University of North Carolina Press, 1991); and Frances Willard, *Writing Out My Heart: Selections from the Journal of Frances E. Willard, 1855–1896*, ed. Carolyn De Swarte Gifford (Urbana: University of Illinois Press, 1995).

98. Bordin, *Women and Temperance*, 41. The cross-pollination between the suffrage and temperance campaigns in the South was, in Marjorie Wheeler's words, "less automatic" than in other regions. See Wheeler, *New Women of the New South*, 11.

99. Stanton to Clara Dorothy Bewick Colby, 25 December 1887, *Woman's Tribune*, 21 January 1888.

100. On Willard's relationships with other women, see Gifford's analysis in Willard, *Writing Out My Heart*, xii–xiii, On Willard's political strategies see Suzanne M. Marilley, Frances Willard and the Feminism of Fear," *Feminist Studies* 19 (1993): 123–146.

101. To sample the evangelical language of a typical union See, Minutes, West Philadelphia Woman's Christian Temperance Union, 2 February 1886, and 6 April 1886, Manuscript Division, Historical Society of Pennsylvania, Philadelphia (hereafter PHi). On the conversion metaphor, see Carolyn De Swarte Gifford, "Frances Willard and the Woman's Christian Temperance Union's Conversion to Woman Suffrage," in Marjorie Spruill Wheeler, ed., *One Woman, One Vote: Rediscovering the Woman Suffrage Movement* (Troutdale, Ore.: NewSage Press, 1995), 117–134.

102. Minutes, West Philadelphia Woman's Christian Temperance Union, 1883–1887, Manuscript Division, PHi.

103. Frances E. Willard, ed., *Woman and Temperance* (Hartford: Park, 1888), 241. For a discussion of the WCTU's entrance into politics, see Mari Jo Buhle, *Women and American Socialism, 1870–1920* (Urbana: University of Illinois Press, 1981), 63; and Bordin, *Women and Temperance*, 3–14.

104. Willard, "Address to the Woman's Congress," Philadelphia, 1876, as quoted in Willard, *Woman and Temperance*, 457.

105. Willard, *Woman and Temperance*, 351. See Gifford's analysis, "Frances Willard and the Woman's Christian Temperance Union's Conversion," 127.

106. Alice Stone Blackwell and Marie C. Brehm, "Suggestions for Franchise Superintendents," WCTU Leaflet (Chicago, n.d.), 8, in *History of Women Microfilm Series*, item no. 8927 (Woodbridge, Conn.: Research Publications, 1983). These publications were used extensively in the South, where the WCTU, by and large, did not eagerly embrace woman suffrage.

107. Stanton to Colby, 25 December 1887, as printed in *Woman's Tribune*, 21 January 1888.

108. Ibid.

109. Matilda Joslyn Gage to Stanton, 20 July 1888(?), as quoted in Stanton to Colby , 20 July 1888, *Woman's Tribune*, 18 August 1888. Gage expressed her opposition to the "Christian Party in Politics"—an umbrella term she used to cover both Catholic and Protestant activities, including the Catholic Congress, parochial schools, the National Reform Association, the American Sabbath Union, the WCTU, and the national ministerial bodies. When she met with hostility in the woman suffrage movement because of her anti-church views, she attempted to form a more radical society, the Woman's National Liberal Union (1890).

110. Frances E. Willard to Susan B. Anthony, 15 August 1888, Ida Husted Harper Collection, CSmH.

111. Anthony to Frances E. Willard, 23 August 1888, National Woman's Christian Temperance Union Archives, Evanston, Ill.

112. Ibid.

113. On the rift between woman's rights advocates during Reconstruction, see Ellen Carol DuBois, *Feminism and Suffrage: The Emergence of an Independent Women's Movement in America, 1848–1869* (Ithaca: Cornell University Press, 1978), 162–202; DuBois, ed., *Stanton-Anthony Reader*, 90–92.

114. Stanton, "To the Women of State of New York," 11 December 1854, as printed in *Lily (Seneca Falls)*, 1 January 1855.

115. Antoinette Brown to Stanton, 28 December 1854, Blackwell Papers, DLC; Lucy Stone to Susan B. Anthony, 31 December 1854, Ida Husted Harper Collection, CSmH.

116. Stanton to Olympia Brown, 12 October 1889, as printed in the *Woman's Tribune*, 2 November 1889, 276.

117. Stanton to Matilda Joslyn Gage, 19 October 1890, reprinted in *Liberal Thinker* (Syracuse, N.Y.) 5 January 1890.

118. *Woman's Tribune*, 22 February 1890.

119. The instructions to vote for Anthony for president appeared in *Woman's Journal*, 1 March 1890. For Stanton's comments on Blackwell, see Stanton to Clara Colby, 6 March 1890, Clara Colby Collection, CSmH.

120. Stanton to Colby, 6 March 1890.

121. Ellen Carol DuBois, *Harriot Stanton Blatch and the Winning of Woman Suffrage* (New Haven: Yale University Press, 1997), 50.

122. Stanton, *Eighty Years*, 245.

123. This controversy is explored in depth in the final chapter. Lucy Stone died in 1893, but her daughter Alice Stone Blackwell joined her father, Henry Blackwell, in discrediting Stanton's Bible.

124. Stanton to Matilda Joslyn Gage, 19 October 1889.

125. Stanton, "Mrs. Stanton on the Sunday Resolution," *Woman's Journal*, 11 February 1893, 47.

126. See, for example, Stanton, "Shall the World's Fair Be Closed on Sunday?" *Woman's Journal*, 25 February 1893, 41–43; Stanton to Eliza Wright Osborne, 10 March 1893, Garrison Papers, Sophia Smith Collection, Smith College, Northampton, Mass.; Stanton to Editors, *Woman's Journal*, 18 March 1893, 88. In the antebellum woman's rights movement there had been a historic connection between anti-Sabbath agitation and woman's rights, see Isenberg, *Sex and Citizenship*, 76, 85, 87. Stanton continued to assert that connection, but it was not one that was widely held among Freethinkers in the 1890s who focused exclusively on the issue of the separation of church and state. At the New England Convention of Freethinkers in 1896, the organization advocated for the abolition of the following: church exemption from taxation, employment of chaplains by the military, religious services held by the government, the use of the Bible in public schools, the use of the judicial oath, Sunday observance laws, and laws implemented to enforce Christian morality. See *Boston Investigator*, 1 February 1896.

127. *Woman's Journal*, 18 March 1893, 88.

128. Stanton to Colby, 6 March 1890.

129. Stanton, "The Solitude of Self" as quoted in DuBois, ed., *Stanton-Anthony Reader*, 252; Stanton to Colby, 8 December 1892, Clara Colby Papers, WHi.

4. "A Great Feature of the General Uprising": The Revising Committee and the *Woman's Bible*

1. Elizabeth Cady Stanton, *Eighty Years and More: Reminiscences 1815–1897*, introd. Ellen Carol DuBois, afterword Ann D. Gordon (1898; rpt. Boston: Northeastern University Press, 1993), 393; Stanton, interview, "The Revising Committee," New York *World*, 17 March 1895.

2. *Atlanta Constitution*, 1 February 1895; *Atlanta Journal*, 1 February 1895; *Woman's Tribune*, 16 February 1895.

3. Stanton, interview, "The Revising Committee." See also Susan B. Anthony and Ida Husted Harper, eds., *History of Woman Suffrage*, vol. 4 (Rochester, N.Y.: Susan B. Anthony, 1881), 237. Stanton's difficulty in rallying a committee demonstrates how differently reformers responded to Stanton and to Shaw. Shaw, an ordained minister, was able to challenge clergy without causing alarm; an agnostic like Stanton was not permitted as much latitude.

4. Stanton, *Eighty Years*, 452–453.

5. Stanton to Clara Colby, 2 February 1895, Clara Colby Papers, State Historical Society of Wisconsin, Madison (hereafter WHi). Colby's financial difficulties in sustaining the *Woman's Tribune* are well documented in her correspondence to Elizabeth Harbert, the editor of the *New Era*. See the letters from Clara Colby to Elizabeth Harbert, Box 3, Folder 34, Elizabeth Boynton Harbert Collection, Henry E. Huntington Library, San Marino, Calif. (hereafter CSmH). For a study of Clara Colby and the *Woman's Tribune*, see E. Claire Jerry, "Clara Bewick Colby and the *Woman's Tribune*, 1883–1909: The Free Lance Editor as Movement Leader," in Martha M. Soloman, ed., *A Voice of Their Own: The Woman Suffrage Press, 1840–1910* (Tuscaloosa and London: University of Alabama Press, 1991), 110–128.

6. Stanton to Colby, 2 February 1895. Stanton promised Colby that any money to be made in the project would be divided among those who actually did the work.

7. Stanton interview, "The Revising Committee;" Isabel (Lady Henry) Somerset to Stanton, 5 June 1895, Theodore Stanton Collection, Elizabeth Cady Stanton Papers, Rutgers University Libraries, New Brunswick, N.J. (hereafter NjR). As I discussed in the Introduction, Carrie Chapman Catt was also listed erroneously as a committee member; her name appeared in the book's frontispiece of volume one. Catt had written a speech on woman suffrage and the Bible, and Stanton may have assumed that her fellow New Yorker shared her views. According to Catt's earliest biographer, Catt had agreed to join the committee. When she learned "how the subject was to be treated," she resigned. For Catt's unpublished manuscript from 1890, see Carrie Chapman Catt, "Woman Suffrage and the Bible," Carrie Chapman Catt Collection, New York Public Library. Catt's interaction with Stanton is mentioned in Mary Gray Peck, *Carrie Chapman Catt: A Biography* (New York: H. W. Wilson, 1944), 87–88.

8. Somerset to Stanton, 5 June 1895; see also Stanton to the Revising Committee, *Woman's Tribune*, 15 June 1895, 93, 95. Stanton defended her actions in this open letter to the revising committee.

9. Somerset to Stanton, 5 June 1895.

10. Susan B. Anthony to Stanton, 24 July 1895, Anthony Family Papers, CSmH. For an account of the suffrage campaign in California, see Gayle Ann Gullett, *Becoming Citizens: The Emergence and Development of the California Women's Movement* (Urbana: University of Illinois Press, 2000).

11. Stanton, "About the Woman's Bible," *Woman's Tribune*, 15 June 1895; Stanton to the Revising Committee, 15 June 1895.

12. Anthony to Stanton, 24 July 1895.

13. Stanton to the Revising Committee, 15 June 1895.

14. Elvira N. Solis to Stanton, 10 April 1895, and Solis to Stanton, 14 April 1895, Theodore Stanton Collection, Elizabeth Cady Stanton Papers, NjR. Solis recommended Henrietta Szold of Baltimore, who was known to be a Hebrew scholar.

15. See, for example, Stanton to Alexandra Gripenberg, 6 May 1895, and Stanton to Theodore Weld Stanton, 16 April 1895, both in Theodore Stanton Collection, Elizabeth Cady Stanton Papers, NjR.

16. The names of committee members as they appeared in volume one included: Stanton, Phebe Hanaford, Clara Bewick Colby, Augusta Chapin, Mary Livermore, Mary Seymour Howell, Josephine K. Henry, Mrs. Robert G. Ingersoll, Sarah [sic] A. Underwood, Catherine F. Stebbins, Ellen Battelle Dietrick, Cornelia Hussey, Lillie Devereux Blake, Matilda Joslyn Gage, Olympia Brown, Frances Ellen Burr, Mrs.[Carrie] Chapman Catt, Helen H. Gardener, Charlotte Beebe Wilbour, Lucinda Chandler, M. Louise Thomas, Louisa Southworth, and Martha Almy. In addition, Ursula Gestefeld's name appeared under the heading: "Comments by."

17. See, for example, the tributes to the Revising Committee by the Coalition Task Force on Women and Religion in the introduction to Stanton and the Revising Committee, *The Woman's Bible* (New York: European Publishing Co., 1895; rpt. Seattle: Coalition Task Force on Women and Religion, 1974),vi–xviii (hereafter *Woman's Bible*, and cited in my text by volume and page number). See also the tribute to Stanton and the revising committee in Carol A. Newsome and Sharon H. Ringe, eds., *The Women's Bible Commentary* (Louisville: Westminster/John Knox, 1992).

18. Stanton's biographer Elisabeth Griffith makes little mention of the committee: "none were prominent either as feminists or scholars." See *In Her Own Right: The Life of Elizabeth Cady Stanton* (New York: Oxford University Press, 1984), 259, n. 54. Maureen Fitzgerald's foreword to *The Woman's Bible* focuses on establishing the importance of religion to Stanton's thought and feminism. Consequently, the revising committee is not central to her essay; however, she points out that Stanton was supported by Gage, Colby and Brown in her religious battles in the NWSA. See Stanton, *The Woman's Bible*, foreword Maureen Fitzgerald (Boston: Northeastern University Press, 1993), xxi. The historian Barbara Welter gives the committee a more thorough treatment in Stanton, *The Original Feminist Attack on the Bible*, introd. Barbara Welter (New York: Arno Press, 1974).

19. Susan Wixon, "The Woman's Bible," *Women's Tribune*, 9 November 1895.

20. The figure for volume two is difficult to determine. Five of the commentaries published were attributed to Ellen B. Dietrick who had died in 1895, presumably after she had submitted her contributions to Stanton. Three commentaries were authorized anonymously, raising the question of how many different authors were covered by this by-line. In any case, Stanton signed 38 of the 63 commentaries in the second volume. As I discuss in Chapter 5, many of the more reluctant members of the revising committee wrote letters at Stanton's prompting for the second volume.

21. Although the base of her political work was in Nebraska, Colby spent a great deal of time in the 1880s–1890s in Washington, D.C., where her husband was an attorney in the Harrison administration. Colby moved the *Woman's Tribune* to Washington in 1888 for the International Council of Women.

22. The "foreign members" are particularly underrepresented in Stanton's correspondence. None contributed commentaries to either version. Two—Irma von Troll-Borostyani and Ursula Bright—contributed letters to the appendix of volume two.

23. Welter includes an amusing précis of *Fettered for Life* in her introduction to *The Original Feminist Attack*, xxvii. For biographical information on Blake, see Edward T. James, Janet Wilson James and Paul S. Boyer, eds., *Notable American Women: A Biographical Dictionary* 3 vols. (Cambridge: The Belknap Press of Harvard University Press, 1971), 1: 167–169 (hereafter *NAW*). Blake devoted considerable energy to marketing her writings as a source of income. In 1884, for example, she sold "fashion letters" to newspapers at the rate of five dollars a letter. She also offered fictional accounts—"not woman suffrage simply a story of New York life"—on the same installment plan. See Lillie Devereux Blake to Elizabeth Boynton Harbert, 8 April 1884, Harbert Papers, Box 3, Folder 20, CSmH.

24. Stanton, "Preface," 31 December 1892, in Patricia G. Holland and Ann D. Gordon, eds., *The Papers of Elizabeth Cady Stanton and Susan B. Anthony* (Wilmington, Del.: Scholarly Resources, Inc., 1992), series three.

25. *NAW*, 2: 27. See Beryl Satter, *Each Mind a Kingdom: American Women, Sexual Purity, and the New Thought Movement* (Berkeley: University of California Press, 1999), 126–127.

26. See Satter's fascinating interpretation of this novel in *Each Mind a Kingdom*, 127–134.

27. *NAW,* 1: 355.

28. In a column titled, "Zintka Lanuni's Corner," written in the third person, Colby shared the childhood quests and questions of her adopted daughter. See for example, *Woman's Tribune,* 30 April 1898, 36,where Colby described teaching Zintka to read. Later in Colby's career, references in Colby's correspondence suggest a troubled relationship between mother and daughter; like everything else, her daughter seemed to pose a financial burden on Colby's limited resources. See, for example, Olympia Brown to Clara Colby, 14 October 1907, Colby Collection, CSmH. According to *Notable American Women,* as an adult, Zintka Lanuni performed in Wild West shows before marrying and moving to Mexico. A more in-depth account of Colby's relationship with her daughter can be found in Renée Sansom Flood, *Lost Bird of Wounded Knee: Spirit of the Lakota* (New York: Scribner, 1995).

29. Earlier studies underestimated the religious fervor among secular feminists. See Ellen DuBois, "The Limitations of Sisterhood: Elizabeth Cady Stanton and the Division in the American Suffrage Movement, 1875–1902" in Barbara J. Harris and JoAnn K. McNamara, eds., *Women and the Structure of Society: Selected Research from the Fifth Berkshire Conference on the History of Women* (Durham: Duke University Press, 1984), 166. My earlier work on this project emphasized a secular/evangelical dichotomy among reformers and underestimated the New Thought influence on the *Woman's Bible.* See Kathi L. Kern, "Rereading Eve: Elizabeth Cady Stanton and The *Woman's Bible,* 1886–1896," *Women's Studies* 19 (1991): 371–383.

30. Olympia Brown to Isabella Beecher Hooker, 26 June [1875–1876], Isabella Beecher Hooker Correspondence, Stowe-Day Foundation, Hartford, Conn., as quoted in Ann Braude, *Radical Spirits: Spiritualism and Women's Rights in Nineteenth-Century America* (Boston: Beacon, 1989), 47. Braude develops an argument for the close association—theologically, socially, and materially—between Universalism and Spiritualism.

31. Braude, *Radical Spirits,* 70.

32. The commentator is Clara Neyman.

33. Frances Lord to Elizabeth Morrison Boynton Harbert, 27 October 1886, Harbert Collection, Box 5, Folder 74, CSmH. Lord was a student of the Chicago based New Thought healer Emma Curtis Hopkins who did not call her practice "Mind Cure," but rather Christian Science or Harmony. Stanton, however, always referred to Lord's interest in faith healing as the "Mind Cure." See Satter's account of Lord, *Each Mind a Kingdom,* 2, 82, 164,193.

34. Lord to Harbert, 7 May 1887, Harbert Collection, Box 5, Folder 74, CSmH. On "chemicalization," see Satter, *Every Mind a Kingdom,* 89–90, 95.

35. Louisa Southworth to Elizabeth Morrison Boynton Harbert, 9 July n.y. [probably c. 1887], Harbert Collection, Box 7, Folder 109, CSmH. References in the letter to Southworth's "enrollment" work in the suffrage movement would place the letter around 1887 when she served on the national enrollment committee for the NWSA.

36. Satter, *Each Mind a Kingdom,* 79–110.

37 *NAW,* 2: 27.

38. Stanton initially introduced Lord to Underwood via correspondence, but then seems to have depended on Underwood for news of Lord's activities in Chicago. Compare, for example, Stanton to Benjamin and Sara Underwood, 15 April 1887, with Stanton to Sara Underwood, n.d. August 1887, Stanton Papers, Vassar College Library, Poughkeepsie, N.Y. (hereafter NPV).

39. See Lucinda Chandler's comment on the Book of Judges where she offers this advice, *Woman's Bible,* 2: 30–31.

40. "Lucinda B. Chandler," in Frances E. Willard and Mary Livermore, eds., *A Woman of the Century* (Buffalo: Moulton, 1893), 165.

41. Stanton to Sara Underwood, n.d. August 1887.

42. Stanton to Elizabeth Smith Miller, 31 October 1886, Theodore Stanton Collection, Elizabeth Cady Stanton Papers, NjR. In Stanton's letter to her svelte cousin, she claimed her own "too solid flesh" was a spiritual handicap: "What blinds your eyes to the beauty of occult literature, I can't imagine. It cannot be overabundant flesh!" See also Stanton to Rachel Foster Avery, 12 January 1887, Susan B. Anthony–Rachel Foster Avery Papers, University of Rochester Library, Rochester N.Y.; Stanton to Sara Underwood, n.d. August 1887; and Stanton to Benjamin and Sara Underwood, 15 April 1887.

43. Stanton to Sara Underwood, 1 November 1887, Stanton Papers, NPV.

44. And she did not hesitate to lecture others, either her daughters or women readers, on her practices and attitudes toward the body. See for example, Stanton's discussion of menopause and menstruation with her daughter Maggie: Stanton to Margaret Livingston Stanton Lawrence,15 June 1895, Scrapbook no. 2, Stanton Papers, NPV: "I never saw the slightest variation in my health either beginning nor ending the monthly period." See also Stanton, *Woman's Tribune*, 28 December 1895, 163, where she accounts for her good health in terms of her moderate eating habits and sensible dress.

45. Stanton, *Elizabeth Cady Stanton as Revealed in Her Letters, Diary and Reminiscences*, ed. Theodore Stanton and Harriot Stanton Blatch, 2 vols. (New York: Harper, 1922), 2: 337. The incident was recorded in her diary on 25 January 1899.

46. Stanton to William Henry Blatch, 7 November 1883, Theodore Stanton Collection, Elizabeth Cady Stanton Papers, NjR.

47. For references to recurring illnesses suffered by Chandler (spinal injury) and Henry (undisclosed physically frailty), see their respective entries in Willard and Livermore, eds., *A Woman of the Century*, 165, 372. Catherine Stebbins to Elizabeth Morrison Boynton Harbert, 16 September 1885, Harbert Collection, Box 7, Folder 105, CSmH, mentions recurring illness and difficulty in traveling. Helen Gardener was described as having "long been an invalid confined to her room," in the *Open Court*, 3 May 1888, 930–931. Ellen Battelle Dietrick died suddenly in surgery, but William Lloyd Garrison Jr. in her obituary described her strength being exhausted by excessive political work. See *Woman's Exponent*, 15 December 1895, 89. Lillie Devereux Blake suffered an illness in 1905 from which she never entirely recovered. Blake died in 1913 institutionalized in a sanitarium in New Jersey. See *NAW*, 1: 169.

48. Chandler also wrote to Harbert about stomach problems, (Chandler to Harbert, 3 November 1884, Harbert Collection, Box 3, Folder 31, CSmH). She also complained of being too weak to deliver a paper to the ICW (Chandler to Harbert, 21 March 1888, Harbert Collection, Box 3, Folder 31), of fatigue and "trying brain taxation" (Chandler to Harbert, 8 April 1899, Harbert Collection, Box 3, Folder 31), and of desiring to "be free from the needs of mortal body" (Chandler to Harbert, 21 March 1902, Harbert Collection, Box 3, Folder 21). Chandler's health problems were compounded by her poverty. She peddled books for a source of income in the 1890s but was unable to support a full-time residence. She wrote to Harbert in 1893—offering Gage's *Woman, Church and State* for sale—and mentioned her homelessness: "I shall stay in Dansville at least three weeks as I have no place on earth to abide[,] circumstances will guide my movements." (See Chandler to Harbert, 26 September 1893, Harbert Collection, Box 3, Folder 31). In 1902, she wrote, "I cannot report any prosperity *temporal*. My situation is not delightful as a homeless floating speck on life's sea, only uncertainty and dependence on the bounty of friends. (See Chandler to Harbert, 21 March 1902).

49. Susan B. Anthony to Thomas C. Gage, 18 May 1900, Gage Papers, as quoted in *NAW*, 2: 6.

50. Stanton to Sara Underwood, 23 January 1898, Stanton Papers, NPV.

51. *Free Thought Magazine* 16 (1898): 334.

52 Willard and Livermore, eds., *A Woman of the Century*, 165. The social history of medicine in the nineteenth-century United States has demonstrated that illness was both gendered and class-bound. Middle-class women often suffered from "neurasthenia." See, for example, Tom Lutz, *American Nervousness, 1903: An Anecdotal History* (Ithaca: Cornell University Press, 1991).

53. Members of Sorosis included Wilbour, Thomas, Livermore, Neyman, Chapin, and Hanaford as a vice president. The Society for Political Study was a club founded by Blake and presided over by Hanaford in 1896–1898. The Association for the Advancement of Women/Woman's Congress involved Chapin, Hanaford (vice president, 1874) and Stebbins. The International Council of Women involved foreign members of the *Woman's Bible* committee: Alexandra Gripenberg (Finland), Irma von Troll-Borostyani (Austria) and Isabelle Bogelot (France). Members from the United States included Thomas, Hanaford, Chandler, Stanton, Gardener, Gage, and Colby, as well as numerous women tangential to the committee, including Harbert and Hooker. The WCTU claimed members in Brown, Chandler, and Chapin.

Chapin was also one of the organizing forces behind the World Parliament of Religions, to which several committee members gave or sent speeches.

54. Catherine Stebbins served as the corresponding secretary for the Detroit Equal Suffrage Association. Louisa Southworth was the vice president of the NWSA of Ohio. Before moving to Chicago, Sara Underwood participated in the NWSA of Massachusetts in 1885. Mary Seymour Howell was president of the Albany (N.Y.) suffrage society in 1883. Josephine K. Henry was an official lecturer in the Kentucky Equal Rights Association in 1890. Clara Colby served multiple terms as president of the Nebraska NWSA/NAWSA between 1885 and 1898. Frances Ellen Burr served as an officer of the Hartford Equal Rights Club in the 1880s. Lillie Devereux Blake was president of the New York City Suffrage League, 1886–1900. Cornelia Hussey served as vice president of the New Jersey NWSA in the 1880s.

55. Gage was alternately president (1875), secretary (1878), and vice president (1882–1887) of the New York State Woman Suffrage Association. Blake was chair of the executive committee (1878) and president (1879–1890). Neyman was chair of the executive committee (1882) and foreign corresponding secretary (1887). Howell served as secretary (1885) and corresponding secretary (1887). In addition to general membership in the NWSA, *Woman's Bible* collaborators also served on committees together. For example, Colby and Blake shared a NWSA committee assignment in 1882. Southworth and Colby worked together on enrollment and representation issues in 1887.

56. Ellen Battelle Dietrick, who served briefly as corresponding secretary of the merged NAWSA, is the one exception. Dietrick was based in Boston and may have had better relations with the New England wing of the movement.

57. Liberal defections included the Women's National Liberal Union (1890) with Gage, Gardener, and Burr. The Federal Suffrage Association (1892), based in Chicago with strong New Thought/Freethought ties, included Olympia Brown (vice president at large); C. S. Darrow (auditor); and Louisa Southworth, Isabella Beecher Hooker, and Abigail Scott Duniway, as division presidents. The National Legislative League (1900) was founded with Blake (president), Stanton (honorary vice president) and Josephine K. Henry (vice president at large). The Federal Women's Equality Association/Federal Suffrage Association (1902–1913) was revived with officers from the Freethought wing of the NAWSA including Brown and Clara Colby. Finally, the Congressional Union (1913) led by Alice Paul and Lucy Burns, was joined by Olympia Brown.

58. Susan B. Anthony to Stanton, 8 January 1897, letter fragment, Anthony Family Papers, CSmH. English and American feminists were interested in Gandhi and Indian nationalism in part because Annie Besant, the world's leading Theosophist after the death of Madame Blavatsky, was engaged in this campaign. As a result of the Depression of 1893, Jacob S. Coxey led jobless men on a march on Washington in 1894 to press for government relief. On Besant's role in Hindu nationalism, see Nancy L. Paxton, "Complicity and Resistance in the Writings of Flora Annie Steel and Annie Besant," in Nupur Chaudhuri and Margaret Strobel, eds., *Western Women and Imperialism: Complicity and Resistance* (Bloomington: Indiana University Press, 1992), 158–176.

59. The constellation of relationships among *Woman's Bible* colleagues included several overlapping orbits. One such path connected Gage with Brown, Chandler, Gardener, Harbert, Colby and Stanton. Chandler, for example, visited Gage in 1893 and wrote letters to promote the sale of Gage's *Woman, Church and State*. (See, for example, Chandler to Harbert, 26 September 1893, Harbert Collection, Box 3, Folder 31.) Gage and Brown visited repeatedly during these years as well. (See, for example, Gage to Harbert, 12 April 1879, Harbert Collection, Box 4, Folder 50, CSmH.) Gage saw herself as having a shared vision with Stanton, "N[ot] even Susan B. Anthony has [as] closely approached the depth of . . . Mrs. Stanton's soul as myself for between us is a sympathy [of] thought deeper and wider than she cares to reach." See Gage to Harbert, 26 October 1885, Harbert Collection, Box 4, Folder 50. In addition, Stanton wrote a preface for Gardener's novel *Pray You Sir, Whose Daughter?* (1892). Colby offered both Gardener's book, *Facts and Fictions of Life*, and Stanton's books as premiums for subscriptions to the *Woman's Tribune*. Another network within the committee existed among the Universalist ministers: Brown, Chapin, and Hanaford. These women worked together to establish a place for

women clergy in their denomination and occasionally substituted in each other's churches. Patterns of friendship and visiting solidified the ties among various members. For example: Stanton visited Southworth in her Cleveland home in 1888; Blake visited Stebbins in Detroit in 1888; Burr established ties through correspondence and visits with Stanton through the Hartford Equal Rights Club; and Gardener formed a close relationship in the early 1880s with Robert and Eva Ingersoll. A sampling of obituaries illustrates the personal and theological connections among members. On the death of Matilda Joslyn Gage, see Clara Colby, *Woman's Tribune,* 25 June 1898; also Lucinda Chandler, Sara Underwood, and Stanton, "Matilda Joslyn Gage Obituary," *Free Thought Magazine,* 16 (1898): 334–337. On the death of Ellen Battelle Dietrick, see Josephine K. Henry, *Woman's Exponent,* 15 December 1895, 89. Brown published a biography of Clara Colby in the wake of her death; see Olympia Brown, *Democratic Ideals: A Memorial Sketch of Clara Bewick Colby* (Racine, Wis.: Federal Suffrage Association, 1917).

60. Stanton to Colby, 8 December 1892, Clara Colby Papers, WHi.

61. Stanton, *Eighty Years,* 372.

62. Stanton, *Woman's Tribune,* 1 June 1895, 85. See also *Woman's Bible,* 1: 64.

63. These categories of interpretation are based on the frameworks developed by Elisabeth Schüssler Fiorenza. She posits four models of biblical interpretation: 1) the "doctrinal approach" which "understands the Bible in terms of divine revelation and canonical authority;" 2) the "positivist historical exegesis" (or historical-critical scholarship) which is "modeled after the rationalist understanding of the natural sciences;" 3) the "dialogical-hermeneutical interpretation" which reflects "on the interaction between text and community, or text and interpreter;" 4) "liberation theology," an interpretive model that draws on the "recognition that all theology, willingly or not, is by definition always engaged for or against the oppressed." Fiorenza has maintained that the *Woman's Bible,* for the most part, remains "within the parameters set by the first two interpretive models." However, she points out that Stanton's discussion of the patriarchal language of the Bible "resorts to the third model of biblical interpretation which stresses the interaction between text and situation." While Stanton's insight—that the biblical texts themselves were androcentric—provided the impetus for her fourth model, a "feminist critical hermeneutics of liberation," the *Woman's Bible* itself "centers on questions of the theological rejection/legitimization of the Bible" and does not develop in the direction of a liberation theology. See, Elisabeth Schüssler Fiorenza, *In Memory of Her: A Feminist Theological Reconstruction of Christian Origins* (New York: Crossroad, 1983), 4–6, 13, 27.

64. A discussion of the practices of intensive and extensive reading can be found in Cathy Davidson, "Towards a History of Books and Readers," *American Quarterly* 40 (1988): 7–17. In fact, popular resistance to the revised New Testament of 1881 underscored a deeply rooted practice of intensive Bible reading. Scholars of reading have maintained that cheaper materials made available by revolutions in printing fostered a change in reading as well. Readers with increased access to more publications began to read extensively, and less intensively. In contrast, cheaper Bibles made widely available seemed not to alter reading practices.

65. Stanton to Elizabeth Smith Miller, 21 July 1897 [date incorrect], Elizabeth Cady Stanton Papers, DLC. Stanton may have preserved the concept of a religious "fetish" from Auguste Comte's Positivism. On Comte's critique of fetishism in religion, see August Comte, *August Comte and Positivism: The Essential Writings,* ed. Gertrude Lenzer (New York: Harper, 1975), 462.

66. This passage offered another lesson to contemporary women's politics: the importance of a united front among women. "The daughters of Zelophehad were fortunate in being all of one mind," Stanton noted. "None [were] there to plead the fatigue, the publicity, the responsibility of paying taxes and investing property." Stanton generally exhibited a low tolerance for those women who stood in the path of women's advancement, but the hypocrisy in this case was particularly galling. "When the rights of property were secured to married women in the State of New York in 1848, a certain class were opposed to the measure, and would cross the street to avoid speaking to the sisters who had prayed and petitioned for its success. They did not object, however, in due time to use the property thus secured."

67. Stanton's tone frequently borders on the anti-Semitic.

68. Commentator Phebe Hanaford serves as a good counterexample. See 1: 142.

69. This passage is more than ironic, because it was published during the depression era of the 1890s and the height of the Populist movement.

70. Although these nineteenth-century commentators made a sharp distinction between Stanton's "plain English" passages and "esoteric" readings, both methods frequently drew upon a dialogical model of analysis. The emphasis on the Bible as "a record of the soul," for example, privileges a dialogical analysis that focuses on the interaction between the text and the interpreter.

71. A theory of heterosexual attraction informed much of Stanton's thinking about theology and religious practice. In 1881 she wrote: "The woman worships the male God and the male Christ as man never can. He is to find his Deity through his opposite." Divine motherhood, according to Stanton, would serve a dual purpose. It would restore women's self-respect which had been lost in the erasure of the feminine from the God-head. It would also provide men their "opposite" to worship and to attract them to the church. See Stanton, untitled speech to Free Religions Association, *Free Religions Index*, 23 June 1881.

72. A snake, according to Adam Clarke, could not walk upright. Therefore, his reasoning went, the animal must have been an ape of some sort.

73. The full quote: "brilliant jewels, rich dresses, worldly luxuries."

74. Matthew Henry as quoted in William Jenks, ed., *The Comprehensive Commentary on the Holy Bible* 5 vols. (Philadelphia: American Publishing House, 1891), 1:32.

75. Thomas Scott as quoted in Jenks, ed., *Comprehensive Commentary*, 1:33.

76. Jenks, ed., *Comprehensive Commentary*, 1:28.

77. Fiorenza has suggested that Stanton's analysis did not evolve a liberation theology model of interpretation in which the Bible is read and interpreted to combat oppression. The *Woman's Bible*'s reading of Eve, however, is perhaps an apt illustration of this model. See Fiorenza, *In Memory of Her*, 27.

78. Stanton, "To the Women of the State of New York," 11 December 1854, as printed in *Lily*, (Seneca Falls, N.Y.) 1 January 1855.

79. Rosalie M. Stevenson to Editor, *Women's Penny Paper*, (London) 19 October 1889, 11.

80. Helen Hamilton Gardener, "Men, Women and Gods," in *Facts and Fictions of Life* (Chicago: Kerr, 1893), 44.

81. Chandler authored a series of anti-Catholic articles in Clara Colby's *Woman's Tribune*, 1889.

82. For this interpretation, see Antoinette L. Brown (Blackwell), "Exegesis of I Corinthians, XVI, 34, 35; and I Timothy, II, 11, 12," *Oberlin Quarterly* 4 (1849): 358–373. My thanks to Jackie Pastis for bring this source to my attention.

83. In this passage Chandler drew upon a textual-hermeneutical approach by juxtaposing Jesus and Paul. For an explanation of this interpretive model, see Fiorenza, *In Memory of Her*, 14.

84. William Buell Sprague, ed., *Women of the Old and New Testament: A Series of Portraits* (New York: Appleton, 1849); Harriet Beecher Stowe, *Woman in Sacred History: A Celebration of Women in the Bible* (1873; rpt. New York: Portland House, 1990); Grace Aquilar, *The Women of Israel* (London: Groombridge and Sons, 1870); Francis Augustus Cox, *Female Scripture Biography* (Boston: Lincoln and Edmands, 1831).

85. Stowe, *Woman in Sacred History*, 25.

86. Ibid., 28.

87. Aquilar, *The Women of Israel*, 53.

88. Stowe, *Woman in Sacred History*, 29.

89. Sprague, *Women of the Old and New Testament*, 38. Ninetenth-century discussions of Hagar drew on discourses of race as well as sexuality. See Janet Gabler-Hover, *Dreaming Black, Writing White: The Hagar Myth in American Cultural History* (Lexington: University Press of Kentucky, 2000).

90. Both readings—Stanton's "plain English" and Colby's "esoteric"—were using a dialogical model of analysis, but as we will see, they differed greatly in terms of whether the meaning inhered in the words or in the symbolic code signified by the words.

91. As I have discussed elsewhere, Colby's reading of this passage of the Bible was shaped by her New Thought beliefs but also by the experience of her husband's marital infidelities. Specifically, Leonard Colby had a liaison with a household employee that resulted in the birth of a son in 1893. See Kathi Kern, "The Private Life of a Public Family: Clara Colby, Lost Bird

and the Search for Spiritual Love," Berkshire Conference on the History of Women, University of North Carolina, 7–9 June 1996, Berkshire Conference of Women Historians Collection, MCR-S. Leonard Colby's marital infidelities are well documented in Clara Colby's correspondence; see, for example, Clara Colby to Maud Miller, 19 September 1893, Clara Colby Papers, WHi; see also Flood, *Lost Bird of Wounded Knee*, 147–165.

92. The esoteric realm, according to Chandler, consisted of "higher and finer vibrations" which were invisible. These vibrations could be sensed, however, by intuition and feelings. See Lucinda Chandler to Elizabeth Harbert, 21 March 1902.

93. Stanton to Clara Colby, quoted in *Woman's Tribune*, 23 February 1895.

94. Matilda Joslyn Gage to Clara Colby, 17 May 1895, and 30 May 1895, Matilda Joslyn Gage to Stanton, 28 May 1895, and Stanton to Clara Colby, c. 30 May 1895, all in Colby Papers, WHi. See also Copyright Registration for Woman's Bible, chapter 1, submitted by C. D. B. Colby, U.S. Copyright Office, Copyright Records Maintenance Unit, Copyright Records Books, registration no. 29883AA.

95. Stanton, *Eighty Years*, 328–329.

96. Ibid., 329. Gage to Colby, 30 May 1895. See also Gage's letter to Harbert in which she described the following incident: "When in Dakota I found an album written with my motto . . . [and] Mrs. Stanton's name signed, I placed quotation marks at each end." Gage to Harbert, 3 November 1885, Harbert Collection, Box 4, Folder 50, CSmH.

97. Stanton, *Eighty Years*, 329.

98. Stanton to Clara Colby, 16 February 1895, Colby Papers, WHi.

99. See, for example, Stanton to Mrs. Unknown, 28 July 1896, and Stanton to Mrs. White, 14 July 1896, both in Stanton Papers, NPV; Stanton to Clara Bigelow Hall, 30 January 1899, Hall Papers, DLC. I have been unable to confirm Elisabeth Griffith's claim that the *Woman's Bible* was a best-seller. Stanton's financial records were completely destroyed, and therefore the only information about the numbers of books published and sold is anecdotal. Stanton's children, Theodore Stanton and Harriot Stanton Blatch, included this footnote in *Elizabeth Cady Stanton as Revealed*: "Before the end of the first year the first part had gone through three American and two English editions, 20,000 copies having been called for. The first American edition of the second part was 10,000 copies." Generally, a nineteenth-century "best-seller" is defined as a book that sold in excess of 500,000 copies. In all likelihood, Stanton's Bible did not qualify. See Griffith, *In Her Own Right*, 212: "*The Woman's Bible* was a best-seller; it went through seven printings in six months and was translated into several languages." See also Stanton, *Elizabeth Cady Stanton as Revealed*, 2:329, n. 1.

100. Susan B. Anthony to Clara Colby, 18 December 1985, Clara Colby Collection, CSmH.

101. Stanton, interview, New York *World*, 17 March 1895.

5. "The Bigots Promote the Sale": Responses to the *Woman's Bible*

A portion of this chapter appeared in Kathi L. Kern, "Rereading Eve: Elizabeth Cady Stanton and the *Woman's Bible*, *1885–1896*," *Women's Studies*, 1991, 19 (3–4): 371–383.

1. Susan B. Anthony to Clara Colby, 13 December 1895, Clara Colby Collection, Huntington Library, San Marino, Calif. (hereafter CSmH). For her part, Stanton felt that the birthday celebration would have been "more appropriate" had it been sponsored by her own organization, the National American Woman Suffrage Association, not by the National Council of Women. See Elizabeth Cady Stanton, *Eighty Years and More: Reminiscences 1815–1897*, introd. Ellen Carol DuBois, afterword Ann D. Gordon (1898; rpt. Boston: Northeastern University Press, 1993), 458.

2. *Des Moines Leader*, clipping, n.d.; *Hartford Seminary Record*, clipping, n.d.; *Albany Evening Journal*, clipping, n.d.; *Trenton Gazette*, clipping, n.d; as quoted in "Press Comments," "The Woman's Bible" Circular, Stanton to Margaret Olivia Slocum Sage, 20 April 1899, enclosure, Margaret Olivia Slocum Sage Collection, Emma Willard School Archives, Troy, N.Y. (hereafter *Woman's Bible* Press Excerpts).

3. As quoted in Elizabeth Cady Stanton and the Revising Committee, *The Woman's Bible*

(New York: European Publishing Co., 1895–1898; rpt. Seattle: Coalition Task Force on Women and Religion, 1990) 2: 7–8; all subsequent citations are to this edition (hereafter *Woman's Bible*, and cited in my text by volume and page number).

4. As quoted in *Free Thought Magazine* 14 (1896): 396.

5. As quoted in "Mrs. Stanton, The Woman's Bible and the Clergy," ibid., 54.

6. As quoted in *Free Thought Magazine* 14 (1896): 396.

7. As quoted in the *Woman's Tribune*, 11 April 1896, 1.

8. "A Striking Sign of the Times: A Chapter from the Woman's Bible," *Our Hope* 2 (1896): 34.

9. *Chicago Christian Advocate*, clipping, n.d., *Woman's Bible* Press Excerpts; Josephine K. Henry "The Woman's Bible" *Free Thought Magazine* 14 (1896): 233.

10. *Woman's Tribune*, 28 March 1896, 1.

11. Alexander Kent, "The Woman's Bible," sermon delivered 19 January 1895 [*sic*], reprinted in *Woman's Tribune*, 7 March 1896, 25–27; all subsequent quotations are from this sermon.

12. Margaret Sangster et al., "Is the Woman's Bible a Success?: A Short Symposium by Five Women," unidentified clipping, n.d., Elizabeth Cady Stanton Papers, Library of Congress (hereafter DLC).

13. "New Woman's New Bible," *Truth* 21 (1895): 249.

14. See, for example, Stanton to Andrew Dickson White, 19 April 1896, Andrew Dickson White Papers, Manuscripts and Archives, Cornell University, Ithaca, N.Y.

15. Sangster et al., "Is the Woman's Bible a Success?"

16. "A Woman's Good Confession," *Truth* 21 (October 1895): 453, which excerpts Amelia E. Barr's article from *Ladies Home Journal*.

17. Sangster et al., "Is the Woman's Bible a Success?"

18. Annie Bronson King, "Apropos of 'The Woman's Bible,' " *Critic*, 25 January 1896, 63–64.

19. Stanton to Editor, 29 February 1896, *Critic*, 28 March 1896, 218–219.

20. Ibid.

21. "The Woman's Bible," *Critic*, 9 May 1896, 331.

22. Jeannette Gilder, as quoted in Sangster et al., "Is the Woman's Bible a Success?"

23. See Stanton to Elizabeth Smith Miller, 2 October 1895, 23 April 1897, 21 July n.y., Elizabeth Cady Stanton Papers, DLC. See also Anthony to Colby, 13 December 1895.

24. Susan B. Anthony to Olivia Bigelow Hall, 8 January 1896, Olivia Bigelow Hall Papers, DLC.

25. Anthony to Colby, 13 December 1895.

26. Martha Strinz, a German observer, suggested that Stanton's unscholarly treatment of the Bible had actually retarded the cause of woman's emancipation. Martha Strinz, "Die Geschichte der Frauenbewegung in der Vereinigten Staaten von Nordamerika," in Gerbrud Baumer and Helene Lange, eds., *Handbuch der Frauenbewegung*, vol. 1. (Berlin, 1901), 469. My thanks to James Albisetti for this citation. Even the *Boston Investigator*, the Freethought newspaper in which volume two appeared, was lukewarm in its praise: "Much of the comment is, from the unorthodox standpoint, reasonable and even strong; but much of it also is prolix, rambling, and pointless. Some of the comments . . . are far-fetched and trivial even to silliness, and thus are calculated to cast ridicule not only upon the Scripture . . . but upon the very cause these women have most at heart, namely the emancipation of women." See *Boston Investigator*, 1 February 1896.

27. Dubuque (Iowa) *Telegraph*, clipping, n.d., *Des Moines Leader*, clipping, n.d., *Woman's Bible* Press Excerpts.

28. *Springfield Republican*, 6 December 1896.

29. Stanton to Clara Colby, 8 February 1896?, *Woman's Tribune*, 8 February 1896, 14.

30. *Chicago Inter Ocean* 7 May 1898, as quoted in *Free Thought Magazine* 16 (1898): 346.

31. For an excellent analysis of the ideological alternatives to "woman's sphere" in the 1820s, see Lori D. Ginzberg, " 'The Hearts of Your Readers Will Shudder': Fanny Wright, Infidelity, and American Freethought," *American Quarterly* 46 (1994): 195–226.

32. *Washington Evening Star,* 23 January 1896.
33. *Woman's Journal,* 1 February 1896, 34. Avery was not actually present at the meeting to read her report.
34. *New York Mail and Express,* 25 January 1896, clipping, Susan B. Anthony Scrapbook, 25, DLC.
35. *Washington Evening Star,* 23 January 1896.
36. *New York Mail and Express,* 25 January 1896.
37. *Washington Evening Star,* 23 January 1896. The vote to table carried 59 to 16. Rachel Foster Avery, ed., *Proceedings of the Twenty-Eighth Annual Convention of the National American Woman Suffrage Association, held in Washington DC, January 23–28, 1896* (Philadelphia: Alfred J. Ferris, 1896), 93–95.
38. Stanton to Colby, 24 January 1896, 25 January 1896, Clara Colby Papers, State Historical Society of Wisconsin, Madison (hereafter WHi).
39. *Proceedings Twenty-Eighth Annual Convention,* 29. Stanton wrote to her son Theodore, "Susan did not know what the actors in the farce proposed." Stanton to Theodore Stanton, 2 March 1896, Theodore Stanton Collection, Elizabeth Cady Stanton Papers, Rutgers University Libraries, New Brunswick, N.J. (hereafter NjR).
40. Stanton to Colby, 28 January 1896?, Clara Colby Papers, WHi.
41. Ibid.
42. *Proceedings Twenty-Eighth Annual Convention,* 91.
43. *Woman's Journal,* 29 February 1896, 66.
44. As quoted in *Woman's Tribune,* 1 February 1896, 10.
45. Susan B. Anthony to Mary Stafford Anthony, 13 January 1895, Isabel Howland Papers, Sophia Smith Collection, Smith College, Northampton, Mass.; Anthony to Clara Colby, 14 January 1895, Clara Colby Collection, CSmH. Another indication of the differences in organizing in the South was the fact that southern chapters of the WCTU did not usually support woman suffrage. See Marjorie Spruill Wheeler, *New Woman of the New South: The Leaders of the Woman Suffrage Movement in the Southern States* (New York: Oxford University Press, 1993), 11.
46. "The Woman's Bible," clipping, n.d., *Greenville Daily News,* Laura Clay Papers, Box 1, Folder 12, University of Kentucky Libraries, Lexington (hereafter KyU). The editor also lambasted the book's anti-male content: "All this sounds like burlesque or insane raving, but it is sober, serious fact. The first volume of "Woman's Bible" has been published . . . by women . . . who usually present three very full names, as the manner of the advanced woman is[.] The keynote of the whole thing is a most vindictive hatred of everything male. It is evident that in the opinion of these talented sheologists the Almighty was guilty of serious error, if not of crime, in creating men at all." The editor suggested that the source of this acrimony directed at men was the collaborators' disappointments in love. They "have not been appreciated by persons of the opposite gender as highly as some of their sisters who were not so advanced and rather more attractive. Some of them possibly drew blanks from the matrimonial lottery."
47. A. Viola Neblett to Laura Clay, 23 November 1895, Clay Papers, Box 1, Folder 11, KyU. See also the speeches of national organizers at the NAWSA convention, *Proceedings Twenty-Eighth Annual Convention,* 55, 57. Wheeler has pointed out that the perception of regional religious differences was a frequently invoked symbol in the "Lost Cause" rhetoric of Confederate apologists. The North was perceived as "atheistic" and the South as "God-fearing." Southern white women's allegiance to Christianity was an intrinsic component of southern values and the Lost Cause. When they attempted to organize in the South, northern women reformers—who, southern men insisted, "despised the word of God"—threatened this crucial aspect of southern nationalism. See Wheeler, *New Woman of the New South,* 5–7.
48. See for example *Washington Evening Star,* 23, 25, 29 January 1896; *New York Mail and Express,* 25 January 1896; *Washington Post,* 29 January 1896.
49. *Woman's Tribune,* 1 February 1896, 10.
50. *Proceedings Twenty-Eighth Annual Convention,* 93–95.
51. Charlotte Perkins Gilman was "Mrs. Stetson" at this time. For her reaction to the Bible

debate, see Charlotte Perkins Stetson Gilman, Diary, 28 January 1896, Charlotte Perkins Gilman Papers, Schlesinger Library, Radcliffe Institute, Cambridge, Mass. (hereafter MCR-S).

52. Stanton had spent considerable effort in the 1880s authoring resolutions condemning religious orthodoxy. See Chapter 3.

53. Gilman, Diary, 28 January 1896.

54. The issue of generational conflict is a crucial factor in this debate, and I am not the first to note it. Aileen Kraditor wrote that "a new generation of conservative women came into the suffrage movement to achieve the victory that the Stantons and Anthonys had made possible." See Kraditor, *The Ideas of the Woman Suffrage Movement, 1890–1920* (1965; rpt. New York: W. W. Norton, 1981), 85. Ellen DuBois has also pointed out that the generational and political tensions between Stanton and the younger women Anthony had recruited to the movement. See DuBois, ed., *The Elizabeth Cady Stanton–Susan B. Anthony Reader: Correspondence, Writings, Speeches* (1981; rev. ed. Boston: Northeastern University Press, 1992), 190. Stanton had her supporters among this generation of suffragists, but they were outnumbered and politically marginalized for a variety of reasons, but especially their religious beliefs and their work on the *Woman's Bible*.

55. The roll call of votes is printed in Susan B. Anthony and Ida Husted Harper, eds., *History of Woman Suffrage* vol. 4 (Rochester: Susan B. Anthony, 1902) 264, and in the *Proceedings Twenty-Eighth Annual Convention*, 93–95. In terms of the geographical issue, whereby the delegates from the South or West might be expected to have supported the resolution, much of the voting record disproves the leadership's theory. To cite one example, both representatives of South Carolina, where a major organizational drive had been conducted in 1895, opposed the censure. The regions of the South and West were underrepresented at the convention in Washington, but still the fact that delegates from those regions typically split their votes on the resolution indicates that the perception of the importance of condemning the *Woman's Bible* in order to continue organizing there was one held by the national organizers, but not unanimously by the representatives from those regions in question.

56. *Proceedings Twenty-Eighth Annual Convention*, 76.

57. The other was Virginia Young from South Carolina. The nine women who worked in national organizing in 1895 and voted in favor of the resolution included Carrie Chapman Catt, Laura Clay, Annie Diggs, Mary Hay, Laura Johns, Helen Morris Lewis, Anna Howard Shaw, Anna Simmons, and Elizabeth Yates. This combination of forces also dominated the discussion in support of the resolution. Of the eleven speakers who argued in favor of the resolution, all but two were either of the "new leadership," national organizers, or Stanton's longtime rivals, e.g. Henry Blackwell.

58. Several of the women who were national organizers were the only delegates representing their states: Annie Diggs from Colorado, Mary Hay from Indiana, Elizabeth Yates from Maine, and Helen Morris Lewis from North Carolina. The organizers who hailed from delegate-rich states were, in every case, able to count all—or all but one—of their votes in favor of the resolution of censure. In Massachusetts, all three delegates from the state association Henry Blackwell presided over voted for the resolution. The one delegate from the vestigial Massachusetts-National (pre 1890 unification) sided with Stanton.

59. Carrie Chapman Catt, "Woman Suffrage and The Bible," 13, 14, 16, 37–40, 45, Carrie Chapman Catt Papers, Manuscripts and Archives, New York Public Library, New York, N.Y. (hereafter NN). Of the new leaders who assumed power in the late 1890s, Anna Howard Shaw, a Methodist Protestant minister, and Laura Clay, an Episcopalian, were the most evangelical in their espousal of liberal Protestantism. Ironically, Rachel Foster Avery, the most vitriolic in her condemnation of the *Woman's Bible*, was the most spiritually eclectic of the new leaders. Avery was a Quaker who studied Christian Science in the 1880s. Although their religious views were at odds with Stanton's, the new leaders opposed the *Woman's Bible* more because of its effect on their political strategy than its affront to their personal religious views. For a flavor of Anna Howard Shaw's religious views, see Chapter 2, and the text of a speech that appeared in *Woman's Journal*, 30 May 1891. A discussion of Laura Clay's theology can be found in Paul E. Fuller, *Laura Clay and the Woman's Rights Movement* (Lexington, Ky.: University Press of Kentucky, 1975), 7, 8, 19–20, 50. Avery's study of Christian Science is documented in the following

correspondence: Rachel Foster Avery to Elizabeth Boynton Harbert, n.d., Harbert Papers, Box 2, Folder 15, CSmH. For a general discussion of religion in the woman suffrage movement in the South, see Evelyn A. Kirkley, " 'This Work is God's Cause': Religion in the Southern Woman Suffrage Movement, 1880–1920," *Church History* 59 (December 1990): 507–522.

60. Stanton, *Elizabeth Cady Stanton as Revealed in Her Letters, Diary and Reminiscences*, ed. Theodore Stanton and Harriot Stanton Blatch, 2 vols. (New York: Harper, 1922), 2: 290. The entry is from 1 November 1892.

61. Anthony to Lillie Devereux Blake, 17 February 1896, Lillie Devereux Blake Papers, Missouri Historical Society, St. Louis (hereafter MoSHi).

62. Anthony to Blake, 7 February 1896, Blake Papers, MoSHi.

63. Ibid. Anthony to Colby, 26 February 1896, Clara Colby Collection, CSmH.

64. Anthony to Colby, 26 February 1896. Anthony informed Colby that "Mrs. Stanton sent me your letter in which you say 'Miss Anthony is like putty in the hands of her young lieutenants.' "

65. Anthony to Colby, 10 February 1896, Clara Colby Collection, CSmH.

66. Ibid.

67. *Stanton-Anthony Reader,* 188–191.

68. Anthony to Colby, 10 February 1896.

69. Mary Gray Peck, *Carrie Chapman Catt, A Biography* (New York: H.W. Wilson, 1944), 88–89, Stanton to Colby, 5 February 1896, Clara Colby Papers, WHi.

70. Anthony to Colby, 10 February 1896.

71. Stanton to unknown (probably Charlotte Perkins Stetson Gilman) 28 February 1896? Gilman Papers, MCR-S. This document has been partially destroyed. My thanks to Diane Hamer of the Schlesinger Library for helping me to piece it together.

72. Stanton's marginalia, Grace Ellery Channing-Stetson to Stanton, 4 March 1896, Elizabeth Cady Stanton Papers, DLC.

73. Stanton to Colby, 5 February 1896.

74. Ibid.

75. "Elizabeth Cady Stanton Convicted of Heresy," *Free Thought Magazine* 14 (1896): 183.

76. Ibid., 184–185.

77. Henry B. Blackwell to Editor, 23 March 1896, *Free Thought Magazine* 14 (1896): 335.

78. Editorial, *Free Thought Magazine* 14 (1896): 337.

79. Jean Brooks Greenleaf to Editor, 24 March 1896, *Free Thought Magazine* 14 (1896): 334–335.

80. Lucy Coleman to Editor, *Free Thought Magazine* 14 (1896): 390.

81. Josephine K. Henry, "The Woman's Bible," *Free Thought Magazine* 14 (1896): 239.

82. Helen Gardener, "On the Woman's Bible," *Free Thought Magazine* 14 (1896): 398.

83. One wonders if Green had read the *Woman's Bible*; he repeated the common misperception that it was a revision of the Bible. *Free Thought Magazine* 14 (1896): 269.

84. Editorial, *Free Thought Magazine* 14 (1896): 333.

85. Stanton to Theodore Stanton, 2 March 1896, Theodore Stanton Collection, Elizabeth Cady Stanton Papers, NjR.

86. Anthony to Colby, 10 February 1896.

87. Stanton, *Elizabeth Cady Stanton as Revealed,* 2: 281.

88. Anthony to Stanton, 2 December 1898, Anthony Family Papers, CSmH.

89. Anthony and Ida Husted Harper to Colby, 18 January 1898, Clara Colby Collection, CSmH.

90. Anthony to Colby, 19 January 1896, and Anthony and Ida Husted Harper to Colby, 18 January 1898, Clara Colby Collection, CSmH.

91. Anthony to Colby, 18 December 1895, Clara Colby Collection, CSmH.

92. Anthony to Stanton, 24 July 1895, Anthony Family Papers, CSmH. "Indian" is a reference to Colby's adopted Native American daughter, Zintka.

93. Ibid.

94. Anthony to Stanton, 2 December 1898.

95. Anthony to Stanton, 24 July 1895.

96. Anthony to Stanton, 2 December 1898.

97. Anna Howard Shaw, *The Story of a Pioneer*, with Elizabeth Jordan, ed. Rowena Keith Keyes (New York: Harpers, 1915, 1929), 214–215. See also Anthony to Anna Howard Shaw, 8 September 1897, Dillon Papers, MCR-S, in which Anthony refers to Theosophy as "the least attractive speculation of all."

98. Anthony to Elizabeth Smith Miller, 12 March 1897, Gerrit Smith Papers, Manuscript Division, NN. Anthony declined the suggestion that Stanton visit, explaining that Ida Husted Harper, her biographer, was occupying the guest room. However, Anthony did extend several other invitations to women reformers to visit that summer, including Frances Willard and Charlotte Perkins Gilman.

99. Josephine K. Henry to Laura Clay, 19 January 1899, Laura Clay Papers, Box 2, Folder 17, KyU.

100. The work of this committee had become so important that Catt was listed on the convention program as one of the NAWSA's officers. Ultimately Anthony became concerned that the committee on organization had become too powerful. She moved to dissolve it in 1900, but Catt staunchly resisted. Anthony won using the power of the executive committee.

101. The other committee members were Julia B. Nelson, Emma Smith De Voe, Helen Morris Lewis, and Emmeline B. Wells. See *Proceedings Twenty-Eighth Annual Convention*, 200. From Oregon, Abigail Scott Duniway, unlike the great majority of woman suffragists, did not support Prohibition. In 1897 Duniway used her own newspaper to charge the "eastern influence" in the suffrage movement with causing the defeats in the state campaigns in California and Kansas. The mutual distrust between Duniway and Anthony's lieutenants would culminate in 1906, when the national organization would take over her statewide campaign in Oregon, essentially forcing her resignation. The woman suffrage amendment lost in 1906 in Oregon, despite the "invasion" of the national.

102. *Proceedings Twenty-Eighth Annual Convention*, 80. Blake grandfathered Susan B. Anthony into her proposal.

103. See, for example, Anthony to Colby, 8 September 1896, Clara Colby Collection, CSmH, and Blake to Anthony, 21 April 1896, Blake Papers, MoSHi.

104. Anthony to Blake, 9 April 1896, Blake Papers, MoSHi.

105. Anthony to Blake, 15 May 1896, Blake Papers, MoSHi.

106. Anthony to Blake, 7 February 1896. The money to be made "in the field" was not a handsome salary, but as Anthony advised Colby: "You would make a vastly greater [financial] success in the field . . . than you ever can with your paper." See Anthony to Colby, 9 April 1896, Colby Collection, CSmH.

107. Blake to Anthony, 2 April 1896, Blake Papers, MoShi. Anthony to Blake, 15 May 1896.

108. Anthony to Colby, 13 January 1896, Clara Colby Collection, CSmH.

109. Olympia Brown to Colby, 19 June 1909, Clara Colby Collection, CSmH. Wealth also enabled a suffragist to prevent her own "annihilation," as Brown put it. Several years into Anna Howard Shaw's presidency, several of the other leaders, including Rachel Foster Avery, became dissatisfied and wanted to make changes in the NAWSA. Avery was subsequently on the "outs," yet, according to Brown, "Mrs. Avery is allowed to exist in a mild shadowy way because she has money & because she is too well known & established to be absolutely annihilated and because she is no speaker" and, consequently, was not perceived as a legitimate rival.

110. Anthony to Colby, 9 April 1896, and 26 July 1896, Clara Colby Collection, CSmH. Anthony also noted repeatedly that Colby had been unable to commit for the entire duration of the campaign and that this had been the cause of her elimination from the California campaign.

111. See Anthony to Colby, 12 February 1897, Clara Colby Collection, CSmH.

112. Anthony to Stanton, letter fragment dated 8 January 1897, Anthony Family Papers, CSmH. Anthony also apparently subsidized the *Woman's Tribune* at various points of crisis. In a letter to Colby, Anthony wrote: "Don't ask this Committee for any pay for anything—nor say aught of my doings with you to anybody." Anthony to Colby, 12 March 1894, Clara Colby Collection, CSmH. Four years later Anthony had to decline Colby's request for "some individual or for the Association to pay you or your creditors $1500" in the event of Colby's death. See Susan B. Anthony to Clara Colby, 20 April 1898, Colby Collection, CSmH.

113. It was this coterie of leaders whom Alice Paul, Lucy Burns, and other young militants abandoned to form the Congressional Union in 1913 and later the National Woman's Party. Ultimately, Laura Clay had a falling-out with Catt and the NAWSA over her "states rights" opposition to the Nineteenth Amendment. See Marjorie Spruill Wheeler, *New Women of the New South: The Leaders of the Woman Suffrage Movement in the Southern States* (New York: Oxford University Press, 1993), 160, 164–165. See also Carrie Chapman Catt to Alice Stone Blackwell, 18 November 1930, 1 August 1941, Carrie Chapman Catt Papers, DLC.

114. On a number of occasions, as I noted in Chapter 4, Stanton's "liberal" followers attempted defections to form more progressive suffrage societies. The lack of success of these defections, in part, lay in the fact that Stanton was tired of organizations and would not volunteer her services. In 1892 Olympia Brown and Isabella Beecher Hooker tried to form one such organization. They wanted "Mother Stanton" to be the president, but she replied: "Under no circumstances would I accept any office in any association. I want really to be free from all anxiety & friction." See Isabella Beecher Hooker to Stanton, 26 April 1892, enclosure with note in Stanton's hand, Olympia Brown Papers, MCR-S. Gage founded the Woman's National Liberal Union in 1890. Blake organized the National Legislative League in 1900. Colby formed the short-lived Federal Suffrage Association with Olympia Brown in 1892 and revived it as the Federal Woman's Equality Association in 1902.

115. Anthony to Colby, 18 December 1895, Clara Colby Collection, CSmH. With the merger of 1890, the Blackwell paper was chosen as the "official organ" of the NAWSA. Colby received no funds officially and was dependent on her subscriptions. She went heavily into debt to keep the *Woman's Tribune* alive. She learned to set type and ran the press herself out of the basement of her Washington home. See Olympia Brown's discussion of Colby's paper in *Democratic Ideals: A Memorial Sketch of Clara Bewick Colby* (Racine, Wis.: Federal Suffrage Association, 1917), 32–40.

116. From 1869–1894, NWSA and then NAWSA held annual conventions in Washington D.C. for the purpose of pressuring Congress for a federal suffrage amendment. (After 1894, the meetings rotated to other cities on the odd years.) Over the years, suffragists testified before several house and senate committees, including the House Committee on the Judiciary, the Senate Committee on Privileges and Elections, the Senate Committee on the Judiciary, and the Senate Select Committee on Woman Suffrage.

117. Rachel Foster Avery to Anthony, 14 December 1897, Susan B. Anthony–Rachel Foster Avery Papers, University of Rochester Library, Rochester, N.Y. (hereafter NRU).

118. Anthony to Avery, 13 October 1897, Anthony-Avery Papers, NRU. Avery to Anthony, 24 November 1897, Anthony-Avery Papers, NRU.

119. Blake to Anthony, 19 November 1897, Anthony-Avery Papers, NRU.

120. Avery referred to Blake as "the fair Lillie" in Avery to Anthony, 18 December 1897, Anthony-Avery Papers, NRU. Blake's main responsibility within the newly merged NAWSA, chairing the committee on legislative advice, was dissolved by the new leadership.

121. Anthony to Avery, 21 December 1897, Anthony-Avery Papers, NRU.

122. See, for example, Anthony and Avery's extensive correspondence in preparation for the fiftieth anniversary of Seneca Falls. The reference to "Mzoomdar and all the other Orientals" was made regarding a speech by Elizabeth Harbert, a known New Thought healer and a devoted supporter of Stanton. Avery's position was particularly ironic given her own enthusiastic study of Christian Science in the 1880s. Avery to Anthony, 24 November 1897. For Colby's participation in the Jubilee, Avery offered her the topic "Indifference and Opposition of Women" on which to address the congressional hearing. When Colby did not respond in what Avery thought a timely manner, Avery replaced her with a Southerner, Virginia Clay Clopton, and then wrote to Colby to inform her of her decision. "I feel almost sure that you will be glad to be relieved of the duty . . . and that you will agree with me that it is wise to get this speaker from the far South." Avery to Colby, 13 January 1898, Clara Colby Collection, CSmH.

123. Avery to Anthony, 14 December 1897. Avery's strategy—the "narrow platform and 5 minute speeches"—had, according to Stanton, alienated some of the older workers, including the Reverend Antoinette Brown Blackwell who had been "treated very disrespectfully by Susan's little cabinet of girls." Stanton offered Lillie D. Blake a list of "dissatisfied" women "who

were retired from the movement because of snubs by Rachel Foster Avery, *et al.*" See Stanton to Blake, 31 March 1900, Blake Papers, MoSHi.

124. Stanton, interview, *New York Herald*, 8 February 1900, clipping in Susan B. Anthony Scrapbook, no. 33 DLC.

125. Stanton to Blake, 14 June 1899, Blake Papers, MoSHi.

126. Blake to Elizabeth Harbert, 28 April 1900, Harbert Papers, Box 3, Folder 20, CSmH.

127. Carrie Chapman Catt to Alice Stone Blackwell, 18 September 1930, Carrie Chapman Catt Papers, DLC. Kathleen Barry, Anthony's biographer, has written that Anthony and Stanton "needed each other in much more subtle and dynamic ways than a rigid . . . categorization of their relationship could ever reveal." See *Susan B. Anthony, A Biography of a Singular Feminist* (New York: New York University Press, 1988), 65.

128. Elisabeth Griffith, *In Her Own Right: The Life of Elizabeth Cady Stanton* (New York: Oxford University Press, 1984), xv–xvii; Ellen Carol DuBois, *Harriot Stanton Blatch and the Winning of Woman Suffrage* (New Haven: Yale University Press, 1997), 246–261; Shaw, *The Story of a Pioneer*, 275.

129 Olympia Brown to Colby, 19 June 1909.

130. *Watchman*, 30 January 1896, 9.

131. *Springfield Republican*, 6 December 1896.

132. *Proceedings of the Annual Convention of the Woman's Christian Temperance Union, 1896*, National Woman's Christian Temperance Union Papers, Microfilm edition of the *Temperance and Prohibition Papers*, University of Michigan, Ann Arbor, 1977.

133. *Free Thought Magazine* 16 (1898): 514.

134. Stanton to Foremothers' Dinner, *New York Times*, 22 December 1895, 5.

135. Stanton to Elizabeth Smith Miller, 19 April 1897, Elizabeth Cady Stanton Papers, DLC. Stanton also recorded what appears to be the same conversation with Jewish women in her diary on 19 April 1895. See Stanton, *Elizabeth Cady Stanton as Revealed*, 2: 312–313.

136. See also Judith Plaskow, "Anti-Judaism in Feminist Christian Interpretation," in Elisabeth Schüssler Fiorenza, ed., *Searching the Scriptures: A Feminist Introduction* (New York: Crossroad, 1993), 117–129. For a historical analysis of nineteenth-century Jewish women's beliefs and religious practices, see Karla Goldman, *Beyond the Synagogue Gallery: Finding a Place for Women in American Judaism* (Cambridge: Harvard University Press, 2000).

137. Stanton to Mary Clemmer Ames, 20 June 1880, printed in Stanton, *Elizabeth Cady Stanton as Revealed*, 2: 169–170. In this letter Stanton also refers to the passage of prayer in which Jewish men thank God that they were not born women. Stanton's letter to Ames concluded: "But from this don't conclude that I am a Jew-hater; on the contrary some of my dearest friends are Hebrews. But this synagogue service is a disgrace to them and to the century." In editing their mother's correspondence, Harriot Stanton Blatch and Theodore Stanton submitted this letter to Felix Adler for clarification; he responded that Stanton's translation of the passage was technically correct but taken out of context. This particular phrase, he noted, "sounds so harsh and is capable of such sweeping misinterpretation." See Stanton, *Elizabeth Cady Stanton as Revealed*, 2: 170.

138. "Bigotry and The Woman's Bible," *Free Thought Magazine* 16 (1898): 433.

139. T. B. Wakeman, *Free Thought Magazine* 16 (1898): 164; "Editorial Department," *Free Thought Magazine*, 14 (1896): 584; "Elizabeth Cady Stanton, The Woman's Bible and the Resolution Passed at the Woman's National Convention," *Free Thought Magazine* 16 (1898): 329.

140. "Editorial," *Free Thought Magazine* 14 (1896): 52.

141. Henry, "The Woman's Bible," 234.

142. Ibid.

143. The Comstock laws gained notoriety for their use in the prosecution of birth-control advocates, but the first person arrested under the statutes was Victoria Woodhull. For an analysis of Comstock, see Nicola Beisel, *Imperiled Innocents: Anthony Comstock and Family Reproduction in Victorian America* (Princeton: Princeton University Press, 1997).

144. Parker Pillsbury, "Parker Pillsbury on The Woman's Bible," *Free Thought Magazine* 14 (1896): 265.

145. "Editorial," *Free Thought Magazine* 14 (1896): 52.

146. Henry, "The Woman's Bible," 237.

147. Ibid., 238.

148. Stanton to Elizabeth Smith Miller, 25 December 1896[?], Elizabeth Cady Stanton Papers, DLC.

149. Stanton to William Lloyd Garrison Jr., 6 January 1896, Garrison Papers, Sophia Smith Collection, Smith College, Northampton, Mass. On Julia Smith's translation, see Kathleen L. Housley, *The Letter Kills but the Spirit Gives Life: The Smiths, Abolitionists, Suffragists, Bible Translators* (Glastonbury, Conn.: The Historical Society of Glastonbury, Conn., 1993), 80–89.

150. Stanton to Colby, 14 January 1896?, 28 January 1896, Clara Colby Papers, WHi.

151. Edwin G. Mauger to Clara Colby, 26 August 1897, Clara Colby Papers, WHi.

152. Anthony to Stanton, 30 September 1895, Anthony Family Papers, CSmH; also Anthony to Clara Colby, 18 December 1895. A few years later, Colby determined she would have to close down her radical paper if she hoped to get any work from the NAWSA. (Her friend Olympia Brown called this strategy a "delusion." "It was not the Tribune they feared, it was you."): Olympia Brown to Colby, 19 June 1909.

153. Anthony to Colby, 16 January 1894, Clara Colby Collection, CSmH.

154. Stanton to Colby, 25 March 1898, Clara Colby Papers, WHi.

155. Anthony to Stanton, 2 December 1898, Anthony Family Papers, CSmH.

156. See for example, Stanton to Antoinette Louisa Brown Blackwell, 16 September 1897, Blackwell Family Papers, MCR-S.

157. See also, the letter from Irma von Troll-Borostyani calling for a recognition of "scientific materialism" and the "progressive evolution" of social relations (2: 190). The letters Stanton appended to volume two originally appeared in various issues of the *Boston Investigator*.

158. Stanton, *Elizabeth Cady Stanton as Revealed*, 2: 329.

159. *Chicago Inter Ocean*, 7 May 1898, as quoted in *Free Thought Magazine* 16 (1898): 346. Even other liberal reformers regretted the title. A British Liberal member of parliament, John Pennington Thomasson, wrote, "the title is inappropriate [and] gives no idea of what the book is. It suggests an expurgated or manipulated Bible. It might have been called " 'Woman in the Bible, considered by Women.' " His wife concurred: "we had not known just what your book 'The Woman's Bible' was like [and] I did not much like the idea of it, from its name—now we see the 2nd Part we see that it is most instructive [and] we shall like to see Part I." John Pennington Thomasson and Katherine Lucas Thomasson to Stanton, 7 January 1899, Elizabeth Cady Stanton Papers, DLC.

160. *Springfield Republican*, 6 December 1896.

161. Stanton to Theodore Weld Stanton, 4 September 1898, Theodore Stanton Collection, Elizabeth Cady Stanton Papers, NjR. Stanton took another unlikely approach to marketing her book: she advertised it as a romance. In a column in the *Boston Investigator*, Stanton wrote: "One lady had just purchased fifty copies of 'The Woman's Bible' to read all about the meeting of Isaac and Rebecca at the twilight hour, 'When she dismounted from her white mule and gracefully dropped her veil to hide her charms.' " Stanton, "The Woman's Bible," *Boston Investigator*, 13 February 1897.

162. Stanton to "friend," 1 March 1898, Theodore Stanton Collection, Elizabeth Cady Stanton Papers, NjR.

163. Stanton, "Reading the Bible in the Public Schools," *Free Thought Magazine* 16 (1898): 471.

164. Ibid.

165. Stanton, "The Duty of the Church to Woman at this Hour" *Free Thought Magazine* 20 (1902): 189, 191. Stanton first articulated these ideas in her speech she informally called "Has the Christian Religion Done Aught for Woman?" See "Manuscript Address by Elizabeth Cady Stanton at Prince's Hall, London, England, June 25, 1883," 74, Elizabeth Cady Stanton Papers, DLC.

166. Stanton, "The Duty of the Church," 192, 194.

167. Stanton to Josephine K. Henry, 23 June 1902, Theodore Stanton Collection, Elizabeth Cady Stanton Papers, NjR.

168. Stanton, *Commonwealth*, 16 May 1896. In a later article Stanton fused her Positivist beliefs with her new interest in socialism, arguing the importance of the recognition of the "feminine element" for socialism to work productively. See Stanton, *Commonwealth*, 29 July 1899 and 24 June 1899.

169. Stanton to Theodore Weld Stanton, 26 January 1898, Theodore Stanton Collection, Elizabeth Cady Stanton Papers, NjR.

170. Stanton to Victoria Claflin Woodhull Martin, 4 October 1898, Martin Papers, Special Collections, Morris Library, Southern Illinois University, Carbondale.

171. Stanton's phrenology reading is published in DuBois, *Stanton-Anthony Reader*, 271–274, and in Griffith, *In Her Own Right*, 230.

172. As quoted in Theodore Tilton to ECS, *Free Thought Magazine* 16 (1898): 287.

173. Stanton to Blake, 14 June 1899. In other letters Stanton wrote near the end of her life, her tone is more bitter, less resigned. In the summer of 1901, for example, she was trying to raise money to publish a collection of her speeches and was frustrated by the lack of support she received from the younger women. She wrote to Harbert: "If my suffrage coadjutors had ever treated me with the boundless generosity they have my friend Susan, I could have scattered my writings abundantly from Maine to Louisiana. They have given Susan thousands of dollars, jewels, laces, silks and satins, and me, criticisms and denunciations for my radical ideas." Stanton to Harbert, 25 July 1901, Harbert Collection, Box 7, Folder 102, CSmH.

174. Stanton to Blake, 14 June 1899.

175. Stanton, *Elizabeth Cady Stanton as Revealed*, 2: 338.

176. Anthony to Avery, 21 December 1897.

177. Stanton to Blake, 14 June 1899; Stanton, *Elizabeth Cady Stanton as Revealed*, 2: 338, 302.

Index

Italicized numbers indicate figures.

Aaron, 91
Abbott, Francis, 63, 97
Abolition, Final, 23–24
Abolitionists, 16, 18, 23, 47, 94–95
Abraham, 152, 154, 163–164
absent healing, 146
Adam, 79, 86–87, 95, 153, 155, 159–160
Adler, Felix, 66, 209, 269 n.137
age of consent laws, 141
Agnosticism, 52, 64, 109, 176; maleness of, 46
Ahlstrom, Sydney, 69
Albany, N.Y., 26, 38, 149
Albany Evening Journal, 173
Almy, Martha, 139, 256 n.16
American Bible Society, 52
American Equal Rights Association (AERA),
    18, 56, 130
American Protective Association, 152
American Revising Committee, 71–75,
    78–79, 242 nn.80–81
American Sabbath Union, 254 n.109
American Woman Suffrage Association
    (AWSA), 98, 121, 129, 130–131, 189, 195
Ames, Mary Clemmer, 269 n.137
Andover Theological Seminary, 242 n.76
androgyny, 156; spiritual, 165–166
Anglo-Saxons, 106
Anthony, Mary, 185

Anthony, Susan B., *105, 128, 186, 188*; adora-
    tion of, 4, 271 n.173; and clergy, 97; dele-
    gation of power of, 201–203; early career
    of, 17–18; Gage critical of, 124–125; ghost
    writers for, 198–199; and *History of Woman
    Suffrage*, 19, 50, 92, 94; and NWSA/
    NAWSA, 99, 126–127, 129, 131, 185, 200,
    203, 204–206; and "nieces," 183, 193, 203–
    204; racial views of, 110; and Revising
    Committee, 137; and religion question, 60,
    94, 98, 118, 120–121, 127, 187, 199, 213,
    267 n.97; and Seneca Falls, 4; and Stanton,
    35, 53, 93, 132, 213, 220; on Stanton, 21,
    51, 125–126, 171–172, 222; and Willard,
    125–127; and *Woman's Bible* debate, 171,
    179–180, 183–187, 189, 191–194, 198; and
    Woman's Tribune, 212, 267 n.112
anticlericalism, 92, 106, 126
anti-Sabbath agitation, 254 n.126
anti-Semitism, 209, 217–219, 248 n.15. *See
    also Woman's Bible*: anti-Semitism in
Antislavery movement, 17, 45, 129
Apocrypha, 158, 228 n.35
archeology, 154
Arena, 142
"Aristocracy of Sex," 111
Association for Advancement of Women,
    148, 258 n.53

astrology, 152, 216
astronomy, 216
Astruc, Jean, 156
atheism, 176, 264 n.47
Atlanta, Ga., 135–136
autobiography, genre of, 47–48; of Stanton
    (*see Eighty Years and More*)
Automatic or Spirit Writing, 64, 146
Avery, Rachel Foster, *105*, 203–206, 264
    n.33; and NAWSA programs, 268 nn.122,
    123; religious views of, 265 n.59; wealth
    of, 267 n.109; and *Woman's Bible*, 182, 184,
    186, 189, 194–195

Banner, Lois, 232 n.27, 234 n.39, 239 n.17
Baptists, 82, 89, 136
Barnes, Albert, 173
Barr, Amelia, 176
Barry, Kathleen, 269 n.127
Barton, Clara, 162
Bayard, Edward, 42, 231 n.23
Bayard, Tryphena Cady (sister), 42. *See also*
    Cady, Tryphena
Bederman, Gail, 82, 233 n.37, 244 n.119
Beecher, Catharine, 55, 120
Beecher, Henry Ward, 120, 249 n.48
Beman, Nathaniel, 41, 43–44, 237 n.76
Besant, Annie, 53, 199, 239 n.14, 247 n.5,
    259 n.58
Bible, 63, 86, 99; authorship of, 153, 157; and
    Christian Science, 61; and "civilization,"
    214; cultural relativism of, 152–153; demo-
    cratic content of, 95–96; divine inspiration
    of, 77, 85, 100, 162, 184; esoteric,
    165–166, 213, 215–216; expurgated,
    218–219; as a fetish, 152, 260 n.65; and
    gender roles, 78, 82; higher criticism of (*see*
    higher criticism); liberal defense of, 213–
    214; literal reading of, 46, 164, 215–216; as
    man-made, 46, 157–158, 161; multiple
    meanings within, 77, 88–89, 151, 211–212,
    246 n.160; obscenity in, 210, 217; rational-
    ist critique of, 66, 214–215; reading of, 77,
    79; impact of science on, 69–71, 76, 243
    n.100; symbolic interpretation of, 86–90;
    translation of, 211–212; and woman's
    rights, 88, 95, 101, 173, 176, 189, 191, 212,
    213–216; and women's sexual exploitation,
    210–211; and women's subordination,
    45–47, 61, 67–68, 76, 90, 99, 191,
    209–211, 213–216, 219, 244–245 n.129
Bible commentaries, 45, 76–78, 78–82
Bible convention, 103–104, 249 n.44
Bible debate (NAWSA), 181–198
biblical criticism, 72, 135, 151, 153–154, 156

Bilimoria, Eleanor D., 7
Birney, James G., 23
Blackwell, Antoinette Brown, 99, 101, 119,
    127, 129–130, 213, 268 n.123
Blackwell, Alice Stone, 121, 129, 132; and
    Woman's Bible, 183, 189, 192–194, 196,
    203, 205, 213–214
Blackwell, Elizabeth, 82, 213
Blackwell, Henry, 18, 129–132, 183, 189,
    195–197, 231 n.11, 265 nn.57, 58
Blake, Lillie Devereux, 2, 97, 259 nn.54, 55,
    57, 268 n.123; and clergy, 141; death of,
    258 n.47; defense of *Woman's Bible* by,
    182–183, 187, 192; financial hardship of,
    202, 256 n.23; marginalization of, 200–
    205, 221, 258 n.47, 268 n.120; and Revis-
    ing Committee, 140, 142, 149, 256 n.16,
    258 n.53, 260 n. 59; *Woman's Bible* contri-
    butions of, 154, 160
Blatch, Harriot Stanton (daughter): and edu-
    cated suffrage, 115; and *Eighty Years*, 3,
    132; and Mind Cure, 62; and Stanton, 50,
    52, 64, 92, 192, 269 n.137; and *Woman's
    Bible*, 98–99, 103, 139, 262 n.99
Blatch, Nora, 92
Blatch, William Henry, 52
Blavatsky, Helena, 93
Bloomer, Amelia, 102
Bogelot, Isabelle, *105*, 140, 258 n.53
Boston, Mass., 16
Boston Investigator, 62, 213
boyhood, 22, 46
boy culture, 33–34, 234 n.47, 235 nn.54, 60
brain: sex-based differences in, 107–109; of
    Stanton, 108–109; and suffrage, 106–109
Braude, Ann, 144, 228–229 n.37, 240 n.34,
    257 n.30
Bright, Ursula, 140, 215–216
British suffrage movement, 52–53, 99
Broughton, Virginia, 89
Brown, David, 78–80
Brown, Ira, 242 n.75
Brown, Jerry Wayne, 242 n.76
Brown, John, 196
Brown, Olympia, *145*; and clergy, 97–98; fi-
    nances of, 202; and immigration, 114; mar-
    ginalization of, 204, 267 n.109, 270 n.152;
    and NWSA, 149; and Revising Commit-
    tee, 140, 144, 256 n.16, 258 n.53, 259 n.59;
    and Spiritualism, 144; and suffrage splinter
    groups, 206, 259 n.57, 268 n.114
Brumberg, Joan Jacobs, 241 n.63
Bruno, Giordano, 196
Buddhism, 93, 120
Buechler, Steven, 112, 245 n.143

Burns, Lucy, 259 n.57, 268 n.113
Burr, Frances Ellen, 2; and Revising Committee, 136, 256 n.16, 260 n.59; and Stanton, 140; and suffrage splinter groups, 259 n.57; suffrage work of, 149, 259 n.54; and *Woman's Bible*, 151, 155, 158, 165–166, 168
Butler, Judith, 235 n.58

Cady, Catherine (sister), 22
Cady, Daniel (father), 15, 29–30, 35, 39, 40, 47, 236 n.71; influence on Stanton of, 39–40; and law books story, 38; law practice of, 37; parenting of, 27; and slaveowning, 22, 29, 232 n.26
Cady, Eleazer (brother), 15, 22, 30, 35, 234 n.42
Cady, Elizabeth, 22; attitude toward girls of, 32–35; and boarding school, 41–44, 237 n.74; and boyhood, 29–37; conversion to rationalism of, 42; failed conversion of, 41–45; and father, 30–31; and Simon Hosack, 30–32; physicality of, 31; and plagiarism, 33–35; scholarly aspirations of, 30–31; and Peter Teabout, 25–28
Cady, Harriet (sister), 32
Cady, Margaret Livingston (mother), 15, 22, 27, 30, 47, 232 n.25
Cady, Tryphena (sister), 22, 42, 231 n.23
Cain, 155
California, suffrage campaign in, 137, 201–202
Campbell, Flora, 38, 236 n.63
Catholic Church, 51, 219; critique of Protestantism by, 73, 77, 244 n.119; and manliness, 210; and Paul, 246 n.161; and Revised New Testament, 73
Catholic Congress, 254 n.109
Catholic World, 73
Catt, Carrie Chapman, 94, 108, 139, *190*, 256 n.16, 265 n.57, 268 n.113; and Bible debate, 184–185, 189; liberals critical of, 194–197; and marginalization of radicals, 201–206; and "Mrs. Catt's Bible," 5; and Nineteenth Amendment, 5; religious views of, 191, 265 n. 59; and Revising Committee, 5, 255 n.7
celibacy, 246 n.161
Chandler, Lucinda, 140, 149, 258 n.53; financial hardship of, 258 n.48, 259–260 n.59; illness of, 148, 258 nn.47, 48; New Thought views of, 117, 151; and Paul, 161–162; and Revising Committee, 256 n.116; Social Purity views of, 117, 146–147; and Spiritualism, 144; *Woman's Bible* contributions of, 158–159, 161–162
Chant, Laura, *105*

Chapin, Augusta, 140, 144, 256 n.16, 258 n.53, 259 n.59
Cheney, Ednah, 213
Chenoweth, Alice. *See* Gardener, Helen Hamilton
Chicago, 62, 103, 146–147, 259 n.57
Chicago Christian Science Church, 142
Chicago Inter-Ocean, 216
Chicago Moral Education Society, 147
childbirth, 155; as curse, 80, 87; as redemption, 80, 244 n.128
China, 67
Christian Party, 254 n.109
Christian radicalism, 95–96
Christian Science, 52, 69, 71, 118; connections to New Thought, 61–62; and esoteric interpretations, 154, 158; faith healing of, 146; and immortality, 120; at ICW, 119; and Revising Committee, 144; and science, 106; in woman's movement, 142, 268 n.122. *See also* Eddy, Mary Baker
Christian Science Healing, 146
Christian Spiritualism, 120
Christian state, 88, 104, 125
Christianity, 59, 66; and "civilization," 127; and Darwinism, 69; and elevation of woman, 67, 86, 98, 214; emasculated, 78; and feminism, 13; and imperialism, 67, 169; and individual conscience, 46; male, 82; morality of, 63; and sexual differentiation, 252 n.76; supportive of women's emancipation, 178–179; and women's subordination, 68, 96, 106, 118–119, 175
Christians: and ICW, 118; racial views of, 109; in suffrage, 88, 90
Church: as public, 244–245 n.129; and racial prejudice, 47; and state, 184; as supportive of suffrage, 133; women's silence within, 81, 85, 95; and women's subordination, 67, 119, 219
Church of Our Father, 181
Civil War, 17, 64, 100
"civilization," 85, 233 n.37
Clark, George Whitfield, 173
Clarke, Adam, 158
Clarke, Edward, 251 n.61
Clay, Laura: and Bible debate, 182, 184; and Josephine K. Henry, 200; and NAWSA, 203; and NAWSA organizing, 189, 265 n.57; religious views of, 206, 265 n.59; and states rights, 268 n.113; and *Woman's Bible* in the South, 185
clergy, 44–45, 90, 99, 141; Baptist, 136; Congregationalist, 97; conservatism of, 107; as enemy of women, 85, 96–97; and Genesis,

clergy (*cont.*)
159; Presbyterian, 173; status of, 120;
Universalist, 174–175, 259–260 n.59;
Stanton on, 91; and woman's rights, 95;
women as, 259–260 n.59; and women's
speech, 95–96; and women's subordina-
tion, 46, 96, 210–211
Cleveland, Ohio, 146
Clinton, Catherine, 246 n.146
Clopton, Virginia Clay, 268 n.122
Coalition Task Force on Women and Reli-
gion (Seattle), 7
coeducation, 84
Coffin, G. Y., 185–186
Coleman, Lucy, 197
Colenso, John William, 70, 72, 153, 179
Colorado, 85
Columbian Exhibition. *See* World's Fair
Colby, Clara, 2, 92, 122, *143*; and California
campaign, 202, 267 n.110; and copyright
controversy, 171; education of, 142; esoteric commentaries of, 151, 154, 164–165;
and defense of *Woman's Bible*, 174, 182–
185, 187, 192–195; disagreements with
Stanton, 164–165, 168, 212–213; financial
hardship of, 202, 212, 255 n.5, 257 n.28,
267 nn.106, 112, 268 n.115; influence on
Stanton of, 61–62; and ICW, 258 n.122,
270 n.152; marginalization of, 150, 200–
210, 206, 268 n.122, 270 n.152; marital
discord of, 261–262 n.91
Colby, Leonard, 142, 261–262 n.91
comparative religions, 63
Comstock, Anthony, 210
Comstock Law, 210, 269 n.143
Comte, Auguste, 54–58, 93, 110, 260 n.65
Congressional Hearings on Woman Suf-
frage, 203, 204–205, 268 n.116
Congressional Union, 145, 259 n.57, 268
n.113
Constantinople, 52
Constitution, 111
Conway, Ellen Davis, 53
Conway, Moncure, 53, 67, 92
Corinthian women (biblical), 80–81, 87
Corinthians, 80
Cornell University, 63
cosovereignty, 95
Cott, Nancy, 112
coverture, 37
Coxey, Jacob, 150, 259 n.58
creation story (Genesis), 59, 86–87; compet-
ing accounts of, 79, 95, 156; and Pauline
doctrine, 79–82; political consequences of,
97

"criminal," *113*
Critic, 176–178, 179
Custom House scandal, 234 n.40

Darwin, Charles, 63–64, 68, 69–70, 71, 91,
152, 157, 241 n.70
Darrow, C. S., 259 n.57
David, 91
Davis, Paulina Wright, 94, 95
A Daring Experiment, 141
Deborah, 45
Declaration of Independence, 26, 55
Declaration of Sentiments, 55, 95
Delaware, suffrage campaign in, 201–202
Democratic party, 201
Depression of the 1890s, 13, 85, 259 n.58
Descent of Man, 68
Detroit, 149
Devil, 22, 41, 73. *See also* Satan; serpent
dialogical interpretation, 151–152, 158–159,
160, 164, 260 n.63, 261 nn.70, 90
Dietrick, Ellen Battelle, 2; as author, 141;
death of, 256 n.20, 258 n.47; illness of,
147; in NAWSA, 259 n.56; obituaries of,
260 n.59; and Revising Committee, 256
n.16; *Woman's Bible* contributions of, 157,
161, 168
Diggs, Annie, 265 nn.57, 58
Dilke, Charles, 104
Dilke, Margaret, 104, *105*
divine inspiration, 73–75, 88, 100, 184
divine motherhood, 261 n.71
Divine Science, 61, 62
Divine Within, 61, 120
divorce, 17, 84–85
Dix, Dorothea, 162
Dix, Morgan, 141
Doane, W. C., 73
doctrinal interpretation, 260 n.63
domestic science, 84
domesticity, 85–86
double standard, 165, 211
dower rights, 235–236 n.61
Douglass, Frederick, 112
Doxology, 73–75
Drew Theological Seminary, 71
DuBois, Ellen Carol, 10–11, 193, 206, 226
n.11, 227 n.22, 229 n.39, 231 n.18, 232
n.25, 239 n.16, 265 n.54
Duniway, Abigail Scott, 201, 259 n.57, 267
n.101

"Eastern" religions, 154
Eddy, Mary Baker, 69, 146; biblical interpretations of, 89, 158; and Christian Science,

52; and Ursula Gestefeld, 142; influences on New Thought of, 61–62

Edger, Henry, 56–57, 60

Edmunds-Tucker Act, 84

"Educated Suffrage," 109–110, 112, 114–116, 169, 205

education, higher, 84, 108, 220

Egypt, 58

Eighty Years and More, 12, 14–49, 68, 132; boyhood in, 30–37, 48; connections to *Woman's Bible* of, 21, 39, 48–49; and controversy with Gage, 170; conversion narrative in, 47; as historical document, 20–21; and memory, 20; political goals of, 20; politics in, 37–40; publication of, 216; religion in, 15, 40–46; repeated plots of, 21–22, 46; repressed stories in, 22, 28–29; reviews of, 19; sale of, 19–20; slavery in, 23, 47; writing of, 211

Eisenstein, Zillah, 227 n.22

election of 1888, 124

electorate, 115

Emancipation, 17, 26, 232 n.29

enfranchisement, 110–116

Episcopalians, 52, 73

Equal Rights Association of South Carolina, 185

esoteric interpretation, 151, 155–156, 158–159, 164–165, 167, 261 n.70

esoteric realm, 262 n.92

Esther, 45

Eternal Mind, 61

ethical culture, 66

eugenics, 115, 155

evangelical Bible scholars, 71–76, 79–82

evangelical clergy, 81–82, 85–86. *See also* clergy

Evangelicalism, 63, 78

Evans, Walter Felt, 61–62

Evanston, Ill., 146

Eve, 79–81, 86–87, 88, 91, 95, 153, 158–160; evangelical interpretations of, 79–80; inferiority of, 80; as intellectual, 159; sinfulness of, 12, 80, 244 n.124; and women's subordination, 80

Washington Evening Star (D.C.), 182, 185

evolution, 63–64, 69, 87, 115, 119–120, 157, 196

evolutionary republicanism, 252 n.76

Fabian socialists, 53

Facts and Fictions of Life, 141

faith healing, 61, 145–148. *See also* Christian Science; Mind Cure; New Thought

fall, the, 158–160

Fawcett, Milicent, 101

Federal Suffrage Association, 259 n.57, 268 n.114. *See also* suffrage splinter groups

Federal Woman's Equality Association, 206, 259 n.57, 268 n.114. *See also* suffrage splinter groups

federal woman suffrage amendment, 84

feminine element: as catalyst for revolution, 119, 127; Comte's concept of, 54–55; in Genesis, 156–157, 175; in Reconstruction debates, 37, 110; and socialism, 270 n.168; Stanton's changing view of, 112. *See also* Positivism

feminism, 13, 239 n.19

feminist biblical hermeneutics, 151

feminist theologians, 9

fertility rates, 83

festivals, African American, 26–27, 233 n.35

Fettered for Life, 141

Fifteenth Amendment, 29, 110, 130

Finney, Charles G., 41, 44, 68, 237 nn.73, 74; and new methods, 43; in Troy, 42

Fiorenza, Elisabeth Schussler, 8–9, 228 nn.32, 35, 247 n.167, 260 n.63

First Presbyterian Church of Johnstown (N.Y.), 40

First Presbyterian Church of Troy (N.Y.), 43

First Principles, 69

Fitzgerald, Maureen, 227 n.22, 229 n.42, 237 n.83, 256 n.18

Flood, Renee Sansom, 257 n.28

founding fathers, 55

Fourth of July, 24–26, 233 n.34

free love, 66

Free Religious Association, 59, 63, 66

Free Religious Index, 66

Free Silver, 152

Free Thought Magazine, 63, 142, 195–198, 209–211, 217–219

Freethinkers Convention, 254 n.126

Freethought: anti-Semitism of, 209; challenge to Bible of, 71; Christian response to, 86, 98; connection to free love, 66; critique of Christian morality, 63, 66, 210, 215; feminist adaptation of, 54, 66–68; and Free Silver, 152; Gage's espousal of, 119; and gender, 241 n.57; history of, 63–68; and secularism, 240 n.45; views of science in, 69, 106–109; in woman's rights, 104, 106–109, 118. *See also* Freethought suffragists; Stanton, Elizabeth Cady

Freethought press, 213, 217–219

Freethought suffragists, 96–98, 101, 104, 147–149, 205, 219; alliance with New

Freethought suffragists (*cont.*)
Thought suffragists, 125; and Anglo-Saxon supremacy, 115–116; critical of Christian state, 125; isolation of, 125; racial views of, 115–116; and views of body, 106–109; and views of science, 106–109, 129, 251 n.61; and *Woman's Bible*, 151, 154–155; and WCTU, 122, 124–125

Gage, Matilda Joslyn, *105*; and autograph controversy, 170, 262 n.96; as Baptist, 144; and copyright controversy, 169–170; critical of Anthony, 127; critical of Christian Party, 254 n.109; critical of Willard, 124; critique of Christianity, 66–67, 119; defection from NAWSA by, 131, 133, 259 n.57; espousal of Divine Motherhood by, 118–119; espousal of feminine element by, 119, 127; and Freethought, 66–67; and *History of Woman Suffrage*, 19, 67; at ICW, 118–119, 258 n 53; illness of, 147–148; marginalization of, 204; and New York State Woman Suffrage Association, 259 n.55; and NWSA, 97, 149; and Revising Committee, 140, 151, 256 n.16, 259–260 n.59; as Theosophist, 144; writings by, 141–142
Galatians (Book of), 88
Gandhi, 150, 259 n.58
Garden of Eden, 158
Gardener, Helen Hamilton: beliefs about body of, 115–116; brain donation of, 250 n.58; and brain debate, 106–109; defection from NAWSA by, 133; defense of *Woman's Bible* by, 197; illness of, 147, 258 n.47; and ICW, 106–109, 250 n.52, 258 n.53; popularity of, 250 n.60; and Paul, 161; pseudonym of, 141; religious views of, 141–142; and Revising Committee, 136, 256 n.16, 259–260 n.59; "Sex in Brain" speech of, 106–109, 118; Social Purity views of, 114–115, 141; as Southern, 140; and suffrage splinter groups, 259 n.57; use of science by, 116; views on heredity of, 252 n.79; writings of, 141
Geary Bill, 251 n.63
General Training Day, 26
generic man, 166
generational conflicts, 94–95, 247 n.7, 265 n.54, 268 n.123. *See also* National American Woman Suffrage Association: generational tensions within
Genesis, 61, 78–79, 95–96, 155–160; creation accounts in, 72; literal reading of, 79
Geneva, N.Y., 93–94
geology, 154

German higher criticism, 71. *See also* higher criticism
Gestefeld, Ursula, 2; and Chicago, 140; and Christian Science, 142, 146; criticism of Stanton by, 167; illness of, 142, 146–147; and Revising Committee, 256 n.16; and spiritual equality, 165; *Woman's Bible* contributions of, 151, 155, 166, 215; writings of, 142
Gifford, Carolyn De Swarte, 123, 228 n.35
Gilded Age, 13, 51, 86
Gilder, Jeannette, 179
Gilman, Charlotte Perkins Stetson, 115, 187–189, 194
Ginzberg, Lori, 228 n.37, 241 n.57, 263 n.31
God, 48, 59, 66, 93, 164; communication with, 177; existence proved by science, 70, 119; as Father, 118; fear of, 22; female nature of, 62, 118, 120; in humanity, 59; as justification for reform, 122–124; as male and female, 165; as masculine, 59, 118–119; as Mother, 118, 156; Mother-heart of, 89; as Mrs., 50; as Over-Soul, 120
Gordon, Ann D., 43, 226 n.11, 230 n.3, 231 n.15, 236 n.68
Gospel of Prevention, 123
Gradual Manumission Act, 23–24, 232–233 n.30
Greek Testament, 31, 72, 242 n.92
Green, Horace L., 142, 196–198, 209
Green, William Henry, 72
Greenleaf, Jean Brooks, 197
Greenville Daily News (S.C.), 185
Griffith, Elisabeth, 206, 234 n.39, n.40, 236 n.67, 256 n.18, 262 n.99
Grimke, Angelina, 29
Grimke, Sarah, 29, 227 n.27
Gripenberg, Alexandra, *105*, 140, 258 n.53
Groth, Sophia, *105*
gynecology, 80

Hagar, 163–164, 166, 261 n.89
Haggerty, James, 35
Hall, Jacquelyn Dowd, 22, 232 n.23
Hammond, William, 107–109
Hanaford, Phebe, 2; and Association for the Advancement of Women, 258 n.53; and ICW, 258 n.53; newspaper work of, 142; and Revising Committee, 136, 256 n.16, 259 n.59; and Society for Political Study, 258 n.53; and Sorosis, 258 n.53; as Universalist clergy, 142, 144; writings of, 142
Harbert, Elizabeth: and ICW, 117, 119–120, 258 n.53; marginalization of, 204–205;

New Thought healing of, 146–148; New Thought views of, 119–120, 268 n.122; recruitment of, for Revising Committee, 135, 259 n.59
harmonial religions, 61–63, 144
Harmony, 62, 257 n.33
Hartford, Conn., 149
Hartford Seminary Record, 173
Hatch, Lavinia, 201
Hawthorne, Rev., 135–136
Hay, Mary, 265 nn.57, 58
Haygood, Rev., 173–174
Heavenly Mother, 156, 165
Heilbrun, Carolyn, 47, 231 n.16, 238 n.86
Henry, Josephine K.: correspondence with Stanton of, 220; critique of Church and clergy by, 209–210, 215; defection from NAWSA of, 205, 259 n.57; defense of *Woman's Bible* by, 197–198, 209–210; and *Free Thought Magazine*, 147, 209–210; illness of, 147; Kentucky suffrage activities of, 149, 259 n.54; marginalization of, 200–201, 203; and NAWSA, 192; and Revising Committee, 140, 256 n.16; as Southern, 140
Henry, Matthew, 173
hermeneutics, 151, 260 n.63
Heroines of Freethought, 142
Hewitt, Nancy, 228 n.37
Higginbotham, Evelyn Brooks, 89
higher criticism of the Bible, 51, 70–72, 78, 216
higher education, 84, 108, 220
Hindu nationalism, 259 n.58
Hinduism, 93
historical-critical interpretations, 78, 151–152, 155, 161, 260 n.63
History of the Warfare of Science with Theology, 63, 211
History of Woman Suffrage, 19, 50, 67, 92–94, 102, 132, 141
Hodge, Charles, 69, 71, 241 n.70
Hodges, Graham, 26
Holley, Marietta, 21
Holy Spirit, 48, 59, 62, 77, 85; as feminine, 165
Home Protection, 83, 123
Hooker, Isabella Beecher: as Christian Spiritualist, 120; defection from NAWSA by, 259 n.57, 268 n.114; and ICW, 120, 258 n.53; and immortality, 127; marginalization of, 204; and Mother Spirit, 121
Hopkins, Emma Curtis, 62, 146, 257 n.33
Hosack, Simon, and Bible commentaries, 81;

as contrast to Daniel Cady, 31; death of, 32; influence on Stanton of, 231 n.23; as mentor, 30, 35; as minister, 40, 44–45; poverty of, 235 n.50; slaveowning of, 32, 233 n.32, 235 n.50; as surrogate parent, 28, 31–32, 234 n.49
House Committee on the Judiciary, 134, 203–204, 268 n.116
Howe, Julia Ward, 88, 101, 251 n.61
Howell, Mary Seymour, 149, 204, 256 n.16, 259 n.54, n.55
Huldah, 45, 91
Hussey, Cornelia Collins, 139, 256 n.16, 259 n.54
Huxley, Thomas, 240 n.45

"idiot," *113*
"ignorant vote," 115
Illinois, 185
immigration, 51
immigration restrictions, 169, 205
immortality, 127–128, 148; proven by science, 101, 120
immutable laws, 54–58, 66, 93. *See also* Positivism
imperialism, 13, 169
indentured servitude, 23
Index, 63–64, 67, 100, 142
Indians, 214; stereotype of, *113*
individual conscience, 55, 68
infanticide, 67
Ingersoll, Eva, 139, 256 n.16, 260 n.59
Ingersoll, Robert Green, 65; agnosticism of, 52; career of, 64; and divine inspiration, 77; and Gardener, 141, 260 n.59; oratory of, 69; as source of controversy, 212; and Stanton, 50, 64; views on Bible of, 63
intelligence, 115–116
International Council of Women (ICW), 93, *105*, 103–109, 116–121, 124, 148, 258 n.53; and evangelical Christianity, 121; New Thought influence in, 116–118; organization of, 103; religious debates within, 103–109, 116–121; and Revising Committee, 103–104, 118; scandal at, 104; science debates at, 106–109
intuition, 159, 166
Irish independence, 18
Isaac, 163, 270 n.161
Isenberg, Nancy, 20, 95–96, 225 n.1, 229 nn.37, 42, 230 n.7, 231 nn.17, 18, 254 n.126
Ishmael, 163–164
Isis Revealed, 93–94

Jerusalem, 58

Jesus, 59, 62, 71, 74, 85, 197; and androgyny, 166; and Anthony, 185; compared to Comte, 56; compared to Stanton, 196; and Constitution, 124; corrupt disciples of, 56; corruption of teachings of, 67; as inspiration for reform, 48; insulted by Freethinkers, 98; invoked at ICW, 118, 121; as radical, 196; reverses woman's curse, 87; supercedes Paul, 89; and woman's rights, 95, 101, 162; women loyal to, 89

"Jesus the Emancipator of Women," 123

Jewish matriarchs (biblical), 163–164

Jewish mysticism, 168

Jim Crow Segregation, 13, 116

Johns, Laura, 187, 265 n.57

Johnstown, N.Y., 15–16, 25, 40–41, 94; slave population of, 24, 232 n.29

Johnstown Academy, 30–31, 35

Joly, Nicholas, 50

Judaism, 168, 208, 248 n.15

Judas, 197

Kabbalah, 154–155, 158, 165, 168

Kansas: and campaign for woman suffrage, 18, 58, 132, 145; and municipal suffrage, 84

Keefer, Bessie Starr, *105*

Kent, Alexander, 174–175

Kentucky, 149; Equal Rights Association of, 200

King, Annie Bronson, 176–177

King James Bible, 72–73, 75

Kingsford, Anna, 94

Kirkpatrick, D. M., 174

Kraditor, Aileen, 11, 109–110, 112, 229 n.40, 265 n.54

Kuklick, Bruce, 241 n.78

Ladies Home Journal, 176

Lanuni, Zintka, 257 n.28

law schools, 84

Lawrence, Margaret Stanton (daughter), 192, 230 n.1

Leach, William, 54, 239 n.23, 241 n.67

Lears, T. J. Jackson, 70, 78

Das Leben Jesu, 71

Lerner, Gerda, 227 n.27

Lewis, Helen Morris, 265 n.57, n.58

liberal Protestantism, 78, 86–90, 177; clergy of, 73; and Genesis, 87; and Paul, 87. *See also* clergy; progressive orthodoxy

Liberal Suffrage League, 133

liberalism, 60

liberation theology, 260 n.63, 261 n.77

Library of Congress, 170

Life of Jesus, 71

"lieutenants" of Anthony, 193–194, 200–203, 266 n.64, 267 n.101, 268 n.123. *See also* National American Woman Suffrage Association: generational conflicts within

Livermore, Mary, 101–102, 148, 256 n.16, 258 n.53; and *Woman's Bible*, 136, 139

Liverpool, England, 92–93

Livingston, James, 232 n.25

Loades, Ann, 227 n.21

Locke, John, 66

London, England, 53

Lord, Frances: and Christian Science, 62; illness of, 144–145; influence on Stanton of, 60, 93; and Harbert, 144–145; and Emma Curtis Hopkins, 257 n.33; and Mind Cure, 103, 147; New Thought career of, 60, 144–146; and Revising Committee, 139; and Theosophy, 60, 93; and *Woman's Bible*, 99–100, 103

Lord's Prayer, 73–75

Lutz, Alma, 234 n.39

lyceum, 18, 46

lynching, 169

Maine, 84

Man's Bible, 179

Married Woman's Property Act, 16, 39, 152, 206, 260 n.66

Mary (mother of Jesus), 118, 215, 219

masculine element, 59, 156–157, 175

Massachusetts, 149

Massey, Gerald, 94

materialism, 167, 270 n.157

matter, 61–62, 119–120

Mauger, Edwin, 212

McLaren, Priscilla Bright, 53, 140

medical schools, 84

medical science, 107–109

Meech, Mary Elizabeth, 7

Melish, Joanne Pope, 23, 232 n.28

Men, Women and Gods, 106, 141

Mendum, Ernest, 213

menstruation, 258 n.44

Mental Cure, 61

metaphysical stage, 54–57. *See also* Positivism

metaphysics, 120

Methodist Episcopal Church, 248 n.14

Methodist Protestant Church, 88

Methodists, 52, 82, 120, 124, 185

Metropolitan Opera House, 172

Michigan, 84

Mill, John Stuart, 104, 180

Miller, Elizabeth Smith: and Bible, 102; and Mind Cure, 62–63; and occult, 257 n.42;

skepticism of, 257 n.42; and Stanton, 35, 62–63, 69, 93–94, 208, 211; and Theosophy, 93–94; and *Woman's Bible*, 179

Milton, Abbey Crawford, 5

mind, 61–62, 115–116; relationship to matter, 119–120

Mind Cure: beliefs of, 60–62; and Christian Science, 60–62, 257 n.33; as a "delusion," 103; and immortality, 120; invoked at ICW, 120; and New Thought, 257 n.33; and Revising Committee, 103, 144–148; rise of, 52; spiritual power of, 118; Stanton introduced to, 60–62

ministers. *See* clergy

miracles (biblical), 66, 153, 165

monogamy, 156

Moody, Dwight, 52

Moore, Margaret, *105*

moral revolution, 110, 112, 117

Mormons, 46, 52, 84, 237 n.82

mortal mind, 61

Moses, 91, 152–153, 157, 165

Mother God, 62

Mother Spirit, 120

motherhood, 83; enlightened, 166; of God, 118; involuntary, 215; and moral regeneration, 82; voluntary, 18–19

Mott, Lucretia: invoked in Bible debate, 187; as "pioneer," 95; as prophetic figure, 21; as religious thinker, 94; Stanton's admiration of, 35; Stanton's memories of, 16, 230 n.6; in *Woman's Bible*, 162

Mount Sinai, 153

"Mrs. Stanton's Bible," 179, 185

muscular Christianity, 78, 244 n.119

mysticism, 142

Mzoomdar, 205, 268 n.122

Naomi, 91

Nashville, Tenn., 4–5

National American Woman Suffrage Association (NAWSA): Congressional hearings of, 203–205, 268 n.122; conservatism of, 181, 206; emphasis on ballot of, 134; financial concerns of, 202, 205–206; formation of, 129–131, 204; and free speech, 182, 187, 193; generational tensions within, 4, 133–134, 182–183, 193–195, 197–198, 200, 203–206 (*see also* generational conflicts); marginalization of radicals within, 198–206, 268 nn.120, 122; national party delegations of, 201–202; organizing work of, 184–185, 189, 201–202, 265 nn.55, 58, 267 nn.106, 109; presidency of, 131–132, 205; religious position

of, 4, 134, 196; splinter groups of, 133, 145, 149 (*see also* suffrage splinter groups); Stanton's leadership of, 132; and Sunday closings, 133–134; and *Woman's Bible* censure, 2, 5, 181–206, 216, 264 n.39, 265 nn.57, 58. *See also* NAWSA committees; NAWSA conventions

National Citizen and Ballot Box, 142

National Council of Women, 172, 262 n.1

National Divorce Reform League, 84

National Guard, 142

National Legislative League, 205, 259 n.57, 268 n.114

national purity, 115. *See also* Social Purity

National Reform Association, 124, 254 n.109

National Woman's Party, 145, 268 n.113

National Woman Suffrage Association (NWSA): compared to AWSA, 130–131; conventions of, 97–98; formation of, 18, 130; and ICW, 103; leadership of, 98; merger with AWSA of, 129; and religion, 96–98, 125, 129, 248 n.14; and Revising Committee, 148–149, 259 n.55; resolutions of, 51, 97–98; and Stanton's anticlericalism, 125–127, 132; and WCTU, 121

Native Americans, legends of, 155

natural selection, 70

"natural spheres," 81–82, 156–157, 159–160

natural theology, 70

nature, 69, 79–82

NAWSA committees: business, 204; executive, 183; on legislative advice, 268 n.120; on organization, 201, 267 n.100; on plan of work, 201, 203; program of, 204

NAWSA conventions: of 1890, 114, 131; of 1895, 135, 192; of 1896, 174, 181–192, 198, 200–201; of 1897, 203; of 1898, 203–204; changes in, 268 n.123; and Congressional hearings, 268 n.116; resolutions of, 184, 189, 191; speaking assignments at, 204–205; and Stanton's attendance at, 135

Neblett, Viola, 185

Nebraska, 84

Negro Training Day, 26

New Hampshire, 84

"new" immigrants, 83

neurasthenia, 258 n.52

New Testament, 87; supportive of woman's rights, 101

New Testament, Revised Version: changes in, 73–75, 242–243 nn.93, 94; defense of, 243 n.99; reaction to, 73–76, 175, 242 n.85, 243 n.102; and reading practices, 260 n.64; rejection of, 71–76; sale of, 72, 242 n.81

New Thought: Anthony's reaction to, 199;
beliefs of, 60–62; challenge to the Bible of,
71; concept of soul within, 157; esoteric
interpretations of, in *Woman's Bible*, 154–
155, 157; espousal of, at ICW, 104, 116–
118, 120; feminist aspects of, 62; and gender, 148; history of, 60–62; and motherhood, 166; practices of, 252 n.86; and Revising Committee, 142, 146–148; rise of,
52; and Social Purity, 117; and spiritual
power, 127; and whiteness, 252 n.75; in
women's movement, 60–62, 64, 106, 146–
148, 257 n.33; and *Woman's Tribune*, 142
New Thought suffragists: alliance with Freethinkers, 125; disagreements with Stanton
of, 212; esoteric interpretations of, 151,
165–166, 215–216; and faith healing,
147–149; at ICW, 104, 116–117; marginalization of, 205, 268 n.122; Social Purity
views of, 116–117; and *Woman's Bible*, 151,
165–166, 215–216
New York City, 17, 64, 172
New York City Suffrage Association, 149
New York State, 23, 84
New York State Woman Suffrage Associa-
tion, 149, 197, 259 n.55
New York Times, 75
New York World, 56, 136
Newcastle Liberal Women's Union, 104
Newman, J. P., 118
Newman, Louise, 114, 241 n.63
Neyman, Clara, 148–149, 151, 258 n.53, 259
n.55
Niagara Falls, N.Y., 42, 44, 237 n.81
"nieces" of Anthony, 183, 192, 204. *See also*
"lieutenants" of Anthony
Nightengale, Florence, 162
Nineteenth Amendment, 4–5, 145, 268
n.113
No Place of Grace, 70
Noah's ark, 153
North, the, 111
Numbers (Book of), 152–153, 210

Oberlin College, 101, 129
occultism, 120, 141
Ohio, 149
Old Testament, 79. *See also* Bible; Penta-
teuch
Oliver, Anna, 82
Open Court, 63, 64, 142, 146
organic state, 54–56. *See also* Positivism
original sin, 67
Our Hope, 172, 174
Over-Soul, 93, 120

paganism, 173
Parker, Theodore, 45, 165
Patton W. W., 91, 97
Paul: advice to men by, 179; and Catholics,
244 n.119; compared to Christ, 89; compared to Satan, 89; as a contemporary, 91;
and evangelical clergy, 78, 80; irrelevance
of, 199; letters of, 78; literal interpretation
of, 87; and masculinity, 246 n.161; as reformer, 88; Stanton's "interview" with,
90–91; translation of, 244–245 n.129; and
women's speech, 52, 80–82, 95; and
women's subordination, 76, 78, 80, 87–89
Paul, Alice, 259 n.57, 268 n.113
"pauper," *113*
peace, 220
Pennsylvania, 84
Pentateuch, 71, 153
*Pentateuch and the Book of Joshua Critically Ex-
amined*, 70
The Perfect Way, 94
Perkins, Sarah, 214
Peterboro, N.Y., 23
Phillips, Terry Greene, 111
Phillips, Wendell, 111
phrenology, 220
physical culture, 220
physicians, 107
Pillsbury, Parker, 210
"Pioneers" of suffrage, 13, 94–95, 101,
203–204
"plain English" interpretations, 151,
153–154, 158, 163–165, 167, 177, 261
n.70
polygamy, 46, 152
Popular Commentary on the New Testament,
78
Popular Science Monthly, 106
Populism, 152, 261 n.69
Positive Religion, 56. *See also* Religion of
Humanity
Positive Science of Society, 55
Positivism: and atheism, 54; compared to
Theosophy, 93; and Comte, 53–60, 260
n.65; conservatism of, 55–56; immutable
laws of, 66; and feminine element, 37;
feminist adaptation of, 58–60; Gage's espousal of, 119, 127; as a religion, 62; and
slavery, 56; and socialism, 59; Stanton's
engagement with, 53–60; in *Woman's Bible*,
151, 167–168; and worship of science, 110
Positivists, British, 54
Price, Abby, 95
Priesthood of Humanity, 56
Princeton University, 69

progressive orthodoxy: historians use of term, 246 n.162, 250 n.50; at ICW, 106; origin of term, 242 n.76, 246 n.162; positions of, 88–90; and WCTU, 121; and Willard, 253 n.96; in woman's movement, 88–90, 104, 178, 191
progressive revelation, 177
Prohibition, 85, 122
Prohibition Party, 124–125
property: laws and women's wages, 16–17; rights, 162. *See also* Married Woman's Property Act
prostitution, 68, 215, 219; within marriage, 117
Protestantism: commercialization of, 51–52; effeminacy of, 244 n.119; failures of, 70; and imperialism, 52; and leisure, 52; liberal, 69–70; moral superiority of, 115; relation to science, 69–71; resurgence of, 51–52; women's dominance of, 82; and women's roles, 86. *See also* Christianity; liberal Protestantism; progressive orthodoxy
public sphere, 10

Quakers, 95
Quimby, Phineas, 61

race: as "irrelevant," 114; progress of, 115; segregation by, 40; and suffrage movement, 106–116; suicide of, 83, 87; "unconsciousness" of, 112–114
reason, 48, 66, 120
Rebekah, 165, 270 n.161
reform, fragmentation of, 220–221
Reconstruction: and citizenship, 37; Constitutional debates of, 56; and educated suffrage, 109; and Fifteenth Amendment, 18, 130; millennial hopes for, 110, 112; as "Negro's hour," 110; and Positivism, 110–112; resurrection of, 132; Stanton's memories of, 29, 99–100; and woman's rights, 116
religion: fear within, 22; new, 51; and science, 63, 106–107, 241 n.78; and sexuality, 159; as side issue, 130; suffocation of, 22; and women's subordination, 15, 133
Religion of Humanity, 53–60, 66, 96
religious liberals, 125
religious liberty, 92, 98, 129, 187; rights of, 95
religious publishing, 72
religious radicalism, 94–96
Religious Outlook, 78
"Reminiscences," 134. *See also Eighty Years and More*

Republican Party, 29, 64, 110, 201; Anthony's support of, 124–125; "betrayal" of, Stanton by, 111; radicals within, 111; and woman suffrage, 18
Revising Committee (of *Woman's Bible*), 136–150; advertised, 100–101, 136; affiliations of, 148–149; anti-Catholicism of, 252 n.75, 261 n.81; anticlerical writings of, 141; anti-Semitism of, 168–169; attractiveness of, 264 n.46; authorial careers of members of, 140–144; connections to suffrage of, 140, 148–150; conservative women and, 100–101, 137; and constructions of gender by, 10, 106–109, 115, 157–163; and contributions to *Woman's Bible*, 139, 150–169; declined invitations to join, 101–103; defense of, 177; demographics of, 140; diversity among, 9, 100, 140, 144; and educated suffrage, 114–116; embellishment of, 138–139; exegetical strategies of, 10, 228 n.35, 150–169; financial hardship of, 140, 202, 258 n.48, 267 nn.106, 112; and Freethought suffragists, 136–137; historians' assessment of, 256 n.18; illnesses of, 146–148, 258 n.47; international members of, 140, 256 n.22; linguistic limitations of, 101; marginalization of members of, 149–150, 198–206; membership of, 256 n.16; and New Thought practices, 144–148; proposed structure of, 100; obituaries of members of, 260 n.59; phantom members of, 5, 136, 207; racial views of, 106–109, 114–116; radicals within, 140; relationships among members of, 150, 259 n.59; and religious experimentation, 144; scholarly aspirations of, 100; Social Purity views of, 141–142, 146–148; ties to Chicago of, 140; and twentieth-century feminists, 138; Universalists among, 144, 249 n.31
Revising Committee (of *Woman's Bible*) recruitment, 100–103, 136–137; of conservatives, 137–138; failures of, 127, 134; of international members, 138; of Jews, 138; for volume two, 213
revival methods, 237 nn.73, 76
Revolution, 18, 54, 142, 210
"rib" story (Genesis), 79, 86–87, 95, 153, 156; and androgyny, 166; and monogamy, 166
Richmond, Va., 207
Robinson, Harriet, 101–102
Rochester, N.Y., 42, 174, 200
Rose, Ernestine, 94, 209
Rothman, Sheila, 245 n.143

Rotundo, Anthony, 34, 234 n.47, 235 nn.54, 60
Rupp, Leila, 249 n.47
Ruth, 91
Ryan, Mary, 25

Sabbatarianism, 220
Sagesse, Convent de la, 50, 152
St. John's Episcopal Church (Johnstown, N.Y.), 40
Sambo, 111
Sangster, Margaret, 176
Sarah, 152, 154, 163–164
Satan, 173, 243 n.94. *See also* Devil
Schaff, Philip, 71–72, 75, 78
Scatchered, Alice, *105*
Scoble, John, 45
Science: ambivalence toward, 75; faith in, 48, 69, 106, 154; at ICW, 119; impact on Christianity of, 71, 214; as materially based, 106; and Positivism, 56; as proof of God, 119; relation to spirit, 69, 106, 119; status of, 68–70; in support of Bible, 81; in woman's rights movement, 106–109; and women's subordination, 106–109
Science and Health, 61, 146
"Science of Being," 146
scientific racism, 108–110
Scott, Thomas, 80
Scripture. *See* Bible
scriptural biography, 163
Searching the Scriptures, 8–9
Second Great Awakening, 41
secular suffragists, 257 n.29. *See also* Freethought suffragists
Secular Union, 63
secularism, 10–12, 53, 239 n.14, 240 n.45. *See also* Freethought
secularists, 53–54
secularization, 70, 76
Senate (U.S.), 84; Committee on the Judiciary of, 268 n.116; Committee on Privileges and Elections of, 268 n.16; Select Committee on Woman Suffrage of, 203, 268 n.116
Seneca Falls, N.Y., 16–17
Seneca Falls Convention, 16, 95, 150, 184; commemoration of, 4, 103, 268 n.122; as "first" convention, 20, 225 n.1; Stanton's role in, 4
"separate spheres," resurgence of, 82, 245 n.143
serpent (in Genesis), 79, 89, 158–159, 261 n.72
Servia, 92–93

Sewall, May Wright, *105*
"Sex in Brain," 106–109, 118, 141
sexual difference, 116
sexual intercourse, women's right to refuse, 18–19, 117
sexual violence, 210–211, 215, 219
Shattuck, Harriette, 101
Shaw, Anna Howard: and Anthony, 199; and AWSA, 121; as minister, 197, 255 n.3; and NAWSA, 132, 135, 201–203, 206, 265 n.57, 267 n.109; religious views of, 88, 365 n.59; and *Woman's Bible*, 184, 189
Simmons, Anna, 265 n.57
Sinnett, Alfred Percy, 94
slavery, 96; in Cady family, 22; final abolition of, 26; and historical amnesia, 23; in New York State, 23–25, 230 n.8; and white supremacy, 232 n.28
Smith, G. Vance, 73
Smith, Gerrit, 23, 47
Smith, Julia, 211
Social Purity movement, 117, 146–148, 220, 252 n.85
Society for Political Study, 148, 258 n.53
Sodom and Gomorrah, 58
Solomon, 91
Somerset, Isabel (Lady Henry), 136–137, 139, 163
Sorosis, 148, 258 n.53
soul, 62, 93, 144, 191, 215; as agent of change, 118; as feminine, 166; as masculine and feminine, 166–167; relation to body of, 106, 117–118, 120, 147, 158, 166; as sexless, 116, 157, 165–166, 168
South, the: clergy of, 185; nationalism of, 264 n.47; religious conservatism of, 185
South Place Chapel, 53
Southworth, Louisa, 2, 146–147, 256 n.16, 259 nn.54, 55, 57, 260 n.59
Spencer, Herbert, 68
spiritual equality, 119
spiritual motherhood, 215
Spiritualism, 61, 139, 144, 157
Stanton, Daniel (son), 234 n.40
Stanton, Elizabeth Cady, 36, *36*, *105*, *128*, *186*, *218*; and abolition, 28–29; and Felix Adler, 66; and aging, 1, 148, 191–192; agnosticism of, 46; and Susan B. Anthony, 17, 98, 198–200, 205–206, 259 n.59, 267 n.98, 269 n.127; anticlericalism of, 129, 133, 236 n. 63, 248 n.14; anti-Semitism of, 168, 208–209, 217–218, 269 n.137; and atheism, 12; as "author" of *Woman's Bible*, 102–103, 150–151, 226n.4; and AWSA, 98, 131; and Bible, 44, 48, 58, 64, 99–100,

152, 169, 184, 216, 220; and Bible reading, 77; birthdays of, 15, 49, 83, 92, 172, 191, 262 n.1; and Blackwells, 129–132; blindness of, 1, 4, 211, 221–222; and body, 62–63, 147, 258 n.44; brain donation of, 250 n. 58; and brother's death, 15, 30–31, 234 n.42; and Catholicism, 51, 219; childbearing of, 16; and childhood, 15, 21–22, 30, 40; and childrearing, 22, 28; and clergy, 44–45, 67, 97, 99, 135–136, 152, 221; and Clara Colby, 61–62, 135–136, 164–165, 170, 183–184, 193–195, 212–213; and Comte, 60; and controversy, 216–217, 220–221; convention attendance of, 51, 118, 184, 191–192; conversion narrative of, 41–44, 68, 237 n. 74; critique of Bible, church, and clergy of, 1–2, 12, 19, 46, 51, 53, 58–59, 67, 76, 90, 92, 94–98, 150–151, 152, 177, 219, 251 n.63; and cultural revolution, 12, 58–59; and Darwin, 68–69; disengagement from suffrage of, 1–2, 13–14, 19, 49–51, 53, 60, 99–100, 129, 131–134, 171, 184, 191, 193, 198, 205–206, 213, 220–221, 268 n. 114, 271 n.173; on divorce, 84–85; as editor of *History of Woman Suffrage*, 19, 102; as editor of *Woman's Bible*, 150–151, 167, 213–216; and educated suffrage, 109–110, 116; elitism of, 195; in England, 51–53, 92–93, 99, 103–104; on esotericism, 167, 212, 216; in Europe, 19, 45, 92; faith of, 40, 53–60, 220, 222; faith healing of, 147; and father, 29, 37–40; as feminist theologian, 6, 8–9, 12; and Fifteenth Amendment, 24, 111; in France, 50–51; and Freethought press, 64, 195–198, 213, 217–219; and Matilda J. Gage, 67, 169–170, 259 n.59; and Helen Gardener, 108–109; on gender, 37, 112–116; on God, 59, 66; as grandmother, 92, 233 n. 36; hair of, 35; health of, 50, 147, 251 n. 61; and heterosexuality, 261 n. 71; and higher criticism, 71, 76, 153, 154, 216; and hired reader, 14, 211; historical reputation of, 3–4, 6; humor of, 15, 47–48, 175; and immigration, 111–112; and individual conscience, 44, 241 n.67; and Robert Ingersoll, 64, 240 n.50; on Jesus, 123; and Judaism, 153, 163, 269 n.137; letters of, 184, 194–195; and lyceum, 90; and Mind Cure, 62–63, 147; and memory, 21, 43–44, 231 n. 15; and natural rights, 59; and NAWSA censure, 183, 194–195, 198; as NAWSA president, 131, 182, 221; as NWSA president, 18; parents of, 27; and Paul, 12, 90–91, 161, 130; phrenological interpretation of, 220; physical immobility of, 1, 14, 184, 191–192, 204; physicality and appearance of, 35; and plagiarism, 33–34, 170; Positivism of, 56–58, 60, 66, 93, 239 n.31, 241 n.67, 270 n.168; on prostitution, 219; and publication expenses, 271 n.173; racism of, 6, 8–9, 30, 37, 106, 109–116, 251 n.63; and reading, 93–94; and reason, 216, 220; and Reconstruction, 17–18, 29, 56–58, 99–100, 110–112, 130, 132; religious experiences of, 40–46, 48, 51, 55, 58–61, 93–94; and religious liberty, 26, 30, 98; religious radicalism of, 8, 130; religious views of, 3–4, 59–60, 93, 157, 227 n.22, 261 n.71; religious writings of, 51, 54–60, 64, 68; reminiscences of, 231 n. 23 (*see also Eighty Years and More*); residences of, 230 n.1 (*see also* specific cities); response to critics of, 211–212, 216–217; and Revising Committee, 100–103, 138–139, 147, 149–150; on same-sex education, 33; and science, 68–69, 107–109, 216; as secularist, 6, 10–12; self-presentation of, 35–36, 235 n.58; socialism of, 59, 169, 220, 270 n.168; as storyteller, 21, 28; and suffrage splinter groups, 131, 268 n.114; and Peter Teabout, 25, 40; and Theosophy, 93–94, 247n.5; travel of, 51, 93, 104, 191–192, 200; and Benjamin and Sara Underwood, 64, 101, 103, 147; and universal suffrage, 29, 112; and WCTU, 122, 124; and A. D. White, 211, 240 n.49; and Emma Willard's Academy, 32–35; and *Woman's Tribune*, 135–137, 212; and women's conservatism, 14, 64, 211; writing productivity of, 1, 14, 211. *See also* Cady, Elizabeth; Stanton, Elizabeth Cady, speeches of

Stanton, Elizabeth Cady, speeches of: in Albany, 39, 236 n.68; to American Equal Rights Association, 56; before Congress, 37, 39; on "Educated Suffrage," 205; "Fear," 42–43; to Free Religious Association, 59, 66; "Has Christian Religion Done Aught for Woman?" 19, 53; on immigration restrictions, 205; in Kansas, 58; as propaganda, 183; publication of, 271 n.173; "Reconstruction," 110–111; at Seneca Falls, 16; "Solitude of Self," 37–134, 234 n.48; to World Parliament of Religions, 59–60

Stanton, Henry Brewster (husband), 16, 22, 29, 234 n.40

Stanton, Henry B., Jr. (son), 66

Stanton, Robert (son), 179, 183, 192, 230 n.1

Stanton, Theodore (son), 3, 138, 192, 198, 217, 240 n.49, 262 n.99, 269 n.137
states rights, 268 n.113
Stebbins, Catherine, 140, 144, 147, 149, 150, 256 n.16, 258 nn.47, 53, 259 n.54, 260 n.59
Stone, Lucy, 18, 94, 132, 196; and Fifteenth Amendment, 129–130
Stowe, Harriet Beecher, 120, 141, 163
Strauss, David F., 71
Strinz, Martha, 263 n.26
Strong, James, 71
The Subjection of Woman, 180
suffrage, African American, 110–116
suffrage movement: aging members of, 127–128; division of, 129; efforts to broaden, 127; expediency arguments of, 11, 109–110; generational conflicts in, 11, 94–95, 110 (*see also* generational conflicts; NAWSA, generational conflicts in); and immigrants, 109–116; and Indians, 109; membership of, 121; racial politics of, 11, 109–116, 127, 239 n.11; religious differences within, 11, 53, 104–107, 116–129, 120–121, 127, 129; reunification of, 129–133; and sex scandals, 249–250 n.48. *See also* American Woman Suffrage Association; National American Woman Suffrage Association; National Woman Suffrage Association; woman's rights
suffrage splinter groups, 259 n.57, 268 n.114. *See also* NAWSA, splinter groups of
suffragists: African American, 114; northern, 116; southern, 116; white, 114–116. *See also* Freethought suffragists; New Thought suffragists
Sumner, Charles, 17
Surgeon General, 106–109
Syracuse, N.Y., 95
Szold, Henrietta, 255 n.14

Talmadge, Thomas De Witt, 67, 73, 74, 74, 86, 98
Talmud, 86, 162
Taylor, Barbara, 239 n.14, 241, n.57
Taylor, Helen, 104
Teabout, Mariah, 24–25
Teabout, Peter, 22–23, 24–29, 31, 35, 40, 46–47, 232 n.27, 234 n.38, 236 n.71
teachers, women as, 162
technology, 69, 155
temperance movement, 17, 83, 121–129, 146, 220
Tenafly, N.J., 18
Terborg-Penn, Rosalyn, 114

theology: liberal, 69; and women's subordination, 133
Theosophy, 60, 93–94, 119–120, 127, 199, 239 n.14, 259 n.58, 267 n.97
Thomas, M. Louise, 139, 148, 256 n.16, 258 n.53
Thomasson, John P., 270 n.159
Thomasson, Katherine, 270 n.159
Tilton, Elizabeth, 249 n.48
Tilton, Theodore, 220
Timothy (Book of), 79, 89–90
Topeka (Kans.) Board of Censors, 207
Toulouse, France, 50, 152
Train, George Francis, 18
Transcendentalists, 45, 155
Trinity, 59, 165
Troll-Borostyani, Irma von, 140, 258 n.53, 270 n.157
Troy, N.Y., 41–44, 237 n.74
Troy Female Seminary, 32, 35, 41–44, 60
"true woman," 81
Truth, 176
Turner, James, 70, 237 n.81, 240 n.46

unbelief, 70, 82, 98
"uncle," 233–234 n.38
Uncle Tom's Cabin, 141, 233–234 n.38
underground railroad, 23
Underwood, Benjamin, 64, 66
Underwood, Sara: and Chicago, 140, 146; contribution to *Woman's Bible*, 214–215; and Freethought, 64, 68; and Mind Cure, 147; newspaper work of, 142, 146; and occult, 148; and Revising Committee, 256 n.16, 260 n.59; and Stanton, 64, 68, 90, 101, 103, 140; suffrage work of, 149, 259 n.54
Union College, 30, 33
universal suffrage, 18, 29, 112, 130
Universal Truth, 62
Universalists, 73, 144
University of Michigan, 20
Upton, Harriet Taylor, 183, 189
Utah, 84

Van Dyke, Henry J., 81
Vashti, 45
venereal disease, 215
violence against women, 215
Voltaire, 50–51, 152
voluntary motherhood, 18–19, 252 n.85
voting, 123

Wakeman, Thaddeus, 68
Walker, Jane, 7

Washington, D.C., 97, 103, 174, 181
Washington, George, 186
Washington territory, 84
Watchman, 77, 207
Wells, Ida B., 115
Welter, Barbara, 227 n.22, 256 nn.18, 23
Western Reserve University, 84
"What Has Christianity Done for Woman?"
 19. *See also* Stanton, Elizabeth Cady,
 speeches of
Wheeler, Marjorie Spruill, 116, 253 n.98,
 264 n.47
White, Andrew Dickson, 63, 211
White, Shane, 24, 233 nn.34, 35
white supremacy, 116
Wilbour, Charlotte Beebe, 139, 144, 148,
 256 n.16, 258 n.53
Willard, Emma: female seminary of. *See also*
 Troy Female Seminary
Willard, Frances E., *113, 126*; and biblical
 interpretation, 78; Christian politics of,
 124–125; and clergy, 87, 90; contribution
 to *Woman's Bible* of, 214; conversion to
 suffrage of, 48, 83, 123; opposition to Revising Committee by, 163; relationship
 with women of, 122; religious views of, 96,
 120, 253 n.96; and Revising Committee
 controversy, 207; and *Woman's Bible*,
 136–137, 139
Williams, A. B., 185
Wilmore, Ky., 185
Wixon, Susan, 139
"woman": as category, 9, 228 nn.30, 31; as
 moral force, 110
Woman, Church and State, 67, 14
Woman in the Pulpit, 87
The Woman Who Dares, 142
woman suffrage, 83, 220. *See also* American
 Woman Suffrage Association; National
 American Woman Suffrage Association;
 National Woman Suffrage Association;
 suffrage movement; woman's rights
Woman's Bible: advertisement of, 217; and androgyny, 156, 165–166; anti-Semitism in,
 155, 158, 162, 168–169; antisuffragists use
 of, 4–5; appendix of, 213; beginnings of,
 62, 71, 99–103; biblical criticism in, 151,
 153; Catholic Church in, 161; collaborative nature of, 1, 138; comparative religion
 in, 152–153, 155; connection to *Eighty
 Years*, 15, 40, 48–49; contrasted to Stanton's speeches, 179–180; controversial title
 of, 2, 174–175, 180–181, 207, 216, 270
 n.159; copyright controversy of, 169–170,
 262 n.94; and creation story, 156, 162;

critics' failure to read, 2, 182, 208, 210,
 266 n.83; critique of clergy in, 156; critique of Stanton in, 150, 167, 216; and
 Darwin, 158; defense of, 177–178, 209–
 211, 214–215; description of, 2; as deter-
 rent to suffrage, 102, 184–185; diversity of
 views within, 9, 150, 163–165, 167–169,
 213–216; elitism of, 10, 168–169; essen-
 tialism of, 8–9; eugenics in, 154–155; and
 Eve, 88, 158–160; female aspects of God
 in, 156; and feminist issues, 7–9; financial
 liability of, 212; financing of, 170–171,
 255 n.6; and free speech, 182, 193; and
 gender equality, 165, 167–169, 178; and
 Genesis, 155–160; goals of, 78, 151–152,
 177; as historical document, 6, 9; and individualism, 169, 178; interpretive strategies
 of, 151–154, 157, 167, 260 n.63 (*see also*,
 historical-critical; esoteric; dialogic; "plain
 English"); and Indians, 160; layout of,
 151–152; marketing of, 270 n.161; and
 monogamy, 156, 164–166; New Thought
 influence in, 157, 161, 164–165, 167–168;
 in the 1970s, 7–8; organization of, 150–
 151, 178, 182; and Paul, 161–162; and
 Pentateuch, 103, 135–136; plan of work,
 136; as political tool, 46, 99–100, 169;
 Positivism in, 54, 151, 156–157, 168, 175;
 proposed, 98–103; Protestantism in, 169;
 publication of, 171, 198, 216; publicity of,
 185, 192, 207, 216–217; reading strategies
 in, 151, 160; renewed effort, 135–136; removed from libraries, 209–210, 217; resolutions of censure against, 184, 189, 192,
 194–198, 207–208, 216–217; response to
 2–3, 19, 172–181; response to, by Christian women, 176; response to, by clergy, 2,
 5, 173–174, 180, 185, 209–210; response
 to, by critics, 176–179; response to, by Eu-
 ropeans, 263 n.26; response to, by evangelicals, 3, 172–173, 176, 185, 207; response to, by Freethinkers, 174, 195–198,
 209, 263 n.26; response to, by Jews, 208–
 209; response to, by liberals, 179–180, 270
 n.159; response to, by press, 172–173, 175,
 180, 207, 209, 216; response to, by Southerners, 173, 185, 189, 192, 207, 264 n.46,
 265 n.55; response to, by suffragists, 2,
 181–198, 203, 213–217, 221; sale of, 171,
 216–217, 262 n.99; scholarly credibility of,
 177, 212, 263 n.26; separatist nature of,
 167, 179; serial publication of, 135–137,
 139, 149, 183, 184, 203, 212; Social Purity
 beliefs in, 164–166; Spiritualist influence
 in, 144, 157; Stanton's authorial control of,

Woman's Bible (cont.)
   136–137, 139, 150, 256 n.20; style of, 180,
   182–184, 194, 207, 209, 263 n.26; suspended work on, 104; textual analysis of,
   150–169; Theosophy in, 165, 167–168;
   tone of, 178, 181; translation in, 154, 161,
   165; use of "common sense" in, 152, 156,
   161–162, 177; use of history in, 151, 153,
   157; use of occult in 152, 154–156, 158;
   use of science in, 151–152, 154–158, 160,
   168; and "woman's nature," 159, 162; and
   women's emancipation, 173, 178, 209–211;
   and women's speech, 162; as work in
   progress, 136; writing of, 211
Woman's Christian Temperance Union
   (WCTU): censure of *Woman's Bible* by,
   207, 216–217; and Christ, 124; and Christian Party, 254 n.109; connection to
   AWSA of, 121; domestic rhetoric of,
   122–123; evangelical practices of, 122–
   124; franchise department of, 121, 123–
   124; membership of, 121; as political
   movement, 122–124; progressive orthodoxy of, 121–127; and Revising Committee, 148, 258 n.53; scientific temperance
   campaign of, 115; in South, 253 n.106,
   264 n.45; Willard's leadership of, 122–127;
   and woman suffrage, 11, 48, 53, 121–127
woman's clubs, 207, 209
Woman's Congress, 123
Woman's Journal, 133 134, 192, 195, 197; as
   NAWSA organ, 268 n.115
Woman's National Liberal Union, 254
   n.109, 259 n.57, 268 n.114
"woman's nature," 35, 107–108
"woman's piety," 47, 174, 209–210
Woman's Place Today, 141
woman's rights movement: antebellum conventions of, 10, 16, 95; doldrums of, 10–
   11; religious debates within, 10, 86–90, 104,
   129–130, 228–229 n.37; religious roots of,
   10. *See also* American Woman Suffrage Association; National American Woman Suffrage Association; National Woman Suffrage Association; suffrage movement

"woman's sphere": alternatives to, 263 n.31;
   conservative uses of, 82–83, 85, 175, 221;
   immorality of, 97; rejection of, 10, 46; relation to *Woman's Bible* of, 181; subversive
   uses of, 83
Woman's Tribune: and alternative religions,
   143–144; Anthony's criticism of, 150, 203;
   Colby's work on, 61, 212–213; defense of
   Woman's Bible in, 174, 193; financial hardship of, 171, 267 n.112, 268 n.115; and
   Native Americans, 142; and New
   Thought, 143–144; production of, 268
   n.115; radical politics of, 270 n.152; refusal to publish Stanton in, 212–213; serial
   publication of *Woman's Bible* in, 136–139;
   as vehicle for Stanton, 124–125
Woman's World, 146
women: declining status of, 82–86; differences among, 108–109; economic dependence of, 235–236 n.61; moral authority
   of, 83, 88, 90; as preachers, 88–89, 118; religious superstition of, 152, 211; speech of,
   88; spiritual emancipation of, 212; as
   teachers, 81
Women in Early Christian Ministry, 141
"Women and Skepticism," 97
The Women's Bible Commentary, 228 n.31
Women's Federal Equality Association,
   145
Women's Loyal National League, 17
Women's New York State Temperance Soci-
   ety, 17, 122, 129
Women's Suffrage Press Association, 148
Woodhull, Victoria, 14, 249 n.48
Woodrow, Wilson, 145
"Work Among Mothers Campaign," 123
World Antislavery Convention, 16, 45
World's Fair, 133–134, 194
World Parliament of Religions, 59, 133, 142,
   148, 239–240 n.32, 259 n.53

Yates, Elizabeth, 265 nn.57, 58
Young, Virginia, 265 n.57

Zelophehad, daughters of, 152, 260 n.66